Annie S. Wolf

Pictures and Portraits of Foreign Travel

Annie S. Wolf

Pictures and Portraits of Foreign Travel

ISBN/EAN: 9783337211554

Printed in Europe, USA, Canada, Australia, Japan

Cover: Foto ©Andreas Hilbeck / pixelio.de

More available books at **www.hansebooks.com**

PICTURES AND PORTRAITS

OF

OREIGN TRAVEL.

BY

EM'LY

"A man may see how this world goes. with no eyes.
Look with thine ears."
                                        KING LEAR.

PHILADELPHIA:
E. CLAXTON & COMPANY,
No. 930 MARKET STREET.
1881.

IF IT CONTAIN

A WORTHY SENTIMENT,

AN ORIGINAL THOUGHT, AN HONORABLE AMBITION,

IT IS NOT DUE TO VANITY BORN OF FLATTERY,

BUT TO YOU,

MY DEAR MOTHER,

WHOSE PEERLESS NATURE AND ANGEL VIRTUES

ARE MY SWEETEST MEMORIES;

AND I TRUST, IN THOSE DARK DAYS WHICH,

AS THEY COME TO ALL LIVES, MUST COME TO MINE ALSO,

MY LOVE OF BOOKS AND DEVOTION TO MY PEN MAY PROVE

MY SOLACE AND MY STRENGTH.

"I am in this earthly world; where, to do harm,
Is often laudable: *to do good, sometimes
Accounted dangerous folly*."
SHAKESPERE.

PICTURES AND PORTRAITS

OF

FOREIGN TRAVEL.

LETTER I.

> "Adieu, adieu! my native shore
> Fades o'er the waters blue;
> The night-winds sigh, the breakers roar,
> And shrieks the wild seamew.
> Yon Sun that sets upon the sea
> We follow in his flight;
> Farewell awhile to him and thee,
> My native Land—Good night!"
> BYRON.

LIVERPOOL, February, 1878.

I ANTEDATE my first page at Liverpool, England, on board the steamship "City of Richmond," which I am officially assured will arrive in the Mersey Saturday evening; and I sit in my cabin wondering how I shall feel when I arrive in a foreign land, and whether the journal I design keeping during my stay abroad will ever be finished, and if so whether it will prove pleasant reading to my friends at home. For many days I have been confined to my room, submitting martyrlike and resignedly to the tortures imposed on me by my turbulent enemy, "Old Nep." For many nights I have lain in my berth (which, by the way, was not the most luxurious couch that ever female's tender limbs rested upon), listening to the incessant heart-throbs of this marvellous iron horse, trampling down the mighty waves, and carrying me many thousand leagues from my country and my home. As I contemplate new ambitions, fresh scenes, and curious studies, the countless possible calamities by which I am surrounded are forgotten. The seagulls that have been tracking the course of the vessel since noon, resembling giant snowflakes drifted by the wind, seem to have folded their beautiful wings in rest, while the gentle waves rock them to sleep on the bosom of the blue sea. These birds live from the offal of the ship, but never come aboard, as they are affected by sea-sickness the same as human beings.

"We have had an unusually calm voyage," so my good friend the stewardess says; the only reply I have to make is, "that the sleeplessness of these 'calm' waters has created in me sensations of a most unpleasant, not to say, hypochondriacal character."

In these leaves I shall endeavor to avoid the safe and easy habit of borrowing ideas from the guide-books, or the equally seductive thievery of reflecting the impressions of former travellers. I have often thought what delightful sketches could have been written by those who crossed from New York or Philadelphia to Liverpool in the first ocean steamers. They got the cream of novelty, and their readers were almost as much gratified as themselves; but now that nearly every one goes to Europe, and that many know far more of other countries than of their own, and that it is the fashion to say you have been "abroad," a review of rambles in foreign climes must be something more than a mere copy of what has been written a thousand times. Any one, however, who is blessed with the usual forty-eight ounces of that material instrument of thought, impulse, or perception, that reigns supreme in man, and who uses his eyes and ears, can find plenty of texts to elaborate wheresoever he may journey. The old, old world is forever new to such minds, every fresh face is a fresh theme, and nothing is so sure to quicken thought as the habits of another people. These will be the books that I shall attempt to study during my absence, and if I can succeed in interesting my friends beyond the vast sea ever so little, my labors will be the labors doubly of love and duty.

Nine days isolated from the great world! Nine days afloat upon the beautiful but treacherous sea! Nine days of oblivion!

* * * * *

No doubt Liverpool is a pleasant city in good weather, but when we rode along its broad streets it was dismal and wet to a degree; still, withal, it had a pious look, for it was Sunday morning, and the people were on their way to church. The two great lions in front of St. George's Hall, and the equestrian statue of Queen Victoria, with Prince

Albert on the opposite pediment, told me I was in England, and the impression was confirmed as we entered the gloomy corridor of the London and Northwestern Hotel. Everything was rich, dark, and heavy. The coffee-room was cheerless like the rest; the elaborate decorations, the silent servants, the dignified lady clerk in the office, who was at once bookkeeper and manager, the massive stairway, were all so many natural introductions to a country that I had expected to find more remarkable for strength and money than for grace and beauty. The bad tea, the execrable coffee, hard bread, cold toast, and immense muttonchop, minus savor, which constituted our breakfast, were the initials to a long series of the same monotonous fare.

The almost constant absence of the sun has a depressing effect. The atmosphere is not keen and cold as in America, but dark and penetrating, and the universal use of bituminous coal gives rather a Pittsburg taste and smell to the air.

There is no Adams Express nor Western Union Transfer Company in England, so we hailed a "four-wheeler" to convey us, in the inside, and our "traps" on the outside, to the hotel. I marvel some enterprising Yankee does not come here and establish one of the baggage transfer companies for which our country is renowned. He would have no competitors to struggle against. Now, here is an opportunity for one of our young men; will he take the advice of a woman?

The "hansom" is an unpretentious "one-hoss shay," resembling somewhat our light buggy-wagons. It has only two seats, doors that close over the occupants, and it is also provided with a glass window that may be lowered over the face in inclement weather. The driver is perched high in a little box at the back, and the reins pass over the top of the carriage. I wonder if this curious equipage is an improvement on, or whether it is fashioned after the same model of the first public carriage that the inhabitants of Liverpool had the privilege of hiring of Mr. James Dimoke, in the middle of the eighteenth century. In those days Miss Clayton was the happy possessor of the only private turnout in this city, so on the occasion of a grand party, ball, or opera, when Miss Clayton was using her own brougham, and Mrs. —— had hired the only one at the extensive livery stables of James Dimoke, the other ladies of Liverpool were conveyed in sedan chairs.

I was surprised to find so few ladies on the street. The women were almost without exception slattern and careless, and I should have left with a wrong opinion had I not had an opportunity to be present at the reception of the chief magistrate of Liverpool, Mr. Forwood, at the "City Hall." Assisted by his accomplished wife, the event attracted all the better classes, including the nobility of the neighborhood. What must be the wealth of a country when the mayor of one of its cities entertains and is honored like a monarch? The City Hall was the first English public building I had seen, and the saloons where the Lord Mayor of this commercial town, with a population of 500,676, received his guests, were infinitely superior to the chambers in the White House, at Washington, as superior, indeed, as the home of a *parvenu* cotton-spinner is to an old feudal castle.

Mr. Forwood is a tall, elegant man, about thirty-six, evidently the junior of his wife by a couple of years, who is the veritable type of an English woman,—a ponderous figure clad in the very softest and heaviest of Bonnet silks. Her reception toilet of pale sage was bordered with knife-plaiting and *russes*, richly draped with the same material, and myrtle-green velvet bands embroidered with cut crystals of emerald, ruby, and topaz, formed the garniture. The costume was completed by an exquisite bonnet of the same shades. Mrs. Forwood is a comely but not handsome woman. She was exceedingly cordial in her manner of greeting an American, and the pleasant words she spoke of my country (for she has visited the United States), thrilled me with kindly emotions for my English cousins, and greatly tempered the odium with which I had always regarded the nation that had held, and hoped to retain *us* their vassals.

Was it not in this nation, and from this very port of Liverpool, that that most infamous and inhuman source of emolument, the African slave trade was opened? As early as 1766 Liverpool had already gained an unenviable notoriety in this despicable traffic—the purchase and sale of human beings—the liberation of whom cost us years of bloodshed, death, and desolation, in the succeeding century. In a bill of lading, dated shortly after we had crossed the meridian of the last century, for slaves shipped to Georgia, then a portion of South Carolina, I see that these poor creatures were branded with particular marks, by red-hot irons, the same process used on cattle, and with equal indifference. And in the year 1806–1807, when this odious trade was abolished, 185 African slave ships sailed from Liverpool carrying 49,213 slaves.

The docks are unsurpassed by any in the world; these masterful constructions stretch along the Mersey for five miles on the Liverpool side, and two miles on the Birkenhead side, covering with dry-docks two hundred acres, together with nineteen miles of quays.

An attempt at forming something like a dock in the old Pool was made in 1561, as a shelter for ships in bad weather, by defending the entrance with massive stone piers; and for a century this harbor was sufficient for the limited commerce of the period. The development of traffic caused the necessity of a regular dock, and in 1709 an act was passed making the first dock at Liverpool for the security of all ships trading to and from this port; it was called the Custom House Dock. These were the early foundations of the existing enormous system. The present business wealth and importance of Liverpool is chiefly owing to its magnificent docks, which are among the greatest works of modern times, considering the obstacles surmounted; unlike most docks they are built in the river itself by inclosing within a sea-wall, five miles in extent, a portion of the beach of the Mersey, and afterward excavating the part thus reclaimed to a proper depth. Most of these docks communicate with each other, and have separate entrances, so the ships may pass from one to the other, without being locked out in the river, and back in the dock again.

The sugar refineries and soap factories are very extensive. What with the murky atmosphere, and what with the soot arising from the soft coal, I doubt not but the demand for the latter product exceeds the supply.

It was cold and inhospitable when we rode through Sefton Park, but the hedges surrounding the homes of the aristocracy within their limits were green, luxuriant, and well-combed, and the silver plates, or the letters carved on the massive stone portals, told not the names of the owners of these mansions, but the name of each estate itself, such as "Maple Grove," "Oak Lodge," "Stanley Park," and "Worcester Place."

LETTER II.

> "Thus,
> Thus upon London do I lay my sword."
> JACK CADE.

LONDON, February, 1878.

LONDON! Great London!! But no. Of that hereafter. Eager as I am, dear, silent little friend, you who never interrupt nor contradict me, to tell you of this bewildering world of a city, I must relate to-night only how I came into it. Were I to follow my impulses, and pour into you all my first impressions, those who may peruse my pages later on would exclaim: "But how was the great capital reached? Em'ly says not a word of her manner of transit from the most gigantic commercial port to the political, moral, intellectual, literary, artistic, and social centre of the world. Did she ride, walk, fly, or make the passage in a balloon?"

I came on the "metals," to use the English word for rails. We were registered for London this morning at the booking-office of the London and Northwestern Station, in Lime Street, Liverpool. Of course I felt a woman's curiosity about an English railway station, which I think I can attribute to the effect upon my mind of Frith's great picture that hung in the British Art Section at our Centennial Exhibition. It was admirably descriptive of the scene that greeted me this morning. What a motley throng! What a torrent of travel! The bright, ruddy-faced schoolboy on his way to Rugby, the burly manufacturer returning to his mills in Manchester, the detective and the pickpocket, the gambler and the priest, the lord and the farmer, the lady and the maid, the stately dowager and the hoydenish English miss, ungainly and inelegant in the extreme, with none of the grace and *chic* of the fair American and brilliant French girl, who followed, all mingling in the *mêlée*. How different from our dépôts at home! Yet with all how precise and orderly! Already I have learned that I must not use the word *dépôt*. John Bull does not comprehend its significance; with him it is invariably "station." I was struck by the enormous sale of papers, and the vast book-stalls; and gazed at the crowds clustered around them, and then at the character of the literature, and was delighted to notice that a large number of American works were offered to customers. Over the door of the first-class waiting-room I read in large letters: "For ladies only." This command excludes a husband, for under no circumstances whatever is a gentleman permitted to enter the hallowed precincts. He is obliged to tarry elsewhere, and join his wife, or his sister, or his sweetheart on the platform.

Every station is provided with a restaurant and bar, for the English are a nation of eaters and drinkers, and these dining-rooms are always filled to repletion on the arrival and departure of the trains; furthermore they are always attended by young women. Not the imaginary pretty barmaid, but pert, flashy, loudly dressed creatures. The great hotel and saloon system, managed by the partnership of Spiers & Pond, who are coining fabulous sums by their franchises, is said to employ over five hundred girls as bartenders. When I expressed my horror at this method, an English lady told me that the most popular man in Liverpool, Mr. Samuelson, who had held the post of mayor, previous to Mr. Forwood, owned several hundred beer shops, and had secured his election by the money and patronage thus collected and organized.

When the herald for departure sounded, there was no hurrying nor rush for seats, but the passengers were shown to the carriages according to the class indicated on their ticket. Before entering, I paused to look at this novel, at least to me, conveyance, with a door on either side of each compartment. Very pleasing and luxurious indeed was the interior, as much so as our American drawing-room cars. The upholstering was navy blue cloth, finished with silk cords and button (you see, woman-like, I jot down the details), an ominous color, and I marvelled if this hue was to pervade my entire tour. As I sank into my place I observed that our carriage contained six passengers, three on each sofa, face to face. This was the extent of its seating capacity, as the sofas are divided into three sections by projecting arms. The places thus formed are spacious for one, and much space is squandered; but I presume that this precaution has been adopted by the circumspect English, as a means of preventing the *accidental* occurrence of travellers becoming too closely allied while confined in these flying prisons. There lingers in my mind recollections of a catastrophe that transpired in one of these carriages, despite this preservative, which created a vivacious gossip on both sides the Atlantic.

Another delectable custom of foreign travel is being

locked in the carriage by the guard, and left. In such a case one's sensations are far more apprehensive when *left* in company than when *left* alone. Had I been a *young* lady, I should have been agitated and ill-at-ease, but as the fact stands, a married one, with Mr. "Em'ly" at my side, I settled myself to scan my companions—two Americans and two English. There was no shrill whistling, nor blowing, nor shrieking, nor shifting trains; no pushing cars back and forth, no clanging of chains, no unexpected collisions of carriages in the effort to get off—such delights we have all enjoyed at home—but we moved as smoothly as if the metals had been oiled, and away we flew to London, six hours distant.

For many years there was great inconvenience to travellers, in consequence of the circuitous *route* they had to make by existing lines, and from the extreme points at which their city termini were situated. The companies that occupy the north, northeast, and midland districts of Liverpool, were obliged to convey all their passengers in an omnibus from a station near the Brunswick Dock to the southern end of the town, entailing an expensive and vexatious transfer of baggage. Now all the annoyance of this wasteful system is obviated by the construction of a station in the centre of Liverpool, adjoining the Adelphi Hotel, which branches from the existing line contiguous to the Brunswick Dock, and is used in common by these companies for passengers and general traffic.

As I was fresh to the sight and to all my surroundings, I began to study and compare. The morning was cold, the atmosphere gloomy and dank, and I was chilly, without the accustomed luxuries of American travel. Long copper canisters, filled with hot water and placed under the feet, were intended to supply the absence of fire. With this accessory, one might have been comfortable enough, had not the English perseveringly kept the windows lowered. Result: an ugly cold and an ill temper. There was no conversation save amongst the Americans; of course we were full of the strange scenes and novel situations, but I could see that if John Bull did not talk he was an eager and hungry listener. At length silence reigned, and I looked out upon the country side, by which we were flying at the rate of forty miles an hour. A dense veil of mist hung upon the landscape. How earnestly I desired the appearance of the sun to dispel all this melancholy fog, and by his influence glorify and irradiate the picture, for I could discern the beauty of the section through which we were passing.

It is winter, yet the grass is green, the trees are in full leaf, and the hedges strong, dark, and glossy. The little brown cottages are neat, prim, and cosey; very few exist out of the large towns, and those we noticed on the roadside were in clusters.

Without exception, the stations were quiet and deserted. At Crewe the doors were unlocked, and a fresh re-enforcement of foot-warmers supplied. This act I hailed with grateful emotions. It is a town of almost entirely modern growth, and the home of numbers of the railway officials of the London and Northwestern Road, who have here a vast establishment for the manufacture of everything essential to railways.

When we reached Rugby, and I saw the train depositing its burden of grammar school boys, I longed to follow, not to school, but to Bilton Hall, formerly the home of the celebrated English essayist, Addison. Dr. Johnson says: "Whoever wishes to attain an English style, familiar but not coarse, and elegant but not ostentatious, must give his days and nights to the volumes of Addison." Remembering this, I was eager to saunter in his footprints through "Addison's Walk," a long avenue or favorite promenade in his garden, hoping that I might be imbued by some enduring essence of the poet's literary merits and grace.

The more frequent clusters of habitations, the faint and flickering lights in the distance, that were growing clearer and more definite every moment, the towering spires, the volumes of smoke issuing from the numberless chimneys, were all evidences of our approach to a great city. Fifteen minutes more and we were in Euston Square Station, London, surrounded by at least a hundred porters and hackmen, all clamoring for patronage, and each one adhering to us with as much persistency as if they expected we could engage them all. I endeavored to describe the dépôt at Liverpool. This one in London exceeds my power. It is confusion worse confounded.

LETTER III.

"What, then, is to insure the pile which now towers above me from sharing the fate of mightier mausoleums? The time must come when its gilded vaults, which now spring so softly, shall lie in rubbish beneath the feet; when, instead of the sound of melody and praise, the wind shall whistle through the broken arches, and the owl hoot from the shattered tower; when the garish sunbeam shall break into these gloomy mansions of death; and the ivy twine around the fallen column; and the foxglove hang its blossoms about the nameless urn, as if in mockery of the dead. Thus man passes away; his name perishes from record and recollection; his history is as a tale that is told, and his monument becomes a ruin."—WASHINGTON IRVING'S WESTMINSTER ABBEY.

LONDON, February, 1878.

WHEN I entered the *atrium* of the Westminster Palace Hotel, several evenings ago, I was awed by the grandeur of its architecture and appointments. The flood of light from the chandeliers, and the blazing fire in the glowing grates, on either side of the hall, were cheering signs of comfort and luxury. But the ample stone stairway and silent corridors, the floors of marble and vaulted ceilings, gave to it a monastic air. I was conducted to my apartments by a natty little English maid in a pale pink cotton gown, carrying a candle that shed a ghostly glimmer. Throwing open the door of a room that was dark and damp, she bade me enter. Depositing the tallow, she was about to make her exit, when I requested her to "light the gas." Gazing at me in amazement, she informed me that there was no gas in the chambers. In one corner I saw a grate of rather limited compass, and inquired if she could light the fire? Replying in the affirmative, the young woman in the pink cotton gown, in midwinter, vanished.

Left alone, I dwelt upon the stone floor, cheerless fireplace, absence of gas, and the old-fashioned bureau, surmounted by a little toilet mirror—a counterpart of one I remember in my grandmother's attic, when a child, still retained by the family as a genealogical relic—and then, like a meteor, it flashed upon me that I was not in America, at the Continental, Philadelphia, or the Fifth Avenue, New York, but in London. The London, that is so old, that nothing certain is known of its origin; the London that Ammianus Marcellinus, who flourished in the reign of Julian the Apostate, termed an *ancient* place, called *Londinium;* that appears as a Roman station during the sovereignty of Claudius; that was first fortified by Constantine the Great, and one of the theatres where some of the world's grandest scenes have been acted. Could I expect modern comforts in a city that had existed previous to the Christian era? I had said adieu to the *Progressive Youth* one bright day, almost three weeks ago, and was now living amidst the memories and habits of the centuries. I was buried in these reflections when my attendant in the summer toilet reappeared, with requisites for the fire, and a copper ewer of " 'ot water," which I sadly needed, after my long ride. Very soon the flames were leaping and dancing in the chimney, and a hospitable glow pervaded the chamber. The one virtue of English bituminous coal is the readiness with which it ignites.

It was about seven o'clock when we left the hotel, and passed on our way to find our first dinner in this world and wilderness of brick and mortar. Eager to see the mighty hive, we directed our footsteps to the Café Royal, the famous French restaurant, in Regent Crescent. The din of the populace was like the roar of Niagara, and the whole picture was a mixture of lights struggling through a humid, hazy atmosphere, a vast crowd in streets slimy with mud, crashing vehicles, over-dressed women, and foreign-looking men. It was neither Broadway nor Broad Street. I was like one of many gazing into a mighty arena where some wild carnival was *en force*—a theatre with a background of fire, and laughter, and clamorous music. But I was hungry, and hurried onward to the "Café Royal." There was magic in the words; they breathed of *Tortue Claire, Soles au vin blanc, Tête de Veau, Vol-au-Vent,* and *Filet de bœuf au champignons.* I had already tested English cooking *ad nauseam.* The Café was filled to overflowing, and for some moments we despaired of seats, till a young gentleman, with a swallow-tail coat, white cravat, and a marked foreign accent, led us through seemingly endless apartments, filled with people packed like sardines. But order came out of the chaos; and finally anchored, I began to unravel the tangled skein. There were many French and Americans, some Germans, and few English. The lady bookkeeper, perched behind her high desk, gave her orders to the army of waiters like a true commandant. But the dinner—delicate, dainty, and delicious! Shall I rehearse all the fresh and savory tidbits of this meal? No! That would be uncharitable! Eight o'clock, and with it cigars! Smoking is in order at that hour—the habit of the Latin countries; so we fled out into the street, under the stars—stars! No, into the dense floating vapor, to inhale the fog. Mingling in the mass of humanity, we wandered on to Piccadilly. Before me rose a formidable pile, one illumination from turret to foundation-stone. It was the Criterion, a theatre and restaurant combined; dining-rooms on every floor, kitchen in the fifth story, and the theatre three stories under ground. It was too late to attend the play, but as my English friend who accompanied us had determined that we should see all that was possible this first night in London, he proposed for us to look in at the great bar-room. He swung open the door, and I, ardent for novelty, followed. A pandemonium indeed! I should have liked to study this medley of men; but before I had obtained a first glimpse, we were waved back by the helmeted sentinel who was on guard at the entrance, with the polite, but decided remark: "No admittance for *ladies* at the bar after nine o'clock." Thus was I greeted on my arrival in a foreign land. My husband then informed the outlying picket that I was not a "*lady*" who sought admittance to the bar, but only an American woman who wished to look in. Here, at least, the sterner sex had it all to themselves, but not so in the surging myriads outside. Where were they all going? Ah, I fear me, they were all blent in one dread course, down, down, to the dark shores of sin and misery, and death!

The first sight of a great city is very like the first sight of the ocean: it overwhelms you. There is so much of it and so little of yourself, that you feel like a feather tempest tost, and a painful sensation of loneliness, or rather nothingness, crept over me, as I walked back, past the house where Charles I was executed, Westminster Abbey, and the House of Parliament, all seen through a cloud of blue-gray mist. For over two thousand years this tide of humanity, now quite four millions of souls, has been growing and going, increasing and unceasing, living and dying, each life valuable to its possessor and valueless to its neighbor. With these reflections I retired to—prayers. I rested superbly, and when I wakened the next morning it was still dark, but my monitor warned me of the hour of nine, so I rose and dressed by candlelight, for the fog seemed to have gathered more densely than ever. It was becoming monotonous.

My first sensation on entering Westminster Abbey was that of a cold, cavernous, grave-like chill. The twilight glamour was very odd. The day was so dark, that even the illuminated windows were vailed, but soon my eyes became accustomed to the influence of the royal sanctuary. What added to the religious emotions that thronged through my mind, was the dead silence of the immensity, only broken by the occasional intoning of the vast organ, blended with human voices, rehearsing a symphony for a coming service. No loud talking; the uncovered gentlemen followed the ladies through the long aisles, and studied the carved effigies of the departed heroes and statesmen, kings, queens, princes and poets, or deciphered the fading inscriptions on the crumbling tombs. No one can be indifferent to the atmosphere of Westminster Abbey. You almost come prepared to yield to it; and you expect much and are not disappointed. No traveller, old or young, leaves it without increased reverence for the great Englishmen of the past, or without gathering information, never to be forgotten. When you recollect that this old abbey is situated on a spot originally surrounded by the waters of the Thames, and that there is a record in the old chapter-house, showing that the celebrated Domesday Book, compiled in the time of William the Norman, was kept there, you have some idea of the vast antiquity of this venerable pile. I could have passed days instead of hours within its precincts. Old as it was, it was very fresh and new to me. The dead were not dead, but so many living lessons. The red and golden windows, the wainscoted choir, the mosaic pavements, the altar-piece, the screens, each a precious memento of the ages, recalled my youthful readings, and added to the fascination of the majestic temple. In fancy the royal ghosts rose from their marble beds and gave to every legend a realistic glow. Henry III; Edward I and Queen Eleanor; Edward III and Queen Philippa; Richard II and Queen Anne, and glorious Harry V of Agincourt, Crecy and Poitiers; and I can well believe how the enthusiastic poet thrills with the fire of his new awakening as for the first time in his life he stands before the monuments and memorials of Shakespeare, Spenser, Milton, Dryden, Addison, Garrick, Goldsmith, Sheridan, and their contemporaries.

I stood by the stone laid over the grave of Charles Dickens, and I recalled the delight I had extracted from *Little Nell*, *David Copperfield*, *Nicholas Nickleby*, *Christmas Carol*, and all the other lovely creations of his myriad mind. But is there no memorial to Byron? "No! we are too good for that," answered an English lady at my side. Yes, they are too good for that, I mused; they reserve their idolatry for profligate kings like the second Charles, and for *roués* like the "first gentleman of England," Beau Brummel's friend, the dissolute Prince of Wales.

LETTER IV.

"Two scraps of foundation, some fragments of lace,
A shower of French rosebuds to drop over the face;
Fine ribbons and feathers, with crape and illusion,
Then mix and derange them in graceful confusion.
Inveigle some fairy out roaming for pleasure,
And buy the slight favor of taking her measure;
The length and the breadth of her dear little pate,
And hasten a miniature frame to create;
Then pour as above the bright mixture upon it,
And lo! you possess such a love of a bonnet."
ANONYMOUS.

LONDON, February, 1878.

FROM the earliest ages France seems to have been the originator and sovereign of costumes and customs. In the year 55 B.C., when Julius Cæsar invaded Britain, he found the inhabitants of Kent the most enlightened, and Tacitus says "they were near and like the Gauls," from whom they had acquired the arts of *dressing*, spinning, dyeing, and weaving wool. Somewhere I have read that the early Britons lived continually *in puris naturalibus*, but Cæsar himself corrects that vulgar error when he tells us that even the least civilized were clad in skins, while those in the southern districts, like the Gauls, were not only completely, but splendidly attired. That they punctured their bodies in numerous devices of animals, flowers, and leaves, stained them blue with their favorite herb, *glas lys*, and flung off their garments when about to rush into battle, we have ample authority. Even the famous tartan plaids were first woven in France, for are they not to this day called "the garb of old Gaul"?

As I strolled along Regent Street, Oxford Street, Bond Street, and the Strand, I saw that these people still assume to follow the fashions set by their neighbors across the Channel, for all the shops were made attractive by the display of Paris bonnets, Paris costumes, Paris mantles, and Paris shoes and stockings, and gloves. And as I looked at these beautiful goods, and then at the myriads of plain, cumbrous females passing by, I marvelled who the purchasers and wearers of these dainty confections could be. Certainly not these heavy, stolid women, who filled the streets and added to the oppression of the atmosphere. It seemed to me that some Women's Rights or Goody-Goody society had just adjourned, and these women with the large feet, whose size was enhanced by rough leather boots, cut low around the ankle, and the broad flat heels, short black dresses, and heavy cloth coats, generally a straw bonnet in February, and invariably an umbrella, were returning from the *séance*. They all appeared to have been *blocked* out after one model. Surely these Parisian morsels should revolutionize the unbroken conformation of these British Venuses. No! Unlike all other nations, the Englishwoman is never Gallicized by a French toilet; and the potency of the salient points of her form Anglicizes the most ravishing French tidbits.

In Regent Crescent I noticed the most exquisite gloves, combinations of two delicate shades of kid—*eau de nile* embroidered with myrtle, and myrtle cuffs; *ciel bleu* and flesh tint; *écru* and brown; pink and fawn—and I longed to possess these novelties, yet I never saw a pair worn by any of the ladies at entertainments. The gentlemen I note in my saunters are universally more careful in their attire than their sisters, being at all times well shod and well gloved. This seems to be a reminiscence of the ages, for gloves were very generally worn in the twelfth century, and prior to that period the sleeves were made long enough to draw over the hand, and thus stood in *lieu* of the later perquisite. And I mourn, as a vision of Chestnut Street floats before me, thronged by my countrymen on their way to the office or counting-house in unblacked boots and ungloved hands, generally thrust deeply into the recesses of their pockets.

There are innumerable *coiffure* establishments, with showy window dressings, and again I ask, by whom are they patronized? For surely the prototype from which Mrs. Bull and her heifers have copied, could not have been conceived by any of these artists. The hair of the London female without variation is parted in the centre and drawn down very closely behind the ears to the nape of the neck, where it is twisted into an exceedingly small coil, about the size of an ordinary lemon. No crimps, no curls, no puffs, no braids! This austere and rigid headdress has the stamp of age and durability, verily: it looks as if it were coeval with the Saxons and Danes. It cannot merit the displeasure of the clergy, and make an occasion for them to declaim from the pulpit against the fashionable follies of the fair sex, which was a frequent event in the fourteenth and fifteenth centuries, when the *coiffure* of the ladies was compared to horned snails, to hearts, to unicorns, and even to a gibbet, for indeed, the reticulated headdress, spreading out on each side, when covered with a veil, might be fairly assimilated to the cross tree of those days. Later on, Addison, in the *Spectator*, likens the steeple "headgear" to the *commode* or *tower*. This gothic building might have been carried much higher, had it not been for the zeal and determination with which the famous monk, Thomas Conecte, fought it down; he travelled from town to town to preach against the monstrous ornament. By his eloquence he so warmed and animated the women against this absurdity that they threw off the *commodes* in the middle of his sermon and made a bonfire of them. While the holy man was in their midst this enormity vanished, but when he had departed, it reappeared, and as Monsieur Paradin says, "the women that, like snails in a fright, had drawn in their horns, shot them out again as soon as the danger was over." From the earliest dates we see that the British frizzed and arranged their hair, after the style of the French, in the most elaborate fashion; the problem is, why the ungraceful severity of the present reigning mode?

I have always regarded the English lady as rather a moral than an artistic creation,—a production of sherry, brown stout, roast beef and leather. She is plain and unprepossessing. I have met English girls with a profusion of exquisite golden hair, but they have none of the delicate flesh-tints and classic contour that generally accompany the same sunny shade of hair at home. I cannot rhapsodize over their soul thrilling eyes, nor sylph like forms! The figure is firm and ample, and speaks loudly of a robust appetite, healthy exercise, and no tight lacing. That this nation of women did fall victims to this evil in the twelfth century we are sure, and in the romance of the "Lay of Syr Launfal," written about the year 1300, Lady Triamore is described as—

"Clad in purple pall,
 With gentyll body and *middle small*."

In London, everything may be procured for money, except taste; that is a commodity in which the bovine Johns do no traffic. The Londoners, however much they may deny it, fly over to Paris to buy modes for themselves, and I can frankly say, they derive no benefit from their visits. A vast deal of pretension and little effect is eminently characteristic of the English costume. And why is this? when all that is *recherché* and effective, embraced in a female outfit, is exhibited at the conspicuous *bijouteries* of Peter Robinson and Marshall and Snellgrove, on Regent and Oxford Streets!

How odd it seems to me, to be compelled to remove my bonnet, before I am permitted to occupy a first-class seat at any of the theatres! And how incongruous to see the ladies at the circus in a plain cashmere dress, and their hair liberally decorated with flowers.

Americans who come abroad and expect to purchase goods for absolutely nothing are always disappointed. There are shops in London where articles may be bought at really very low figures. But, to become posted in these establishments, one must live in a city for some time, or possess a valuable acquaintance, who may render such a service. Strangers must pay for their ignorance in whatever country they roam.

The great jewelry shops are very unlike ours. Instead of adorning the windows with statuary and painting and ceramics, as we do at home, they expose the greater portion of their stock to the eye of the passer-by. And very beautiful and ornate are their displays. Frequently I linger at the shop-windows in old Bond Street, and feast my eyes upon the diamonds, pearls, and rubies, the pale-pink coral, and the delicate blue turquoise, these, combined with spark diamonds, enjoy a prominent position among the costly ornaments of the present day.

LETTER V.

> " No sun, no moon !
> No morn, no noon !
> No dawn, no dusk, no proper time of day :
> No sky, no earthly view ;
> No distance looking blue ;
> No road, no street, no t'other side the way.
> No top to any steeple,
> No recognition of familiar people ;
> No travelling at all, no locomotion,
> No inkling of the way, no motion ;
> No go by land or ocean,
> No trail, no post ;
> No news from any foreign coast !"
> THOMAS HOOD.

LONDON, February, 1878.

THE fog continues to envelop the great metropolis like a pall. Dismal indeed is the aspect. It is a funeral dirge in vapor; a dream of darkness; a vision of gloom; a melancholy antiphony. The bright sun is extinguished, and the stars do wander darkling in eternal space, rayless and pathless, and the vicious earth swings blackening in the air; morn comes and goes, and comes and brings no day, but men do not forget their passions. Were it not for the infinite variety of diversion in London now, life would become intolerable to the stranger and traveller. To minister to the appetites of every age, sex, condition, seems to be the general study. And that such efforts are not vain, is proved by the vast multitudes who flock hither, at all seasons, to enjoy the great metropolis. Here the musical critic, the literati, the blasé pleasure-seeker, indulge their propensities, and here the prodigal, the man of science, the traveller, the inventor, gather as to a harbor and a home. London is an endless encyclopædia for the uses and improvement of mankind.

Regardless of the cloud upon the surface of the earth, yesterday we took the underground railway to Baker Street, Portman Square, to pass a couple of hours in the Museum and Historical Gallery of Madame Tussaud.

Underground railways are the outgrowth of the last twenty years. The facilities for travel on the surface in London became insufficient, and then began the subterranean surveys. *Tunnels in the earth* do not require the drill or the explosive; but the permanent walling and arching requisite to safety, are frequently more expensive than blasting the solid rock. Yet in this populous hive the danger to property and to person make the tunnel preferable, regardless of cost. So they mapped the lower mundane regions as Agassiz mapped, and searched, and sounded the floors of old ocean; and now lower London, or rather invisible London, has almost as many miles of road permeating it, as the unseen arteries and fibres that permeate the human frame. We procured our tickets at Westminster to Baker Street Station, over two miles distant, for two pence apiece. I descended a long flight of steps, and found myself in a clean, well-lighted cellar. There was no sepulchral air; it was very like any other dépôt. Long platforms, thronged by busy mortals, with bright faces; bookstands, the walls illuminated with showy playbills and advertisements. I saw a crimson star in the distance, and then the train shot into the station like a comet. There was opening and slamming of doors; the railway guards boisterously shrieking the name of the station in unintelligible sounds; a rush out of the incoming passengers, and a rush in of the departing. I was pushed into a carriage by an official, and again the door was slammed in such a way as to lead me to believe that the guard who made the most noise received the largest salary, and that they were all in competition. This was my first acquaintance with a railway in a tunnelled city. The door was locked, and off the comet shot, to thread its way through long caverns, past open spaces, where the route crossed the upper streets, past other comets flying in an opposite direction. Baker Street! was shouted by the guard, which I never could have recognized, had not my eye caught the words on a sign. Again I was pushed out like a parcel. Mounting to the outer and upper atmosphere, I found myself in a broad airy street, full of shops and people, hansoms, broughams, organ-grinders, and gin-palaces—a wild din of life.

A short walk brought me to the famous exhibition. Madame Tussaud's gallery is Westminster Abbey in wax, but it is not a sepulchre; it embraces the living as well as the dead celebrities. It is neither so choice nor so chaste as the great Cathedral, as we find here all the notorieties, from Lydia Thompson to Jesus Christ: the ballet-dancer and the tragedian, the murderer and the murdered, the king and the clown. These effigies are lifelike and artistic, and very often capital copies of the originals, particularly the counterparts of English celebrities. But oh! how Madame has blasphemed in wax, murdered in mechanism, and travestied in spermaceti, the great ones of America. Her ideal of General Grant is a fair-haired boy of nineteen, that of Abraham Lincoln, a black-bearded clergyman in " swell clothes." But nothing could have been more valuable than the historic groups of the royal families of England, from the Normans down. There sits Bluebeard, Henry Tudor, his six wives clustered around him, each one looking serene and radiant in the sunlight of this magnanimous (?) man's favor; his hand rests upon the young prince's head—the future Edward VI—and sweet Anne Boleyn wears the famous yellow dress in which the capricious monarch loved to see her. I was ever so much interested in Madame Guelph, as Her Majesty is called; her nine children and four of her grandchildren are near her, with the handsome and virtuous Prince Albert; slightly in the background, and on the right of the Queen, is seen the man who combines " the genius of Bolingbroke, the wit of Canning, and the eloquence of Burke"—the omnipotent Premier. I was much impressed by the wonderful likeness of the hero of Wagram, Marengo, Austerlitz, Eylau, Friedland, and by the eloquent relics of his soldier, domestic, and consular life. The figures of the ill-fated Louis Napoleon, and the beautiful and queenly Eugénie are side by side. They are all here; from the old man, Emperor William, and Bismarck of Germany, to the sad Czar of the Russias; from the Chinese teaman to the Ameer of Afghanistan; from the white-haired Emperor of Brazil to the Viceroy of Egypt; the youthful kings of Italy and Spain; and Thiers, Guizot, Trochu, Gambetta, and Cassignac.

Madame Tussaud, the disciple of the art of the ancient Verrochio and Orsino, was a native of Berne, Switzerland; at an early age she was placed under the supervision of her uncle, M. Curtius, who was artist to Louis XVI, and by him she was instructed in the fine arts. Later she was summoned to the palace as the artistic adviser of Madame Elizabeth, the sister of the hapless king. Passing much of her time at the Tuilleries and Versailles, she became acquainted with the nobility and genius of the French court. One of her ablest works is the portrait model of the celebrated wit, Voltaire. In 1802 she bade adieu to France with her valuable collection of figures, to exhibit them in the principal cities of Great Britain and Ireland.

The ceroplastic art seems to have degenerated with the

centuries, and at present it is held in low esteem. The power, skill, and ingenuity manifested in the major portion of the Tussaud collection should impart to the art some of the pristine glory by which it was hallowed in the days of Michael Angelo, who did not deem it below his merits to produce wax-figures. Such representations were held in high repute by the early Romans, who placed to the honor of their ancestors their wax-figures in the vestibules. That time may not revive this usage I sincerely hope; I should not fancy it cheerful to have long-departed grandmothers and grandfathers constantly hovering over our portals.

Madame Tussaud was an economical genius (a rare specimen indeed), for my English guide, who had been attending the museum from childhood, told me that the same figures were made to serve many purposes, that the cloths and faces, with slight remodelling of noted characters in one decade, had been used for others in the decade previous.

It is a short ride from Baker Street to the "Doré Gallery" in New Bond Street, where the celebrated *chef-d'œuvre*, "Christ leaving the Prætorium," is still attracting thousands, though it has already enjoyed five long years of sovereignty. I studied this picture for some time before I fully appreciated the wealth and art and time expended on it; it is so vast and powerful that it dazzles you, one must pause until mind and eye expand sufficiently to comprehend the movement and multitude, the light and the shade, the glow and the gloom of this splendid conception. It possesses the vigor of Angelo without his contortions, the power of Rubens without his dramatic effect, the radiance of Tintoretto, the sweetness of Rafaelle, the melancholy of Guido, and the harmony of Van Dyke. Gustav Doré, to use an old metaphor, not only mixes his colors with fine oils, but with brains.

The picture illustrates one of the most pathetic incidents in the early sacred drama. See! There is the sublime actor in the snowy and seamless raiment, the crimson dew of his precious blood is upon his brow, as he descends the steep steps of the Prætorium. The assemblage seem awed into silence by *His* grief and gentle dignity, for *He* is "exceeding sorrowful unto death." There, against the background of gathering gloom, and volcanic darkness, are Pontius Pilate and Herod; Judas shrinks from the reproachful gaze of his master; a momentary flash of vivid feeling crosses the face of a boy, as if struck by one of the soldiers and you imagine you hear the exclamation of pain. Close by is the august but crushed Virgin mother, but far more touching was the spectacle of Magdalene; she it was who claimed my tears and sympathy. True, Mary the mother is bereft of her *Son*, but to the other Mary there has fallen utter misery, desolation, and solitude. She has lost all, for she has lost her Saviour, who drew her from the fathomless gulf of sin and death; she has lost her Guardian, who led her straying feet into the golden paths of virtue; she has lost her King, who protected and loved her; and she has lost her God, whom she worshipped.

LETTER VI.

"Once I was pure as the snow—but I fell;
Fell, like the snow-flakes, from heaven to hell;
Fell to be tramped as the filth of the street;
Fell to be scoffed, to be spit on, and beat.
Pleading,
Cursing,
Dreading to die,
Selling my soul to whoever would buy,
Dealing in shame for a morsel of bread,
Hating the living and fearing the dead."

BEAUTIFUL SNOW.

LONDON, February, 1878.

I HAD not been a resident of this foreign city long, ere I was impressed by the terrible disparity between the extremes of wealth and the extremes of poverty. The rich are very rich, and the poor are very poor. The rich learn to rule, while the poor learn to obey. London is great in its opulence, great in its mendicity, great in its virtue, and great in its vice, and these extremes are frequently so closely allied, as to be next-door neighbors. While in Liverpool, I attempted to draw the line between the dissipations and the distresses of the poor, and I speedily reached the conclusion that the chief cause of pauperism was rum; that much of it issued from the excessive use of gin and beer. That which originated in a custom, ultimately became a necessity. The two-pence or three-pence begged on the sidewalk and invested in this vile poison, if expended on bread and coarse meat, would prove the salvation of thousands of these wretched creatures. But oh! what is this demon that pursues mankind? Legions of fresh and healthy recruits falling in the ranks each year to be led along the dark shores of sin to the seas of death. Is there nothing to stop its ravages? It spreads its gloomy wings over happy homes, it is the mother of murder, the progenitor of defalcation, the parent of lies. Crime in whatsoever attitude it may appear is the inevitable offspring of this defiling fiend. It devastates families and pollutes the brightest mind.

It was only when I came to London that I realized the force of these impressions, for it is only here that I have seen the piteous and pitiful depravity of my own sex; not the poor painted butterflies who flicker and fall in the fiery gulf of the dazzling sin of the streets, but those who suffer simply from cureless destitution, who wander apparently all through the long night without shelter or food, and scarcely any clothing; bleared and bloated women clamoring for more whiskey or struggling with their imbruted husbands. This direful pauperism, together with vice, has led to an organization of beneficent ladies in London, which, thank God, is not necessary in our happy country. A large hall is procured amidst the very haunts of the destitute and reckless classes, and during the severe and dreary winter nights many noble women of exalted rank remain here, to receive and reason with the poor fallen outcasts who are conducted hither by friendly policemen from the slums and narrow lanes. The varied emotions that rend the bosoms of these frail strays as they issue from the dark and dismal highways to the light, and warmth, and welcome of these great parish halls, where hot coffee and homely food are provided for them, have more than once roused my womanly sympathies. Some of them are conspicuous in their tawdry finery, and generally under the influence of gin—others are shoeless and hatless—locks dishevelled, face and hands soiled — others shivering through their threadbare clothes, and again those who wear a hostile and defiant mien; all unsexed by the frequent contact with privation and sin. But oh! to see the soothing, tender, and forgiving manner of the clergymen and humane ladies, who greet the fugitives as they enter from the cold and cheerless outer world. There are no reproaches, no long sermons, no moralizing, but now and then a touching hymn and a plaintive prayer for the rescue of the wanderers, which go directly to the heart. I have seen the tears coursing down the rouged and whited cheeks of these ill-starred girls from the purlieus of the music-halls and gin-palaces.

There seems to be a strange fascination in a great city for these depraved beings. They prefer the filth in which they exist, and would rather starve in its dens and alleys, or be confined in the lowest of its prisons than emigrate to other countries, or honestly toil for sustenance; and the method employed by some of the paupers to gain this living is worthy of a special chapter. The street Arabs are simply multitudinous. They are a fraternity of their own, indigenous to London, without parallel in any other section of the world, generally in league with the older ruffians, men and women, adepts in all kinds of wickedness, ever ready to face any risk or run any danger. They pour down upon and besiege the foot-passengers in hordes. They attach themselves to your person, and adhere with the utmost tenacity. When you hail a hansom or four-wheeler, in the twinkling of an eye you are surrounded by as many evil spirits as sprang upon "old Rip" on that eventful evening in the Catskills when he took his nap, and these English manikins emanate from every corner in the same mysterious manner. There is the old man, the ragged girl, the dirty boy, and the consumptive woman with the baby hidden under her scanty shawl, all eager to render some service, and receive compensation.

A couple of days ago, as I was walking up Parliament Street, a little boy sprang before me and proceeded to throw summersaults on the pavement for quite a block, and it was only when he demanded pay, that I became aware that these feats of agility had been indulged for my special delectation. Further on two little girls started off on a waltz for my amusement, and they, of course, wished pennies for their pains. Now these children all belong to some of the older alms-seekers, who stand on the curb turning their sightless eyes, withered hands, or deformed and offensive limbs into capital. There are regular companies formed by the beggars, and each one perambulates his own circuit; sometimes they exchange beats in order to equalize their receipts. They are numerous in St. Giles, Seven-dials, King Street, Shoreditch, and St. Paul's Churchyard; there are restaurants and public houses in the vicinity, and even places of amusement entirely supported by mendicant patrons, who congregate at these resorts at night and spend considerable of their earnings(?)

in hot suppers and liquor. But even the landlord who subsists from the bounty of such characters, does not entertain the most exalted opinion of their moral rectitude, for the forks, knives, and spoons are chained to the tables.

Another profitable source of emolument is the shoe trade. These bullies or swaggerers, excite charity for shoes, by appearing on the streets barefooted, their feet scarified and scabby; the old shoes begged they translate into new ones which they sell, and thus net a sum each day that enables them to live well.

Vice is one of the admitted facts of this awful London, even organized vice, vice in all degrees; but then so is virtue. The wealthy tradesmen and the aristocracy do many graceful acts of charity in secret, and those who are in the habit of declaiming against the luxury and extravagance of the nobility, do not know what enormous sums are paid by some of the latter to relieve the poor. Yet, the rule of oppression prevails too entirely throughout the United Kingdom to make a happy and healthy community. I heard some melancholy stories about the poor in Wales, in what are called the nail factories, that I should have rejected as untrue had not the facts been given to me by a member of the House of Commons. Delicate young women work more arduously, than our southern negro slaves ever worked, for the support of drunken husbands, whose only escape from the workhouse is by the patient and uncomplaining toil of their wives. Suspension of labor in the collieries, cotton mills, brickyards, and lace factories, has produced a state of affairs that baffles description.

These are some of the figures of British pauperism, as I contrast them with other countries. A few years ago England paid $30,000,000 or $16 a head for the support of her poor, while in France the cost for their poor was only $3,400,000, or $2.64 a head. In 1873 there were eight hundred and fifty-five thousand six hundred and eighty-nine paupers in England, and the cost of these in 1860 was $36.25 apiece. In Germany, $7, and in France only $2.50. So British pauperism is ever in the ascendant. Even the *word* found its birth in England in the seventeenth or eighteenth century, to describe that condition of penury where self-support is not attempted, and where the basest vices are bred. Pauperism dates back to the reign of Henry VIII., when the breaking up of the feudal system and the dismantling of the monasteries, threw very many people upon their own endeavors for support. Extreme poverty was the consequence, but a law was passed to the effect, that "valient beggars and idle loiterers" were to be avoided, and only the old and feeble, and the halt were to receive alms, the able bodied men to be put to work. But when the daughter of Anne Boleyn ascended the throne the law was revolutionized, and for the first time a legal right was given to every one to claim relief. Very often the condition of the pauper was superior to that of the independent laborer; if the wages of a parish were considered insufficient for the support of a family, allowances were granted, and more money bestowed for the maintenance of an illegitimate than for a legitimate child. Of course such laws only tended to spread the infection of immorality and sloth.

What a contrast our blessed country forms to this doleful state of government! There is very little native pauperism at home. All of this terrible plague that we have in the United States is foreign-born, or of foreign extraction. We have towns and villages where not one pauper is to be found. Why? It is a question readily answered. The influence of liberal education, the self-respect imposed by political and social privileges, the low prices of land and the right of every man to become a property holder. If England would follow this example of her truant offspring, and educate rather than relieve her masses, the gigantic evil would be greatly abated. So noble a country should labor to remove this foul stain from her escutcheon. No community can be happy while men are allowed to "look to charity as a fund on which they may confidently depend."

LETTER VII.

"Here is the nursery of Art,
Here millions gather glad to see,
The treasures of this mighty mart,
Taken from worlds long past, and yet to be."
ANONYMOUS.

LONDON, February, 1878.

HAD I come abroad previous to the grand pageant which signalized the cetenary of our independence I am quite sure I should have raved about all the wonderful things in this whirlpool of a London. But the education I received in art, science, and invention, while attending that microcosm of marvels, disciplined me to examine more soberly the beautiful creations that were novelties to Americans before the International Exhibition. And so these exquisite displays do not surprise me now.

Therefore, passing through the South Kensington Museum I was a little like the Indian who saw nothing in the white man's country to stir his stolid nature. I was about to add, the institution has cause to be jealous of our Philadelphia Exhibition, but I will attempt no comparisons, they are always odious. Left by itself this great museum would be the *ne plus ultra* of schools and galleries. If I attempted to describe South Kensington Museum, I should fail to be original. I could only walk in the footprints of my predecessors. Thought is sure to dull and dampen the ecstasy of the neophyte in a foreign country. We crave to be novel, and yet how impossible when so many older and wiser judges with all these facts in their memories, devote their best energies to this old world! When I entered this repository of curiosities I was stunned by the dead silence. Silence seems to be one of the characteristics of the English—silence of motion and of speech. In the vast hotels we never hear a footfall nor a loud word despite the stone floors and lofty ceilings, and here I find the same quiet order. All is dumb as death! Perhaps you have noticed the eloquence of unspoken solitude at times. Some one has said "order was heaven's first law," and order is always stillness, but such complete noiselessness as we have here is oppressive.

There were numbers dispersed through the *salons*, and as I watched them in the distant alcoves and sheltered retreats, they grew into a multitude of men and women; but they moved rather like shadows than substances, and they spoke only in whispers. They conveyed knowledge and ideas to each other by signs, and pointed to the catalogues, to paintings, and statues, and maps, and cases. This silent language is contagious, and as I studied them I unconsciously sank into their fashion, and lost my own identity in the voiceless concourse. My words were hushed, and I began to converse by motions, not from choice, but the spell was upon me. I soon became accustomed to and rather enjoyed the speechless conversation. I speedily found myself holding colloquies with the objects, antique and recent. Every statue, relic, chart, fossil, and engraving could articulate ideas to my hungry mind. I passed two days in this splendid academy, and feel that it ought to have been two weeks. Shall I tell you of the living at the side of the skeletons, or of the living before their portraits? Shall I tell you of science, of which I know little; or shall it be politics, of which I know nothing? What interested me most was the wealth of art, skill, ingenuity, and novelty in snuff-boxes, fans, ceramics, and medallions.

A collection of snuff-boxes, in étuis, gold, enamel, jewelled, etc., loaned by Mr. C. Goding, fills several large cases, and I bent over these exquisite morsels until head and heart reeled. The prodigality of expense, time, and genius on these gewgaws is marvellous. Gems by famous Dutch, French, and Italian artists adorned the collection. There was one of scaly gold resembling a serpent's epidermis; the lid was embellished with a matchless mosaic of Venus and Adonis upon the emerald and velvety turf, at their feet babbled a silvery brook, casting a spray over tiny pebbles. The goddess was endeavoring to cajole the cold and chaste youth, who received with utter indifference the proffered favors of the divine coquette. There were splendid enamels containing devices and legendary emblems in diamonds, some of jasper, some of block-crystal, others of sardonyx, and choice moss-agate. There were the productions of all nations and of all ages, proclaiming how for centuries the inhalation of volatile dust was the ruling fashion of society in Europe. The estimated value of this array of snuff-boxes is thousands of pounds sterling.

The next cases that engaged my woman's time and attention were those containing fans. One section was consecrated wholly to a curious and elegant exhibition of fans, mostly the compilation of one lady; many of exquisite French design; satin, tulle, gauze, parchment, and the so-called chicken-skin; and these were beautified with paintings by such clever craftsmen as Marie Bonheur, A. Soldé, Edouard Moreau, and others of equal subtlety. There was the novel Pompadour that forms a perfect oval when expanded, and the folding fan of Catherine de Medicis; the eccentric Lombard shapes of the seventeenth century, and brilliant tuft fans of peacock and parrot feathers with jewelled handles. Fans of wood and fans of ivory; fans of great elegance from Rome, Greece, and Egypt, and even from the fatherland of fans, China. I have heard it contended that fans are a feminine appendage, and in the countries where the use of fans is a national custom, the salient characteristics of the natives are pre-eminently effeminate. But I have no fair samples to offer. They are as essential to a gentleman in Japan and China as his boots, and I am sure the Turk contradicts any such doctrine. True, he wears petticoats, but do you believe the fan and farthingale could effeminate the stern, tyrannical Giaour?

In this collection may also be classed two cases of miniatures, the property of Earl Beauchamp; a blazoning of gold and fine painting on ivory by the illustrious artists of his day, likenesses of his family in a variety of gorgeous costumes and head-dresses; several of pretty Nell Gwynne and Kitty Clive, and the beautiful Duchess of Devonshire. The renowned Mr. Beresford Hope displays a vast amount of ecclesiastical utensils, clocks, ivory carvings, and enamels; among them a curious cross of gold, incrusted with Cloisonné enamel, one of the earliest specimens made in Constantinople, in the eleventh century. Beautiful samples of *Vitro di Trina*, or glass lace-work; specimens of Schmelze, Avanturine, Millefiore, of the colored glass of Venice, and numerous vessels of early Venetian manufacture, having a horny hue and texture. In the western arcade is the harpsichord of Handel, a curiosity in its way; but it recalled to my mind the stories I had heard of his uncontrollable temper, and I was rather surprised to see it in such excellent repair, for the musical genius had rather a careless way of disposing of things, as well as people, when he was in a rage. Then, again, I remembered that he had never loved a woman. Can a man have music in his soul, who has never experienced the divine passion? Near it stands a spinnet, dated 1577, made by Annibale di Rossi, of Milan; the case was of pear-tree wood, and beautifully incrusted with ivory, ebony, pearl, lapis-lazuli, malachite, and Egyptian alabaster; and here also was the curious little German finger-organ that formed a portion of the household adornments of the great ecclesiastical reformer of the sixteenth century, Martin Luther. But I cannot recapitulate all I have enjoyed of Raphael's cartoons, and precious stones, and intaglios, pearls of vast size, and various colors, the historical "Mexican Sun Opal," and marvellous specimens of amber, containing fish and lizards, and numerous agates, bearing miraculous representations of the human face.

Here the devotee of ceramic art may feast upon the confections of the centuries. What a banquet has been spread to allure him! Pottery of all nations and epochs. First: The jasper vases of Wedgwood, in black, and white, and blue, and soft green, with white figures *en relief*, and the majolica by the same artisans, that surpasses all similar wares of the present day in modelling and coloring. Then Minton stoneware and Minton plaque. I cannot leave this chapter before I tell you of a chaste and elegant dinner service I have seen of this choice porcelain, on exhibition in a window near Pall Mall, opposite Haymarket. It is of turquoise blue, soft, yet brilliant in tone, and adorned by carefully drawn swans, in shades of mellow gray and white, wading among the long lush grass. Attending this service were a pair of figures about two feet high, of the same exquisite make and hues, representing a lady and gentleman of the Court of Louis XVI. Whenever I pass this cynosure, I endeavor to distract my attention by any object in an opposite direction, but the magnet conquers, and when I gaze I am enthralled; it is so temptingly beautiful. Twice I have ventured into the sanctuary to price and prey upon it; and as I look and linger, two fiends tear at my heart, as they did at good Launcelot Gobbo's; mine are the fiends of a luxurious desire, and a scanty purse. The fiend —desire—is at mine elbow, and tempts me, saying, "take it, gratify your taste." "No," says my meagre enemy on my right, "take heed, honest lady, take heed; scorn such frivolities." Then courageous desire says, "Rouse up, be of brave and positive mind." Then, replies the slim and hungry opponent, "My honest friend, you are an honest woman's child; beware!" Then flattering desire says, "Imagine it upon your table at home, the beauty enhanced, when in combination with fine linen, pure crystals of sparkling wines, shining silver, laden with luscious fruits, seen through the glow of colored lights; how pretty the little French lady will be on the *étagere*, when not called to the dinner-table." And I am about to yield, when the other voice whispers, "Caution, prudence, go your way!" and I go! Through sheer madness, I "run away with my heels" as Gobbo did. But the Minton porcelain of pale blue with its white swans haunts me nevertheless.

Further on are specimens of jewelled Copeland and Sévres, Henri Deux and Palissy, and many worthy adaptations from Majolica, Palissy, and Della Robbia, produced in England.

The windows of the refreshment-room of the South Kensington Museum and the corridor leading to it, are combinations of the most beautiful stained-glass fragments

I have ever seen. Much of this same glass has been taken from the famous windows of Saint Chapelle in Paris.

Outside, the building is not stately as our Philadelphia Exhibition Hall, although a series of magnificent edifices surrounded by twelve acres of ground, the cost of which was $300,000. Since the erection of the first structure at $75,000, a group has been added. This section of opulent London is intersected by miles of massive and forbidding mansions. Within these lordly palaces there are light, and warmth, and hospitality, sweet women, and sweeter children; but the outer face is lifeless and dreary, and I soon learned how few of these favored classes walk the streets. They are like precious jewels closed in a casket, to be seen only on special occasions. They saunter in their own grounds, and when they venture beyond those limits, are always in costly carriages.

LETTER VIII.

"His faith and works, like streams that intermingle,
  In the same channel ran;
The crystal clearness of an eye kept single
  Shamed all the frauds of man."
                      JOHN GREENLEAF WHITTIER.

"No dear mother ever upon me smiled—
  Why is it, I wonder, that I'm nobody's child."
                      PHILO H. CHILD.

                    LONDON, February, 1878.

I WAS greatly interested in the accounts that floated to America of Dean Stanley's welcome to General Grant, when the ex-President visited Westminster Abbey shortly after his arrival in London last July. How the gray old cathedral was suffocatingly crowded; how all the Americans and thousands of the English were present to tender kind salutations to the unostentatious hero; and how the Dean at the close of his sermon addressed the great soldier directly. Such an honor was indeed a novelty; it is the dead, and not the living, who are glorified in Westminster, and the venerable scholar and ecclesiast is not in the habit of praising men in power. I heard him speak a few days ago, but was not near enough to catch his tones nor to gather in his thoughts, and had, therefore, formed no opinion of him until after my social call at his home in the ancient monastery yesterday.

In one of the dreary and crumbling traverses of the abbey we found a door leading to the Dean's private chambers. By a huge brass knocker we made our presence known, which was speedily answered by a youthful servant. I feared we would not be granted an audience, knowing so well how heavily he is pressed by other duties, from which there is no escape. The charge of the great Abbey is in itself an exacting task, and then the visitors, the religious bodies, and his literary exertions, are so many constant claims upon his time. A member of Parliament, who had for many years resided in the United States, accompanied me, and, upon the presentation of his name, we were graciously received. The room we first entered, and where we waited during the absence of the messenger, was rigidly plain; it presented a rather gloomy aspect, and here and there were placed old religious relics, including aged Bibles, High-Church books, and pictures. While absorbed in the contemplation of these curious ornaments, we were summoned to the Dean's study. We passed through many corridors, and up several spacious stairways of polished walnut and oak. A glad, familiar sight met me in the antechamber; these were Rogers's statuettes, "Coming to the Parson's," and "Rip Van Winkle." I knew that the Dean was partial to America, and had frequently invited American clergy to preach from his pulpit, but this manifest inclination to American art was a welcome to his fireside. The study was a large square apartment, homelike and luxurious. All the appointments were rich, and dark, and handsome. A vast Oriental rug covered the room almost entirely, exposing only a margin of the polished walnut floor. Bookcases extended along the sides, containing the congenial companions of the amiable churchman. On the wall were some portraits of nobility and clergy, by Kneller, Lawrence, Reynolds, etc. The mantel was large, a massive carving of walnut and oak, and in the grate a genial fire was leaping; in its glow stood the old Dean of Westminster. My first impression was: what a large hearth and what a shrunken little man! His greeting was kind, but undemonstrative. He bade us be seated while he remained standing, as we had found him, throughout our entire visit. He is of the Cassius type, "lean and hungry, he thinks too much," and with a scholar-like air. He has very little conversation, and appears to be absorbed by far-away thoughts. He seemed to wait for us to introduce subjects of discussion, and his remarks were invariably polite and laconic. He made a few inquiries about America, and then relapsed into utter silence. When a question was directed to him he seemed to rouse from his distraction in a nervous, epileptic way, and after several moments' hesitancy and deliberation, as if searching through his mind for an exact reply, answered simply, intelligently, and deliberately. An English lady had told me that no marriage was valid solemnized after twelve o'clock, noon, according to the Established Church of England. This statement seemed incredible to me in view of the fact that marriages take place at every hour of the day and night in the United States. I felt quite sure she was jesting with a stranger to English laws, or that she had been misinformed, so I carried the case to Dean Stanley himself. He assured me that what my friend had told me was correct. All marriages, according to the canonical law of the High Church, are null and void after noon, unless by special license from the Right Honorable and Most Reverend Archibald Campbell Tait, Archbishop of Canterbury, and that is only granted in extreme cases.

Arthur Penrhyn Stanley is a son of the late Bishop Edward, and nephew of the first Baron Stanley of Alderly, where the Dean was born December 13, 1815. He was a favorite pupil of the eminent English historian, Dr. Thomas Arnold, while the latter was head master at Rugby School. When he was only nineteen he gained a scholarship at Baliol College, Oxford, and at twenty-two he gained the Newdigate prize for his English poem, "The Gypsies." After many years of admirable official migration, when he was forty-seven, he married Lady Augusta Bruce, daughter of Lord Elgin; she was the Queen's most intimate friend, and acted as one of her ladies-in-waiting until her death in 1876. The Dean is still very near to her Majesty, although not a member of the Tory party. He holds a powerful hand in public affairs, and is much beloved by the English. On the Sabbath I heard him speak I noticed many ladies sending messages and cards to his apartments after he had retired.

Accustomed to hear of extravagant salaries to clergymen at home, I made some inquiry of one of the chapter clerks at Westminster, and learned, that while Dean Stanley receives only £2000, or $10,000 a year, Archbishop Tait, the Primate of all England, is paid $75,000; the Archbishop of York, $50,000; the Bishop of London, $50,000; the Bishop of Durham, $40,000; the Bishop of Winchester, $35,000; and the Bishop of Bangor, $21,000. There are twenty-six other bishops whose salaries are from twenty to twenty-five thousand dollars per annum, and all this great aristocracy supported by still other bishops, deans, deacons, and archdeacons, secretaries, clerks, and innumerable minor dignitaries, some of whom are paid as high as fifteen, ten, and five thousand dollars each, for attending to their religious duties. Of course, this great establishment is a puzzling problem to an American woman, but in contrast with our republican system in America, it seems a monstrous outlay of money when added to other expenses, to pay for the Established Church.

I had heard much of the singularly fresh and brilliant style of Canon Farrar, one of the Dean's assistants, and desired to see the new celebrity. Last evening he spoke in the Church of St. Andrew's, corner of St. Andrew's Street, Holborn Viaduct, and I am obliged to confess I was disappointed, alike in his thoughts and diction. His text, "Modern Martyrs," was one capable of marvellous elaboration, yet he seemed to fail in its treatment. His manner is somewhat graceful, but he lacks fire. He has a soft dulcet English voice, but it has none of the clear and electric American ring. Much of his sermon was inaudible, although the church was filled. The English make a demigod of a clergyman who is not comparable to numbers of our ministers who really enjoy no special celebrity, barring the Reverend Beecher, for whom I entertain the utmost admiration, not as a divine creation, but as an orator, a statesman, a philosopher, and a thinker; it is the subtle eloquence in which he clothes his ideas, that thrilled my whole being when I first listened to him.

Last Sunday I attended holy service in the chapel attached to the Foundling Hospital in Guilford Street, Bloomsbury Square. It is one of the objects that never fail to interest the stranger, and is as full of novelty to the Englishman, for the very natural reason, that it has been the depository for armies of anonymous English children. And I enjoyed it for the other reason, that I had ever felt anxious to see how such institutions are managed. Until after I had made this visit and became interested in these homes for the little unfortunates, I had formed no conception of the statistics of these European establishments. The foundling hospital in Rome has the capacity of retaining 3000 little ones, and one in Naples receives 1900 annually at the turning-box at the door; every foundling has a number fastened about its neck to aid its future recognition. The hospital in Florence grants to the girls a dowry of 235 francs on the event of their marriage, and from 1855 to 1865, 1403 girls received this reward. From 1863 to 1866, the Italian hospital received 33,222 children. Eighty-three of these institutions exist in Italy alone. The statistics of the Russian system are appalling. In the year 1864, there were 6181 foundlings in the St. Petersburg institution, and from 1862 to 1864, 35,387 were admitted to the one in Moscow. Those of Vienna received 54,478 infants, from 1863 to 1868. Both ancient Greece and Rome were furnished with these establishments, and in Athens the forsaken children were exposed in a pillar placed in the public market.

Old Captain Coram, founder of the London Foundling Asylum, was a seafaring man who, several centuries ago, donated to the city fifty-six acres, which has now so increased in value, as to be covered by great squares and flower-gardens, and handsome houses; and thus this hospital stands in one of the most beautiful districts of the gray metropolis. Over 500 outcasts, girls and boys, from mere infancy to the age of fifteen years, joined in the service of the church, and I afterwards saw them at their dinners in the long well lighted hall. The children *must* all be illegitimate, and the mother is not permitted to visit her little one after placing it here, unless she mingles in the throng of visitors on Sunday. After it has received the prescribed amount of education and is about to be apprenticed out, then she has a right to claim it. In the building are preserved cases of trinkets, cards and other mementos found on the waifs, as they are deposited with the keeper. Nothing could have been more beautiful than the day I visited this imposing spectacle. Some of Hogarth's most valuable productions, who was a great benefactor to this charity, adorn the walls, and several fine statues are preserved in memory of Captain Coram and his worthy successors.

LETTER IX.

"The boast of heraldry, the pomp of power,
   And all that beauty, all that wealth e'er gave,
Await alike the inevitable hour:—
   The paths of glory lead but to the grave."
                              GRAY.

"Among mankind we are all born alike
Of father and mother. None excels
Another in his nature, but the fate
Of evil chance holds some of us, and some
Good fortune favors, and necessity
Holds some in bondage."
                    SOPHOCLES.

LONDON, March, 1878.

I HAVE ever regarded the study of heraldry the height of folly, and while many of my friends love to dilate on the subject, I prefer to study something more useful. I never had any time to give to that prodigious mass of conceit, "Burke's Peerage." What has an American lady to do with armorial bearings, descents, precedence, ceremonies, and processions? Unlike some Pinchbeck patrician sisters, I never had the slightest inclination to purchase from my stationer a counterfeit crest, nor to shield my shortcomings by a blazonry of borrowed dignity or genealogy. The ambition of every American should be to merit a title of real nobility, then may he proudly wear it.

I passed yesterday morning in the Herald's College, Benet's Hill, Doctors' Commons, and became interested so much in the science as to feel authorized to disprove the axiom of the men, that women are always attracted by gewgaws, and I reproach my sex for being too ready to yield to the accusation. I hope those who may visit the College of Arms and converse with Mr. Stephen I. Tucker, the Rouge Croix pursuivant, will not freely give way hereafter. This institution is a huge monument of the vanity of men. Not that my sex are not fond of the signs of blue blood and ancient ancestry, but it is invariably the male who originates and carries these empty honors; the female is only the reflection of the lords of creation, save indeed, when she is mistress, like Queen Victoria. Yet I learned from one of the friends of the Lord Chamberlain, that even Her Majesty obeys the mandates of her ministers in her rules of court and in the choice of the ladies of her household.

While Mr. Tucker was showing us through this receptacle of the parchmented and vellumed title-deeds of the British nobility, he related some amusing stories of the numberless communications they receive from persons craving information as to their relationship with the old families. Frequently Americans are sure a vast fortune is soon to be theirs on account of their claimed connection with one of these ancient houses, and there are also numbers of such expectants in England. The Herald's College is often pestered by these waiters upon fortune, who sometimes lose their wits in the wild search for riches that never come. In America we have no such institution as the "Herald's College," and yet many of our people are constantly sighing for borrowed robes. Neither have I any respect for those who would deny their ancestors, forgetting, like the ostrich that hides its head as the storm approaches, that what they hope to conceal is only made more public by their struggles. And those who exist in and on their grandparents, are still more worthy of contempt, for they are brave in feathers not their own; to me it seems equally absurd to blush for, or to boast of one's forefathers. Still the "Herald's College" was interesting and novel, for here I saw for the first time the value of mere titles and tassels. The apparent fact is that virtue and worth are too rarely recognized. The original merit may be virtue, worth, bravery, benevolence, but the sin and shame of the whole system is, that the most worthless inherits the most worthy, and, far worse, the vices of the last heir are always condoned by the glorious deeds of his progenitor a thousand years ago.

Mr. Tucker, sensible and practical as he is, showed us the collective autographs, rolls, missals, and archives of the great English houses for many centuries, but did not make an argument for them. These reminiscences at first aroused my pity, such pity as I had often felt for a dear friend who was making a dunce of himself, till I saw how all the English bow down before these relics, how they worship a lord or a lady, a duke or a duchess, and how (naturally enough) the be-praised families accept the adulation, as if they had earned it. So it was not for me to attempt a reformation, nor to condemn the English nobility if they become fools like their parasites.

The "Herald's College" was founded by Richard III. in

1484. The chief is the Duke of Norfolk, one of the leading Catholic peers, and the office is an heirloom of his house. There are three kings of arms, six heralds, and four pursuivants. These officers attend on court occasions in royal costume. The scarlet coat embroidered with gold, and gold buttons, cocked hat, and pantaloons with broad gold stripe, and a small sword, gave to handsome Stephen I. Tucker the appearance of a masonic knight. It was a sort of theatrical uniform, or holiday fancy-dress, and as I write I feel quite sure my gracious friend will charge my criticism to my democratic rearing. I presume I was obtuse, but it was a long time before I could comprehend that the objects of the " Herald's College" were to preserve all the pedigrees of the British nobility and gentry, the records of royal coronations, marriages, christenings, funerals, visits of kings and princes, also official reports of cavalcades, processions, tournaments, and combats. The royal funerals alone fill sixty-five folio volumes. The immense libraries are crowded with books, portraits, and engravings, to preserve veneration for rank among the people. These documents and records are very often necessary to settle questions of title to lands, but the general object is to keep alive respect for aristocratic forms. I was much impressed by this regard for old customs. At home almost every family has peculiar habits, generally hard enough to explain to strangers, or to justify to ourselves, and this is the case in London. I was shown an account of Sir Gervase Clifton, who had been a widower six times; also a volume, the work of a monk of the 14th century, "The Pedigree from Adam to the Saxon Kings." He tells us after "Adam had lived 930 years he died of the gout." Lady Juliana Berners says that "Adam was a gentleman," and in one sense she does not transcend the bounds of reason. But when John Guillim, the rouge croix pursuivant of the 17th century, ascribes coat-armor to the tribes of Israel, I think he has allowed his imagination rather free play. Mr. Tucker's ancestor and namesake, Stephen Tucker, was licensed by Henry VIII., July 2, 1519, " to use and wear his bonnet upon his head, as well in our presence as elsewhere, at his liberties." The great mass of books, papers, and vellums, were kept in perfect order, and as they relate to thousands, and are frequently consulted, their preservation requires a prodigious outlay of money. The Queen appoints all the heralds, and their homes are in the college. Mr. Tucker presented us to his charming family, and when I left I felt that the winter day had been profitably passed, though I was unsatisfied; having tasted of this enigmatical science, I hungered for still further knowledge.

The mysteries of coats-of-arms are indeed curious. The precious stones, topaz, pearls, rubies, sapphires, emeralds, amethysts, and diamonds, are in constant use, each emblematic; also the colors, red, yellow, blue, white, orange, purple, and black; and the planets, sun, moon, stars, Jupiter, Venus, Mercury, and Saturn. How soon we learn that the precious stones are for nobility, the planets for princes, the various colors for higher or lower degrees; which is the dexter and which the sinister side of the field; and thus we are able to read the hieroglyphics of heraldic bearings by the effigies of men, women, and children, beasts, fruits, and flowers. Lions gardant, saliant, couchant, dormant, and passant, seem to have been one of the earliest charges; we see them on the shields of the great houses of Northumberland, Cadogan, North, Westminster, Fitzhammond. The meaning of such charges as fleur-de-lis, clarion, and the fylfot is obscure; they are, therefore, called doubtful. Learned scholars do not hesitate to devote themselves to this study, as if it had a visible use other than to keep alive form, degree, obedience, and reverence among men. The struggle for precedence amused me. Every rank has its place, and none dares to precede his superiors. Ridiculous anecdotes are afloat of the disputes of men, but the gossips say that ladies are far more severe and particular, especially those of ancient family. Serious dissensions occur, and the royal households are not exceptions to bursts of feminine temper. The Queen, Princess of Wales, princesses, duchesses, the wives of kings, or brothers of the Queen, daughters of the Queen, come first, and then the other grades of nobility, down to the wives of clergymen, and lawyers, and burgesses; but there is no place for the consorts of tradesmen or mechanics, and those of scientists, artists, and scholars are excluded. The clergy and lawyers come last on the roster.

The titled families take not only the precedence, but absorb most of the offices and attentions of the court. An American now and then engineers herself into the charmed circle, but it is paid for by much intrigue and humiliation; and after her object is accomplished, she is discussed and canvassed disparagingly by the British sisterhood.

Since I have been in London, incidents have come to

my knowledge by which I am taught social caste is as strong in England as it ever was; and I am sorry to add that those who cannot boast a coat-of-arms of their own, nor a long lineage, are generally too anxious to enjoy the patronage of their more fortunate fellow-creatures.

LETTER X.

"Home of the Grosvenor's high-born race,
 Home of their beautiful and brave,
Alike their birth—and burial-place,
 Their cradle and their grave!
Still sternly o'er the castle-gate
Their house's Lion stands in state,
 As in his proud, departed hours,
And warriors frown in stone on high,
And feudal banners 'flout the sky,'
 Above his princely towers."
FITZ-GREEN HALLECK, AMENDED.

* * * * *

"A world of busy workers, who nobly toil
 The greater world to clothe and charm,
Men who take vast wealth from sky and soil,
Coin gems for ornaments, and guns to harm.
Such is this glowing City—such this home
Of modern art, a new and dazzling Rome,
Where labor rules supremest king,
And bright inventions choicest offerings bring."
ANONYMOUS.

BIRMINGHAM, March, 1878.

It was a day very like our Indian summer as we strolled through the famous town of Chester, in Cheshire; passing through the old city gates, lingering in our walk upon the original Roman walls, and upon the antique and tottering bridges that span the Dee, and pausing to feast our eyes upon the exquisite specimens of pottery in the shops hidden under the *rows*, as they are called here—roofed galleries extending along the sidewalk, where pedestrians may shop, protected from the rain when the weather is inclement. I enjoyed these novelties under the kind guideship of General Lucius Fairchild, American Consul at Liverpool. He lives so near the ancient seat, and has so many friends in the vicinity, that, as well as having the pleasure of his genial society we garnered much information from his intelligent descriptions of the interesting and picturesque country around us.

Chester has become almost an American town; not in its inhabitants nor its customs, but because it is largely visited by our country people, and is also the central point for an immense amount of English traffic and travel. A flood of overpowering historical recollections enveloped me as I paused to think and gaze upon the busy town upon the high road between London and Ireland; it is the very spot upon which to draw comparisons between the old, old times and the new ones. The Romans were here with the twentieth legion in A. D. 60, and many descriptions of ancient relics are found at this day, speaking loudly of the early possessors. Old as Chester is, it is very clean and very much improved, although there is a visible effort to hold on to the vestiges of the original Roman occupation. Here, indeed, was the archetype of the many pictures I had seen of English towns. The narrow lanes, low, red-tiled roofs, spotless dimity curtains stretched across the lower window panes, rows of earthen flower-pots and little green plants, gave to it a provincial air.

The books that have been written about this one town would fill a respectable library, especially those by Americans. I will not loiter upon the old, footbeaten path, but try to preserve some idea of the famous Eaton Hall, the magnificent estate of the Marquis of Westminster, the richest peer in England, the owner of a large portion of the great murky metropolis, whose income is simply incalculable. The ancestor of this Norman lord was the Earl Hugh Lupus, the nephew and favorite of the Norman conqueror, who, like many of those ancient chiefs, after living through years of vice, expiated his sins by constructing the Abbey of St. Warburg, from which the old cathedral, within a few years splendidly improved, may claim its origin.

The fair and opulent demesne on which Eaton Hall stands, is over sixteen miles in length, and some seven miles broad, nearly as vast as the entire city of Philadelphia, Fairmount Park inclusive, and this is not all; the mighty Marquis of Grosvenor, or Westminster, is the happy possessor of a large part of the city of Chester. We drove, in our little English wagonette, out to this historic domain, about three miles from this still more historic town. As we approached, the great iron gate supported by the stone portals of the outer lodge, was swung back upon its creaking, rusty hinges, by the keeper's daughter, a little ruddy-faced English girl in a crimson dress, who dropped us a courtesy, and cast upon us a coy glance from under her lashes, that meant pennies. We drove for miles through long avenues, skirted by huge oaks and firs. Although much of the grounds are under cultivation, there are vast sections devoted to the ornamental, and to large herds of deer,—that were grazing by thousands,—not for human consumption, but simply for the sport of the noble Marquis and his titled guests. We obtained a glimpse of the costly castle; of the hall 450 feet long, in which the Marquis resides when at home, of a floor 40 feet square, that cost $8000, of the great corridor extending 500 feet, of the spacious drawing-room, with the ceiling of heraldic shields, and honeycombed in tracery of cream color and gold, the walls rich in their treasures of art, by Rubens and West, of the still more spacious library, with its colonnades of pillars on either side, and heavy gothic windows, and oaken shelves, overladen with the rarest books. The grand stairway is a prodigy; two colored marble Egyptian statues stand on either hand as you ascend the long flight of steps, which run from the centre right and left to the second gallery, and thence to the private apartments on the higher story. Land and sea have been ransacked for gems to adorn this luxurious pile. Here are inclosed precious articles of *virtu*, paintings, statuary, mosaics, and frescoes. During the hunting season this nobleman entertains many hundred guests, and his tenantry alone are from five to seven hundred. The whole edifice, exclusive of stables and out-buildings, covers a space of 700 feet in front. 1600 guineas were expended upon the pavement of the main floor.

Tapestries, damasks, shields, vases, chandeliers, and a world of precious treasures of art, have been purchased and placed in the interior, while outside you are enchanted with fountains, vistas, Italian gardens, long walks, and endless arrangements for the enjoyment of those who prefer the chase, or the drive, or the pleasures of the angler. Apart from the historic pieces, and portraits, and old armor, is a choice collection of racing pictures, illustrative of the fabulous sums of money that have been squandered on blooded horses by the luxurious Grosvenors. The portraits of the animals belonging to this family for more than a hundred years occupy a prominent place in the household. This house of Westminster, or Grosvenor, has been collecting wealth and adding to all its territory since the Norman invasion. I was enraptured by the gardens and conservatories, which, though it was early spring, were filled with every variety of exotic shrub and flower, including exquisite pieces of native growth, making altogether a bewildering multitude of color and a weight of odor that recalled the simile of the poet when he speaks of the rose dying of aromatic pain.

As I entered the central avenue, I was greeted by a vision of entrancing beauty. The floral-fretted walls extended and gradually contracted in the far perspective; from the lofty and vaulted glass roof hung the delicate sprays of a vine bearing tiny crimson stars that had clustered and wreathed their tendrils into a network and fringe overhead. Far, far down this gallery, the effect was that of a cloud of sea-foam in mid-air, tinged by the lurid glow of the sinking sun. It was a poem of radiance and perfume from the breath of heaven. Then there were the scarlet and pink and white lilies, the sweet modest violets, the cold chaste bridal-wreaths, the lusty velvet roses, and the bronzed and glossy margins of box; and you may be quite sure I did not quit this Eden till I had secured fragrant trophies of my memorable visit.

The old racecourse, where the Chester cup is annually run for, has a history of its own, and there is no finer English scene than the struggle for this cup in May. In 1540 a custom began, by which a silver bell, costing 3s. 6d., was annually given by the saddler's company "to him who shall run the best on horseback." This arrangement was subsequently changed, and it was decreed that that "horse which with speed did overrun the rest, had the best cup then presently delivered, and that horse which came second, next the first, before the rest, had the second cup then also delivered."

Cheshire, in which Chester is placed, is perhaps the richest county in England in old houses; many of the churches are very beautiful, and it is noted for the number of its aristocracy and wealthy proprietors; but among its old estates you will find few, indeed none, as extensive as Eaton Hall. The country is so gridironed with railroads, that with its limited territory you pass from one place to another without the slightest difficulty. So bidding adieu to our friend, General Fairchild, we passed into Warwickshire, and found ourselves at The Great Western Hotel, Birmingham, a few hours after leaving Chester. Warwickshire is one of the wealthiest territories in the world, and Birmingham the largest manufacturing town in England, and is claimed without an equal in any other country. Far different from Liverpool, brighter, cleaner, and more intelligent, it is called "the toy-shop of Europe," from the number and variety of its manufactures. I had no time to stop to examine the churches and shops, theatres and cemeteries, and so hired a hack and a guide, and made a rather close survey of the manufactories, all of them very curious and interesting to me. It is the great headquarters of buttons; buttons of brass, copper, cloth, shell, bone, wood, and porcelain. The gilt buttons for military and other uniforms employ thousands of persons; millions of cloth buttons are sold annually, also linen buttons, hooks and eyes, and pearl and bone buttons. Swords and guns and pistols are made in immense quantities in Birmingham. The gold and silver plate in jewelry trade is very large. 30,000 wedding rings annually pass through the assay office. 70 ounces of gold leaf are used every week, and 150,000 ounces of silver are used annually. I was completely astounded by the manufacture of brasses and bronzes. The Birmingham workers in iron are renowned all over the world. The glass manufacturers, and the manufacturers of steel pens are also very interesting; they claim that Birmingham supplies the world with pens.

We drove through Aston Park, by the sweet waters of the Rea, along the eastern slopes of the undulating hills of red sandstone, and into the suburbs as far as Stafford and Worcester. The new court of assizes, that is in course of erection, is quite as large and as handsome a building as our new post-office promises to be; the town cannot claim half the population of Philadelphia, including that portion beyond city limits.

Opposite my window is one of the beautiful arcades or galleries of shops that one finds all over Europe; and after the lamps were lighted I sauntered through it to note the diversity of fancy articles of native manufacture that embellished the windows. A pleasant place to pass half an hour; a clean walk, a glass roof, brilliant goods displayed, and it seemed to be a general rendezvous for luxurious idlers.

LETTER XI.

"Thou soft flowing Avon, by thy silver stream,
Of things more than mortal sweet Shakespeare would dream;
The fairies by moonlight dance round his green bed,
For hallow'd the turf is which pillow'd his head."
                                            GARRICK.

STRATFORD-ON-AVON, March, 1878.

A RIDE of about half an hour on the rails brought us into this quaint old town of the myriad-minded poet. The atmosphere was salubrious and hazy when we quitted Birmingham, and the blue glamour of the long English twilights was weaving itself around the horizon. Of the beautiful section of Warwickshire through which our route lay, I saw little; the glimpses I caught of the rich farms, luxuriant valleys, and gentle-flowing streams, were not satisfactory through the obscuring mists. When we drew up in the little station in Stratford-on-Avon, only twenty-six miles distant, we were greeted by "an eager and a nipping air" and a driving shower of hail. A rickety omnibus conveyed us to the Shakespeare House, where the chambers are designated by titles from the immortal plays, one over each door. As you enter the hall there are tables and escritoires of the heavy English style, a bust of Shakespeare, and memorial engravings. Over the dining-room I noticed the appropriate quotation, "may good digestion wait on appetite." I was assigned the apartment bearing the inscription, "Midsummer Night's Dream." I could attach no point to this motto on which to hang a vision. I only knew that it was a large room containing three beds, the walls in a state of utter dilapidation, and the windows, illy fitted to their frames, were shaken all through the night by the wind, while the hail pattered violently against the glass. These circumstances did not inspire the delightful sensations suggested by the title. The bridal-chamber is labelled "Love's Labor's Lost," the same that had been occupied by Olive Logan several months ago when she passed through Stratford. Has this most incongruous prefix been inadvertently placed here, or is it the work of some melancholy pessimist?

On the second floor of this little hotel are some valuable old paintings by Rembrandt, Sir Joshua Reynolds, and early artists of equal celebrity; and the original sign-board of the inn, bearing a dim and defaced effigy of Shakespeare

The proprietor's wife, an Englishwoman of considerable education, was excessively hospitable, and after chatting about her collection of pictures, the ancient house, and the strange maxims that arrest your gaze at every step, she spoke of my obvious state of poor health, and offered her tender care and an alleviation, if not a remedy, for my sufferings while I remained her guest. She left me, and a quarter of an hour afterward a maid appeared with a bowl of what I supposed to be farina gruel and a small vial of a brownish hue, of which she cautioned me, to let the dose be meagre; this warning might have been omitted, as there was but *one* remaining drop; still the words created unpleasant suspicions in my husband's mind, who endeavored to dissuade my imbibing the ominous potion. Despite the entreaties, I took it; I felt that my sands of life were rapidly drifting out into the great ocean of eternity; the ruthless winds were shifting the leaves of my brief book of life, to the page where only one word, *finis*, was written; and so the offered sympathy I accepted; but let my experience serve as a watchword to my American sisters; the following evening I found my landlady's pap and charity put in the bill, after I had praised her as a model! Beware of the sympathetic English proprietress; this is the second one who has charged for benevolence. "The best in this kind are but shadows; and the worst are no worse, if imagination amend them."

My first visit was not to the house where he who became Lord Paramount in English literature opened his eyes upon the light of this world, but to New Place, the home of his ripened genius and industry, where he waited the too early summons of the grim and bribeless reaper. Of his ancient sanctum there remain only a few foundation stones. But here lived and labored the poet; here were his garden, his favorite mulberry tree, his shady walks, and his lawn and orchard stretching down to the margin of the silvery Avon. The morning succeeding the hailstorm was dismal and wet, but the turf in the Shakspeare garden was fresh and green, and the gravel-paths firm beneath our feet. These gardens are cultivated and embellished with beautiful flowers, and in the summer season are open for public enjoyment. By special arrangement they may be procured for picnics and other occasions of merry-making.

In the house attached to New Place, where resides the ancient and interesting warden of the illustrious poet's devastated home, are many silent but eloquent relics of his life and surroundings; a rude clay cast of the "bard of Avon," and a portrait, as also portraits of the noble line of Cloptons and Coombes, whose fair daughter, if my memory rightly serves me, was consigned to a living tomb, and the fact is generally believed to have been the incentive to the melancholy tragedy, "Romeo and Juliet."

We approached Trinity Chapel through a path skirted by tall limes, whose interlacing branches form a shelter overhead, where the cold glimmer of white tombstones is faintly seen through the rank grass, where the sweetly flowing Avon winds like a silken ribbon about the base of the crumbling and ivy-crowned house of God, whose gentle murmur is a dulcet accompaniment to the whistling of the wind among the almost leafless branches. As we waited for the sexton, I noticed a sad-faced woman and child planting flowers around a little grave that had been newly made, and then we passed from the yet untrodden earth of a spring-time burial, into the centuried sanctuary of the immortal dust.

On the left side of the chancel, as you face the altar, is the grave bearing the well-known inscription:—

> Good frend for Jesus sake forbeare,
> To digg the dust encloased here;
> Bleste be ye man y^t spares these stones,
> And curst be he y^t moves my bones.

Printed fac-similes of these characteristic lines of the "poet of the world" are for sale at a shilling each; but by offering a bribe of another shilling, I became the possessor of the identical one upon the tomb. From the entablature just above, the florid and bedizened effigy of sweet William, in scarlet doublet and sleeveless black gown, looked down upon the sacrilegious barter over his dry and whited bones. And then we were requested to contribute to the beautiful new memorial window that is placed very near Shakespeare's tomb, and is paid for from American bounty; it is of exquisite stained glass, and represents the "seven ages," applied to the Bible; four of the panels are already completed. After lingering in the aisles and naves of the old Gothic structure, we turned to the birthplace of the modest wool-comber's poet child. Here everything is redolent of Shakespeare, and the phantom that I had entertained of Shakespeare being made of different clay, and cast in a different mould from the rest of humankind, rapidly faded. He had lived so long ago, I so far away from all that proved his existence, his writings so peerless, his imagination so wild and creative, that I had sometimes believed him a tradition, always divine, but never a myth. I delight to find him human, approachable, and lovable. The old fireplace, the decayed walls, ceilings, and floors, the low-gabled tenement, and the ten treacherous steps that ascend from the kitchen to the chamber where he was born, all seem hallowed by the "great heir of fame," and then I remember that this same house served afterward as a butcher-shop and a tavern, impregnated with the odor of beer, bad gin, coarse meat, and greasy bacon; ah! verily, "to what base uses may we not return, Horatio?"

The walls of the chamber are blackened by thousands of pencilled names, and Scott and Byron are easily read upon the glass window panes. There remain the chairs, the signet ring, the first copy of some of his plays, and even a letter from Richard Quincey, written in 1598, for the purpose of borrowing from the poet thirty pounds, but not one line in the hand of Shakespeare. The little garden attached to the "birthplace" is filled with the flowers so often mentioned in his dramas, and as the old lady who conducted us over the poetical ground handed them to me, she repeated the lines of poor Ophelia, and those that run, "I know a bank whereon the wild thyme blows," etc. I found Mr. J. O. Halliwell Philips not only the god of her idolatry, but the presiding genius of all Stratford-on-Avon; it must be remembered that he purchased over ten years ago "New Place," and presented it to the Crown, after putting it in splendid order. Occasionally he visits the ancient village, and must be, from all accounts, a regular brother Cheeryble, judging by the ecstasies of the woman janitor of the "birthplace." Every one about Stratford, with the exception of the great families, makes a living out of Shakespeare; were it not for the constant stream of tourists, mainly Americans, the old houses and haunts of the idol William, the shops, taverns, and churches, would have a dismal experience. Everything is placed under a rigid system of contribution. The charges are not great, but the system is consistently and steadily maintained.

The great staple product of the vicinage is beer; indeed, the whole neighborhood cultivates the juice of the hop, just as all classes drink the tempting brew. The memorial theatre, which seems to have originated from the fund started by David Garrick, one hundred and ten years ago, to construct a statue to Shakespeare, is in rapid course of erection, and when completed, will be one of the finest in the kingdom. It is entirely too large, however, for the town, which has a population of not more than 4000. Only on rare occasions can it ever be put to profitable use.

LETTER XII.

"He was not of an age, but for all time,
And all the muses still were in their prime,
When like Apollo he came for to charm
Our ears, or like a Mercury to harm."
BEN JONSON.

WARWICK, ENGLAND, March, 1878.

THE charm of English life is a residence or sojourn in the country during the spring and summer, but as my programme carries me on the Continent for the opening of the Paris Exposition, I am obliged to improve an English winter as best I can. The country side of England is always lovely, even in March, and the climate is much less dismal and inhospitable than that of London.

Warwickshire, the county in which Stratford is placed, has been, from its central situation and physical periphery, called the heart of England. It is a little world by itself; a world of wealth in mineral and agricultural products, a world of learning, of aristocracy, of poetry, romance, history, ancient records, and modern progress. The railway radiates all through the section at exceedingly low fares, cab hire is reasonable, and the distances between the various show places, village inns, cities, and towns, in this particular county, are so short, that many travellers, when the weather is fine, prefer to walk. A week might be spent in Stratford and its vicinity, and you would reap a golden harvest of pleasure and information.

While at the Shakespeare house I heard of many of my country people who come there in June or July, and loiter around the place sanctified by the great master, his predecessors, and followers; interesting in their Roman remains and attractive in recent ancestral homes. The river Avon flows through Warwickshire on its way to the Severn; it beautifies and freshens the borders of lovely English

6

abodes, passes smiling, thrifty hamlets, sombre castles, irrigates rich farm lands, murmurs at the poet's grave, and coils around the old county-towns with their venerable churches and towers.

Alcester, seven and a half miles from Stratford, a small market town, the seat of a Roman encampment, as proved by the discovery of ancient bricks, coins, and urns of human bones, is now a modern factory of needles. Alcester is at the confluence of the streams Arrow and Alne, a short distance from the ancient castles of the Beauchamps and Grevilles, two miles from Coughton Manor, the home of the ancient family of Throckmorton since the reign of Henry IV. The same little town is bordered, equally distant, on the southwest by Ragley Park, the patrician estate of the Marquis of Hertford, with its castle, park, lakes, and peerless gardens. Charlecote, four miles from Stratford, indissolubly associated with Shakespeare, is the ancient family seat of the Lucys, whose ancestor, Sir Thomas Lucy, is said to have bitterly persecuted Shakespeare, because the latter, on several occasions, made free with the Knight's deer, which favor (?) the poet returned by attaching immortal and merciless ridicule to him as *Justice Shallow*. The old homestead is of brick in the Elizabethan style, the great hall wainscoted in oak, containing marvels of ancient and richly carved furniture, and many valuable paintings. Charlecote Church, near by, was rebuilt by the same family. The Cloptons and Combes, families contemporary with Shakespeare, had their estate on the Avon, so that the entire vicinage is dotted with noble castles and opulent homes.

Shottery, where Shakespeare wooed — or rather *was* wooed by Anne Hathaway, is only a mile from his birthplace. There is nothing here to awaken pleasant recollections, and I was rather glad that some doubts were thrown upon its authenticity. Even the relics purchased from here by Garrick, as sanctified by confederacy with the great poet, were most probably the constructive frauds of an enterprising auctioneer or collector.

My visit to Stratford left a sad impression. It is odd indeed that there remains nothing satisfactory of Shakespeare's ways of life, either in London, or at his village home. There was quite too much surmise and speculation. The most living things about him are his plays, and even these are doubted by some and openly conceded to others. For so great a mind, it is painful how little has been left by himself or found by antiquarians! Dwelling upon these facts, like thousands of others who have preceded me, I was cheered by the following lines, that I copied from the crumbling walls of Shakespeare's house, written by sweet Washington Irving in 1821—fifty-eight years ago. It is the most solacing excuse for Shakespeare's *anonymous character* I have seen:—

> "Of mighty Shakespeare's birth the room we see,
> That where he died in vain to find we try;
> Useless the search—for all immortal he,—
> And those who are immortal never die."

When we left Stratford the annual cattle fair was at its height, and as we passed through the picturesque valley of the Avon, we saw vast herds of choice grades in paddocks for exhibition. There were the short-horned Durham breed, the Herefords, that are valuable as working oxen, the Devons, famed for their beauty, the Ayrshires prized for the quantity of milk they yield, and the Alderneys whose EXTRACT is world renowned for richness. I have good reason never to forget the latter breed, and when my experience recurs to my mind I do not contemplate this particular stock with much satisfaction. Several weeks ago my London physician advised me to drink English stout, champagne or cream. The first was less palatable than any drug he could have prescribed, the second too costly, and as I was forbidden still wines I was reduced to the remaining expedient, so I ordered the commissioner at the Westminster to have Alderney cream served to me every morning. Nothing could have been finer, so that it is not the quality of which I complain but the price; when I received the account I discovered that I had been building up my health upon a foundation of cream at two dollars a quart! Now, do not look aghast as I did. I endeavored to persuade myself that I had forgotten my table of English money, or that my *entire* bill amounted to eight shillings. I rang for the commissioner and advised with him. He assured me the bill was correct and seemed to be surprised that cream had declined to eight shillings, the usual price being ten! I had always heard the capabilities of the Alderney highly spoken of and for the first time I realized how *high* they were.

What a beautiful spot is Warwick! These sweet English towns are much more attractive than wild, 'wildering London. Here one has such a supreme sense of rest, away from the gloom and clamor of ponderous houses and noisy streets, away from the vast palaces where great questions of state are discussed, away from that ceaseless whirlpool of trade.

After we had deposited our luggage and engaged rooms at the Warwick Arms we strolled out through the streets of the town. I noticed cleanly highways, beautiful residences, extensive shops, and then wandered toward the eminence on which the castle stands, lingered upon the new stone bridge that girds the same beautiful Avon ever in our wake wheresoever we may turn. The picture was one of unrivalled beauty. The sky was pale blue, flecked with filmy clouds, and the sun just sinking behind the western hills, shed a rosy glow through the hazy atmosphere. It was much such an afternoon as we frequently have at home in early spring. The luxurious shrubbery in the vast park bent low to rest on the gentle waters they bordered. Shakespeare must have been referring to this sweet river when he said:

> "The current, that with gentle murmur glided
> Thou know'st, being stopped, impatiently doth rage;
> But when his fair course is not hindered,
> He makes sweet music with the enamelled stones,
> Giving a gentle kiss to every sedge
> He overtaketh in his pilgrimage;
> And so, by many winding nooks he strays,
> With willing sport to the wild ocean."

The ancient willows droop to kiss the ripples as they pass, and others like them in Denmark are undoubtedly alluded to by Queen Gertrude, in the passage where she tells Laertes of his fair sister's death, beginning:

> "There is a willow grows ascaunt the brook,
> That shows his hoar leaves in the glassy stream."

On the odorous English road, the rustic lads and lassies doffed their hats and dropped us courtesies, as they came to or from their country homes in the neighboring shires of Stafford, Leicester, or Worcester; from the hills of Fenny Compton, the valley of the Stour, or the Dale of the Red Horse; from the Northwest, near the red marl and sandstone mounds, and from the vicinity of Morton Hill and Dunsmore Heath; some trudging their way on foot, while those from a greater distance rode in their cosey wagonettes. Then we sauntered through the obscure lanes at the rear of the castle walls, where ruddy-faced babies played in the mire, with the poultry, and where low-thatched cottages were as clean and orderly as the splendid palaces across the river; and as I retraced my steps to the quiet little hotel in the town, I marvelled if I should enjoy the interior of the home of the mediæval Earls of Warwick, as much as I had my afternoon ramble on the country side.

LETTER XIII.

"Old castles on the cliffs arise,
  Proudly towering in the skies;
Rushing from the woods, the spires
Seem from hence ascending fires;
Half his beams Apollo sheds
On the yellow mountain-heads
Gilds the fleeces of the flocks,
And glitters on the broken rocks."
JOHN DYER.

WARWICK, ENGLAND, March, 1878.

MY first work this morning was to visit Warwick Castle, which I was as anxious to see as all who have preceded me. Had a register been kept of these thousands it would have been as curious as any in history. So we rang the bell at the great iron gate, which was swung back by the old janitress, who acts as a sort of lady abbess, or as I have heard her called "jailoress" of the old pile. She looked like one of the weird sisters who met Macbeth upon the heath to tell him of his future greatness, and as we entered the stone-canopied avenue, we were greeted by a ruddy young English girl at the door of the porter's lodge whom the old witch presented as her "servant-gal." This woman who must be at least eighty, told us that she had been retained by the Neville family since childhood; and for ever so many years she has day after day repeated the stories of Guy of Warwick, and sounded the vast metal porridge-pot with the flesh-fork in which the smoking stew was prepared for him and his warriors, and from which his successors have drunk their draught through the centuries. It is now used as a punch-bowl with a capacity for 102 gallons, and on the occasion of the coming of age of the present earl, the antiquated Hecate saw it "thrice filled and emptied." The armor, consisting of helmet, shield, sword, and breastplate of this legendary Guy, are preserved here and weigh 111 pounds. Among other relics are trophies of his exploits on Dunsmore Heath. Our historian told us of the vast number of Americans who track hitherward *en route* to London; "Ah yes," she said, "I have been here many a year; they never fail us, and they are the most liberal of all my visitors." This sly hint of the shrewd old crone I very well comprehended, but I had the shilling ready and as she spoke I almost felt as if I stood in the presence of one of the old dependents of the "king-maker."

We reached the castle by a cavernous path hewn through the solid rock, by a long ascent, and heard the dull crush of the sodden gravel beneath our feet in this novel vault-like tunnel. At the terminus of the wonderful granite formation our path lay between a colonnade of tall and venerable trees whose interlacing branches were heavy with nature's tear-drops, and the weeping willows and sweeping cedars made mournful music on the cloudy morning. As I advanced my thoughts reverted to the long ago, when came hither the lords and ladies of dead kings to visit their opulent and half-royal entertainer, who gladly consented to bankrupt himself to gratify his sovereign. In my mind's eye I saw again the cavalcades of knights and kings and queens, radiant in powdered curls, golden lace, crimson plush, and ermine, treading the paths I now trod, coming from the surrounding country and from great London town ever so many centuries ago. They came to visit my lord and lady, holding high revel in yonder gray monastic towers which burst upon my vision as I reached the plateau on which the glorious monument stands. How supremely beautiful and lovely! The air was mild, and the sward smooth and green. My eyes have become accustomed to these English landscape scenes, that seem reproduced in India ink, and partially obliterated by having had a moist sponge passed over them. I now appreciate their artistic points, but at first they formed a dismal contrast to our intensely clear and brilliant American pictures.

All was silent as the grave, for the great people were away off in London, and their palace was left in charge of the servants and seneschals. We ascended a long flight of steps on our left and passed into a marble vestibule overarched by a Gothic canopy; but we had to tarry for no one is in a hurry here; all classes take their time, the servants are slow, the peers are slower, and all is slow except the telegraph and steam, and they wait for no man, "nor woman neither." Then the door was opened unto us, and I found myself in the halls where earls had been born and bred since the days of William the Conqueror. To the right lay the grand baronial hall with its richly carved and gilded roof of Gothic architecture, its Venetian marble floor, and antique wainscoting; on the east wall were hung the armor, swords, and matchlocks of a long line of baronets. Many of these treasures remain as trophies of victory, wrested in battle from their vanquished foe in the days of Edward I, II, the campaigns of the Black Prince, the reigns of Henry VI, Edward IV, and subsequent ages. On the opposite wall were long windows set in deep embrasures, and equally distant between each of these were the effigies of the former lords of this fair demesne clad in armor and mounted upon their favorite chargers. From this point I viewed the situation of the hill. Towers were all around us; the castle, the cathedral, the donjon-keep, and the high walls made the level at the head of the stony walk a sort of inclosure. Looking down upon the Avon, a hundred feet below, we saw it softly and silently lapping the base of the mighty rock, the foundation of this stronghold of "ancient and chivalrous splendor."

To add to the romantic and unequalled scene is the densely wooded portion of the park, which has been allowed to go unkempt and uncombed; also the dilapidated remains of an ancient bridge; and farther up, the beautiful stream is crossed by a new stone structure with picturesque adornments; the plains of the Feldon and the woodland of the Arden may be seen, and in the far distance above all, and beyond all, are the mist-capped heights of Worcestershire and Gloucestershire. As I waited in this hall historical memories deluged my brain—memories that seemed to waken into life in the midst of the blazoned armorial bearings and heraldic devices of this noble house. And as I pondered in this atmosphere of ancient glory, our *cicerone*, the palace guide, appeared. He was a faded, *blasé*, drowsy, rheumatic English servant, who received us with a supreme sense of indifference that proved his calling. We followed him into the great hall, and banqueting hall, where everything was gorgeous, lordly, and artistic, but, unhappily, very new, for, of course, the necessary repairs have been made since the disastrous fire in 1871. But in the state-bedroom, known as the "Queen Anne

Chamber," the magnificent appointments remain in their original state; here all the furniture has the rigid straightness of that period. The bed of crimson velvet is the same occupied by Queen Elizabeth when she visited Warwick. The chairs, square and antique, were upholstered in crimson velvet, enriched by an arabesque pattern in *appliqué* of sea-green and white satin, stitched with golden thread; doubtless the handiwork of royal fingers long since crumbled to dust. In this room are the world-renowned tapestries, picturing the gardens of Versailles, the pleasures of seeing these in nature I have daily in contemplation. To designate individually the treasures of art in oil, marble, buhl, marquétrie, parquétrie, mosaic, bronze, and porcelain, scattered through the gilt drawing-room, cedar drawing-room, red drawing-room, Milady's Boudoir, and the Chapel Passage, I should be minute and tiresome. Here the artists of all decades and countries are represented by glorious monuments of their genius and assiduity; Salvator Rosa, Teniers, Gerard Dow, Vandervelde, Vandyke, Rubens, Van Mieris, Paolo Veronese, Zucchero, Lely, Murillo, and even Raffaelle are here. Our rheumatic friend pointed to pictures, statuary, old arms, and relics of special interest, signed us to windows to view the splendid outside combinations of sky, water, and foliage, and now and then mumbled a sort of idiotic catalogue of the surrounding history. The display of fire arms excited my interest, for I saw that the pistols three or four centuries ago were made very nearly after the model now so prevalent in America, and which we claim as our invention. I thank the present Earl of Warwick for the apparent care of this treasure-house of English history, and will not complain of the sullen conduct of his gouty subordinate. I enjoyed to the fullest extent all I came to see; a splenetic attendant could not prevent that. I had my shillings ready to preserve us from his malediction, and retired into the garden to stroll by the ancient moat, through the charming pleasure-grounds and winding paths, bordered by the stately cedars of Lebanon. And the old gardener in the meanwhile told us of the kindness of the present Earl to his servants, and catalogued in chronological order his issue. We paid the old fellow a shilling for his courteous replies to our questions, and then he insisted we should enter the greenhouse to see the famous vase, nearly seven feet high, and twenty-one in circumference, with quaint handles of twisted snakes; a magnificent piece of Grecian art, carven from one solid block of purely white marble. It was found at the bottom of a lake in the Emperor Adrian's villa, at Tivoli, one of the exquisite suburban palaces of Rome, and was purchased by the ancestor of the present Earl, from Sir William Hamilton, ambassador at Naples in the last century. Of course I had the curiosity just to peep into the dungeon beneath Cæsar's Tower, where the names, devices, and sentences in English and French, cut into the walls, were a sad reminder what the wretched captives who pined within these charnel-houses did to beguile the weary hours. And then I attempted to mount the summit of Guy's Tower, where the guide assured me I could obtain the finest possible view of the surrounding counties for many miles; but when I had less than half accomplished my tedious task, I abandoned it, and was obliged to rest before I retraced my steps over the steep and rickety stair. No doubt it would have been a creditable feat to have completed the ascent, but I never aspired to glory of that description. After doing this proud offspring of the ages, I returned to my little boudoir in the Warwick Arms, where I write to you, the eyes of Lord Leigh, another of the grand moguls of the vicinage, peering down upon me from the opposite wall. Within an hour I am going to bid adieu to the native town of the erudite scholars, Walter, of Coventry, and John Rous, and post across this enchanting section of England to the other historical and romantic points in opulent Warwickshire.

LETTER XIV.

"With Leicester, Lord of Kenilworth, in mournful robes, was seen
The gifted, great Elizabeth, high England's matchless queen.
Tressilian's wild and manly glance, and Varny's darker gaze,
Sought Amy Robsart's brilliant form, too fair for earthly praise."
                                                CHARLES SWAIN.

LONDON, March, 1878.

BACK again in old London, under the shadow of Westminster Abbey, within sight of Westminster Hall; the darkly-flowing Thames to my left, with the dense veil of black fog that London may indeed call its own, hanging low over the city, and Big Ben's deep-mouthed voice bidding me an honest welcome!

Yesterday morning after completing a bargain with the Jehu of the Warwick Arms, to drive us to Leamington, about ten miles distant, for the sum of fourteen shillings, which I considered excessively reasonable, remembering our American tariff, another enterprising cabby offered to do the same work for ten shillings. Of course, I was somewhat provoked, not alone on account of the four shillings, but I felt the trick of the first sharper like an insult to my intelligence. I could not repudiate my promise, however, to the former, but endeavored to reduce him to the price of his rival, without effect; he said his rival did not know his business, that he could give us no history of the country through which our route lay; "but I, madam, am acquainted with every rood of the ground, and can relate all the hinteresting hanecdotes." The last persuasive promise settled the matter; who would forego the benefit of such a store of knowledge for the paltry sum of four shillings? As we turned our backs upon the home where Richard Neville, the frank and hospitable "king-maker" had lived and governed, I found the conveyance comfortable, and the driver reasonably intelligent, as he drove over the broad smooth English roads and past the comfortable English homes, pointing out the great estates and naming their titled owners. He had opened his budget and I allowed him to prattle on. He related the story of Ethelfleda, Alfred's daughter, who fortified and contributed to the prosperity of Warwick; he repeated pages of Dugdale's narratives, and of the Roman occupation, but he evinced special delight in dwelling upon the glories of the "king-maker;" how his bravery had attached to his interests the military; how his gifts and friendship were always regarded as genuine; how the people in general, and particularly his retainers, were more devoted to his iron will, than to the English law; and by his fulness of soul how he had conquered all *men's* affections. Our rural communicant said nothing of the ancient Earl's conquests over female hearts; I presume that he left to conjecture.

It is March, and although there is no snow on the ground, nor ice in the streams, there is sufficient chill in the air to cause me to draw my fur cloak around me; but this was a secondary discomfort in the midst of these storied scenes. Oh! for the bright winter skies of my own dear home just now—nothing could be more cheering than to ride through this lovely country in our incomparable weather. Art and nature combine to make rural England a small realm of loveliness, and, notwithstanding there are many gloomy days between December and April, still the best English homes are abodes of almost royal luxury, and when spring and summer follow, that which has been done by wealth to beautify the roads and the fields, and the entire country, makes the scene one of indescribable splendor! Yes, it deserves just this one word splendor.

A very short ride of a mile brought us to Guy's Cliff, familiar to all of us as the chosen home and tomb of the fabled hero who slew the giant Colbrand, and whom the early metrical romances make a champion against the Danes. Now this point presented to Jehu a rare opportunity to paint a poetic picture of the famous old legend, and he proceeded to "horate." The cave where lived and died the said Guy, was scooped with his own hands from the rock. It is treason to harbor a doubt of the fact; for the legend tells us:—

"There with my hands I hewed a house
 Out of a craggy rock of stone ;
And lived like a palmer poor,
 Within that cave myself alone."

I am rather incredulous as to the last line of this poetical autobiography; the old story tells us that the fair Phillis would hie hither to bestow alms upon the solitary man, and receive in return his saintly counsel(?). Phillis never recognized in the hermit her husband, whom she believed to have long since died, or to be a captive in the Holy Land. Phillis, unlike Juliet, was not easily won; she did not tell Guy, at their first interview, to deny his father and refuse his name, and for that name which was no part of him to take all herself; nor did she exclaim, "In truth, I am too fond," and then ask "Dost thou love me?" and before Guy could reply, answered her own question by "I know thou wilt say—Ay ;" and clinched the contract by adding, "And I will take thy word." And then implored him to swear fidelity by something more constant than the moon. Oh no! Phillis lived in more provincial days, and bore a greater resemblance to Penelope, who was so loath to make a final decision. Guy's sweetheart was a perverse young lady, who frowned, and said him nay; who required deeds of high intrepidity from her suitor before she yielded her affection and liberty; all of which he wrought for the love of this woman, for he was in the very summer of the tender passions; and then after years—oh ye gods pity us!—true to his sex he regretted that he had caused so much mischief and bloodshed for the sake of *one* in this world of women, and he betook him to a life of penance in a stony abode from sheer remorse. Tradition tells us that he did not disclose to her his identity till he was dying, but I have a sly notion that these two understood each other all along. The spot is one of surpassing beauty, and if Phillis retained any of the powerful witchery of her youth, that goaded Guy to his valiant exploits, he did not suffer the many privations during his hermitage, attending a life of asceticism.

Here was another of those exquisite rural English pictures. The verdure was soft and green, the river gentle, except where it had been dammed (mechanically), and then it impetuously foamed and raged, to help the evolutions of the old mill; the rocks were moss-grown and ivy-wreathed, and the rustic foot-bridge across the Avon in a rapid state of decay. The mansion is quite modern, and the residence of the Hon. Mrs. Percy, who was "at home;" at such times it is never shown to visitors; but after enjoying the fresh fields, the paths trod by the chantry-priests of other days, the groves of stately elms, the avenues overshaded by firs, we remounted our little chaise and proceeded on our way over the Kenilworth road. Not far beyond the Cliff, and on the opposite side of the highway is Blacklow Hill, the scene of the execution of Piers Gaveston, Earl of Cornwall, the favorite of Edward II, and the hated enemy of Guy de Beauchamp, Earl of Warwick. Gaveston had stigmatized Warwick as "the black hound of Arden," and when the latter attacked Deddington Castle, where Gaveston was lodged for safety, he was at once captured and taken to Warwick Castle, and thence to the wooded elevation scarcely more than a mile distant, where he paid for his spite with his head. This place of execution was alone marked by an inscription on the rock, now quite obliterated, until Mr. Greatheed, the father of Mrs. Percy, present owner of Guy's Cliff, erected a stone cross to the honor of "the minion of a hateful king."

There had been a hunt at one of the great manors in the neighborhood, and as we wended our way toward Kenilworth we had a fair view of a flock of natty English lordlings in red jackets and jockey caps skimming across the country on their spirited coursers, followed by their grooms. As we entered the town I was impressed by the modern appearance of its architecture. The buildings are all humble and comfortable, and reminded me very much of the outskirts of the little town of Freehold, in Monmouth County, New Jersey. When we reached the Castle of Kenilworth there was a heavy shower driving upon us. You who have been in England can appreciate the delight of these unexpected and penetrating downpours. Meanwhile we paused in a veritable little country tavern opposite. Pray do not be shocked at our haven of rest, for there was no more aristocratic inn available, and you know "drowning men catch at straws," but we improved on that by taking a "hot Scotch" without the straw. The sky was clearing as rapidly as it had clouded, and I went out to get my shilling's worth of the magnificent ruin. The gate-house is the only habitable portion of the building, which is occupied by the keeper, who wore the garb of those in the employ of royalty, and his daughter who sold photographs of the gray old towers reft of all their former glory. I made my way over the grass-grown path by a gentle ascent to the eminence where all that remains of the castle are found. Immediately beneath me lay a wide and undulating expanse of greensward, luxurious pines, miniature lakes, drained moat, and precipitous ravines; to the east was the church spire and the *débris* of the Augustine Monastery, covered by a veil of mist, and at my right the unroofed and dilapidated halls, where we can read tales of history and romance, love and hate, crime, misery, stratagem, and prodigality, from the days of Geoffroi de Clinton to those of Robert Dudley and Cromwell's commissioner. Is it necessary for me to repeat the memories that floated back through three hundred years as I stood in the shelter of this crumbling and skeleton structure? The rivalries of Sussex and Leicester, the wrongs and sorrows of Amy Robsart, the villanies of Varny and Lambourne, the constancy of Tressilian, and the splendid pageant of the Virgin Queen. Ah! surely poor Amy, you were an outcast and prisoner, while your husband, the parasite and favorite of royalty, had a queen for his guest! And as I turned toward the Donjon keep nature seemed to mourn and weep for the foul murder of the beautiful girl three centuries ago.

Our path to Leamington was broad and level; something smoother than an ordinary turnpike, more like cement, perhaps a macadamized road, and when we entered the fashionable English spa I felt as if I had been translated to my native land, so modern is this sweet town upon the Leam. It impressed me as very much like our beautiful Williamsport, in Lycoming County, Pennsylvania. Leamington Priors is the outgrowth of the last forty years, its cause of prosperity being attributed to the medicinal qualities of its mineral waters. In 1784 a saline spring was discovered by one Benjamin Satchwell, a village shoemaker, and to him may the now flourishing resort offer all thanks for its rise and affluence. Here we took the train for London, ninety-seven miles distant, where we arrived about nine P.M.

LETTER XV.

"I waited for the train at Coventry;
I hung with grooms and porters on the bridge,
To watch the three tall spires; and there I shaped
The city's ancient legend into this:—"
TENNYSON.

LONDON, March, 1878.

I REGRET that I did not stop over long enough at Kenilworth to run across the country to the ancient city of Coventry, only five miles off. It is chiefly attractive by the story of the lady Godiva, woven into immortal verse by the British poet-laureate, Alfred Tennyson. But I was not idle, having collected a good deal of information from several kind people whom I met at the little country inn near Kenilworth, and afterwards in the station where we were obliged to wait a long time before leaving Leamington for London. Indeed, apart from the beautiful countess herself, Coventry and the surrounding country are very full of history, ancient, monastic, literary, and scientific. The town has over 41,000 inhabitants, and the manufacture of ribbons, silk, and watches so considerable, as to give employment to five or six thousand men, and almost as many women and children; and then there is a large additional population engaged in the same work in the neighboring parish of Foleshill. I specially regretted not having seen what the people in Leamington talk so much about, St. Mary's Hall, a splendid and remarkable edifice, built in 1450, and at present in an admirable state of preservation. It is the headquarters of one of the old British guilds, and is regarded as one of the most magnificent specimens of ancient domestic architecture in the United

Kingdom. Here, and all over this part of England, the name of Lady Godiva is celebrated and preserved as the worshipped saint of the common people. The story is a beautiful one, and I sat and listened for quite an hour as I heard it related by an old village gossip, who tells it for the purpose of securing a few shillings from the passing stranger.

In 1043 the fifth Earl of Mercia and his lady, Godiva, founded and richly endowed a Benedictine monastery on the ruins of a nunnery, destroyed in 1016 by Canute, the Dane. The old legends tell us this monastery was unspeakably grand, a perfect casket, in fact, of gold and silver. Leofric and his countess were both buried in the porch of this priory. Now, whether this Lady Godiva is the same immortalized by Tennyson my informant was unable to say, but the accepted authority of the district, Sir William Dugdale, who was a devout believer in the romance, gives the following account of it: "The Countess Godiva, bearing an extraordinary affection to this place, often and earnestly besought her husband that for the love of God and the Blessed Virgin he would free it from that grievous servitude whereunto it was subject; but he, rebuking her for importuning him in a manner so inconsistent with his profit, commanded that she should thenceforward forbear to move therein; yet she, out of her womanish pertinacity, continued to solicit him, insomuch that he told her if she would ride on horseback naked, from one end of the town to the other, in sight of all the people, he would grant her request. Whereunto she returned, "But will you give me leave to do so?" and he replying "Yes," the noble lady upon an appointed day got on horseback naked, with her hair loose, so that it covered all her body but her legs; and thus performing her journey, she returned with joy to her husband, who thereupon granted to the inhabitants a charter of freedom." . . . The residents of the town, grateful to their beautiful sovereign for the delicate task she had accepted to secure their civil franchises, with one accord withdrew from the highways and windows in order that as little pain as possible should be inflicted upon their royal Eve; but one Tom, by profession a tailor, yielded to the rare temptation, and for his lack of moral valor, had his eyes shrivelled into darkness in his head. There is a grotesque picture of the count and countess set up in Trinity Church; he holds a scroll in his hand bearing these words:—

> "I, Leuriche, for Love of thee,
> Doe make Coventre Tol-free."

The Lady Godiva pageant that was instituted in the reign of the indolent voluptuary, Charles II, has not taken place within the last thirty years, and may confidently be numbered among the jubilees of the past. In its days of youth and prosperity, the festival was one of unprecedented splendor, and was always dignified by the presence of the municipal authorities. Of course, the spectacle of St. George on horseback, and her *uncovered* ladyship, was the principal attraction of the saturnalian revel. The mayor, aldermen, and sheriffs, ancient orders and beneficial societies, with their streamers, decorations, and bands of music, presented a fantastic and bizarre sight.

Out of many of these old places, the haunts of traditionary heroes, martyrs, and saints, imagination creates some of its wildest and sweetest fancies. Within a circle of ten or twenty miles, I find material for a succession of dramas, each with a basis of fact, which time turns into fable, or mystifies into doubt. Shakespeare himself, the sublimest wonder of all, grows more sacred and more *spirituelle* as the ages go on, while Guy of Warwick, and Richard Neville the great "king-maker," and gentle Amy Robsart, and now the fair-haired Godiva, become more and more legendary with the centuries. I like it better so. We are too young in America to have such advantages, and hence the scarcity of our great authors, in comparison with the rich treasures dug out of those ancient mines, and coined into such golden music. There is not an old English house that has not a hoard of precious memories. Even the fireside gossip makes material for future poets and historians, and there is not an old church from the Mersey to the Tweed, from the Irish coast to Dover, that is not the storehouse of ghostly reminiscences.

All over England the early example of London in regard to ancient charities is imitated, and everywhere in the town of Coventry the goodness of the Lady Godiva in relieving the poor is perpetuated in the rude art of the time. Ford's Hospital, founded in 1529, by William Ford, a merchant, for the reception of aged females, has grown in dignity with the years, and has been increased by donations from other parties; there are twenty old women in this beautiful building, who receive 3*s.* 6*d.* per week and coals, and twenty-five other women, called out-of-door recipients, who receive the same amount of money and a ton of coal each year. Then there is Bablake Hospital, founded in 1806, by Thomas Bond, for ten poor men; but subsequent gifts have so augmented its funds, that it now receives over forty persons. Then there is a superb school for boys, founded by Thomas Wheatly, Mayor of Coventry, in 1560; the revenues are $4500 per annum. Then there is St. John's Hospital and free school, founded in 1155, for the sick and poor, and for a free school with an annual income of $5000. There are several other schools and hospitals liberally endowed centuries ago, which, in the progress of time have largely increased by additional bequests and enhancements of land, from which you will perceive how very rich is every part of England. There is hardly a shire or parish in which you will not find one or more endowments, as they are called, for religious, charitable, and educational purposes; most of them beginning ever so long ago, from a very small provision and gathering in value with the growth of the population, and the importance of the real estate set apart by the old-time philanthropists. England is deeply afflicted by the growing curse of pauperism, and the equally dangerous element, millions of discontented laborers, but these charitable preparations against ignorance and misfortune, show not only the great care of the generous leaders of society, but also the great opulence of the kingdom itself.

As I sit in my little room in this cathedral of a hotel, pondering over my sweet swift visit to Chester, Birmingham, Stratford, Warwick, Kenilworth, Leamington, and my flash back to this great, grim, gray capital, I wonder if I shall ever see it all again. How many people cross the ocean from our country to these old places with their minds, if not their eyes shut. They rush through England, Ireland, Scotland, across the Continent, even into the Holy Land, and perhaps away off to India, Asia, and Africa, and are back again in the twinkling of an eye, as it were; and for what? I fear only to boast to those who have been less fortunate. Ah, me! how I commiserate such people. For myself, I am never tired learning from this mighty volume, Experience. It teaches me how small I am (not physically but mentally), and though I love my own dear land, I am never oppressed nor fatigued by the knowledge I gather in these strange, ancient, and suggestive scenes. And still a voice within asks, Shall I ever sit by the sweet English ingleside again? So good-night, my voiceless, patient friend.

7*

LETTER XVI.

> "Sing—sing—music was given
> To brighten the gay, and kindle the loving;
> Souls here like planets in Heaven,
> By harmony's laws alone are kept moving.
> Beauty may boast of her eyes and her cheeks,
> But love from the lips his true archery wings;
> And she, who but feathers the dart when she speaks,
> At once sends it home to the heart when she sings."
> Tom Moore.

London, March, 1878.

At last I have had an opportunity of enjoying the Royal Opera in London. Here long enough to beware of hasty judgments, I will not trust myself to avow them; but I may whisper that I am not quite carried away by a first experience. We secured stalls in the parquette for $5.25 each, and last evening retiring into the secrecy of my closet, I "unclasp'd the wedded eagles of my belt," and proceeded to array me in festive regalia before going to Covent Garden Theatre to see the nobility before the curtain, and the great melodists under the curtain. The opera house is large, heavy, and solid; very English, with a little of the air of musty style that makes age respectable, and goes far to consecrate disabled furniture and dilapidated arras. Although the present stupendous structure has been open only since 1858, it has encountered disaster by fire several times subsequent to the erection of the original edifice, in 1732. In this *bric-a-brac* period, when the antique is the newest fashion, and when to be in the mode we must drag out of old garrets our great grandmother's (those who have had one) spinning-wheel and andirons, and resurrect long-expired spoons, and tea-kettles, and knee-buckles, I supposed such a venerable dame as Covent Garden would have thrown me at once into violent ecstacies. But she didn't!

Though the auditorium of this theatre is larger than our Academy it looks smaller, as the tiers range higher, and are divided into close boxes heavily draped with florid tapestries. Many of these belong to noble families, and when they do not wish to occupy them they are not too proud to let the managers sell them to the highest bidder, and they pocket the money. Red and gold are the prevailing colors, the crimson dominating the whole. We started for the opera with the intention of hearing Madlle. Sarda, but before we had been seated many moments an Italian appeared upon the stage, and at once my heart sank within me, I anticipated disappointment. Our friend from the sunny South told us, in very bad English, " Madlle. Sarda was ill, and, in consequence, opera and *prima donna* were both changed, but we should hear Bertelli and Smeroschi," two names wholly unknown to me. The opera was Verdi's superb creation, *Un ballo in Maschera*, that I had often enjoyed at home, and it was magnificently rendered. So great a city as London is necessarily a centre of musical art. All the eminent singers, and, of course, many that we are even unacquainted with in America float here in the season, to get the highest prices for their genius; and yet Italy and Russia often outbid London for such celebrities as Patti and her new husband, Nicolinni. The orchestra, of at least seventy-five instruments, was full, correct, harmonious, and nobly mastered; and the work upon the stage complete. The recitatives were chaste and strongly accentuated, the arias sometimes sweet and *allegro*, at others sublime and sombre, and the *ensembles* grand. The troupe was particularly strong in its subsidiary force; the ballet brilliant and effervescing in the admirable scenery, and that perfect discipline, which may be called the crowning glory of patience and time. It is readily seen that the opera in London is a government machine, and not a matter of speculation. It is an institution like a great castle, built to last, and not made for the pleasure of the rich merely, or for a spasmodic season.

There was nothing popular about it except the fine repertoire. Even the cheapest places were occupied by the better class of middle Londoners. Americans always seek the best; they travel first class, they dine *à la carte*, they never restrain their physical nor moral appetite for a few shillings, and of course they want the best for their money. In the overpowering tide of travel that sweeps across the Atlantic, the major portion are pleasure seekers, and they act on the principle that they are resolved to enjoy their holiday carousal with all its epicurean attributes. Our party sat in the midst of the *crême de la crême* feeling for the time a sort of millionnaire superiority. I was by no means oppressed because to my right sat a countess and to my left a princess. In this state of supreme complacency I devoted myself to observation. Very unlike, indeed, was the prospect contrasted with the radiant and varied habitues of our Academy of Music. An amplitude of gaudy dress, but wholly incongruous. Ponderous old dowagers in *point d'aiguille* and diamonds, redolent of rare roast beef and port, chaperoned their youthful female relatives. There seemed to be a dearth of gay gallant youths. I missed the fresh maidens accompanied by suitors or friends, that fill our play houses; and then, the sweet newly-created matrons, still in their tyronism, that time and tribulation have not yet robbed of their maturescent bloom. The English girl migrates from a hoyendish school miss, to a square, solid female bovine; nowhere have I seen that stage or age of feminine beauty, so prevalent in America, that is only comparable to a superbly ripe moss rose, full, fragrant, and magnificent. A British fledgling of eighteen or nineteen summers, under the protection of her father's wing, in white silk and white mittens reaching the elbows, and Mrs. Langtry, the reigning English belle, at whom the Prince of Wales has been casting *bull's eyes*, in canary-satin and ten-button black-kid gloves, were the only ladies in the vast assemblage that recalled a vision of our fair ones at home. The opera is always a resort for well-bred indifference, a savage noise in the midst of beautiful music—a place in fact where the so-called cultivated classes rush to display their uncultivated rudeness. Ah! how well these English understand impassive insolence.

Why is it that the most pretentious people in America are often the most offensive in public places? The more elegant the entertainment the more intrusive and noisy they are; and so it is here, as I learn from those who are initiated into the ways and means of the better orders. It was certainly so last night. There was a box full of nobility, so much I gleaned from surrounding comments. They arrived late—9.30 P. M.—and had evidently been dining; in jubilant moods, every one; they were as utterly regardless of the opera as if the vocalists had been plantation slaves. There was no protest against their rude patronage, either on the part of the actors or the audience. I am obliged to confess I have seen the same effrontery at home, but never quite so boisterous and unblushing.

The now familiar science of music takes rank amongst the modern arts. In the early ages, when architecture, painting, and sculpture rapidly rose to perfection, the lyric science seemed to remain a dark and dormant study.

Through the most effulgent epochs of ancient civilization and intellectual splendor, music had no place, even when the brilliant epicurean and artistic sports were national amusements. Nowhere do we read of a musical theorist, composer, or performer, among the master-minds of the mediæval period of *beaux-arts*. Since the history of the creation, the rudest and most barbaric races have endeavored to make the eye and ear slaves to ecstatic and thrilling emotions; but what was intended to gratify the ear, did not progress to the lofty stages of cultivation. The first efforts to reduce to a system and classify its true principles, and reveal its clouded beauties, were apparent at the close of the Middle Ages. Therefore our music is the offspring of the last three or four centuries, and the lyric drama of much later date. Of course, Italy was the cradle where this child of harmony was born, at the beginning of the seventeenth century, and nursed until adopted by kindred nations. The polyphonic compositions were rapidly decaying for want of fresh tissue, and as the spirit of renaissance was fanatically imbued in the patrons of art in this period of scientific revolution, an attempt to establish the homophonous music of the Greek drama was made, and with the aid of the eminent *devotés*, Caccini and Peri, our modern recitative was produced, as the most potent semblance of the chaste and classic cadenza. The foundation of this chanting tone had already been laid by Giovanni Palestrina, composer of the masses, hymns, and *mottetas* that won the encomiums of Pope Julius III, and created the author singer in the papal chapel. Cimaroso, Piccini, and Paesiello, the great composers of the last century, and the numberless ones of the present, do not display any marked changes in the emphasis of their operas, other than the radical division of the aria from the recitative, effected by Alessandro Scarlatti, in the preceding century; he was seventy-six when he died, and composed 118 operas, 200 masses, and 3000 cantatas, and many minor works.

The earliest French operas, that were little more than complete imitations of the Italian, were by Jean Baptiste Lully, whose first introduction into the French capital was as a scullion in the palace of the Princess of Montpensier. He accumulated a vast fortune by his musical genius, and reigned absolute monarch of the stage until the advent of Rameau, who was not more than four years old at the demise of the musical dish-washer. Gluck, however, was the originator of French "grand opera," who struggled with his innovations of style till his sixty-fifth year, before he received a satisfactory appreciation from the Paris public. The light operas of Hérold, Halévy, Auber, and recently Offenbach, seem to have superseded the heavier and loftier works of Mihal, Rossini, and Meyerbeer, in the hearts of the laughter-loving Parisians. The earlier masterpieces, even of our contemporary musical authors, are overruled by their younger progeny; thus, Aïda, and Un ballo in Maschera are of the latest productions of the Italian senator, Verdi; so it is with Balfe, Auber, Hérold, Donizetti, Thomas, Rossini, and Von Flotow, whose Martha is the only one of his operas known at home.

LETTER XVII.

"To the traveller imbued with a feeling for the historical and poetical, so inseparably intertwined in the annals of romantic Spain, the Alhambra is as much an object of devotion as is the Caaba to all true Moslems. How many legends and traditions, true and fabulous, how many songs and ballads, Arabian and Spanish, of love and war and chivalry, are associated with this Oriental pile!"—WASHINGTON IRVING'S ALHAMBRA.

LONDON, March, 1878.

LEICESTER SQUARE is one of the interesting and beautiful sections of the West End. Formerly it was a fashionable quarter; then it fell into disgrace by dint of neglect of the open space, that has been transformed from a depository of refuse into an exquisite public garden at the individual expense of Baron Grant, whose palace in the neighborhood of the Albert Memorial, and *en route* to the South Kensington Museum, is the present marvel and envy of the great metropolis. He was one of the money-kings of England, but has recently been the prey of the merciless fiend Misfortune, and will be compelled to part with, even before he has occupied, his regal home that cost over three millions of our money. The current prophecy is, that the Baron Grant will never rise again; but he is elastic, ambitious, and full of resources, and even now the requiting angel may be hovering over his dreams. He has been once or twice chosen to Parliament, but was deprived of his seat, owing to charges of corruption in procuring votes; and while the newspapers were heaping vituperation upon him for every kind of fraudulent transaction in stocks and bonds, and he was entangled in all manner of lawsuits and contentions, he conceived the idea of rendering a public service by purifying this dismal spot in the heart of London. So in the centre of Leicester Square he planted plots of grass and parterres of flowers, erected fountains, and placed a statue of Shakespeare in the middle, surrounding the whole with seats for the aged and the poor. Leicester Square was the home of the mathematician, Sir Isaac Newton; the artist, Sir Joshua Reynolds, and the free caricaturist, Hogarth. On the east side of the circle, John Hunter, the pathologist and anatomist, lived and gathered his great museum of specimens illustrative of his profession, subsequently purchased by the government for the Royal College of Surgeons. These facts and adornments of Grant add immensely to the attractions of the *Alhambra*, the famous variety theatre of the metropolis and one of the most profitable of the many great resorts of London. This great show-place is called after one of the oldest and most ornate and lascivious of the palaces of Moorish kings, near Granada, Spain, beautifully described by our own Washington Irving in the words I have placed at the head of this chapter. The London architect seems to have had the Spanish Alhambra for his model. Its fountains, dancing halls, conservatories, seraglios, baths and Saracenic splendors are all Oriental; the original palace was a combination of gorgeous magnificence, not only in works of art and lovely women and ravishing music; but in forests, flowers, fruits, singing-birds, delicious fish, and curious animals, and all these are sought to be imitated in the dazzling music hall and ballet of the spectacular temple in Leicester Square. There is an inanimate duplicate of the palace at the Crystal Palace, Sydenham, which is a marvel of superb Spanish coloring, mediæval ornamentation, elaborate carving and quaint architectural style. This splendid attraction stands on a portion of the ground called after Robert Sydney, Earl of Leicester, who was father of the handsome Sydney, who figured in the Grammont Memoire, published by Count Anthony Hamilton, in 1713—a complete *exposé* of the exploits of his brother-in-law in love and at the gaming-table. It is a spacious structure in the moresque style of architecture, and was first opened by a scientific and literary body, somewhat resembling the Polytechnic, on Regent

Street, under the title of Panopticon; but the night I attended the gilded palace the performance did not bear the slightest resemblance to the instructive discourses and palinodes of that "inspired uniformity of goodness," that Canning used to talk about. Twelve years ago gentlemen *only* attended this wild alluring saturnalia, and although the management still have an arduous task to secure license from the Lord Chamberlain each year, I am obliged to confess I saw nothing there but an exquisite musical extravaganza. A magnificent orchestra, such as the theatres of London only have, a ballet of 175 or 200 beautiful young women—not female wrecks, rendered dazzling by the aid of paint and calcium lights, such as constitue our home-ballets,—and an audience chamber thronged by quite the same class of ladies that frequent other playhouses. Perhaps there are performances here justifying the caustic indignation of the circumspect, that I did not see. For, if all I have heard be true, there are ambiguous platforms under the same roof where the comedies, farces, dramas, and even tragedies of life are freely enacted. The operetta or vaudeville of "Wildfire" was to me a most brilliant and pleasing feast. The interior is flashingly beautiful, exceeding in size any one of the American theatres, the altitude rising five tiers. To the bonnetless ladies and female ushers I am becoming more and more reconciled each day I linger in the capital, but the imperative six or eight cents for a programme that oftentimes is thrust into the hands of the neophyte, and inadvertently accepted, the peddling of refreshments amongst the audience between the several acts of a play, and the coolness and complacency with which the English ladies call for a glass of wine at the lobby-bars, are customs I cannot vindicate. The first, imposition; the second, indignity; the third, indelicacy. True, the play-bill is unique, containing vignettes of the *dramatis personæ* upon the margin, that might be worthily imitated at home; but I entreat you, shun the extortion and the impudence.

The patriotism of the British, whether inborn of despotic rule or inherent loyalty, is ever apparent, and at all public resorts when a political witticism or local hit is made the hisses and applause are instant and prolonged. I have been present when an audience have joined with one accord in a national chorus. To me, there is nothing more interesting and elevating than a people fired by public sentiment, but not the boisterous demonstrations I have witnessed here. It would not hurt us one bit were the

Americans to borrow from their neighbors beyond the seas a portion of their national zeal; I fear ever since the black and bloody cloud, War, has fallen from our horizon, we have been slowly and surely sinking into a state of indifferent fealty.

All around Leicester Square are bright lights, and surging cosmopolitan crowds. It is the favorite quarter of the foreigners, and abounds in foreign hotels, but the Alhambra is the attractive constellation that sheds radiance over the secondary satellites. After seeing the beautiful statue of Shakespeare in the new park, I sauntered into a neighboring bookstore, and in raking through a heap of literary ashes, discovered a living coal that throws upon the existence of the great poet an indisputable halo. It is an extract from a poem by an English rhymster, Richard Barnefielde, written in 1598, eighteen years before the death of Shakespeare. Whether old or new, it is quite conclusive, and a supreme satisfaction to me to find Shakespeare no myth, and such a proof of his title to his own work; although "rare Ben Jonson's" melodious testimony in his favor ought to silence the clamor of envious tongues.

> "And Shakespeare, thou whose honey-flowing vein,
> (Pleasing the world) thy praises doth contain:
> Whose Venus and whose Lucrece, sweet and chaste,
> Thy name in Fame's immortal book hath placed.
> Live ever you, at least in Fame live ever!
> Well may the body die, but Fame dies never."

By some the Alhambra is classed amongst the music halls of London, but the mode of entertainment now holding the boards of this theatre deserves the title of vaudeville, as the difference between it and the stereotyped London Music Hall is eminent. One of the most popular of these plebeian and independent resorts is Evans's celebrated concert room, famous for its mutton chops, Welsh rarebits, whiskey-punch and brown stout, and its renowned gallery of theatrical portraits. At these concerts, which begin late and last far into the night, the male element prevails; they flock here after the opera and theatres have closed, rather an easy process, as the boxes of the concert hall may be entered from the adjoining Covent Garden Opera House. I have heard the chanting boys, or choral singers of this establishment highly extolled, and have been eager to enjoy their harmony, but lacked the moral fortitude to venture upon forbidden ground,—even in a foreign city,— where, I believe, all Americans are conceded unlimited license. But I loved to linger in the vicinage hallowed by the names of Dr. Johnson, Garrick, Boswell, Goldsmith, Addison, and Pope. Close to Evans's is St. Paul's Church, not the Cathedral, interesting because in the adjacent grounds we saw the grave of Butler, the author of the immortal poem, "Hudibras;" and of Gibbons, the illustrious sculptor, whose flowers carven in wood, needed only color and perfume to make them pass for nature.

St. James Hall, entrance on Piccadilly and Regent Street, an attachment of the famous restaurant, is a gorgeously decorated room, where the Moore and Burgess American Minstrels present to the English a thoroughly American plantation jubilee. It is refreshing to see these English people enjoying this as a novelty. The Oxford Music Hall, the portals of which I ventured to pass, was thronged with a motley crowd, comparatively little smoking and drinking, a cheap place, a dismal repertoire, but the audience exceedingly reputable, that is, while I remained in this bacchanalian *rendezvous*, which was only long enough to take a peep, and then glad to hurry away. For although I had been anxious and curious to see one of these sports for the London mob, I was conscious of a feeling of self-desecration while my inquisitive longing was being gratified. Canterbury Music Hall is on the Westminster Bridge Road, across the Thames; the original building was the first of this class of carnival in London: and Exeter Hall, near Covent Garden, is a better specimen of the same type of amusements, as it is also often used for meetings of religious associations, oratories, and theological disputations.

LETTER XVIII.

> "Is it not monstrous, that this player here,
> But in a fiction, in a dream of passion,
> Could force his soul so to his own conceit,
> That from her working, all his visage warmed,
> Tears in his eyes, distraction in 's aspect,
> A broken voice, and his whole functions suiting
> With forms to his conceit? And all for nothing?
> For Hecuba!" HAMLET.

LONDON, March, 1878.

AND so I felt, as I sat and saw Henry Irving enact his portrait of *Louis XI* at the Lyceum Theatre. He is worshipped here as the Roscius of the British stage. While the ladies sing praises to his melancholy grace and the music of his voice, the critics exhaust adjectives in eulogies of his genius. They do not overrate this English disciple of the Greek drama, and I incontinently yielded to his magnetic influence. I had seen him several weeks before in the weird representation, *The Bells*, where the hero has bidden farewell to content, and dies the victim of a remorseful conscience. Irving is a man whose walk and talk are full of shadowy forebodings, and well adapted for such a character as the superstitious, suspicious, cruel, and faithless King of France. He is not handsome, but possesses the charms of intonation, gesture, and manner that come only to the finished artist—partial Nature's gifts to her favored few. He has a moody and student air, and seems to have thought out all his paces and points; an atmosphere of musty books and meditation clings about him. He is at once attractive and repellent. He has conned French history and the novel of the Scottish story-teller founded upon it, and he has studied the illustrated lists of the costumers of the time. The manner in which he dressed the character honored the author; the facial make-up was as artistic and elaborate as the *Meg Merreiles* of Charlotte Cushman.

The scenes are all laid at and near the Castle of Plessis-les-Tours, where the miserable monarch passed the last years of his life, surrounded by a body-guard of soldiers. He feared that humanity would be as cruel to him as he had been cruel to humanity. He ascended the throne a tyrant, determined to subjugate all the nobles to his will. He was as wise as he was jealous, but he labored to concentrate all power in his own hands. He selected his counsellors from the people, and encouraged commerce and industry, a cause to which Jacques Coeur, the merchant prince of the former reign, had given such impetus. His impulses were low and cunning, and though he was a churchman, he was the type of abject bigotry and superstition. He thought he could propitiate the saints with promises as he did his fellow-creatures—promises that he never intended to redeem—particularly noticeable in his midnight devotions, when he knelt before the image of the Lady of Cléry, after supplicating for the fulfilment of all his worldly projects. He concludes his prayer, according to Sir Walter Scott: "Sweetest Lady, work with thy child, that he will pardon all past sins, and one—one little deed that I must do this night—nay, it is no *sin*, dearest Lady of Cléry, no sin, but an act of justice privately administered; for the villain is the greatest impostor that ever poured falsehood into a prince's ear, and leans besides to the filthy heresy of the Greeks. He is not deserving of thy protection; leave him to my care; and hold it as a good service that I rid the world of him, for the man is a necromancer and wizard, that is not worth thy thought and care—a dog, the extinction of whose life ought to be of as little consequence in thine eyes as the treading out of a spark that drops from a lamp or springs from a fire. Think not of this little matter, gentlest, kindest Lady, but consider how thou canst best aid me in my troubles! and I here bind my loyal signet to thy effigy, in token that I will keep word concerning the county of Champagne (which, by the way, he had pledged several times previous), and that this will be the last time I will trouble thee in affairs of blood, knowing thou art so kind, so gentle, and so tender-hearted." Ah! wily reasoner, how well you plead and flatter! And here we see the shrewd diplomate—without heart or conscience—in his fortress, with none near him but his barber minister, Oliver le Dain; his provost, Tristan l'Ermite; and his physician, Jacques Coitier. He feared to meet his Creator, because he had so blackened the life bestowed upon him. I recoiled from Henry Irving as he played the intriguing, crafty, soulless hypocrite, yet found myself melting toward him the next moment as he addressed a favorite; his every tone a sweet caress. He is one of those who so sink the actor into the character, and so rapidly paint the various phases of life that you alternately hate and sympathize with him until the curtain drops, when, for the first time you dwell upon the creative skill of the consummate artist.

And for the pleasure of the evening passed with the crafty Louis, as interpreted by this gifted young actor, I was indebted to our country's good friend in London, Mr. James McHenry, who is a zealous patron of the drama, and Henry Irving's special champion. The home of Mr. McHenry, Oak Lodge, is a portion of the old Holland estate, Kensington, where the last Lord Holland, nephew of Charles James Fox, died in 1840. Here Fox, Byron, Moore, Addison, Sheridan, and all that galaxy of fast and fashionable Whigs of the olden time, gathered and held high revelry, played their special antics, and plotted their special intrigues, making their clubs and the House of Commons, and old London itself, resound with the gossip of their frequent saturnalias. I looked, or tried to look over the hedges and high walls that separated Mr. McHenry's fair demesne from this paradise of other days, now hermetically sealed against profane eyes, and deserted by the descendants of the great families, who lived and lorded there so long and so long ago. The last Lady Holland is still living, but the glory of the great place has departed. Traffic and population have usurped the lovely domain, for centuries the exclusive retreat of the magnates who ruled the camp, the court, the senate, and the stage. Mr. McHenry, who paid a large round sum for his corner of this delightful suburb, could now sell his property for three or four times what it cost him. And I was told, such is the demand for what is left of the grand old estate, that it will not be long before it is surrendered to the rapacious grasp of remorseless modern innovation.

Of the other countless crowded resorts of London, I have only to say that we give a much better entertainment at home for less money. The best dramatic stock companies here are not comparable to those of Philadelphia and New York. And frequently when I have paid seven or eight shillings for my stall, I wondered if I was not paying for the exquisite adornments of the audience chamber, instead of the play I had come to witness. In contrast with our dollar amusements, fifty cents would be a fair price. True, the artistic and architectural appointments of these dramatic palaces surpass anything we have at home. The Criterion, three stories underground, is a glittering mass of gold and *eau-de-Nile* satin, reached by a stairway panelled with encaustic tiles and mirrors; but the successful comedy of Pink Dominos, that has already passed its 300th representation, I have seen much better acted in America. The

Princess Theatre, where Miss Heath nightly harrows up the best and tenderest emotions of the public by rehearsing the struggles and sins of the beautiful but frail Jane Shore, is dismal to the last degree. Had poor Jane borne the slightest resemblance to the lady who assumes her *rôle*, I am loath to believe she could have numbered Edward IV, Lord Hastings, and Thomas Lynom, the king's solicitor, amongst her *devotees*. Mammon, a capital commercial comedy-drama at the Duke's, is a charming presentation, with Miss Louise Moodie as the heroine. Miss Neilson at the Haymarket, is Miss Neilson everywhere; and so I might continue; and yet all these houses are spacious and invariably thronged.

We are apt to regard the present growth of the drama as altogether more remarkable than theatrical displays before and after the appearance of Shakespeare, and in some respects the assumption is correct. In the time of Charles I–II, and for many years succeeding, there were no women on the stage; men played women's parts, and at an earlier period, at the close of the fifteenth century, passion or religious plays ruled the primitive stage, alike in France and England. One of these, "The Passion of our Saviour," was written so early that the name of the author is lost. A writer by the name of Bale, who died in 1563, the year before Shakespeare was born, wrote seventeen dramatic pieces, some of the titles of which were, "The Baptism of Christ," "Christ when He was Twelve Years Old," "The Lord's Supper," "The Resurrection," etc. Another by the same author, was called " God's Promises," and some of the poetry is of a very doubtful character.

Endless plays were produced, and the absence of all art in their representation made it very difficult to show them. Great religious quarrels resulted from the religious dramas, until finally they were suppressed by the civil governments. When Shakespeare fell into the hands of the illustrious modern tragedians, of whom Garrick may be called the most eminent, women came forth to add to the illustration of his and all contemporaneous and succeeding works; and then grew the art of painting, costumes, and that infinite variety of scenery and architecture which have made the stage in all enlightened nations the most potent ally of public enjoyment and social development. Music was equally advanced, and the drama, aided and beautified by the presence of sweet women, called to its assistance the sister arts, and became one of the most delightful instrumentalities for the entertainment and improvement of mankind.

LETTER XIX.

"O thou sweet king-killer, and dear divorce
'Twixt natural son and sire! thou bright defiler
Of Hymen's purest bed! thou valiant Mars!
Thou ever young, fresh, lov'd, and delicate wooer,
Whose blush doth thaw the consecrated snow
That lies on Dian's lap! thou visible god,
That solder'st close impossibilities,
And mak'st them kiss! that speak'st with every tongue,
To every purpose."
TIMON OF ATHENS.

LONDON, March, 1878.

" FOR they say, if money go before, all ways do lie open." The importance of these words I have learned to realize, though I have hardly looked beneath the surface of this glittering metropolis. The "saint-seducing gold" is all powerful here, as it is at home, and I have already begun to wonder what people meant who talked about going abroad to economize. Of course one can economize here, but he must first learn these old countries, and to gain this knowledge he must pay for his experience, and generally a pretty heavy tax. Then there are those who possess the high talent for suffering and starving, and it matters little where they go or where they stop, for they have set upon a campaign of skimping. Strangers must fee the whole kingdom, and this system is reduced to a science. I grant you a very little goes a great way. It is not the amount to any one that makes the vacuum in the pocket, but the unceasing demand for pennies; and the *pence* is what cheats the American. With us the cent is the penny always, and though we know the fact well, it takes some time for us to become accustomed to it, that a shilling is twenty-five cents, though twelve pence. The waiter that smiles as you give him sixpence, would be content upon one; Cabby knows an American at once and trades upon his contempt for coppers and his weakness for silver. The Frenchman is happy on a s*ou;* the German on a *kreuzer* or *pfennig;* the Italian on a *centesimi*, and the Spaniard on a *real;* it is ever the smallest coin offered by the English to the waiter, but the American disdains anything less than sixpence. Gradually I convalesced from the sixpence folly, and the London restaurants wrought the radical cure. I confess I was captured by a superb dinner—music included

—for "three and six," and exclaimed, with Dominie Sampson, "prodigious!" before calculating the other expenses attending this epicurean but economical feast. "Three and six" are eighty-seven and a half cents; a bottle of red wine four shillings ($1.00); and sixpence for the waiter, swells your account to $1.50 each if two are dining. The fee for the attendant does not remain at the option and generosity of the diners, but is charged in the bill, and then of course, you are expected—no! not expected, but *obliged* to hand the waiter a small gratuity for himself. If you take a hansom to reach any one of the swell restaurants, your outlay for dinner will net quite $2.00; what with the lodging at the hotel, and breakfast, you discover that you are living at about five dollars a day, or more than it would cost at the "Continental" or "Fifth Avenue." No one dines here without wine, and the tariff equals the American prices, for the Englishman is also obliged to render impost to his French neighbor across the channel for the *beuvrage*.

There are many chop houses, and pot houses, and grill rooms, where a gentleman may dine well upon a chop, a snack, with vegetables and bread, for six or eight-pence, but these are scarcely the places for a lady. They are mostly found in the city; Strand, Fleet Street, Cheapside, Cannon Street, and Ludgate Hill. I have made a tour of the better class restaurants, and have finally anchored at the "Café Royal," Regent Quadrant, where I took my first dinner in London many weeks ago. The English are the vilest cooks on this round globe; the talent for ruining all viands they touch seems plenarily developed, and I hailed the French café as a harvest and a home. Here we are served with a savory meal of chicken, vegetables, salad, cheese, bread and butter, ice-cream and wine, for the very modest sum of one dollar. Our *garçon* is a blue-bearded Italian, called Tony, who, besides supplying our delicious bite, is as polite as a dancing-master, as active as an acrobat, and lies like a lawyer.

Perhaps you are saying "fat paunches have lean pates, and dainty bits make rich the ribs, but bank 'rout quite the wits;" but this subject of food has been weighing heavily upon my—brain (?), and I must deliver myself of it. The other afternoon I strolled along the monumental splendors of Parliament Street, the House of Commons and the House of Lords, past old Westminster Abbey, through St. James's Park, past the great India House, through Waterloo Square, and by the four colossal lions of Landseer guarding the towering column of Nelson, in Trafalgar Square. What a throng! and what a medley of wealth and poverty! Beggars pleading for pennies at every step, and the gay and festive young soldiers of the Queen's Guard, with their jaunty little caps tilted on one side, short jackets and close-fitting trowsers, each one as straight as an arrow, and each with a *bonne*, and each *bonne* with a baby. Then the nobility rolling along in their luxurious carriages with liveried footmen and outriders, it was a panorama indeed! We lingered on Oxford Street to look into the dazzling shop windows filled with objects of *virtu*, gold and silver ornaments, and a perfect wilderness of female paraphernalia. Shortly we emerged into High Holborn, and then to the famous restaurant of the same name where we dined. Under the roof of this vast establishment there are many mansions; the grand salon, the duke's salon, the ladies' salon, Lincoln's inn buffet, and the grill room, besides an infinity of cloak-rooms and private dining-rooms. On entering the grand salon at *The Holborn*, for 6 P. M. *table d'hôte*, I thought I was in a fairy palace; it was as light as a flood of gas and wax-candles could make it; the crystal and gilt chandeliers were reflected in a hundred mirrors; the air was filled with the perfume of flowers,—for on each small table was placed a bouquet,—the silvery tinkle of the fountains' spray as it dropped upon the marble basin beneath, with music and the song of birds; music taken from the operas and executed by master hands. We dined in the lower balcony, behind the shadow and within the glow of crimson drapery, from where we could see the well-dressed guests in the large hall just below, and those around us; the waiters seeming as courtly as the company; and this was the *menû:*

Soups.
Purée of Game.   Consommé with Italian Paste.

Fish.
Fillets of Sturgeon, Indian Sauce.   Turbot, Lobster Sauce.

Entrees.
Turtle Croquettes, with Mushrooms.   Fricassee of Rabbit.

Roast.
Ribs of Beef, with Horseradish.

Sweets.
Rhubarb Tart.   Dom Pedro Jelly.
Génoise Glacéau Kirsch.

ICES.

Orange.   Ratafiar
  Cheese.   French Salad.

DESSERT.

Apples.   Oranges.   Pippins.   Olives.
  Almonds and Raisins.

And all of this graceful and elegant feast for three and six. Yet I have heard many American gentlemen say they were obliged to double up on the European *table d'hôte*, as the usual supply is insufficient.

At the New Viaduct Hotel, Holborn Viaduct, under the auspices of Spiers & Pond, the restaurant princes here, an elegant dinner is supplied, but not for three and six; that is one of the silvery resorts. The St. James, on Piccadilly, in connection with the concert rooms, serves almost as good a meal, but not the other accessories, as the High Holborn, for the same sum. At the Criterion there is also a six o'clock *table d'hôte*, but it is still more expensive. The Burlington, on Regent Street, is conspicuous, costly, with dinners *à la carte;* the interior adornments are strikingly beautiful, but we suddenly retreated when we were told we should have to wait at least half an hour for a small dinner. Mr. Blanchard, of the Burlington, is also proprietor of a less pretentious establishment on less pretentious Beak Street, where we obtained a very fair meal at rather a reasonable price. Verrey's, on Regent Street, is select and expensive, and the resort of fashionable ladies during the shopping hours. Simpson's, on the Strand, is famous and constantly thronged, so it requires considerable electioneering to secure a separate table, but I regard the cooking inferior to the others I have tried. Here roast beef and mutton, with potatoes and Brussels sprouts, are the staples; the dissector in white apron, jacket, and paper cap rolls a large barrow upon wheels to the side of your table, and there carves whatever you may choose from a huge round of beef or mutton. The Pall Mall, in Pall Mall, is the aristocratic restaurant of this extremely wealthy and noble quarter. It is pervaded by a solemn and stifling hush. Just out of Carleton Gardens and St. James Park, and in the midst of the clubs—the Athenæum, United Service, the Reform Club, the Traveller's, the Carlton, and Army and Navy—it is at once the rendezvous of the peer and poet, the scholar and the soldier, the man of play and the man of pleasure. The *table d'hôte* at the principal hotels, as the Grosvenor, Langham, Midland, and Charing Cross, are always expensive, never less than six or seven shillings, frequently ten.

The most costly and exclusive hotels of London are not the largest and most prominent where the greater portion of the tide of travel settles. They are to be found in quiet sequestered districts, off from the din of the mercantile world; outside, the counterpart of a large private residence, plain and spiritless; inside, palatial; and they are never advertised.

Much has been written of the quality and quantity of milk and cream in England, yet the price and dearth of ice cream is one of the points to be observed. It is generally a very inferior product, when it is found at all, and sixpence for so much as might be put into a Sauterne glass, frequently a shilling; this depends in what end of the town it is bought. The best is to be had at Gunter's, in Berkeley Square, confectioners to Her Majesty; but believe me, that ice cream has received a too liberal dose of arrowroot or corn starch. Eighty-seven cents for half a dozen of the most diminutive raw oysters you ever saw. One dollar for a dish of clear turtle soup. Seventy-five cents for one portion, and a very small one, of lobster salad. Two dollars for a capon. These figures are quite conclusive that the luxuries of the table are procurable at far lower rates at home. And to those who have been harboring the false conception of going abroad to economize—dispel it at once!

LETTER XX.

> "This royal throne of kings, this scepter'd isle,
> This earth of majesty, this seat of Mars,
> This other Eden, demi-paradise;
> This fortress built by nature for herself,
> Against infection and the hand of war;
> This happy breed of men, this little world;
> This precious stone set in the silver sea,
> Which serves it in the office of a wall,
> Or as a moat defensive to a house,
> Against the envy of less happy lands;
> This blessed plot, this earth, this realm, this England,
> This nurse, this teeming womb of royal kings,
> Feared by their breed, and famous by their birth,
> Renowned for their deeds as far from home
> (For Christian service and true chivalry)
> As is the sepulchre in stubborn Jewry,
> Of the world's ransom, blessed Mary's son."
> SHAKESPEARE.

LONDON, March, 1878.

IN this cloudy country, a "constitutional" is almost as necessary to health as food and sleep, and the "constitutional" of the English is a long stroll or stride of many hours or miles. The practice accounts for the immense feet of the females and the stalwart forms of the males. An English lady in her walking costume is more an object of oppressive respectability than of attraction. One rapidly grows into the customs of a country. I have already learned to prefer walking to riding, even in rough weather, and what enhances the pleasure are the thousand curious sights and scenes which make our jaunts a series of panoramic views. A stranger in London cannot fully enjoy the metropolis from a closed omnibus, a four-wheeler, or a hansom, and, of course, not from the underground railway; therefore we have adopted the Bayard Taylor fashion of taking views afoot.

So to-day we concluded to walk from Westminster to Tower Hill. Of the tower with its many black and bloody legends; its hoary walls and machicolated battlements; its ancient moat and Traitor's Gate; its resplendent halls of armor and chambers of jewels; its bastions and donjon, and its shroud of past gloom, casting shadows over the present sunshine of intelligence and liberty—I will not talk; it is a hackneyed as well as horrible story. But of the approach and immediate vicinity of this mighty monument of bygone vice, slavery, and barbarity, I trust I may dilate without being tedious. The sufferings of Lady Jane Grey, and her husband, Guildford Dudley, Walter Raleigh, Archbishop Laud, Lord Lovat, and the many others, are the threadbare tale of every school-book. This palace and prison is the familiar cenotaph of the ages, and one picture of it suffices for all time. Not so the environs of the venerable pile, for while it remains the same, time with them is ever working changes.

From the Royal Exchange where the bronze equestrian statue of the Duke of Wellington stands in all its conscious opulence of the $50,000 it cost, we crossed to the Bank of England; here I was unable to resist a peep. £100 shares are at par $500, each has risen to £230 or $1150. The yearly salaries of the officers are $1,100,000. The bank manages the national debt, which amounts to $4,000,000,000. "The old lady in Threadneedle Street"—as the English call their bank—is an affluent dowager, as her capital equals nearly $80,000,000. Here I saw the wonderful clock with the sixteen dials, so that a face may be seen from the sixteen distinct offices of the bank, through which all day long wild crowds are rushing to and fro. Here they shovel the bullion, and weigh the gold pieces, instead of counting them; it all seems very strange to us, but mistakes occur rarely. With a scoop, they cash a check for $1000 in a second. The bank notes are printed by a singular process, and forgery is rendered impossible. The hordes of people, and the busy officials, the cries in the street, the din of traffic, the dull, heavy roar of the unceasing ocean of hauling, make a terrestrial pandemonium. And yet the order of the management of this great temple of Mammon is a marvel of the age.

To the east, we have Cornhill, a thoroughfare of cheap shops, counting-houses, tumble-down taverns, insurance offices, historic haunts, and even poetical reminiscences; for it was in this quarter that Gray was born, and lived years ago, and Daniel De Foe—the author of Robinson Crusoe—carried on the business of stocking-maker, in 1702. But who shall depicture the Stock Exchange? It was a wild day (Saturday) there! A medley of crazy rioters. Frequently the police are necessary to disperse the mob gathered to buy and sell stocks, tobacco, pepper, indigo, and drugs, and the broker is always there to effect the barter. It was a clear day, but the air was rude, and the tumult ruder as we endeavored to thread our way through this modern Babel.

All trades are plied, all classes mingle, all languages are spoken. You are thrust here and there by the extended elbows of a ruffian, by a greasy fish-basket, a heedless boy, wheelbarrows, boxes, and wagons. Suddenly there is a halt midway in the mad tumult; there is a blockade in the torrent of travel on sidewalk and highway, if, indeed, you can distinguish them, as at such a time horses and wagons are driven on the pavement, regardless of human life; and then the air reverberates with the shouts of drivers, porters, beggars, hawkers, guardians of the *peace*, fishwomen, candy and fruit sellers, importunate showmen, and peddlers. At first I was provoked that I had consented to venture in the midst of the human and *inhuman* menagerie, then my mood changed to one of solicitude for my raiment, for my premonition was that I should be vehemently divested of it, and the *tertium quid* was a silent prayer for my life. No man tarried for his neighbor, so I abandoned myself to the current, to gaze upon the strange concourse, and watch the passions on the faces of the multitude, and stare into the kaleidoscope of the windows. If the picture on the highway was exciting and *outre*, it was novel in the depositories that flanked the pavements. Here were shelves of gold and silver coins, next door masses and mazes of old statuary, paintings, engravings, musty books, and bric-a-brac. Past brokers, law-offices, and antique houses, we were carried into Leadenhall Street, the place of markets of meat, poultry, and especially hides. Another world as exclusive in its devotion to creature comforts as what I have just left is to money and speculation. Here is the vast sepulchre, or confined subterranean sea, of light French and German wines; the cellars of H. R. Williams & Co., extending beneath the range of the entire markets, and then we emerged into Lombard Street, the region of the golden gods of Europe and America, and the same where the Longobards of Edward II's reign met to transact their affairs. All here was heavy, and gloomy, and strong; the great dealers of finance seem to avoid glitter. Odd it is that all these treasure-houses are surrounded by marts for the sale of food and grain; and here we came upon Mark and *Mincing* Lanes, the corn markets of the world.

The scene at Billingsgate great fish market and wharf was grotesque and bizarre to the last degree. What a *mélange* of curiously dressed men, and still more curiously attired women! What an atmosphere and multitude of odd-looking and odd-named fish. This wholesale market was made open and free for all classes of fish in 1699, and all the oviparous inhabitants of the water that are imported in British vessels, fresh or cured, are free of duties. The fish in this market are sold by count, except salmon and eels; oysters are sold by measure, and no fish are sold on Sunday, with the exception of mackerel. Much has been written of the peculiar characteristics of the fish-mongers. Time has evidently improved them, as I heard none of the ribaldry and vituperation of the olden days, but they are much rougher, ruder, and more boisterous than the same order at home.

The Thames is to London, life, food, health, and enjoyment. Without its ceaseless current there would be no world's metropolis. However regarded it is vital to London existence. Venice is not more dependent upon her canals, than is London upon the Thames; nor is Holland more indebted to her dykes, and the estuaries of the sea that penetrate into, cleanse, and improve her cities. And the very region I have been visiting to-day proves how indispensable the Thames is to the city it divides. It is bordered by stately edifices, and they produce a most impressive effect. The custom-house is solid, capacious, and most extensive; the long room is 190 by 60 feet, and has an altitude of 55 feet, in the centre; some conception of its extent may be formed, but the rush and crush of business cannot be idealized. Here I had my first real insight of English commerce. Even Liverpool, with its forest of masts, and wilderness of docks, did not impress me like these mighty storehouses on the Thames, that hold the produce of the Mediterranean and America, of the Orient and the Occident. I was bewildered by the scene, yet I labored to retain a few facts of this Trade Colossus. The St. Catherine Docks cost nearly nine millions of dollars, and the wine vaults of the Eastern Docks cover an underground area of 890,545 feet; one vault alone a space of seven acres! On the India Docks six millions of dollars were expended in the beginning, seventy-nine years ago, and they now include three hundred acres of land and water.

Such is the opulence of London, of its world-wide affiliations, of the endless varieties of its traffic. All the delicacies, refinements, luxuries, necessities, inventions and products of the human race, are collected in their gross and rude virgin state. It was a wild blending of foreign sounds, smells, and costumes. There were many ladies and travellers from distant ports, tradesmen, and many like myself taking notes. We had reached the limit of this historical and commercial labyrinthine *locale*, and the melancholy walls of the Tower burst upon us from the hill. We joined the democratic brigade commanded by a "beef-eater," with faded and flaunting ribbons, and proceeded to view that of which we had so often read.

LETTER XXI.

"Ye distant spires, ye antique towers,
 That crown the wat'ry glade,
Where grateful Science still adores
 Her Henry's holy shade;
And ye that from the stately brow
Of Windsor's heights th' expanse below
 Of grove, of lawn, of mead survey,
Whose turf, whose shade, whose flowers among
Wanders the hoary Thames along
 His silver winding way."

THOMAS GRAY.

LONDON, March, 1878.

THE Thames, that vital artery of the English capital, always seemed chiefly important as a commercial stream, till George Eliot, in Daniel Deronda, glorified it into romance and beauty. Taking its rise near Cirencester, it passes Windsor, Hampton Court, Twickenham, Fulham, Chelsea, Richmond, and so on to London, where its shores are crowned by the oldest religious, political, charitable, commercial, and literary monuments. Although the Thames is often repulsive viewed from the many bridges that span it, or from the new and costly embankments, it seems to purify as we penetrate into rural England. All along its banks are the silent abodes of blissful wealth. The great novelist has opened new views of its pastoral beauties, of the lovely regions it traverses, of the hamlets and estates, palaces and retreats, battle-fields, colleges, schools, and churches, it has rolled through and by for centuries. As you travel you find inland towns and villages connected with London by rail and sail down to the North Sea, where the river empties its tribute of darksome waters; its margin is lined with punts and barges plying out into the current. We see it at intervals through the trees a mere coiling ribbon, gradually expanding into a river navigable for vessels of 1400 tons. These towns are flanked by fine hotels, houses, lordly domains, and public gardens. As you approach London you realize that the Upper Thames has become the rendezvous of fashion, frolic, high life, low life, and the ten thousand secrets of a huge metropolis. Here they are largely concealed and steadily increase. The Thames at London is pregnant of dark mysteries and darker tragedies. Few travellers follow its course and rarely see its country side in nature. They visit the Docks, Tower, Tunnel, and Custom-house, linger on the bridges, and stop at Windsor, Richmond, and Kew. They are thus only partially prepared for the endless wealth of London, proved by the superb memorials on its river's banks, brought into bold relief by the sky, and these evidences strengthen their belief in the words of the old Pope, who a century ago said, "If the treasury of Philip Augustus had been put up for sale London could have bought it." Then they dwell upon the fountain of this incalculable wealth—the ocean—and of the Thames, its tributary, and think of what the martyr Sir Walter Raleigh said, " He who commands the sea commands the trade of the world; he who commands the trade of the world commands the riches of the world, and consequently the world itself;" but there! I am transgressing my woman's province. I have no desire to play the *savant*, nor decoy you into the belief that I have all the *mots* and aphorisms of the ecclesiastical, political, and poetic Solomons, at my finger tips. No! I spare you the infliction.

So with the vision of Daniel Deronda in mind, just as the sun was sinking behind the hills, and night was wrapping nature in her dusky cloak, and the little stars were coming out one by one like so many eyes to witness his rescue of the melancholy Mirah who had wandered to the river edge, where it slopes gently from Kew Gardens, and the willow bushes stand thick and close to the margin, I projected my tour of the silent highway, with Windsor Palace, Eton, Kew Gardens, Richmond, Bushy Park, and Hampton Court in prospect. Next morning was balmy and soft, though the month March, and as we passed under the dark arches of the great bridges, the river was sluggish and opaque, the tall spires lost their heads in the misty clouds, and the dim masses of stone fretwork were indistinctly outlined against the hazy sky; but the fishers' boats, pleasure barges, and commercial craft, were steadily ploughing the watery way. The Oxford and Cambridge lads were in their cockle-shell skiffs, practising for the prize competition which will take place in about two weeks. We rested upon our oars close to the Great Western Railway Bridge and viewed Windsor, with its ghostly towers and wooded heights, the famous old beeches with outstretched arms and gnarled trunks, that tell us of the "years of generations." At the feet of these old monarchs is the baby crocus in her cradle of soft, fresh green; she pushes back her blanket, and lifts her sweet sad face to the pale English sun, but a chill gale blows over the bleak Welsh hills, and the new-born crocus shivers and bends her head to her mother—Earth. The willow bushes and long rank grass are dipping into the river, which sparkles as the struggling sun touches its ripples, the anglers are sporting with their rods, and a flock of white sheep are grazing on the young verdure. Yonder on the opposite bank is Eton, the famous school of preliminary instruction for the sons of noblemen and gentry. The main portion of the youths under tuition here are oppidans, numbering nearly nine hundred, the number of the King's scholars who reside within the walls is limited to seventy; the narrow lanes and level highways of the town are full of these oddly dressed oppidans. As we passed many of the lads were out on the greensward, and in these sporting youths I saw the future British poets and statesmen, and thought of their predecessors, Walpole, Bolingbroke, Fielding, Gray, Chatham, Fox, and Wellington, who had gambolled upon the same lawn.

We turned from the chalk hills of Windsor, and pulled toward Hampton Court, past the royal and densely-wooded estates, gladdened by sunny trout-brooks, where the fallow-deer were browsing, and where the dark English roads are bordered by glossy hedges, where the cattle wade among the mossy and slimy stones at the river's brink, within the shadow of the tall elms, where my lord rides out upon his palfry in buckskin or corduroy, while his retainers lay down the hoe and sickle as noon-tide tolls from the curfew tower.

The first glimpse we caught of the palace made it appear like a small town. We lingered upon Hampton Bridge, as we had been told to do, to gain a view of the Gothic turrets of Wolsey, and then passed the great stone portals guarded by the lions, and adorned by the armorial symbols and trophies of the third William. Through a neglected court or avenue that lay between the barracks—a long row of low, dilapidated brick structures on the left, and heavy, decaying incongruous buildings on the right—we reached the regal home of Charles I and II, where the workings of nature and art go hand in hand, where countless names of fame are indissolubly carved, where cling the traditions of the romance and tragedy of three centuries, where the saintly but sybaritic Wolsey held high revel, and his thousand satellites were housed, where the illustrious scriptural tapestries still embellish the walls of the great hall. They are in a perfect state of preservation and illustrate the eight epochs of the life of Abraham. They are elaborate specimens of art, "the higher lights being worked in gold." Each one is bordered by an intricate design in arabesque, where figures, fruits, flowers, and vines intermingle, emblematic of the lessons the subject is intended to teach. Need I recount the high-pitched roof and pendants, the stained glass windows bearing the titles of the six wives of "bluff king Hal?" the banners, and arms, and ciphers of the nobles? the court and chapel? the king's staircase with its essentially French frescoes by Antonio Verrio? The adornments are striking and exuberant, but I am told by superior judgment, they will not sustain criticism. We wandered through the royal bedchambers and *boudoirs*, and long succession of art galleries, where each portrait is an eloquent legend of the past. From the centre window in the queen's drawing-room we looked out upon the garden below, with its brilliant border and level yellow gravel paths, the terraces and mounds of soft green turf, stone vases, a mass of luxuriant bloom, dancing fountains, and through the vista of a long line of lofty and venerable trees, shadowing a footpath, there is a lake ornamented with statues and sparkling *jets d'eau*. Across the highroad to Kingston we entered Bushby Park, with its long colonnades of chestnuts and limes, several centuries old, and not one of them seems to be allowed to grow an inch above the other, making a mighty and mazy arbor of green.

A short row brought us to the celebrated Kew Gardens, extending along the Thames. This extensive collection of living flowers and plants of all kinds, is now national property, but nevertheless we could not forget the time when it was leased to the Prince of Wales, son of George II, afterward George III, nor that the cottage is still preserved as it was left by the ill-fated Queen Charlotte. At present the chief interest centres in its gardens and botanical treasures, said to be the most famous in the world. How soft and velvety the turf! How capacious and well-ordered the green-houses, nurseries, and conservatories, and how wonderful in summer the open beds of various colored flowers, exotic and otherwise, gathered from every land under the sun, and cured and cultivated by all the resources of science and of genius. To this lovely resort continuous and countless crowds repair from multitudinous London, by daily boat and rail Kew Gardens are open every day to the public after one o'clock. Famous Richmond—the Tivoli of England—is a sail of a few moments from Kew, a large town with a population of over 15,000, and beautifully placed on the right bank of the Thames. Its park and bridge, and palatial surroundings, and glorious perspective, will live ever in my memory. The muse of history has lingered long and written much upon this favorite place. Near by Pope and Walpole lived for many years, and here myriads gather during the fine days to enjoy the exquisite scenery, to walk through the historic parks, to punt on the romantic river, or to regale themselves upon the costly dinners at the *Star and Garter*, an experience we were fain to avoid, being unwilling to pay for mere form and style, when we could procure an equally satisfactory repast at one of the less pretentious inns. Our hostel, the *Talbot*, was "neat but not gaudy." We had to wait for quite awhile for our steak and potatoes, and while doing so, witnessed one of those exhibitions which I regret to say are too common in England, a rather decent young lady accompanied by her swain, both considerably worse for too frequent potations. The food was good, and we were ready for it, and we did not complain as we paid our nine shillings, feeling it would be double the amount at the more silvery Star and Garter.

LETTER XXII.

"And throned immortal by his side,
  A woman sits with eye sublime,
Aspasia, all his spirit's bride;
  But, if their solemn love were crime,
Pity the beauty and the sage,
Their crime was in their darkened age.

He perished, but his wreath was won;
  He perished in his height of fame:
Then sunk the cloud on Athens' sun,
  Yet still she conquered in his name.
Filled with his soul, she could not die;
Her conquest was Posterity!"   CROLY.

LONDON, April, 1878.

BARRING the noble (?) classes who come upon the stage of life with their titles generally more developed than their limbs, the most exalted positions in England are held by those who have won renown by their literary efforts. By no other assumption, howsoever lofty, may one claim an *entrée* to the exclusive circle of *sang bleu*, as potent as those whose stockings are of the corresponding hue. Of this class "George Eliot" crowns the lettered heights. Marian Evans, the original of this male pesudonyme, is now about fifty-eight. She was born in Warwickshire, the daughter of an humble curate, and afterward adopted by a wealthy clergyman, who lavishly educated his little *protégé*. But her astounding mental expansion grew out of her tutelage under the philosopher, Herbert Spencer, with whom she studied French, German, and Italian, music, art, and metaphysics, after she had finished at the academy, where only the foundation stone was laid of her great learning. She is the worshipped Calliope here, notwithstanding her *mésalliance* with the celebrated George Henry Lewes, who sincerely loved and honored her. She has no attractions of face, but her mind overrules all else, and though much of the eloquent and peculiar phraseology, which has gained for her so vast an audience, has been attributed to her constant association with Lewes' philosophy, it was her established style before she assumed the voluntary fetters of that mental and sacred fellowship. Her first literary attempt—a translation—was not made until she was twenty-six, and her first novel was published twelve years afterwards. Within a later period she has written several poems that would have made the fame of any other struggling aspirant, but have added nothing to that of the great novelist, and are comparatively unknown. George Henry Lewes is her senior by only three years, and though his first days of student-life were steeped in anatomy and physiology, he afterward wrote fiction, and later became a scientific zealot, and has ever since attracted attention by the ability of his psychological dissertations. I was tempted to study the surrounding country of the Thames by George Eliot's inspired descriptions, and this led to my meditations on the other female writers of London.

Miss Mary Elizabeth Braddon, the daughter of a contributor to the old sporting magazines—which accounts for her heroine, Aurora Floyd, having a predilection for jockeys and the pleasures of the turf, carrying a betting-book, and indulging in such literature as *Bell's Life*—was born in Soho Square over forty-one years ago. Still corresponding under her maiden name, she has married a wealthy gentleman and lives in affluence. She is a prodigious worker, and her novels, plays, and current contributions to periodical literature, are popular and remunerative. She is the editress of the *Belgravia*, a monthly magazine of the type of our *Galaxy*. Her publications have not only enriched the authoress, but as adapted to the stage have proven a source of emolument to actors and managers.

Mrs. Henry Wood, the daughter of Thomas Price, a glove manufacturer, is about sixty years old. For many years the editress of the *Argosy*, a sixpenny monthly and favorite of fiction readers, she has been eclipsed by the brighter luminaries, George Eliot and Miss Braddon. How many tears have been shed over the wayward and misled Lady Isabel in *East Lynne*, and other equally hapless heroines of her dramatized works!

One of the oldest English authoresses and artists is Mrs. Anna Eliza Bray. She studied art under the guidance of Mr. Stothard, whose son she married in 1818. Their congenial life of study and travel was fated to be brief, for scarcely three years had passed when he was killed. His great labor, *The Monumental Effigies of Great Britain*, was completed by his widow, who shortly after married the Rev. Mr. Bray, the author of several theological and poetical books.

Another of these brave women living in London is Florence Nightingale, more eminent for her noble philanthropies in peace and war, though she has written much upon charitable and sanitary subjects. She received all the advantages of a complete education, but her life mission has been to alleviate physical and moral distress. She may be justly called the idol of the good people of England. Though she rarely goes out now, this lady has a claim upon our gratitude for her unselfish sacrifices for suffering humanity. Surrounded by all the luxuries of wealth and refinement, still her heart beats warmly for the afflicted. She has expended immense sums from her private means, and a few years ago, when $250,000 were voted to her by the public in recognition of her splendid services in the military hospitals in the Crimea, she established with that fund an institution for the "training and employment of nurses." And now, after a life abounding in such examples of royal munificence, she relapses, in the autumn of her days, into restful comfort.

Another of the toiling ladies of London is Miss Amelia Blandford Edwards. She is about forty-seven, and a descendant of the Walpole family, as yet unmarried, I believe. She has written many novels and juvenile books, as well as being a constant contributor to five or six magazines.

But no woman in all England, with the exception of the Queen, has had more deserved and greater honors than Angela Georgiana, Baroness Burdette-Coutts, who won fame by the liberal use of her large fortune; the greater portion of it she inherited from her mother, Sophia Coutts, who married Sir Francis Burdette, an effective Parliamentary orator, and the "idol of the London populace." The Baroness is about sixty-five, and was created a peeress in her own right, in June, 1871. Her wealth is as boundless as her generosity, and her features as conspicuously homely as those of the Premier. With $250,000 she endowed three colonial bishoprics in British colonies. With lavish hands she bestows money upon her favorite, the Church of England, but to institutions of science, charity, education, discovery, and art, she is in a like manner liberal She is equally solicitous for the advancement of the drama and music. Henry Irving is her chosen friend, and a braver, more modest, whole-souled woman does not exist.

One of the facts that have ever interested me is the amount of work done by literary and professional women in America and England, and, indeed, in every part of the world. The labors of George Sand, Madame de Staël, Madame de Sevigne, in France; Mrs. Stowe, Julia Ward Howe, Louisa Alcott, Anna Dickinson, in America, and the countless thinkers and writers of England, are prodigious.

LETTER XXIII.

"What hid'st thou in thy treasure-caves and cells,
 Thou hollow sounding and mysterious main?—
Pale glistening pearls and rainbow-color'd shells,
 Bright things which gleam unrecked-of and in vain!
Keep, keep thy riches, melancholy sea!
We ask not much from thee."

HEMANS.

LONDON, April, 1878.

WE set out for Hastings in a burst of sunshine, but alas! our bright experience was short-lived. The gray clouds lowered, the first drops pattered against the window-pane of our carriage. We hoped for a favorable wind that might chase away the threatening storm. But no! the atmosphere was ominous, and at length the storm broke in all its fury. Unlike ours in spring, at home, the tempest did not purify the air; for several days after, the heavens were overcast. Why did this particular war of the elements make such a deep impression upon me? Perhaps because I was at a foreign seaside! Perhaps because I had anticipated glory and met only gloom! But I did not sit down to moralize, and there is "something too much of this."

Hastings is three hours' distant from London by rail. The first station of note after leaving London Bridge, is Chiselhurst, familiar as the retreat of Napoleon III and Eugénie; the scene of his death and burial, and since the growth and peace of the Republic the restful harbor of the beautiful Empress. Then on we dashed through emerald pasture lands and cultivated farms, smiling roadsides framed by glossy, luxuriant hedges, and past the hills, veiled with Nature's cobwebs, where nestle the white cottages and the rude barns. At Tunbridge Wells, an ancient and famous inland watering-place, an humble clergyman, who had been a pleasant *compagnon de voyage*, possessing apparently plenty of brains and little gold, left us. Then our route gravitated gradually toward the sea. The air was full of the smell of salt from the brackish inlets, and over the wide expanse of moorland I saw the naked downs bordering the Channel. From the station we rode along the parade to the Marine Hotel facing the ocean, which was calm enough, but the skies were not bright, the rain was falling in torrents, and the air was soft and warm. I had been anxious to see one of these winter seaside resorts upon the southern coast, where London society rushes to escape the black fogs, where the ocean is as level as the Delaware in June, and the people make gardens in the open air at Christmas. I knew the town must be bizarre and picturesque, and determined to brave wind and weather as soon as I had regaled myself with a substantial English dinner. Beneath my front window lay the gray crested waters of the great main, while close to the rear rose a huge boulder, groined by the finger of Time. The ocean is as fascinating to me as a cemetery. The comparison may appear to you far-fetched, and the taste eccentric; but, nevertheless, whether it be to toss up on the heaving breast, saunter upon the sands, climb the cliffs and jutting crags of the one, while my heart sings second to the mournful melody of the eternal ebb and flow, or to linger by the silent and restful graves of the other, it is the same lesson of eternity.

When Pluvius hid his weeping eyes behind a temporary screen, I ventured out into this model sea and mountain town, lying partly at the base, and partly upon the acclivity of the range of steep hills that shelters it from the northern winds. I started in search of an old friend who I heard was wintering in the soft and genial climate for her health, and as I was referred to one location after another, and numbers innumerable, I studied the beauty of the costly and aristocratic little houses upon the velvety terraces, the windows filled with flowers blossoming in bouquets, the squares fresh and radiant; meanwhile I was being sprinkled in the most liberal manner by the treacherous god, and oh, great spirit of Fashion, pity me! I had on my swell clothes.

I rose from one narrow street to another, and another, and another, sometimes by a few steps, and sometimes by a gentle ascent as they meandered around the old hills; very quaint and very odd are these sinuous avenues over the bold cliffs. In the higher part of the town, I found the atmosphere more bracing and American. I confess I had a full satiety of humidity. These English are like fish; they enjoy the water, and the damp, and cold, and fog; undaunted they waded through the hilly town, umbrellaed and cloaked. The tears of the gods were still unquenched; I had sought my friend in vain, and though I anticipated passing the evening at the Pavilion Theatre, erected at the extremity of the long pier extending far out in the Channel, I returned to the hotel, through the balmy air and the clinging torrents.

A thorough English dinner and the drenching over, both ample and satisfactory, I ensconced myself before the genial sea-coal fire in the cosy sitting-room of the silent English hotel—always silent as cloisters even if filled with company—to enjoy my companion,—a book—for a couple of hours, before retiring to rest under the same roof that had sheltered the Empress Eugénie, when she came to meet her son, the young Prince Imperial, after her escape from the palace of the Tuileries. In this flight she was aided by our fellow-countryman, Dr. Thomas Evans, proprietor of the *American Register*. And then I slept to the chant of the waves, while visions danced through my head of bloody frays, led by Harold the Saxon on one side and the Norman William upon the other; of vast fleets of men of war moored close by; of Matilda the industrious wife of the Conqueror, and her maids of honor engaged in sewing sphinxes, and birds, and dogs, and horses,—oh, such horses!—and trees, and ships, and men upon that great big sampler—the Pictorial History of the Invasion—that she presented to the Bishop of Bayeux.

Next morning was dreary and damp, as I made a tour of the shops—numerous, beautiful, and complete—and the ascent of the rearward hills to obtain a view of the beach thronged by the rude fishermen in fantastic dress, some in their boats, and others upon land mending their nets for future use; the broad marine parade stretching far away along the coast; the town immediately beneath me snuggling close to the rocks for protection; healthy villages crowning lofty summits, and the ghastly desolation of the dismantled castle upon a seemingly perilous cliff. As I retraced my zigzag steps, I descried new comforts and luxuries concealed in cosy recesses. Back again we went through Wellington Square to our hotel, a clean edifice of stone, where our carriage waited to convey us to St. Leonards-on-Sea, the " West End " of Hastings. Our ride was along the sea, then by the side of the lion sea, quiet and calm — but evidently as powerful as the other forces of nature. A continuous façade of white stone houses extends from the East Cliffs to Bopeep; in the bow windows were rather good-looking, clumsy women gazing out upon the world of waters. But there were no blue skies nor pure waves of air; no pleasure barges, nor equestrian parties; no stream of fashion's votaries pouring through the streets, and no promenaders lounging in the arcades, for the overcharged emotions of the gods were still uncontrollable

On we rode past solid, strong structures, until we reached St. Leonard's. What a lovely town! with noble and enduring homes, fine shops, the same features of atmosphere, architecture, luxurious private residences, and none of the horrors of a London winter, as the historical Hastings. Here I observed the same large feet of the ladies, awkward carriage, indifference to dress, and utter lack of taste.

There is no more interesting, beautiful, romantic, and historical spot in England than Sussex County or its shires. Everywhere are found relics, eloquent of Roman origin and occupation; legends of the Norman Conquest; ancient estates and titled castles.

These two seaside towns, Hastings and St. Leonards-on-Sea, even seen through a vail of gloom, more completely fill my ideal than any similar resorts we have in America. Of course I had sketched *my picture* of Atlantic City, Cape May, Long Branch, Spring Lake and many others before visiting them; and upon personal acquaintance I found I had been feeding upon delusion. I had thought to enjoy the seashore, the hotels should be placed directly on the sands, facing mainward, where the roll of the "deep and dark-blue ocean" should be ever dashing against our windows, instead of standing in a paved street half a mile, and frequently a greater distance from the waters. Another feature that always disappointed me at home was the absence of rocks, and every topographical accessory that makes up a beautiful landscape, or rather, marine scene. Here I had it all!

Every year greater numbers of our people are copying the foreign custom of wintering by the sea, and the fact of the beneficial effect of the soft and salubrious salt air upon those suffering from pulmonary complaints must strengthen this fashion. As for me, I should never wish to escape the glory, the fervent clearness, and nipping air of an American winter.

One fact deserves to be studied by the people of Long Branch, Cape May, Atlantic City, Seagirt, and other Atlantic sea-settlements; that from the closing of the summer season to its reopening, they have many long spells of delightfully soft and salubrious weather, and that they ought to profit by the experiences of Hastings.

LETTER XXIV.

> "Deep in the wave is a coral grove,
> Where the purple mullet and gold fish rove;
> Where the sea-flower spreads its leaves of blue
> That never are wet with falling dew,
> But in bright and changeful beauty shine
> Far down in the green and glassy brine.
>   The floor is of sand like the mountain-drift,
> And the pearl-shells spangle the flinty snow;
>   From coral rocks the sea-plants lift
> Their boughs, where the tides and billows flow;
> The water is calm and still below,
>   For the winds and waves are absent there,
> And the sands are bright as the stars that glow
>   In the motionless fields of upper air."
>   JAMES GATES PERCIVAL.

LONDON, April, 1878.

THE Crystal Palace! the beautiful glass temple, with its girders of iron, crowning fair Sydenham Hill, eight miles from London, is a store-house of every department of ancient and modern art and science. Its English and Italian gardens, foreign mediæval architectural courts, and historical portrait gallery, are lessons for meditation, and form an unrivalled preparatory school to a Continental tour. Yet its industrial department was in a state of dishabille when I saw it, and many of its sections were dingy and tawdry. But English wealth, ever apparent, is in nothing so striking as in the copies of expensive and unobtainable originals in this same Crystal Palace: copies of statuary, paintings, plate, armor, castles, tombs, shrines, jewels, ceramics, antiques, and all the spoils of the ages, which are invaluable as so many reflections of the reality. So opulent, indeed, is England, with London as its treasure-house, reinforced by English pride (for they are as fond of their country as a woman of her diamonds), that though the great Palace has not proved a financial success, they will not allow it to fail. Very beautiful and ample are the attractions of this permanent exhibition; but I am still *blasé*, by dint of the splendors of our Centennial. And so in place of rhapsodizing over all that is spread before me at this banquet of pleasure and knowledge, I orally compare and contrast, and my verdict is always: Young America has excelled his parent!

    I lingered long in the Pompeian Court, a copy like that

to be presented by Mr. John Welsh, our good minister in London, to our Fairmount Park, endeavoring to glean some ideas of the exhumed city, where *Deo volente* I shall pass some future days studying the chapters written by ancient art and time. The decorations of the musical court are appropriate and novel; sacred music is typified by David, "the sweet singer of Israel," and Miriam; also pastoral and martial melody by Pan. These are upon the exterior, while the interior is still more beautiful and imposing. Extending quite along the four sides of the court are arched recesses—depositories for the instruments. Over each of these presides the bust of a famous composer. The panels and columns are adorned with playing boys, musical instruments, pipes, and shells entwined with fitting foliage *en bas relief*, and *vis-a-vis* upon the sides are St. Cecilia and the muse Erato *en alto-relievo*.

But to the Marine Aquarium! Here I passed my time, for here I found a congenial amusement in the study of natural science. Of all the 'ologies, this one through all its departments and epochs, from the *genus homo* to the lowest grade of animal life, the *poriphora* or pory class, as sponges, has ever been my pet since my salad days, when I received from the sanctified hand of Archbishop Wood, under the convent roof of the Academy of Notre Dame, the prize for zoology. But some years have elapsed, and having had no subsequent experience with great aquaria, I enjoyed the novel feast with fresh delight. Long did I watch the habits, and study the history of the curious species of the first-class (fish) of animals. Here were the brilliantly and beautifully colored Wrasse that abound on the coast of Norway; and though many writers versed in fish lore tell us that as we ascend into northern seas we find the scales of the water-living tribe losing all the radiant hue peculiar to the tropics, and invariably dull and leaden in color, we here have a strong contradictory proof of the text in this exquisite animal; the male is as beautiful as a rainbow, having ultramarine-blue and greenish-bronze stripes upon the body, while the head is adorned with the most vivid blue and yellow; the female is not nearly so handsome, though flashingly attractive. The Lamprey, with which the reservoirs of Diomed were well stocked,—the fish upon which the first-century Sybarites supped,—were adhering to the rocks and glass of the tanks with their ugly disk-shaped mouths. One of the Sole family was floundering about with the outlines of the human face and features plainly defined upon the obverse. I saw the Stickleback weaving its nest of weeds, which it sewed together with threads exuded from its body, in the same manner as the filaments that the spider uses in the construction of his web. Of course the animals peculiar to British waters were here in great affluence, the White-bait, Whiting, Smelts, Gray Mullet, etc.; and I watched them eating, sleeping, resting, burrowing, and house-building.

It was the first fair demonstration I had of zoophytes or the animal flowers. Their form is that of a beautiful flower and generally of a pale pink or yellow flesh-color, their manifold tentacles bearing a strong resemblance to human flesh. Like the Scriptural Peter, I was not content with the *oui dire* of their animated existence, and determined upon having an exhibition of animal life from these white-blooded creatures. I saw they had motion, and powers of expansion, but these faculties would be common if they possessed only the vegetable nature. I had not long to wait, for soon the keeper came with feed; it was with few exceptions raw flesh; their absorption of organic matter was a conclusive proof of their animalism. This class of creation, more familiar as sea-anemones, are radiate animals, and breathe from the surface of their bodies. They are sensitive to touch, although no nerves have been detected; but they must exist in some species, as they are capable of being rendered insensible by an opiate. I noticed they were all voracious, though they presented a well-fed and healthy appearance, their complexions rosy, and their limbs full; but their tentacles are ever spread in "full blast," to sweep whatever may approach them into the cavities of their stomachs. To secure living prey they eject poisonous darts. Their dinner was conveyed to them from the top of the tank by means of a curved tongs. Each one was fed singly, and as the tongs holding the feed was lowered within level of their reach, all the neighbors of the one who was to receive the prize extended their mouths until you could look into the very pit of their bodies, and then contracted with despair and disappointment. Like all eager feeders their powers of locomotion are limited. The most active and energetic have never been known to accomplish more than six inches of travel in twenty-four hours, and the most slothful scarcely move their position in a life-time. If the aquaria are healthy they often exist forty-five years and even longer periods, giving birth to thousands of young, and evincing no signs of approaching age, a proof of their devotion to the command, "bring forth and multiply." Those that have a taste for travel and no desire to tax their own energies, have the human instinct of attaching themselves to the back or flank of a more ambitious creature, the crustacean. The crab, lobster, or prawn, often becomes so burdened by its parasitic friends, that it abandons its shell in sheer desperation and seeks another home, while another species so resignedly yields all authority to the sycophant, that when it changes its habitation it conveys its vital incumbrance hither. The great lesson taught in this volume is the human power of understanding between these lowest organized creatures. There are many beautiful legends of the zoophytes in connection with ancient warriors whose powers and customs faithfully resembled them.

Full of this interesting study it occurred to me that I might complete it by an examination into the enormous playhouse and museum, "The Aquarium," a few steps from the Westminster Palace Hotel; so paying our shilling we sauntered into this other variegated world, and it only required a few minutes to realize that the title of the great exhibition was in one sense a misnomer. At first intended to be a grand depository of all the ocean tribes, it has rapidly become a receptacle of the works of the human tribes, a sort of caravansera, or *olla podrida*, or general *rendezvous*, not only of fish, and fowl, and birds, and beasts, and flowers, and minerals, but of all the species of the paragon of animals. In one end Uncle Tom's Cabin played to thousands daily by colored Americans, men, women, and children; in another Chinese acrobats, Asiatic jugglers, Swiss musicians, Turkish doctors, the American circus, operatic matinees, wrestlers, dancers, telephone experiments, learned pigs, educated fleas, and finally a wonderful mind-reader, "Little Louie," a girl about ten, trained to a lightning perception, by means of intuitive psychology, and like all those occult practices, quite beyond explanation. Fancy this child standing at her father's side, eyes bandaged, and answering quickly to every question he puts to her, as he passes from her to a considerable distance among the audience, and holds in his hand the special object he receives or takes from a spectator; it may be a watch, or a coin, or a book, or a manuscript, or an inscribed ring, or the tiniest article or animal, while rapid as thought she characterizes the article, its size, its color, and what is most astonishing, the date, the name of owner, and inscription.

Having failed to discover any curious inhabitants of the great deep, I was sufficiently successful in searching for strange material among my own fellow-creatures.

LETTER XXV.

"Search Windsor Castle, elves, within and out:
The several chairs of order look you scour
With juice of balm, and every precious flower:
Each fair instalment, coat, and several crest,
With loyal blazon, ever more be blest!
And nightly, meadow-fairies, look, you sing,
Like to the Garter's compass, in a ring."
MERRY WIVES OF WINDSOR.

LONDON, April, 1878.

SATURDAY was a bright, balmy, British day. The whole town was in a tumult; the two rival colleges, Oxford and Cambridge, were to row against each other on the Thames, and myriads came to see, but we were royally inclined, and the train that carried us to Windsor, stopped at every little roadside station only to be laden by hundreds of country lads and lasses bound for the river race. Before we reached our destination the radiance of the morning had turned to rain, and so we saw Windsor Palace, one of the eight historical homes of the Queen, through a vail of gloom. Our route to Windsor lay through the enchanting valley of the Thames, bordered by the opulent estates of the wealthy nobles. As we moved onward the scene was so fertile, finished, and clean, so like a regal beauty waiting for the robes of spring, that the wonder grew, where the multitudinous poor were hived. Being in Windsor town, what first impressed me was the Merry Wives, or maidens, that thronged the little winding streets. Within the castle court, to ride through the double row of elms, "the long walk," from the York and Lancaster Towers to Snow Hill, where George III is enthroned in all his brazen splendor, was my first step; and I think the most delightful part of my visit to the palace-home was passed under the shadow of the mighty trees that shelter the avenue which all the monarchs of England have trodden. Three continuous miles of such fresh, formal foliage was a banquet for a botanist. To give the history of Windsor would be to relate the history of the kings and courts of England; although William the Conqueror is said to have had a residence here, the architecture of the most ancient towers is not earlier than the twelfth and thirteenth centuries; but so much of the original edifice has undergone alteration, and so much has been added to it, that the authors of its first towers are almost as fabulous as Noah's Ark. The castle as we now see it, is with very few exceptions the creation of Sir Jeffrey Wyatville, in the reign of George IV, against the tyranny of whose father our ancestors warred and won. Never had I so esteemed American liberty until I came here to learn the pomp and wretchedness, the glory and gloom, the contumacy and despotism of the dead monarch, though as I looked at the portrait of George III, all my resentment melted into admiration and pride for the artist, Benjamin West, a member of the Royal Academy, and an American. And as I gazed I recollected with still greater exultation the loyalty of the republican painter in the darkest hours of our contest, even while he was surrounded by royalty. One day when Benjamin West was engaged on the King's portrait, the castle was in a tempest of hilarity at the news of a victory over the transatlantic rebels. The King appealed to him to learn the cause of his silence, adding, "Why do you not join in our rejoicing?" To which Mr. West made the ready and haughty reply, "I cannot feel pleasure in hearing of misfortunes to those among whom I was born and passed my early days." Even the arrogant monarch was moved by the pathetic and noble retort, and replied, "Right, right, West! Good sentiment, and I honor you for it."

In those days, the sovereigns made their London homes in the quaint old jail-like castle of St. James, at the foot of the Park, the meadows that Henry VIII had converted into a pleasaunce. This dingy brick structure, originally a hospital for leprous women, is really the only edifice of the kind in all the capital that contains salons sufficiently spacious for royal levees, but George IV pined for a more sumptuous residence, and therefore transferred the court to Buckingham Palace, at the western end of St. James's Park and immediately opposite Green Park.

The Queen had gone to Osborn Castle, in the land of cakes, so the whole of this grand collection of the centuries was open to our inspection, except the private apartments, and after paying due respect to the mausoleum of the Prince Consort, the Virginia water, which is famous and artificial, and the ruins which did not awaken in my bosom any emotion of reverence, for they are also fictitious—they are said to have been brought hither from Tripoli, and their entire history is veiled in obscurity that is impenetrable—we passed to the royal stables, of endless chariots, phaetons, wagons, and barouches, most of them gifts from foreign powers, a mass of splendor that remains unused at least six months in the year. Her Majesty has her stables in London, Osborn, and Balmoral amply stocked, and though she is constantly peregrinating, the domestic appointments of the palaces are stationary. Of the horses retained for the pleasure of royalty eighty-five are at Windsor, sixty-five at Osborn, and eighty in London, to say nothing of the Government equipages.

The terraces and gardens, fountains and parterres. the Vandyck room, the Zuccarelli room, the Sir Thomas Lawrence or Waterloo Chamber, I must slight for the Round Tower, the most antique of the massive battlements over which the royal standard floats when the Queen is at Windsor. Mounting two hundred and seventy steps, we finally reached the acropolis, from which our brusque and ruddy soldier-guide pointed out the luxurious regions round about, including the territory of twelve opulent English counties, transcendently fascinating, though seen through a shroud of vapor; alternating with spires, domes, river, forest, road, rail, ships on water, and steam trains on land, all bound up in history, poetry, and romance. It was like a dream of enchantment. Then this *bovine* son of Mars asked me if I knew what river lay so tranquil and tawny below us and was lost amidst the hills and dales. When I answered, "Certainly; the Thames," he took up the refrain, saying, "Yes, the Thames; the greatest river in the world. You have no such stream in your vast stretch of country. True, your Mississippi is larger, but I tell you this is the greatest of all rivers;" and with these words he clapped his mouth together as if he had delivered his *ultima um*. I confess I was amazed at the abrupt assertion, and could no more summon the moral courage to reply, than to a young mother, when she announced that the shapeless mass of rose-colored flesh in the cradle —which more intimately resembled a zoophyte than any animated object I ever saw—was the most beautiful and wonderful of all heaven-born creatures. Such is the love and pride of Fatherland that the Britons have bequeathed to their offspring.

To our right was Henry the Eighth's Gateway, the trysting-place of the polygamous monarch and the young and attractive Anne Boleyn. It was here that he came to meet her when he bestowed the title of marchioness only as an *avant courier* of the jewelled diadem that awaited her.

Slightly to the left, on the opposite side of the Thames, Eton College and Park, presenting a very different aspect from the one that met my eye a couple of weeks ago, when I rowed up the river Now the hall was closed and the greensward deserted; the students had gone home for the Easter holidays.

To our rear lay Frogmore, the home of the Duchess of Kent, now the residence of her grandchildren, the Prince and Princess Christian of Schleswig-Holstein.

Below is the Home Park, where once stood Herne's oak, immortalized by the poet in the *Merry Wives of Windsor*. The spot is marked by a sapling of the same family.

Away off is the green meadow of Runnymede, separated from Charter Island only by a narrow estuary of the Thames, as calm and sleepy in the misty noontide, as if it had not witnessed the wrested signature of King John to the great charter of the insurgent nobles and clergy for the rights and liberties of the people in the thirteenth century. With the aid of a lorgnette I plainly saw the Stoke Poges churchyard, where Thomas Gray wrote his famous *Elegy*, and close to the Round Tower where I stood, is the castle curfew that "tolls the knell of parting day." In this same belfry the butcher, Mark Fylton, was confined and eventually hanged, for breathing scathing rebukes upon the King's incontinent and untimely love for the fair daughter of Sir Thomas Boleyn.

Descending the tower with a view by the way of the Queen's dining saloon, where she entertained our soldier President and his spouse less than a year ago, and where she welcomes the royalty of other lands, we next included what many regard as the most interesting part of this venerable fortress, palace, and historic treasure-house, St. George's Chapel. Smaller than the several cathedrals I had seen, yet wonderfully oppressive and impressive by its chilly silence and the suspended banners of the knights and kings. It was interesting because here the mother and grandmother, Empress and Queen, worships in public whenever she occupies her castle on the Thames. Here many of the great ones were mated and mourned. Here famous Church of England preachers have preached; here all the illustrious men of the realm, courtiers and cabinet ministers, soldiers and statesmen, have worshipped during their prolonged visits on state occasions. Here the Prince of Wales was married to Alexandra, and here the superb voice of Jenny Lind poured her mellow melody through these lofty groined arches, and chanted in her unequalled tones the sacred benison composed by the Prince-consort, Albert, for his eldest son and heir.

LETTTER XXVI.

"Thence with Creed to hire a coach to carry us to Hide Parke to-day, there being a general muster of the King's Guards, horse and foot ; but they demand so high, that I, spying Mr. Cutler, the merchant, did take notice of him, and he going into his coach, telling me that he was going to the muster, I asked and went along with him ; where a goodly sight to see so many fine horses and officers, King, Duke, and others, come by a-horseback, and the two Queenes in the Queene-Mother's coach."—PEPYS' DIARY, July 4, 1663.

LONDON, April, 1878.

OF the lungs of the great metropolis, none is more vital than Hyde Park, the aristocratic resort of the "West End;" bordered by the luxurious homes of Grosvernor Square, environed by royalty, traversed by foot and carriage-roads crossing at all angles, irrigated by the Serpentine, enriched and enlivened by the exclusively equestrian inclosure, Rotten Row—this inelegant title of the most famous bridle-path in the world is really a corruption of *route du roi*—it is at once the haunt of the gay voluptuary, the fashionable *inconnu*, the wealthy *parvenu*, and the centuried *noblesse*. And as I turned from the long line of regal equipages, glistening under the oblique rays of the sinking sun as they wound around Ladies' Mile following the northern bank of the Serpentine, with footmen and outriders in lapis-lazuli liveries, gold lace, powdered periwigs, and silken hose, and a burden of portly dowagers in garish dress—turned to the horsewomen with their jockey grooms in buckskin or corduroy, following at a respectful distance, passing under the solid symmetry of the marble arch, past the colossal bronze of the Wellington Monument, crossing the pillars of the stone bridge that gives access to Kensington Gardens — within the shadow of whose mighty trees, Her Gracious Majesty first saw the light of day — and saw away off the memorial glories of the Albert Cenotaph — the British troops reviewing upon the level sward, to the shrill music of the ear-piercing fife — it all seemed a pageant of the feudal ages. The beautiful Serpentine is an artificial stream fed by the Chelsea water-works, where the lovers of skating and sliding revel in the winter with as much delight as the aquatic zealots in the heated season.

Not so celebrated and universally favored, but larger and equally attractive, is Regent's Park, which was a regal home and gardens in the sixteenth century. It passed into the possession of private individuals subsequent to the annihilation of the Protectorate when the House of Stuart was restored; but recurred to the Crown upon the accession of the Hanoverians, and was converted into a public recreation ground by the Prince Regent, who afterwards became George IV. It is situated close to the northern limits of the dingy metropolis, between Mary-le-bone and Hampstead roads, while Albany and Clarence streets, and Park Road, are upon its immediate confines. Scattered through the park are exquisite private villas closed in by massive strong hedges; majestic terraces of mansions form an outer boundary. A diversity of rural scenery, hill, dale, lake, delightful retreats, and sequestered promenades under leafy canopies by quiet nooks and dreamy avenues, challenge the admiration of the lover of nature. The astrologist may read the language of the planets written upon the azure dome from Bishop's Observatory; the botanist reap a harvest of erudition in the costly hot-beds; the ornithologist gratify his soaring ambitions in the aviaries and branches of the trees; and the mammalogist or herpetologist indulge his propensities among the mammalia and reptiles in the dens and paddocks of the Zoological Garden at the northeastern extremity of the Park. Hyde is the resort of the sybarite, Regent's the retreat of the student.

Of all the pleasure-grounds of London, St. James can boast of the historic and romantic legends of love, intrigue, and dark strategy; perhaps because it was the palace park, and so close to the chambers of political and social royal transactions. The second Charles greatly beautified it, I presume in honor of his fair captor, Nell Gwynn. It was here that the king and she who had been born in squalid poverty, and whose transition through the several rôles of orange-girl, concert-saloon danseuse, fantastical or jocular actress, until she reached the apex of the social column, bided tryst. Varied, potent, and sparkling were the accomplishments of pretty Nelly. The spot seems dedicated to and hallowed by the sovereign lover's example; and is still a rendezvous of successive Romeos and Juliets, Heloises and Abelards, Jessicas and Lorenzos.

Since welcome spring's advent a booth has been constructed in the park where fresh milk and cream is the specialty. To prove the purity of this article, the kine are stationed by; this is for the nourishment of the myriads of poor children sporting upon the sward. If the prices equal those I paid several months ago while patronizing that exceeding moral beverage, the indigent and ill-starred youths of Britain do not indulge in frequent libations. Under the peristyle of old St. James' Palace patrol the guards, with little to heed except the royal mews of the Queen. The Park is at once bond and barrier between the castle and Marlborough House, the city residence of the Prince of Wales. Numerous as are the legends of the Park, they are exceeded by those of the Palace. George IV was born here, but high revel has not been held in these spacious chambers since the days of his father, though many still speak of our ambassador being sent to the Court of St. James. Foreign ministers are now accredited to a country not a court, to a people not a potentate.

Love intrigues, political plots, traffic in honor, barter of human souls, sad leave-takings, deaths, births, and the amalgamation of infants, have left their dark imprint upon the old castle walls, but there is no more amusing chapter in its history than that devoted to the presentation of Mr. and Mrs. John Adams, our first envoy after the peace with England, to the Court of George III and his plain and unassuming queen. On both occasions of Mr. Adams's first meeting with the king and queen he was armed with a lengthy and preconceived address, for which the royal couple were unprepared. The king readily collected his scattered senses and made rather an able reply, but his equally eloquent burst of oratory to Queen Charlotte quite overpowered the little woman,—for though a queen, still only a woman, and not nearly so finished in manners, nor possessing the *aplomb* of the republican ambassador's wife

—and her only answer to his lofty rhetorical explosion was, "I thank you, sir, for your civilities to me and my family, and am glad to see you in this country;" then the queen relapsed into a friendly conversation with the American official, in which all the royal family could take part. When Mrs. Adams and her daughter attended their first "drawing-room," at St. James' Palace, she was quite as *nonplussed* by the initial address of the king as his royal consort had been some time previous by the exalted speech of Mr. Adams. "Have you taken a walk this morning?" he said. Now the entire forenoon had been occupied in donning the court costumes, upon the construction of which so many days had been spent, and the lady was inclined to tell the truth, but upon reflection merely answered in the negative; upon this, the obtuse sovereign drove her to the wall by asking if she "did not enjoy walking?" and now the poor, persecuted female was obliged to offer the base fabrication "that she was rather indolent in that respect." The queen was always embarrassed in the presence of Mrs. Adams, while the latter remained perfectly undazzled by the foreign court. She was a plain-spoken, democratic American, with considerable cultivation and uncommon good sense, and therefore never a favorite at the shrine of arrogant, pedantic, vulgar title-worship.

The prevailing style of city architecture in Great Britain, though stately and imposing, is oppressive. All the famous churches, halls, castles, banks, theatres, and public edifices are either the original plans of Sir Christopher Wren and Inigo Jones, or have been remodelled from their draughts.

The idea of dividing the metropolis into sections, or squares, or places, or parks, or parishes, is a pretty one, and a necessity in a city where there are almost two hundred St. John streets. How should one ever find his destination if the affixes, Berkeley Square, Finsbury Park, Portman Square, Bloomsbury Square, etc., were banished from the directory?

The veritable English hot cross-buns, of which we read so much in our infantile rhymes, are always eaten here on Good Friday morning, so yesterday at breakfast we were regaled by the annual supply.

Among the bigoted millions these cakes are retained from one Easter jubilee to another to prevent whooping-cough in the family.

Indeed, many of the customs that we think American

are borrowed from England, and I am daily surprised at strange practices that need an explanation to make intelligible. The shop windows are filled with Easter eggs, just as the churches were arranged for Good Friday, and Lent was an interval of abstinence, and palms were worn by Catholic and Protestant on Palm Sunday. The British have a thousand inherited follies, which they continue to honor only because they are old. These odd and childish customs are not confined to the common people, but are cherished by the nobility and the throne.

LETTER XXVII.

"These bookmen, what a busy race!
   How happy in themselves and others!
They glorify all time and place,
   And make us human beings brothers.

"What rapture to themselves they give!
   What joy to millions yet unborn!
Thus in their wondrous works they live,
   And turn the night of dulness into morn."
                        ANONYMOUS.

LONDON, April, 1878.

AMONG the wonders of London the British Museum is the first. To recount the attractions it offers and the lessons it teaches would require transcendent genius. It is so all-absorbing, and there is so much of it, that it overwhelmed me. Far different the feeling it excited from that inspired by the Tower, Westminster Abbey, the Parliament Palaces, the Docks, and the Thames. The British Museum is a collection of human progress, a wedding between the past and present; the great threshold upon which to anticipate and look into the future. It is of imposing presence, and under the sunless skies and humid atmosphere of London, apparently venerable. Yet the massive group that bears its name, though projected at the close of the last century, was only commenced in 1823 and completed twenty-seven years afterward.

The approach to this mighty structure is through a spacious court-yard, and under the portals of the Doric entrance hall, thirty feet high; but this altitude is dwarfed by its breadth and depth. At the western extremity is the grand staircase, itself a work of great magnificence, with its walls and gigantic figures; and it was only when I reached the top that I gleaned some idea of the immense temple itself. Through five stupendous galleries of this section I lingered, and endeavored to store away a part of what was spread about me of botany, zoology, mammalogy, mineralogy, to say nothing of the seven galleries devoted to sculpture, and the five to Egyptian, Greek, and Roman antiquities. In this department many of the relics and inventions seem odd and impractical, others warlike, and others serviceable and suggestive.

The English are famous for bequests, and if I could determine the millions bestowed upon this institution by private individuals as well as the Government, my story of the museum would be better understood. Founded by the Sir Hans Sloane collection in 1783, and holding in its halls the most varied subsequent gifts and purchases of invaluable antiquities, the British Museum is not really older than the date of the finish of its chief structures thirty years ago. George IV presented his father's valuable library of 70,000 volumes; then came the Harleian MSS; the Cottonian Library, and priceless objects purchased by the authorities, making one gigantic storehouse of learning. What adds to the interest is the steady incessant contributions of the rich and titled who die without heirs, and have under their own roofs vast deposits of curiosities, collected by themselves or their ancestors, which they do not care to will and fear to scatter, even amongst their distant kindred. To such people the British Museum is a blessing, and by them, not only the institution, but all the striving, studious millions, in the future, are reciprocally blessed. So here they leave their precious gatherings safely, feeling that their names will live forever in a blazonry of fame as well for the motive itself as for the intrinsic merit of their gifts. As we advance in years in America, by a natural sequence, the same practice will enrich our colleges, libraries, schools, and benevolent foundations   Here in this comprehensive microcosm my reflections were not only of the authors and donors, but of the millions that have poured through the corridors, and of the great men and women who have come here to gather food for their literary labors. Admission is free to all three days in every week, from 10 A. M. till dusk, and on Saturday from 12 M. until dusk. A museum

11*

upon which countless sums have been expended, that has been the object of the generosity of princes and magnates, and the living care of Parliament, is thus thrown open to the poorest and the richest.

I lingered by the desks where Thackeray, Dickens, and their associates, read and wrote; and where Macaulay, as trustee and student, sat while he gave shape and fire to the material he had collected for his marvellous history. In the King's Library he took his notes, and referred constantly to the shoal of pamphlets preserved by the third George, and given to the public by his son. Across this threshold have passed far greater monarchs than common kings and queens. You are sure to meet the contemporary celebrities at their desks if you come frequently; and if you yourself be an habitué, at regular intervals you will see such characters as Tennyson, Tyndall, Charles Read, George Eliot, the Baroness Burdette-Coutts, John Bright, Beaconsfield, Rosetti, Swinburne, Edmund Yates, Dean Stanley, Cardinal Manning, Archbishop Tate, Monsignore Capel, Canon Farrar, John Walker, of the *Times*, Levy, of the *Telegraph*, Sir Charles Dilke, Henry Byron, Halliwell Phillips, Gilbert, Sullivan, and all the great and even lesser minds of the bench, the bar, the pulpit, Parliament, and the academy; a host of willing slaves of the pen, citizens of the Republic of Bohemia. To linger and ponder in this magazine of the dead ages, this sagacious preparation for the inspired thoughts of unborn generations, took much of my time, so I went home, returning another day to essay the autographs, letters, manuscripts, royal, baronial and ecclesiastical seals, a wonderful collection. The letters of the dead are ever sadly interesting. They outlive the body, and are the nearest of man's living works. They endure beyond his posterity, and are more precious than print or photograph. Leaving the Greville Library, I mused upon the autograph manuscripts of Martin Luther, the great theological reformer of the fifteenth and sixteenth centuries (in this letter he asserts that disbelief in purgatory is not heresy); of Philip Melancthon (born 1497, died 1560, acknowledging a present of venison); Cardinal Wolsey, " who once trod the ways of glory," to his young friend and aid, Thomas Cromwell (subsequently Earl of Essex), informing him that Richmond Lodge was not yet ready for his reception; Sir Walter Raleigh, directing that bread furnished for voyaging adventures should be prepared, his letter is dated from the court; Sir Philip Sidney, written in French from the court, assuring M. Jean Hotnan of his friendship; Sir Francis Bacon, Attorney General to James I, on arguments in the Star Chamber; and one from our old friend, William Penn, regretting his inability to do a service for a friend; the letters from Ariosto, Michael Angelo, Albert Dürer, Paul Rubens, Van Dyck, Rembrandt, Racine, Corneille, Molière, Voltaire, Prior, Swift, Addison, Dryden, Hogarth, Pitt, Burke, Fox, Washington, Franklin. Byron, Wellington, and the Admiral Nelson to his fair friend Lady Hamilton, on the eve of the battle of Trafalgar, communicating that the enemy's combined fleets were coming out of the port, and that he hoped to finish his letter, dated on Board the Victory, October 19th, 1805. He continued it next day, but it was left unfinished, and a few lines in the hand of Lady Hamilton state that it was found in Lord Nelson's desk, after this action of October 21st, in which he lost his life. There are autographs of numerous English and foreign sovereigns; a signature of Shakespeare, and manuscripts of Pope, Burns, Walter Scott, Dr. Johnson, Ben. Jonson, Macaulay, Queen Elizabeth, Mary, Queen of Scots; many cases of original charters, missals, Hindoo miniatures, Buddhist books, hymns in Ethiopic language, the Gospels on cotton paper in Armenian language, the Koran in minute Arabic characters, poems and albums in Arabic and Persian, seals of the sovereigns of England from Edward the Confessor to her reigning Majesty; seals of bishops and archbishops, of abbots and abbeys, and seventy-five baronial seals of ladies of rank. Such are the jewels found in this gigantic shell—jewels and rarities that come from the ages. Lord Macaulay justly said, "It was one of the glories of his country."

The collection of Henry Weeks, professor of sculpture, on Tichborne Street, is one of the countless instances of scientific philanthropy. It consists chiefly of curious specimens of mechanism. Birds whose songs not only emulate nature, but that hop from bar to bar; mice that gambol nimbly over the floor, and human figures performing upon musical instruments in full band; swans swimming in the water, and serpents winding themselves up trees, all of which is the result of scientific research and experiment.

I could make another long letter on this subject of the British Museum, indeed a book would not do justice to a superficial view; but I am admonished that my stay in London is coming to a close. I must, therefore, hold my pen. It is like a hungry man stopping in the midst of a feast. I have such an appetite for more work in this world's centre, that I feel, if time served, like pitching my tent here for another month. But I must "move on." I have only two days more in the world's massive capital, and must give these to preparation for crossing the channel; and then for the gay Gallic City on the banks of the Seine.

LETTER XXVIII.

"The illustrious house of Hanover
  And Protestant succession,
To these I do allegiance swear,
  While they can keep possession;
For in my faith and loyalty,
  I never more will falter,
And George my lawful king shall be,
  Until the times do alter." UNKNOWN.

LONDON, April, 1878

BEFORE leaving London I determined to take another stroll about the Parliament Palace, and look in again upon the Houses in session. The day was "fine" (I am borrowing from John Bull) and the grass had grown full and bright upon the inclosure, though the clouds drifted by like gloomy spectres. The English climate is ever capricious, and a few flecks of blue, or a scintilla of sunlight, have no longer the power to decoy me into the hope of a genial atmosphere. I have been living here quite three months, and cannot recall a week of ordinarily pleasant weather. The cold spell in March was as severe as at home, but the thermometer here is not so steady as with us. The natives call it "beastly" for its tantalizing treachery. These barometrical changes make a sad people by tempting them into an extravagant consumption of beer, brandy, gin, and rum, even amongst women of the better classes; and the soaking, sunless days, and grim, gruesome nights, produce a sullen, morbid, and sluggish temper. A lady friend, in our hotel, insists that to these four liquors, taken frequently in succession, may be attributed the wife-beatings and riotings common all over the kingdom; and that where high and low imbibe heavy potations, it is not surprising that so much unhappiness exists.

It was about four o'clock in the afternoon when we stood on the new Westminster Bridge, and with our glasses looked over into the esplanade on the river front, where the members of the House of Commons converse, and smoke, and take refreshments at intervals in the long nights of the summer session. Here they are directly within call. I ought to add, that besides other mysterious amusements, there is a subterranean passage which connects both houses with the new Conservative Club, St. Stephen's, facing the Embankment, on the opposite side. As the House does not meet till shortly before five in the afternoon, often sitting far into the night, these retreats on the Thames and in the clubs, are closed to the eye of the multitude, pouring over the broad and sweeping bridge opened on the 1st of July, 1862, and pronounced to be the largest in Europe. The Houses of Parliament or New Palace of Westminster were begun in 1840, and are, therefore, quite modern, but are almost as discolored as the centuried and massive monument of Westminster Hall itself. I had the good fortune to see these historic places in company with a member of Parliament, who courteously secured me an eligible position in the Ladies' Gallery. Dusk comes early in London even in April, and the gallery looked dark as I entered. It was filled with ladies, old and young, and I shortly became accustomed to the dim religious gloom, and as the burners in the great hall before me were being lighted, they came out like planets in a neighboring sky. I had often heard of the jalousies behind which the ladies are hidden who come to see the proceedings of Parliament, with its front of iron fretwork and historic exclusiveness; no man being allowed admission; all so different from the promiscuous throngs that crush into our legislative balconies overhanging the halls of Congress at Washington.

I was anxious to see the faces and listen to the voices of the great leaders of public opinion, but before seeking for them I tried to comprehend the surroundings. Directly below us was the Speaker's throne, and between him and our gallery were placed the seats of the parliamentary reporters for the various journals, and immediately in front of the Speaker,—the desks of the clerks intervening,—were two long, broad benches, the one on the right occupied by the conservative ministers, and the other on the left by the opposition leaders, a large and spacious table between them. I tried with the aid of my printed guide to disentangle these rival statesmen, whose photographs I had seen and studied in the windows of the printshops in Bond Street; but I soon abandoned the task. An intelligent English lady, noticing my disappointment, offered to act as my *cicérone*. Discovering that I was an American, she became quite communicative, and in a clear, cultivated voice, without indicating her bias in politics, she said: "There is Mr. Gladstone, the tall man with a stoop, a prominent nose and thin straggling hair; he is just now taking his seat and pulling his hat over his eyes. Now you see Mr. Bright, but you Americans know him so well by his face that he needs no biography; see, he is now talking to Mr. Bland, the Speaker, the official that we are in the habit of calling the first gentleman in England. The Speaker has not yet called the House to order, which he will presently do. The tall, slender man next to Gladstone is the Marquis of Hartington, the present Liberal leader, and directly at his side is Sir William Harcourt, son-in-law of your countryman, the late Mr. Motley, the historian; these are the Liberals, who oppose almost everything set forth by the Tories, on the bench directly opposite, to the right of the Speaker. The small, sandy man is Sir Stafford Northcote, the Tory leader of the House of Commons, and the direct representative of Lord Beaconsfield. Then you have the Rt. Hon. William Henry Smith, Secretary of the Navy or first Lord of the Admiralty, the owner of the newspaper circulation of the kingdom; Lord John Manners, Postmaster-General, and others."

And so my English friend, who seemed to be a sort of parliamentary directory, continued to describe the great leaders of public opinion in the sombre hall below. Presently the House came to order, and I remained just long enough to hear some of the voices of the speakers and catch some of their points. I noticed that Sir Stafford Northcote always held his hat in his hand as he spoke, and the same was noticeable of Mr. Gladstone and Mr. Bright, but I learned when they spoke an elaborate harangue, they laid down their chapeaux.

Reluctantly leaving my post I hurried with my American friends to the House of Lords. Pausing in the lofty hall, the approach to Westminster Hall, which is of unequalled magnificence, ranged on either side were the figures, larger than life, of the illustrious men, English orators and statesmen, the two Pitts, Fox, Burke, Clarendon, etc. Before descending the flight of steps into Westminster Hall I had a glimpse into the Peers' lobby, and the costly splendors of the House of Lords itself. Of several hundred peers I do not think twenty were present that evening. The Commons are loud and noisy, but the Lords, save on very great occasions, pay very little attention to their legislative duties. To strangers many of the parliamentary customs are difficult to understand. The great big powdered wigs of the lawyers, the crimson plush of the officials, the liveried servants, the omnipresent dignity and adulation, are confusing indeed, especially when the real great ones, like Disraeli, Derby, Stanley, and the various dukes and earls, move around you in the dress of ordinary mortals, and only don their stars and garters on state occasions. I wish I could give you some idea of the interior splendors of this palace of Parliament, but it defies my descriptive powers.

Now for the beautiful and venerable building, Westminster Hall, founded by William Rufus in 1097, and rebuilt by Richard II in 1399, where he frequently kept his Christmas, and entertained ten thousand guests a day; the largest saloon in Europe unsupported by pillars, 270 feet long, 74 feet wide, and 90 feet high. This great hall was designed for royal banquets and coronation feasts; courts of justice were conducted here in early times, the sovereign himself presiding; here, too, courts of impeachment have been conducted, and here William Wallace, Sir Thomas More, Protector Somerset, the lamented Earl Strafford, minister of Charles, and that equally ill-fated sovereign, were tried and convicted. Here also Warren Hastings was subjected to that protracted ordeal for his misconduct in India, defended and opposed by such intellects as Sheridan, Burke, and their contemporaries. The last coronation-dinner was held here by George IV. Outside is a large paved square into which the equipages of the members of the two Houses of Parliament are driven, and from which they pass into their respective halls. As we stood, many celebrated characters who passed were designated to me by name; some were late, evidently just coming from dinner, and others seem to have been sent for for what is a call of the House. Opposite the north front of the hall is the Parish Church of St. Margaret, begun in the reign of Edward I, where many great and noble men are buried; Caxton the printer, Sir Walter Raleigh, Admiral Howard of the fleet in the time of the Spanish Armada, and very many equally distinguished.

I have now heard some of the most distinguished orators of England, and of those who spoke this evening, Sir Stratford Northcote makes the least pretensions to oratory; a pleasing, rather tenor voice; his rhetoric is clear and distinct. Lord John Manners has a bold, manly style. Sir Robert Peel, who took part in the debate behind the ministerial benches, was very fearless, and was followed by a perfect chorus of "Hear, hear, hear." Mr. Bright spoke most like an American, with a rather coaxing voice, yet distinct and capable of rising into a fine volley of eloquence. Mr. Gladstone is evidently very much idolized by his constituents, and the little he said proved that he was master of the Liberal situation. I regretted that I had not heard Lord Beaconsfield in the Peers; but one cannot see everything and everybody, and so I was obliged to economize my opportunities, and to choose my days from the time I had allotted in this great English centre.

LETTER XXIX.

"When France in wrath her giant limbs upreared,
And with that oath, which smote air, earth, and sea,
Stamp'd her strong foot and said she would be free,—
    *   *   *   *   *
Yes, while I stood and gazed, my temples bare,
And shot my being through earth, sea, and air,
Possessing all things with intensest love,
O Liberty! my spirit felt thee there."

                              COLERIDGE.

PARIS, April, 1878.

WHEN we steamed out of Victoria Station this morning, bidding adieu to the damp and dusky capital, the anticipated gayety of another strange world gave a fresh zest to my spirits; but alas! the other vision of the Dover narrows with the short, chopping billows hoisting the boat fore and aft; the rush of waters under the keel; and a host of sick and pallid passengers, with my own white visage as the frontispiece to the tableau, was an antidote to all exuberant expectation.

We started in the early morning before the sun had cut away the gray-white mist and kissed the dew from fresh green nature. After flying along several miles I realized for the first time the transcendent beauty of the English landscape.

The charms of Cheshire and Warwickshire were heightened by the presence of vast wealth and the memory of noble deeds. Here it was not the romance of history and the glory of genius, but nature's radiant features that delighted my senses. Soon Phœbus spread forth his shining morning mantle, and the English spring blushed around us. The open arms of the great limes and maples seemed to court the welcome warmth. The broad stretches and slopes of herbage had grown brilliant and strong under his influence, and the little field flowers shone in vivid lustre under the rays of the sun; and in all this variety and beauty of color I experienced my first ecstasy for anything English. In the months that I had devoted to Westminster Abbey, filled with the splendors of the dead, or to Westminster Hall ablaze with the glory of the living; to the Tower that holds and hides the dark mysteries and miseries of the past, or to the crooked lanes and cramped alleys of the slums of the city that cradle and generate the sin, squalor, and starvation of the present; to the palaces of wealth or to the prisons of crime and cruelty; to the fashion and frivolity of the Royal Opera, or to the hush of the churches; to the homes of the poets and potentates or the holes of paupers; wherever I turned my steps, there seemed something mournful and mortal.

On we whirled through wooded tracts, by rushing rivers, sharp defiles and gentle slopes, till old Canterbury town, with its campanile towers, its decaying gateways that had canopied the two youthful monarchs, Henry VIII and Charles V, on the long-gone Whitsunday, its century-touched cathedrals and baronies were in perspective. Over the vale came the sweet silver chime of the turret-bells, in music as chaste as if St. Thomas à Becket's blood had never marred its peaceful sanctity.

Soon the flowering banks of the Medway and its oft-trod paths by saintlike pilgrims were left far behind, and before us rose the white cliffs of Dover, crowned by castle battlements, protected by watch-towers, and lapped by the dark Channel wave. Upon a soft green hill a flock of white sheep were browsing. The red roof of a farm-house shone against the blue-gray sky, and bare-limbed chubby children were scattering feed to a brood of young fowls. In the peace of the dulcet Sunday noon and hazy English atmosphere, this picture seemed like an animated Creswick, Ruskin, or Birket Foster. More lofty still looked the blinding hills of chalk in the rays of the mounted sun. "The murm'ring surge that on the unnumber'd idle pebbles chafes, cannot be heard so high; and the fishermen that walk upon the beach appear like mice." There was a crush of craft in the strait and at anchor in the harbor of the only existing quay of the Cinque Ports of William. Our royal barge to Calais was moored to the pier; it was not a burnished throne that burned on the water, neither were the sails purple or perfumed; no silver oars, no luscious women reclining upon couches of violets or golden tissue cloth, no smiling, dimpled cupids wielding fans of Oriental dyes, no gallant Mercury or dazzling Apollo. No! in one feature alone did the barque resemble that of Cleopatra when she floated down the Cydnus to meet her Antony, and this was "from the barge a strange invisible perfume hits the sense of the adjacent wharfs."

Crossing the Channel was a ghost that had haunted me long. The strait has been the scene of thousand of calamities, experiments, and expeditions for as many years; and here it tumbles and threatens the human travel that pours over it now as in the long-gone centuries: travel ever changing, but this eternal tide the same.

A crowded boat with a *mélange* of passengers from every nation and speaking every tongue; gross men and *generous* maidens, shrill screams of porters and seamen; a steam and stench of cooking, and as the steamer dropped down the Channel and Albion's snowy banks receded from our view, I descended to the stuffy, noxious cabin. I contemplated distress from the sleepless sea, and am too well acquainted with the nature of my humid, turbulent enemy to take liberties with him. For awhile all went "merry as a marriage bell," and the joyous laughter of those who had been more daring than I, and remained on the upper deck, reached my ear in mockery of my cowardice; but my spirit was strong and my stomach was weak, and I heeded not their taunts. "At length their high-blown pride broke under them," and as I lay with closed eyes and calm soul, I could hear the mourners descending to my level. They arrived in detachments, and sore were their lamentations for their lost ones. The god of the trident had been merciless in his shower of afflictions upon my companions; he had deprived them of their dearest and nearest treasures. To me he had granted all comfort because upon first action I had so submissively yielded all vanity. In this attribute of character at least, a god does not differ from mortal man. When we touched the fair shores of Gaul the afflicted were worn and weary with long suffering and I was comparatively buoyant.

Once upon the soil of Charlemagne and Clovis, the fair land washed by the English Channel and the Bay of Biscay; irrigated by the Seine, the Loire, and the Rhone; and sheltered by the Vosges, Jura, Alps, and Pyrenees, the entire earth's face seemed to have undergone a radical change. I was about to say reform, for such is my honest conviction, but the word would perhaps offend the quiet and puritanic discipline of the isle we had quitted. Here with a Gallic sun pouring down upon me, the light white earth beneath my feet, the brisk, energetic movements, and the shrill, nasal tones of the Frenchman upon every side, the shackles that had oppressed me in the dark metropolis dropped with the first breath of French republicanism. Liberty was all around us! For the first time the soul of the freedman throbbed within me, and then only I defined the weight of royalty that had pulled me down. The carol of birds, the soft, sighing breeze, the running stream, the intensely blue and fervently clear heavens, the young waving wheat, the joyous spirit of the peasant, the willing toil of the farmers, and the happy, thrifty cottage homes, sang one universal cantata of brotherhood, equality, and prosperity.

Before taking our places in the carriage at Calais, our baggage was weighed and registered; here I had my first experience in the Continental custom of paying for the transition of all baggage exceeding sixty-six pounds individually. These figures vary slightly as one passes from one country into another.

Of all travellers the Englishman invariably conveys with him the greatest amount of personal paraphernalia. Such cumbrous articles! To say nothing of the trunks and chests innumerable stowed in the baggage car, several portmanteaus, hat-boxes, bundles of countless umbrellas and canes, the inevitable bath-tub, and frequently a folding-chair, to the horror and inconvenience of all other occupants are brought into the carriage.

Resting here over half an hour for dinner—of course the Englishman eats at every station-bouffet he meets—the shrill, screechy whistle of the French locomotive was blown, and the thin, screechy voice of the French conductor was heard in his native vernacular of "All aboard."

It was all beautiful, all novel, and all sparkling! The white roads wound about the green fields in striking contrast, and here and there in clear outline was the crimson dress of a peasant child. As we passed through the Valley of the Somme this bright, warm Sunday afternoon, the fields were filled with men and woman tilling the ground and sowing the seeds of prosperity and happiness. The majority of the earth cultivators were women past middle age, in coarse shoes tied at the ankle, and blue stockings, short petticoats, and bareheaded, or perhaps a large towel wound about the forehead for protection from the heat; the men always appearing in the blue blouse, the heraldic ensign of the French *ouvrier*.

We seemed passing away from the neatly combed hedges; straggling meagre lines of shrubbery or slat fences taking their place. Great forests of lofty poplars grew in lines as precise as if they had been placed by a master surveyor. After stopping at Crecy, where Edward the "Black Prince" won the feathers more than five centuries ago, that "Albert" the present Prince continues to wear; and at Amiens, the principal town of Picardy, and famous for the treaty here signed which placed the English and French once more upon amicable ground, and for the signal victory and subsequent possession of the German forces in the autumn of 1870—we dashed on to Paris. As we approached the great capital the fantastic mode of trimming and training the trees, and artistic devices of the vegetable gardens greatly impressed me.

Ah! Paris! Dashing, dancing, dazzling, *insouçiant* Paris. I came upon you just as the evening Angelus was chiming forth its sweet and solemn melody. You looked like a newly-arrayed bride, whose snowy garments were yet unsoiled, whose spirit was yet uncrushed by the cares of added years and sorrows, while the sinking sun hung in a halo of burnished gold over your brow!

The little *voitures de place* with *cocher*, in crimson vest and black shiny oilcloth hat, were flying over the cleanly swept streets like so many fire-flies. The great white hotels were joyous with the sparkle of life. The gay boulevards were shaded by tall, waving trees and filled with pleasure-seekers. All along the sidewalks and in front of the *cafés* were clusters of little iron tables and chairs, and knots of happy care-free people chatting and sipping the diluted Burgundy or coffee *au petits-verres*. The mechanic laid down his hammer and trowel, and descended high scaffolds as the church and convent bells rang six. The flower, fruit, and vegetable shops had their merchandise displayed to the purchasing public in inviting and infinite gaudy groups. Passing through the Place de l'Opera to the Rue de la Paix I caught a glimpse of the exterior glories of the New Opera House, and away off directly facing me shone the golden citadel of *Des Invalides*.

Need I say how I enjoyed my first dinner in the delicious little French hotel, after existing upon English cookery for months?

The agitating question was, "What to do after dinner?" One of the sinners of our little *coterie* proposed the theatre, which the saints vetoed at once by a horrified negative exclamation. I objected, not because my religious principles forbade me the pleasure.—*I consider it a duty of a voyager to conform to all rules of all countries*—but the evening was excessively warm, and I fatigued with travel. After much discussion, the wicked element prevailed; has it not ever been so since the seduction of Eve? and we beguiled our pious brethren into a visit to the *café chantant* on the Champs Elysée. All along the Rue de Rivoli the great lamps swung in the dark arches of the colonnades; opposite were the lights and marble urns, and vertical lines of trees of the Tuileries, where the flowers slept, and the insects droned, and the fountain spray fell in silver music. A wild, roving, rollicking concourse jostled each other in the Place de la Concorde, rode in the revolving chairs, turned in the elevated wheels, and enjoyed the delectable luxury of getting sea-sick in swinging boats upon dry land. The booths and vendors of lemonade, pastries, and beer were in the full flush of trade, and from the concert-gardens came the melody of the merry, ambiguous *chansons*. The garden was crowded with the better class of men, women, and children, and a great number from the aristocratic circles, if one may form an opinion from clothing and conduct; there was no intoxication, though the two francs' admission included a very bad glass of beer, brandy, wine, or any other kind of liquor. Upon a small covered stage the actresses and actors sang their songs, cut their antics, turned their somersaults, and seemed to enjoy it as much as their audience.

Back through the starlit, glorious city of Sévigné, and

Maintenon, De Staël, Roland, Recamier, Jeanne d'Arc, Antoinette, Josephine, Eugénie, and all the literary and social lights that have illumined the bright capital, to my sixth-story chamber, looking out upon that panorama in bronze of the victories of the "Lieutenant of Artillery"— the Column Vendôme—I came to sleep away my first night in the White City.

LETTER XXX.

"John Bull for pastime took a prance,
Some time ago to peep at France,
To talk of sciences and arts,
And knowledge gained in foreign parts.
Monsieur, obsequious, heard him speak,
And answered John in heathen Greek,
To all he asked 'bout all he saw,
'T was, Monsieur, *Je vous n'entends pas.*"

DIBDIN.

PARIS, April, 1878.

I CANNOT reconcile myself to the Frenchman's idea of an aristocratic fifth or sixth-story chamber. It is considered decidedly plebeian to occupy apartments on the ground-floor or the *entresol;* these are exclusively for servants. The *premier étage* of the French domicile is in reality our third-story, and when I rise in the morning and gaze through or over the jalousies of my elevated window, upon the pygmian horses and carts, and surging population— dwarfed by the height—a sense of distress, and poverty, and confinement as in an old tower, comes over me. I can sympathize with, not satirize, the little village-girl, who travelled to Paris in search of the recreant lover, whom she had heard was ill, and while mounting five or six pairs of stairs, exclaimed, "Mon Dieu, how poor he must be!" but flung open the door of his *salon* to meet a blaze of light and gold and fresco; Aubusson rugs, and lace, and damask hangings; the sparkle of champagne, the heavy aroma of sweet perfumes, and the laughter of women. It is ever so here; palatial parlors next the roof: all very beautiful and bewildering when you reach the sky-chambers; but the journey is tedious, and there is no American elevator.

There is a rare sweetness in the air of Paris, a radiance indeed so different from London, that I feel already at home in its broad streets, bright society, and happy industries. I so gladly miss the constant fog, that has clung about me for the past three months in the great English city like a wet garment. I like the utter abandon of manner, and the holiday appearance of the multitudes who sit along the boulevards and avenues sipping their *vin ordinaire, café noir*, or absinthe, or eating galette,—a crisp, flaky piece of pie-crust, made as only the French can make patisserie. I like the popular passion for strolling along the highways, and I join the legion of *flaneurs*, as they are called, to saunter along the Boulevarde des Italiens, Haussmann, des Capucines, Montmartre, and in the Rue de la Paix, to gaze in the wide-awake shops; every shop a show, and every show a new invention; from an odd game to a cheap dress, from a figure that talks to a toy full of tunes; from a game that tells fortunes to a watch that is a barometer; from a cane that is an umbrella, to a portmanteau that will kill the robber who would steal it. I like to see the bare-headed, blue-bloused workmen, the white-capped *bonnes* and the babies, the *jeune fille* of the middle class, who never dons a bonnet, but enhances the beauty of her pretty face and large liquid eyes by coquettishly wearing Alsacian bows of black velvet; the paper-capped cooks of the cafés, the *gamins* spinning their tops, and the gay booths with their flaunting exhibitions. It is all so joyous, jolly, and jubilant. A wild scene without intoxication, a saturnalia without open sin, a revelry that stimulates. The population has the appearance of our fellow-countrymen, and one thought is ever paramount, 'tis so like home. Along the new Avenue de l'Opera the dazzling façades of the six and seven-story white edifices stare me almost to blindness. They are just from the artisan's hand, yet the exteriors are scarcely whiter than the ateliers and hotels that have braved the elements many years, so bright and pure is the climate. Row after row of these magnificent new structures have large placards in the windows bearing the words "*à louer.*" A young gentleman in our circle, who possesses a rather limited knowledge of the Gallic tongue, asked me what "*à louer*" (allure) meant? I replied, with surprise, "allure;" you surely understand the word, to decoy, entice, beguile; not realizing my friend was reading the French sign, "to rent," with his English tongue, and his reply was, "What an odd way these French have of wording their signs." Poor fellow! he now believes that the landlords of the Avenue de l'Opera intend to decoy tenants into their property by fair means or foul. The Boulevarde des Italiens is a banquet for the eyes, the ears, the palate, and the memory, in its bazars of *confections*, bijouterie, and display of Disderi photography; in its Grand Opera, Théâtre Cleverman, Théâtre des Fantasies Parisiennes, the Opera Comique, and Théâtre Italien; in its epicurean *cafés*, as the famous Maison-Dorée, Café Restaurant Tortoni, Café Cardinal and Riche; and its ever-varying, never-ceasing flow of life, into the Boulevarde Montmartre; here we passed the Théâtre des Varieties, and I paused to read the playbills upon the boards. I catch the name of Judic, and at once I determine to stroll into this playhouse some evening soon to hear and see the fair, fat Frenchwoman, of whom we Americans have read so much, and whose photographs are floating through the United States in shoals. Right and left are sybaritic restaurants and cafés; cafés occupying the upper stories of theatres and bazars; and so on and on we wander through the changeful kaleidoscope, until the princely establishments degenerate into eating-houses or bouillies, the opera-house into circuses and third-class shows, the *voitures* are few and pedestrians seldom, and we find ourselves upon the very confines of the town. In this *quartier* we came upon the Church of Notre Dame de Lorette, a place of worship celebrated for its interior sumptuous decorations, animated and inert. This highly artistic temple is considered one of the curiosities of Paris, because it is sustained and frequented by an aristocratic and rather ambiguous sisterhood assuming "a virtue if they have it not," whose beauty is splendor, and whose toilets are regal; as a fraternity they wear the name "lorettes" from the oratory in which they pray; if pray they ever do! It seems their only object in assembling in the sanctuary is to fan the flame of envy in each other's degenerate hearts, by the prodigality and anticipated rivalry of costume, and seek expiation of their sins through the medium of their tarnished gold dropped into the *boîte pour les pauvres*.

To hail a fly and ride back through the highways we had trodden, gave us another dazzling effect of the scenes in the changeful drama. The city appeared to be arrayed in carnival regalia, and this I attribute to the inauguration of the Exposition Universelle upon the Champ de Mars tomorrow; but old residents tell me their city is ever so. Paris is a universal playhouse, where the farce, the comedy, the melodrama, and tragedy blend one in the other, but where the curtain never falls. Whether it be an act of sin, sorrow, or shame, a spectacle of pomp and hypocrisy, all are clothed in the garments of pleasure and virtue. These French comprehend the true philosophy of life. Every phase of existence seems to possess its charm for them. Their work is not toil, because they go to it with brave hearts and willing hands and transform it into sport. Happiness is not ostentation and opulence, but the calm peace of occupation and a strong fervent heart. Their domestic tasks and social pleasures are all performed with the zest that a Frenchman alone claims, and so mingled that labor becomes play. In the heart of the industrious Parisian, "all time is a temple, and all seasons summer."

In the Place du Palais Royal, just where the jetties of two fountains were casting their spray in a radiate circle, we dismissed the little French cabriolet and entered the arcades of the edifice that was erected by Cardinal Richelieu.

You dine at the Palais Royal, in the *Café Véfour*, elegantly; and though the price is high, the supply is plentiful—cheap, as you remember that you dine upon and drink in history. The Arcade in which this superb restaurant is placed is gorgeous in gilt, glass, and statuary. It is girdled with the superb shops of Paris, chiefly of jewels and watches. These shops are fairy shows, solitary in the day, but at night thronged with customers and crowds in every costume and from every country, while in the hollow square in front there are dancers to the band that plays at intervals in the afternoon, and a multitude of children. The elegance of the dinners at the *Café Véfour* attracts epicures from all lands; but if you desire to enjoy them at leisure, you must come early. When the tide is in you can hardly secure a chair; indeed, from six to nine, Paris is a great dinner world—eager, hungry, polite, fastidious, if you please, but still violently hungry. After enjoying a plentiful variety, we emerged into the outer world of the Palais Royal. It was a whirlpool of light and life, music and conversation—a Babel of sounds, a Solomon's Temple of splendors. Here we saw the ravages of the Commune, on the 24th of May, 1871, and the restored Palace of the Louvre and the new Hôtel du Louvres. It was an easy stroll along the Rue Rivoli homewards, under the stars, yet every rood of our progress was made instructive by some rare novelty and by the surging mass from the French provinces and the great towns of the European Continent, centring here to be present at the opening of the Exhibition Universelle to-morrow.

LETTER XXXI.

"Ring out false pride in place and blood,
The civic slander and the spite;
Ring in the love of truth and right,
Ring in the common love of Good!"
TENNYSON.

PARIS, May, 1878.

IT is past midnight, and still the shuffle of feet, the hum of voices, the shouts of the revellers, and the strains of the "Marseillaise," are heard in the broad and brilliant street below, as I sit in my upper chamber attempting to organize the impressions of the Exposition—to-day's wonderful pageant of wealth, nobility, and popular enthusiasm—before the memory is dimmed by other splendors.

Yesterday morning when I walked through the unfinished temple of art and industry, legions of mechanics, and decorators, and laborers were busy in the work of completion, or at least striving to reduce the halls from their present state of anarchy to a condition suitable for the reception of princes and potentates. We waded through an ocean of debris, the dust of sweepers, the shavings and shingles of sawyers, and the vibration of hammers, to the English Department, which, under the master-hand of P. Cunliffe Owen, C.B., who is Secretary of the Royal Commission, already wears a garb of completeness, while her surrounding companions are still crude and unfinished. How this vast building was ever to be transformed from chaos to order by the morrow I could not define. After visiting General McCormick in his private sanctum, we met in the American section John Russell Young, the companion and diarist of General Grant, Henry Pettit, the enthusiastic and efficient draughtsman of the American Buildings, and

Monsignore Capel, the hero of *Lothair*, who has received an apotheosis from the London females, whose heads and hearts he sways by his priestly eloquence. He has the portly distinction of a churchman and the subtle elegance of a courtier. A man who comprehends the secrets of winning voluntary concession from all he addresses— socially or professionally—I had longed to see in his pulpit in London. His villa, not far from the confines of the great city, the former residence of the comedian Sothern, a really boronial estate, now has changed from the Sybaritic home of the player to the sanctuary of the prelate.

I will neither compare nor criticize the French national displays now. Such a proceeding would be a gross injustice, and when I do speak of them, if I am not the most impartial judge, forgive me and remember that all my opinions are biassed by one fact: I am an American, and lived in Philadelphia during the incomparable Centennial Exhibition of 1876. But in passing, I may say the exterior of the palaces on the Champs de Mars are artistic and showy without being flaunting; gay without being gaudy; ornate and chaste even in the combination of rude, ruddy fresco, and façades of vivid wooden fretwork, and colored glass, sustained by robust caryatides of the nations over whose heads float the standards and streamers of their respective lands. Whatever a Frenchman touches seems to be made graceful. What his work lacks of pomp and potency, it possesses in delicacy and purity; so it is with the temples nestled on the left bank of the Seine, against the grassy slopes of Auteuil and Passy. Still an emotion of sadness thrills me as I meditate upon the unfinished structures; such utter incompleteness seems to presage failure to the exhibition of the republicans, and a stimulant to the hopes of the Imperialists and Bourbons of the Faubourg St. Germain, who want it to fail. The city is overflowing with strangers, and hotel and café prices are proportionately extortionate.

When I rose this morning there was a rustle and bustle of busy life in the Place Vendôme, in the Rue St. Honoré, in the Rue de Rivoli; and as far as my eye could reach, or the ear catch a sound, there were evidences of pleasure-bent throngs in the motley concourse of pedestrians, the incessant beat of horses' hoofs, and the whirl of wheels. Of course every one was going towards the Champ de Mars; those who were fortunate enough to possess credentials of admittance to royalty would cross the Pont de Jéna, and be ensconced under the peristyle of the Trocadéro, or at one of the upper windows of the Exhibition Building, while the millions of the democracy would crowd the highways and avenues, not knowing or caring so much for the princes or the pageantry as to mingle in and swell the populace. The day dawned fairly, but the sun wore upon his face a sultry smile of treachery, and though we started in a burst of brightness for the installation, by solemn and political ritual of the first industrial, social, and national event under the republican *régime*, before we had crossed the Pont de la Concorde, nature was arduously striving to drown every hope and aspiration of the new government. The situation of those poor deluded mortals in the open *voitures* and *cabriolets*—I was one of the damp, drizzled stars comprising this galaxy—was dismal and desperate to the last degree while heaven's blessings were descending in a watery superfluity. Though my mood was not amiable, I did not indulge it to the top of its bent; there were so many not any worse, and still so much worse off than myself. Hundreds of newly-dressed, fashionably-dressed, and expensively-dressed daughters of Eve waded through lakes of mud and mire, until starched skirts and lofty expectations wilted away together.

After waiting one and a half or two hours in the American section I heard a flourish of trumpets and roll of drums, which announced the approach of the *cortége*. The time passed in anticipating the monarchical and military display was not calculated to promote good temper. Front stalls at the windows were at a premium and unsatisfactory; if you attempted to retain one after securing it, some individual of ineffable *avoirdupois* rested a portion of his burden upon your shoulders, although his own were broader; if a gallant—seeing your discomfort—offered you a chair, your gratitude was quick in all save the acceptance; to abandon your post was to make a voluntary and permanent consignment to the too solid enemy, and so meditating you concluded to rather "bear the ills you had than fly to others that you knew not of."

All around there was a clatter and chatter of French; the Americans were few, and seemed hushed into utter silence by the Gallic gabble. From the Trocadéro, over the Pont de Jéna, sanctified in the baptism of angels' tears, came the Prince of Wales, bright scion of the house of Hanover, fair, fat, and not yet forty. As he passed the

American pavilion he raised his chapeau, and a shout greeted him from the Yankees. It is said Wales has a hearty liking for us Americans, and is a good deal of a republican; but then most royal heirs are democrats until they take the reins into their own hands. The future English monarch has a good face, very like his portraits; and although it poured upon his regal umbrella there was a jolly smile beneath. The old Marshal President MacMahon looked like a bouquet of daisies, his face all pink, and his hair and moustache all white, but with a rather angry and crestfallen air, as if he felt his seat in the executive chair to be insecure, and though loath to relinquish the baton, so far has failed to devise any policy to strengthen himself. He was followed by the ex-king of Spain, husband of the famous, or infamous, Isabella. A little spindle-shanks, hobbling along in all his finery, a poor, useless Hidalgo living in Paris at an immense cost to the Spanish treasury. Then came a huddle of dignitaries lost in puddles of mire; while we were dry they were draggled. Had the day been bright it would have been grand, no doubt; but the democratic gods *rained* down their most impartial favors, even upon the pride and plumes of kings and princes. Princes and sovereigns they were, it is true, and yet only men. And then—well, then I rode home with the weight of this vanquishing conviction—*the parade did not pay for the pains!*

The sun broke through his humid shroud just as he sank behind the wooded heights of Grenelle and Auteuil, gilding the tops of the monuments, and glorifying the open spaces in which they stood. With the closing day the crowd had augmented; grisettes and students of the Latin Quartier; crimson-pantalooned soldiers from the garrisons; the disabled veterans of Des Invalides; the ouvrier of the Rue Saint Antoine; the diplomatists and financiers of the Faubourg St. Honoré; the Legitimist of the Faubourg St. Germain; the wit, artist, and literati of the Chaussée d'Antin; the bourgeois, and the old crone, weather-beaten and time-worn, in black petticoat, white cap, and kerchief folded over her breast, *à la* Marie Antoinette, to be found in every cranny of the city, were gathered in one promiscuous *mélange.* The sun had fallen quite asleep behind the *portes* of the white town; the hour of six had rung through the *arrondissements;* the upper-tendom of Paris were dining in hotel, café and private *salons;* but the great holiday was not over; it was only opening.

As twilight unfurled her dark curtains, busy hands and brave hearts were actively engaged in the labor of decoration. The façades of all the public buildings and even the churches were ablaze with patriotic devices in colored lights, and banners and pennons floated from every window. The great lamps in the colonnades, the lights of the Tuileries, the stars in the dark, clear heavens, had transformed the white macadamized road of the Rue de Rivoli into a sea of brightness. Through it poured a mass of happy, free people from the Rue St. Antoine. Were it not for the weird ruins of the palace staring at us like a spectre, we would be prone to forget to-night that seven years ago the same populace rushed through the same highway, fiends and petroleuses, sowing the seeds of sedition, and sin, and desolation in their pathway. The Champs Elysées that were then a charred and blackened desert are now bright with the glory of a new republic. There is no sad regret for the fate of the fair Austrian, Marie Antoinette, in the Place de la Concorde to-night. Every wall, rampart, and bridge is bathed in a phosphorescence of splendor and pride, and "*Liberté, Egalité, et Fraternité,*" shine not in blood but in fire. To-night the memory of wretched crimes, fruitless prayers, and the guillotine, is dead in the Place de la Bastile. The radiant Palais de l'Industrie, the headquarters of the Teutonic enemy seven years ago, to-night sheds a free French lustre over the Elysée, and all the Rue Royale is dazzling in the halo of the Madelaine.

The night has been a deserved compensation for the dismal incidents of the day to the actors and spectators at the Exposition. I had read of a Paris populace; I had studied the Centennial in 1876, when Philadelphia was deluged by strangers; I had seen the throngs of to-day, but had formed no idea of the sight after twilight on this first of May in the French capital. It was all so wild and tumultuous; I was the atom of the poet and this was really

> "Ocean into tempest tost,
> To waft a feather and to drown a fly."

I was less than a feather or a fly, and in the heedless whirl was borne along like a cloud before a great storm. It was a fantastic, turbulent saturnalia. Yet there was a strange sense of safety in the delirious mass; all were happy, and no one was intoxicated by liquor. The horses were driven to one side, and the glad people filled the broad boulevards with song, and shout, and hymn, and chorus, until I caught the contagion of their ecstasy. There was a pause, an eddy in the great driving current of the great human sea, formed by a side-way in a wide avenue, and I floated into it toward my home. I had seen and heard enough to understand it all. The French were enjoying the first real sense of their liberty in a long lapse of years, and I did not marvel that the welcome draught had temporarily stolen away their senses.

LETTER XXXII.

"The French have taste in all they do,
While we are quite without;
For Nature that to them gave *goût*,
To us gave only gout."

ERSKINE.

PARIS, May, 1878.

I ROSE early this morning to watch the city undergo the cleansing process. The buckets, and tubs, and pans of offal were arranged as primly along the curbs as vases upon a parlor mantel. There was nothing slovenly or repulsive in the sight, even of the garbage. The passion for artistic and artificial effect is innate with the French, and it is apparent in the minutest affairs. The *chiffonnier* and his wife were already at work under my window, raking amongst dust-heaps in the street and ashes and refuse upon the pavement. Sometimes they would lightly toss the contents of barrels or boxes with their long forks—generally a bent wire or nail in the end of a stick—and turn away with an expression of disgust and disappointment, failing in their search for prizes. Over the next pail they would linger, and dive deeper and deeper at each effort. Some of these heaps of debris were veritable *olla podridas* yielding crumpled paper-bags, old rags, pieces of coal, dirty strings, bones innumerable, stale pieces of bread, and nests of snarly hair, which they tucked away with great caution and classification into the several pockets of the long, narrow, leathern sack hanging upon the left arm. The rolls of hair, however dusty and tangled and interwoven they might be with other matter, whether from the moulting of mistress or maid, countess or cook, blonde or brunette, were special booty. These locks rescued from pollution are sold to the *coiffeur*, and after passing through his purifying hands again adorn the heads of us poor, unsuspecting females in puffs, waves, crimps, and frizzles. Then as the wagons came along to cart away the residuum, and the water was turned on at every corner, running through the gutters as pure and limpid as a mountain spring, the weary *chiffonnier* sat down upon the curbstone to take his breakfast of black bread or to gnaw a spare bone, perhaps from the spoils of his morning ramble. Groups of mechanics were shuffling through the streets now, and fair Paris greeted them in her freshly-made toilet.

Inside the toil of the day had also begun. How different and how much more arduous are the tasks of these foreign servants compared with the labor of our *domestiques* at home! Yet here they are all apparently happy, while in America the same classes join in a universal chorus of dissatisfaction. Jeanne, our neat little *femme de chambre*, told me yesterday—her spare English aided by my limited French—she had the care of sixty chambers, all of these containing one or more beds, and that the hot and cold water for these apartments has to be carried over many pairs of stairs, and through many corridors, as they have not the American accessories of stationary washstands; and poor Jeanne's remuneration is not more than fifteen or eighteen francs a month. True Jeanne receives many francs from the ladies and gentlemen whose chambers she arranges, but does it compensate for the weary limbs and aching head when the clock tolls eleven at night? And even then Jeanne is still slowly dragging tin pails of water upstairs. As I listened to the poor girl's story, and marked her amiable nature and inborn courtesy, my heart swelled in sympathy. Thinking of her sorrowful lot my memory took a flying trip to my transatlantic home, where my maid has the insupportable responsibility of one bed-chamber resting upon her each day, and other housework of a light character, with nameless privileges, and three dollars per week; yet she frequently displays the cloven foot at the weight of her burden. As these contrasting pictures passed before my vision, I exclaimed, "You have too much work for one pair of hands. It is far worse than the drudgery of a slave. You should appeal to your employer for an assistant." It was the first time I had ever sown the seeds of insurrection in any household; now I could not restrain my impulse to protect this girl from such unjust and cruel exactions. I felt the germ I had planted, though you may call it seditious, might produce valuable fruit for Jeanne. Sometimes Étienne, who is the *frotteur* and husband of the pretty and beneficent *concierge* at the front *loge*, assists Jeanne spread the linen over the beds if he is in the same hall or chamber polishing the floor. We have no carpets under our feet. The boards are waxed until one may behold his reflected visage upon them, and the centre is adorned by large rugs, and the *frotteur*, with his stiff brush strapped upon the sole of his foot, is always busy scudding over the chambers and corridors.

I like the proverbial politeness of the French. Call it superficial, if you choose; even if shallow it is very fascinating. Inquire a direction of a passer upon the streets, and be it man, woman, or child, discovering you are a stranger, will accompany you two or three squares out of his or her way to set you upon the right path, chattering to you all the while, never conceiving for a moment that most of what is said may be utterly unintelligible. Fortunately I succeed in making myself understood by the natives, but when they orate in their rapid and pauseless jargon, I subside in utter amazement.

During the three months I resided in London, six weeks of which time my friends despaired of my life, not one of the attendants at the hotel offered me the slightest voluntary civility. The second day after my arrival here, Jeanne came to my room with a card of a friend, while I was dressing, and noting my unfinished toilet, she asked to be allowed to hook my dress, or button my boots. Perhaps you are saying, she expected a franc for her kindness; did not her complaisance deserve it? Another instance of the urbanity of this nation took place at the milliner's this morning. Do not sneer! Did you ever hear of a lady coming to Paris and omitting her first duty, to buy a French bonnet? I did not wish to violate the custom of my sex; I had no desire to visit the Exposition until it had reached a more finished state, so I passed the forenoon in millinery, book, and photograph shops, gratifying my personal desires. An establishment in the Faubourg St. Honoré had been highly recommended, and to examine the stock of this magazine I repaired thither. As I strolled toward the Faubourg, again I was impressed by the sobriety of the populace and the absence of beggars. What a vivid contrast the picture forms to the great English metropolis, where ebriety and mendicity are written by a sharp stylus upon at least one half the faces we meet! An equally apparent fact is the extreme neatness of the French women; however meagre the dress, it is always neatly worn, and the hair, if not elaborate, ever tastefully arranged; not so the females on the other side of the Channel.

On my way I passed many noble homes, where the great wooden gates close out the eyes of the rude, inquisitive world from the flowering paradise of the courtyard, of which I caught an occasional glimpse as a servant would pass, or a marquise enter her carriage. At length I reached a stately building, bearing the number I sought; directed to the fourth story by the *concierge*, I ascended and found myself in regal apartments, sparkling in gilt, frescoes, mirrors, and laces. An infinity of *confections* were upon exhibition, and though their construction justified the prices, they exceeded what I was able to pay. No bonnet for less than twelve dollars, and many for twenty-five, and I should have turned away had it not been for the courtesy of the accomplished salesladies. I may apply the word "ladies" in its every acceptation; in manner, in appearance, and in education. Both handsome, the younger past youth, the elder had crossed the meridian of life, and yet either would have "shaken the saintship of an anchorite" by their subtle grace, and liquid voice and talking eyes; and so they succeeded in selling me a bonnet. How could I resist the influence of two such seductive flatterers and liars? They compelled me to be seated before a mirror, and one bonnet after another adorned my pate; for "she was quite sure she could suit madame. If one was too costly there was another, hanging upon the next peg, just as beautiful, for eighteen francs less. If madame did not like the *rouge*, madame should see herself in the *ciel-bleu;* it was just madame's color, but then madame was so easily *coiffed;* madame was—ah! *si très belle* in anything;" and then these two handsome, crafty females indulged in a dissertation in their own tongue, largely interlarded with English, upon my constructive attractions. This last *coup d'état* clinched the bargain. The next "madame" who purchased a more expensive article would be still more beautiful, and would undoubtedly hear her charms extolled in still more winning tones. Still I admire the shrewd philosophy of these people; it made us all happy; they sold their merchandise; I went away in a state of beatitude, in being compared to flowers, and angels, and sunbeams, the calmness of moonlight, and the sparkle of champagne, which would not have been the case had disobliging attendants shown an indisposition to display goods, saying, "Madame, we have nothing that would become you." And as I passed away towards the bookshop, my meditations were upon the cruel fascinations of these French women. With me their influence had been potential; what would such sway be with the opposite sex? I could find little censure for one who yielded to the spell, whether exercised for good or evil.

The literature of the gay city is a marvel. It abounds in such a variety, that even a woman with an infirmity for dress and ornamentation, is startled at the mass of engraving and printing for sale and show. Here, at least, you have what is not to be found in London. There the literary depots are in the railway stations; here books, papers, and periodicals fill the windows and kiosks on the Boulevards in all languages and for every nation. At Madame Michel's, on the *pavé* of the Grand Hotel, I find French, Italian, German, Dutch, and even Greek, Turkish, and Chinese literature. People of all these nationalities flock here to buy and read the periodicals in their vernacular. Of course the French predominates. In comic journalism and caricatures the French excel. We had an example of them as printers and sculptors at our Centennial Exhibition. But now I pause briefly upon the French gift of printed satire. Everybody is ridiculed; no one is sacred or saved from the merciless wit and scathing lampoon of their savage jokes. With a dash of the pencil they transform the most serious statesman into a clown. Mademoiselle Sara Bernhardt's willowy figure is turned into a trail of smoke; the fighting Cassagnac converted into a huge pistol; Victor Hugo, a dying lion, gazing upon the setting sun; Marshal Mac-Mahon, scowling in a gigantic moustache; Gambetta, in kingly robes; Pope Leo XIII, in every conceit of honorable disguise; John Bull, in as many shapes as his peculiar habits may suggest; Brother Jonathan, in all descriptions of stars and stripes; and the world's catalogue of politicians, soldiers, actors, priests, and celebrities of all vocations. And as I overhauled the photographs of living and dead heroes in the shops on the Rue de Rivoli, my ardent desire was to make a collection. I looked, and looked, and was dazed by the endless profusion of famous faces in various guises; but I turned away with saddened purpose as I remembered my limited spaces, and finances, and reflected upon how much farther my journey was to extend.

LETTER XXXIII.

> "Of the hearts that daily break,
>   Of the tears that hourly fall,
> Of the many, many troubles of life,
>   That grieve this earthly ball—
> Disease and Hunger, Pain and Want,
>   But now I dream of them all!"
>
>   Hood.

Paris, May, 1878.

However paradoxical it may seem, the Exposition Universelle is the remotest magnet to the stranger in Paris. The gay city is itself an endless and unfading microcosmic display. Of exhibitions we have had a satiety; at least, until a warrantable interval has elapsed, when we may again show our demonstrations in art, science, and literature, from the lofty pedestal of Progress, and when our national and social development has reached a higher state of civilization. We had an exhibition at Philadelphia, of which this one is, with all its splendor, a feeble lethargic transcript; and we can have exhibitions in every city and town of the two hemispheres which will only be the copies of a great archetype. But Paris—national, political, peculiar, and *omnium gatherum* Paris—stands alone, and can only be enjoyed here; and here there is such inexhaustible enjoyment that the "appetite seems to grow with what it feeds upon."

The exhibition palaces are still disordered and in *dishabille*, while Paris is ever in gala attire. She is alternately the rainbow, the storm, the sunshine, the starlight, and the cyclone, and in each of these phenomenal phases is entrancingly unsurpassed.

I have endeavored in vain to retrospect through the vista of centuries, the ravages of pestilence and famine, the smoke of artillery, the bloody sloughs of battle, the flames of communes, and the devastation of revolutions, and on the banks of the Seine, recall the mud huts of the Parisii, where now stand the noble monuments which perpetuate the memory of crime, commune, and conquest.

Oh! ancient Lutetia, thy primitive mantle dropped before Cæsar's sword, and was trampled into dust by his vanquishing hordes; purged and purified by successive despoilers wert thou, until now, not even an aroma of thy gypsy, pastoral lineage remains to mar the luscious luxuriant flower of thy glorious womanhood.

But who, gazing upon this white-robed *Napeæ*, can forget the other and darker side of her life? I mean the life portrayed by Victor Hugo and Eugene Sue, of the drudging, struggling, sinning Faubourg St. Antoine, that hotbed of indigent insurgents; and upon the Rive Gauche, the Quartier Latin, the home of their reckless student allies? Not so direful, it is true, as when Eugene Sue presented his vividly wrought picture to Louis Philippe, through the medium of his *Mystères de Paris*. The inauguration of the present *régime* has done much toward ameliorating the morals of these arrondissements, as I soon perceived while penetrating the forbidden precincts.

Passing the brilliant shops and hotels of the Rue de Rivoli, the equestrian statue of Joan of Arc, and the fountains into the Rue St. Antoine, which is still broad and brilliant, but from which issue numerous contracted by-ways and alleys, dark and damp, lined by cloud-piercing tenant-houses, grim and grimy, whose outer walls seem sustained by huge boulders against which the wheels of our voiture grind as we ride through the narrow streets. Coarse, toiling, hunted, bloated men are tilted all along the margin of the houses, in ragged blue blouses, and stunted clay-pipes between their tobacco-stained lips. Dirty, halfnaked children wallow at their feet and under the chairs, seeming to cradle pollution and malaria in the folds of their scanty garments. A large lamp projects over the court entrance, and sheds a melancholy glow over the inmates. Some of the women are drawing water in their large tin pails, while others are drowsing under the effects of anisette or absinthe. From the upper windows, fifth, sixth, and seventh stories, are glimmering rays that display the toiling forms and anxious, famished faces of laboring females, some bending over lace frames, some working over tiny forges, welding gold and silver wires; while other hands are soiled in the paint and glue of artificial floral construction. The windows have long been strangers to water or brush, and cobwebs festoon the ceilings, but along the sills are boxes of flowers drooping for want of sun and pure air, and over the walls and blinds bean vines are wreathing their tendrils; a little feathered prisoner or a kitten is seen, perched in many of these languishing arbors. A steam of strong, young spring onions emanates in regular puffs from the inner stories and permeates the atmosphere. The front shops of these houses are alive with the trade of energetic and successful *marchands;* a cobbler, a tinsmith, a *blanchisseuse*, or a restaurant, where the *menû* consists of leeks, radishes, *bouillon*, and *bouilli*, wine, and liqueurs. These people are arduously struggling to make an honest, respectable living, so they may clothe and educate their children, and lift them out of the slough of contamination. But will the fruition of their humble, praiseworthy aspirations be realized? They are young now; hope and ambition are lusty within them. The human buds are bursting in fast succession, but the soil is setoned with virus; the husbandman may choose the sunniest, most sanitary spot in the entire garden, but will not contagion be conveyed, even upon angels' wings, in the breath of heaven, and the limpid current of virtue, turned to irrigate and nurture the nascent plant, will gather the virulence of the sea through which it flows!

Vice is quick and virtue is slow to become root-bound in the embryo procreated and nursed in an atmosphere of corruption. The lessons taught by example exert a more potent and permanent authority than theoretical ones, and here the evil example is ever paramount.

Often there is seen a young woman carrying a bundle,—perhaps a faded silk skirt,—an old woman with a pillow or bolster, or a man with a dingy mirror issuing from the courtyard; they do not stop to chat with their neighbors upon the corners, but cast stealthy glances right and left and hurry on. You wonder where they are going; their manner whispers that they are upon some secret errand bent. They all turn toward the northwest; you need not follow; they are all tracing the one path, to the Mont-de-Piété, in the Rue de Paradis du Temple. It is a curious establishment, but is nothing more nor less than a vast government pawnbroking office, whose profits are devoted to the support of charitable institutions. It seems an incongruous project.

A few steps farther is the Marché du Temple, where hundreds of this same population are congregated to overhaul and perhaps eventually purchase some of the sordid, soiled, trumpery of this wonderful rag-fair. They are truly the "vestments that Time filches away." Here, in one incompatible mass, are the cast off

—" Purple, princely gown,
Of high success ; or ease, like robes of down ;
Or harsh denials, like the camel's hair
The Prophet wore ; or sable weeds of grief ;
Or smooth white burial robes of last relief."

And here the vocabulary most largely patronized bears a similitude to the ribaldry and vituperation of London's Billingsgate. Such a vicinity, of course, is impregnated by thieves, grog-shops, dance-houses, gambling houses, yet when I passed through it was withal orderly in the extreme.

From the Faubourg St. Antoine, across the Pont d'Austerlitz, along the promenade of the Seine, I entered the Faubourg St. Germain, where there exists another population than the Ultramontanists and Bourbons, which is much oftener seen thronging the streets, and filling the highways with shout and revelry. On the Rue Dauphiné and the Rue du Bac, there still reside the offspring of the companions of Madames de Staël and Recamier, it is true; but come into the retreats of the students and grisette of this Quartier Latin, where the aristocratic, conservative incense has evaporated though decorum is preserved, and you will at once observe its resemblance to the district we have just quitted on the right of the river. There is not so much sorrowful, starving poverty visible here; the by-streets are dark and the houses tall and dingy, but the students of art and medicine are full of animation and jollity, swaggering along, linked in each other's arms; or stopping to take a glass of wine at the adjacent cabaret, where the account is only scored off once a month, when the stipulated allowance arrives from the doting parents in the far-away provinces; or going toward the Odéon or one of the café gardens, apparently happy by the side of his favorite grisette.

The conceit I had formed of this class of females was a vain delusion. I had expected to see youthful, natty, sparkling coquettes, whose vocation it was to wink and blink, and waft a salute to every man whom fortune threw across their path; I found neat, modest, confirmed, industrious women, not at all calculated to sway a man by their ravishing beauty nor subtlety, but created and trained for good housewives and vigilant mothers.

The pictures of this section of the city were weird and bizarre, but not disagreeable. If the undeveloped artist or embryo doctor was poor, and compelled to lead a studious life, and to sleep up many pairs of stairs in a stuffy back chamber, they seemed to accept the inevitable philosophically, and embrace the pleasant opportunities of their lives with hungry zeal.

The grisettes were tranquil and content.

The foliage in the garden of the Luxembourg seems forced in its luxuriance for this early season; the lights flash from the summer theatres, and the orchestras fill the air with melody.

In a little gloomy shop two women were picking rags; they were handsome creatures, with full white throats, from which their dresses were turned back, and crimson kerchiefs were knotted over their bosoms; my gaze and attention were arrested by these superb animals, with the dark luminous eyes and wealth of sable hair, set in the engulfing frame of filthy refuse; and as I lingered one flung her lusty, polished arms about the other's neck, and caressed her with a lover's ardent rapture, until the cheerless hole glowed with the fire of passion and youth. To my eyes it was no longer the dismal home of the *chiffonnière*, but a heaven—or hell, God knows which?—of delirious ecstasy.

It was Saturday night when I passed through these scenes, and this community seemed resting in their orgies to stimulate them for the morrow. Yes! Sunday is the grand gala day here; it is the day of frolic and fun, excursions into the suburbs and wild sports in the city.

As I fell asleep after this experience, it was with these reflections: what I saw had instructed me; it taught me the lesson of strife and sin; but I was eager for further erudition in this stratum of society. Intuition warned me that there was much to be yet unfolded. But how to reach these fantastic marvels of Parisian life was the agitating disquisition! My desire grew into a passion, and as I pondered I became wroth with an imaginary tyrant who was thwarting my foolish whim. Soon, very soon, my sad fancy was about to be gratified, to my intense satisfaction and disgust.

The next evening, Sunday, a company of six set out to visit the Cathedral of Notre Dame. We dismissed *cocher*, and applied for admittance at the great entrance of the western façade; here we received no answer, and loath to abandon our project, we applied at many other entrances of the *église* on the isle of Seine without success. We leaned over the parapet of Pont Notre Dame; in the calm, even flow of the beautiful river was reflected the star-spangled canopy above, intensely blue at the zenith, and fading gradually into a pale turquoise in the far west. Upon the massive stone bridges flickered rows of yellow lights, finding their duplicates in the current below; under their dark arches glided the boats with green and crimson lanterns, casting fore and aft long trails of phosphorescent light upon the gently rocking ripples; the broad stone steps of the quay were clean and smooth by the constant lapping of the tame, sweet waves. Oh! why do not hundreds of those wasting, languishing creatures, who are pricking out their eyes with the lace needles, or eking out a miserable existence in a garret hovel, come here on such a night, and "sustained and soothed, wrap the drapery of their couch about them," and let the caressing billows drift their spirits into the "slow and silent stream, Lethe!"

The *fiacres*, with their poor skin-and-bones horses stood along the river-banks; the care-free students and gay companions were coming from their day's outing at Vincennes, Versailles, St. Denis, Neuilly, Sèvres, or St. Cloud, to terminate their spree at a *jardin*. The proprietor of one of the skin-and-bone equipages stepped up to us, and queried: Bullier? I know I looked horrified. At first I thought he was talking about soup or cold boiled meat; but the word contained fascination for me as I discovered that this mercantile driver wished to take us to the great ballroom of the Quartier Latin. Of course the gentlemen answered and emphasized "*non*," the ladies appeared shocked, but still *cocher* lingered, as I questioned an American resident in Paris regarding this enticing Bullier. Then I thought it must be the sight of which I had been deprived the preceding evening, and, at length, we concluded to look at this show, as we would at any horrible curiosity; so *cocher* won his suit.

In a wide rather handsome street there was a blaze of gas-jets, a crowd of *gamins*, youths, and heedless girls, and an orchestra in full blast; this was the Jardin Bullier. We obtained our tickets, two francs each, at the bureau, and descended a long flight of steps to an immense floor where the band played, and hundreds of animals, with human souls, were mingling in the mazes of the dance. There was no botanical beauty in the garden, which seemed to extend in a complete circle around the hem of the *salon*.

It was a narrow, gravel path skirted by withering pines in tubs; here and there a grotto closed in by shrubbery, or a sheltered arbor. But the audience did not care for quiet, sequestered retreats; they preferred to bask in the full glare of the gaslight, and bacchanalian revel. Slovenly waiters were hurrying by with little caraffes of cognac. All was wild and incoherent, but no one in a state of brutish intoxication.

For a few moments we listened and looked at the fantastic scene around us. What we saw and what we heard I will not translate, for

> "Into strange vagaries fell,
> As they would dance."

Every feature of this human menagerie was nauseating in the last degree. Low, imbecile men; miserable, dirty women, marked by the finger of disease and wretchedness. There were no laces, nor paint, nor silk, nor jewels, or the stimulus of champagne to hide the tarnished souls, the tattered reputation, and the decaying bodies of these poor children. But they danced,—danced wildly, as if impelled by a demoniac power, not caring what, or when, or how, and I covered my eyes involuntarily and hurried away with more anxiety than I had shown importunity to come.

LETTER XXXIV.

> "When lovely woman stoops to folly,
> And finds too late that men betray,
> What charm can soothe her melancholy,
> What art can wash her guilt away?"
>
> OLIVER GOLDSMITH.

PARIS, May, 1878.

WHEN last I opened my diary it was to chronicle the horrors of the vast human menagerie of the Quartier Latin, where I had seen the animals in the height of their saturnalian sports on the Sabbath. I never had a prepossession for a circus, a hippodrome, nor any of the curiosities or monstrosities contained in collections of wild beasts, such as educated hogs,—or *uneducated*,—armless girls, double-headed babies, brainless men, or heartless women. No! I will not malign so grossly my sex by applying the epithet to the mongrel creatures who filled the *Jardin Bullier*.

My experience in this bizarre species had been limited until then, and though I do not regret the trial, as I favor the study of animate and inert nature in all its phases, one experiment contented me, and I shall penetrate no deeper into the revolting subject.

Again it is Sunday night, and I come to speak of the beauties of the marvellous market of humanity, the *Jardin Mabille.*

Hush! a lady friend is appalled because I suggest that we should tread these forbidden paths. But why not? I query; had we not the day preceding visited *Les Halles Centrales*, and inhaled the incense of the flower bazaar of the Madelaine? Why shadow in obscurity the fact that we enjoyed and studied this greatest, choicest, and most bewitching, yes, beautiful, most beautiful of all, — the market of human souls: the retreat of the nymph and the haunt of the sibyl?

Just off the Champs Elysées in the Avenue Montaigne is this emporium of fashionable vice. Nature and art have labored hand in hand and heart to heart to transform the nursery into a paradise, and invention seems to have been exhausted in the construction of grottos, groves, arbors, sequestered walks, and secret recesses. The ravines and cascades, gay parterres and gentle slopes, make an elysium. Five francs each we paid to enter this heaven of flowers, flounces, and furbelows. We arrived early, rather too early, for though the angels had trimmed and lighted their lamps, and nature's musicians were filling every nook and wave of air with sweet melody, the candelabras bordering the café and the garlands of Chinese lanterns festooned from branch to branch of the trees, were only dimly burning, and the orchestra was silent in the pavilion.

Our advantage lay in this fact; we had ample time to loiter through the avenues and linger upon the delicious features of the garden, while the fair votaries of fashion and pleasure were still employed donning the ravishing toilet designed to make the wearer's fortune, while annihilating that of some other ill-starred sister. The café is quite as large and much resembling Proskaur's in our Fairmount Park. In the centre of the garden is a highly decorated semicircular building for the accommodation of the band, and about this nucleus cluster females whose loftiest aspiration is to relieve a gentleman spectator of his hat by an intricate flourish of the left toe, while executing the vagaries of the *can-can.*

We found a comfortable seat in a rustic alcove, near the main entrance path, where I could observe all who entered, and very much entertained was I by the devices practised by the frail beauties upon their equally faithless prey. Occasionally a veritable old Darby and Joan couple from one of the near provinces would pass through the glittering throng in a state of bewildered admiration at all they heard and saw, without having the slightest conception of its meaning. It was better so; you know the old adage, "Where ignorance, etc." Had these good, unsophisticated people suspected the perversion of the banquet, at which they were willing guests, they would have denied themselves the otherwise enchanting treat. Oftentimes a country bumpkin, in loose shoes, short trowsers, hands thrust into the very extremities of his pockets, and mouth and eyes wide open, would stand in a stony attitude, gazing and marvelling at the splendor of these creatures, whose images God had formed after his own, and whose souls had been supplied by Satan with the covenant they should return to him after the casket had fallen into decay. There were many sightseers from strange lands like ourselves, and as the brilliant butterflies floated and swarmed amongst the flowers, the lights burned brighter, and the tuning of instruments told the advent of the dance.

The tide of strollers stopped, and by the laughs, and applause, and the shouts of the revellers I knew that fun and frolic were running riot. But I was loath to leave my little retreat, though anxious to witness the dance, yet dreaded lest the exhibition might resemble the sad performance a week ago.

When I did finally move towards the citadel of delight, the array of fashion, elegance, extravagance, and beauty that dazzled my eyes was such as I had never dreamed, even in the wildest flights of fancy. The scene was, even to my *woman's* eye, more exquisite than any of the great picture galleries I had walked, though not quite so enduring, and the fragrance exhaled by the female flowers was equally sweet if not so pure as the bouquets of the market of the Madelaine.

To see that most bewildering of all dances, the *can-can*, executed by Parisians, in Paris, and at the most aristocratic garden of its class in the world, would indeed be a fantastic sight for an American lady, and there were many there besides me. To procure a position close to the actors in the farce was now almost impossible, as the majority of the pleasure-seekers were clustered about them in a series of circles; so I contented myself in the background until some one satiated by the excess of passionless and garish sensuality consigned me a place; and what a spectacle riveted my gaze!

Beside me stood a night-blooming Cereus, excessively handsome and aromatic, in lemon colored satin and garniture of bronze leaves, all of which inevitably fade into nothingness as the daylight approaches.

Before me was another, a sweet moss-rose, in pale-pink silk, a cream-colored mantle embroidered, and a profusion of flaxen golden hair, appearing so gentle and modest, before some rude hand had torn away from her fair face its hood of soft green innocence; the beauty of the full-blown flower had not been marred by unmerciful brutality to the bud, but in the eye there lingered the pensive, pathetic lustre of heaven's own dew. To this sweet plant my heart yearned. I felt that she was no vulgar creation like the devil-may-care hundreds, not only a female, but a *woman*, young and beautiful now, struggling under a weight of sin and wrong, but sure eventually to fill a penitent's grave.

Behind me reposed a glorious damask rose, framed in black satin, and a blaze of diamonds upon her ample neck and arms, as hollow and heartless as a great bladder invented to float upon the foam of this most perilous sea.

The music ceased, and the audience dispersed, so I secured my place at the revel. None of the elaborately attired beauties participated; the dancers were without exception of the lower, poorer type, and the men—well! I need not discuss the male element; he who consents to such an exhibition of himself is unworthy mention.

As much has been written about the Mabille Gardens and against them, as in regard to any other of the myriad sins of the age; and yet the abused resort is always full during its season. You are told that it is not what it was; that it has fallen off; that the world has gotten so much purer; and that people go to these glittering deviltries no more. All I have to say is that such is not my experience. An American resident in Paris spoke of the large sums expended every year to add to its attractions, and, judging by what I saw and heard, the money laid out, and the profits received, show that the business rewards the heaviest and most costly investment. It is not for me to draw the moral. I presume that nobody will uphold this meretricious place, and that even its *acolytes* will not dare to defend the example. But what puzzles me is that many persons who in Philadelphia and New York would run away from places no better, and play prude and precisian if even asked to look in at a German theatre, or concert garden, or a bright saturnalia like Gilmore's in New York, come over to Paris and boldly pay five francs for a sight at the *demi-monde*, who flutter their stained lives in the doubtful penetralia, and walk the glittering declines that lead down to inevitable Hades. And these American *Josephs* and *Clarissas* rarely go alone. They come in crowds. Sometimes the ladies veil their porcelain faces; sometimes the men hide their pious brows; but most frequently they gather in numbers, and when they return home they fold their hands in their laps, and raise the whites of their eyes to heaven, and propitiate offended virtue by saying: "It is an awful place, that *Jardin Mabille*, and very naughty; but we went, like the rest of the world, just to see it for once, so not to have it said that we were afraid to follow the example of others."

LETTER XXXV.

"He was a scholar, and a ripe and good one;
Exceeding wise, fair spoken, and persuading;
Lofty, and sour, to them that loved him not,
But to those men who sought him, sweet as summer."
SHAKESPEARE.

PARIS, May, 1878.

A VERY warm and almost American summer day decided me to make several calls, and return several visits, and as Sunday shines no Sabbath in the French capital, I did not hesitate to use the first morning in the week to pay my respects to an American family, whose home is on the beautiful and broad avenue Josephine. They had adopted the sensible plan, and occupied the floor above the *entresol*, and as they had plenty of money and plenty of opportunities, they were enjoying Paris to the full. As we drew the bell-handle towards us the great doors of the court flew back, and the *concièrge* appeared at her little window.

From her we obtained the direction of our friend's apartments, and passed up a spacious stairway of polished oak and walnut. We were admitted to the antechamber by a gentleman of sable hue, imported from "the States" as special *valet de chambre*. The room was rather small and square, containing only several carved-walnut chairs and a table, but the floor gave evidence of the assiduous toil of the *frotteur*. Here we left parasols, canes, hats, or any other awkward appurtenances by which we might be encumbered, before entering the grand *salle*. Our auspicious brother of the Fifteenth Amendment ushered us into a *salon*, garish in its elaborate decorations in *repousé* of gilt and white and gaudy frescoes. Very few works of art adorned the walls, except those painted in the panels by the deft skill of the artist. The floor was covered by an expensive Axminster; filmy laces and crimson satin draped the deep embrasures of the casement-windows; and even the door-frames were of ornate wooden fretwork tinted by delicate pigments and dazzling in gold leaf. I do not wonder that the richest come here, like Mr. and Mrs. Mackay, and other bonanza kings, to revel in these Old World glories and to squander their easily earned millions, and I am sure you will forgive me when I say, had I been equally fortunate, I would have followed their example at least for awhile. There is one trouble that would not befall me. No glare and no novelty would ever alienate my heart from my country. It is too true that many Americans who come to Paris on a short visit soon grow so much fascinated with this luxurious capital, and therefore out of heart with their own ways at home, as to become regular *habitués;* and this applies not only to the very rich but to those who have very little money of their own. There are countrywomen of mine to-day in this costly city, women of irreproachable reputations withal, who resort to every sort of expedient, and even at times submit to privations simply that they may live a Bohemian's life among these agreeable strangers.

Although the day was warm, the avenues were already crowded with carriages dashing out to the Bois, and the magnificent boulevards, jocund with the wild and varied life of the bright metropolis; and I could well understand the witty remark of the superficial Frenchman when he said "that the opulent barbarians had again taken possession of his luxurious Paris." The occupants of the glittering chariots and shining cafés and decorated highways were the foreigners, from all lands, flocking hitherward to enjoy the Exhibition Universelle; so threading our way through the cheerful and shouting throng, we told *cocher* to drive us to the College de France, just at the rear of the theological and classical school founded by Robert Sorbonne. Every American calls to see Professor Laboulaye, now the chief of that great academy, and a Senator for life in the French Assembly. He lives in the noble institution, which was founded in 1530 by Francis I, containing twenty-nine chairs, and distinguished for its lectures in history, law, and languages, M. Laboulaye himself delighting crowds every Monday, when the Senate is not in session, with exquisite dissertations on such interesting subjects as Washington, the American Constitution, Socrates, Julius Cæsar, etc. M. Laboulaye lives in the simplicity of a cultivated student and scholar, and the plainness of his furniture, the learned confusion of his books, his soft voice and gentle manner, all a marked contrast to the fresh decoration and rather boisterous welcome of my American friends, was very like the austere and quiet rooms of the other great man I had visited in London, Dean Stanley, in Westminster Abbey. And when M. Laboulaye said to me, in his sweet broken English, "You Americans are *so* rich," I received it as a reproach of many of my ostentatious countrywomen. M. Laboulaye, though, as every one knows, a severe Republican, looked and was dressed like a priest; he possessed the rare charm of listening intently to all I said in reply to his graceful questions, Whether I had seen the Exhibition? Whether I liked Paris? How long I intended to remain? Where I lived in America? And whether we would do him the honor to come any Monday and hear him lecture? It was all just as nice as it could be, and when I left his presence I felt the influence of his pure character and honest example, precisely as if I belonged to the French Republic myself.

As we emerged from the College, the streets in that far off quartier were quite deserted, as quiet indeed as Philadelphia on a sunny Sabbath afternoon; so hailing a *voiture* we were rattled off to the Jardin des Plantes, opposite the Pont d'Austerlitz. This is one of the favorite resorts of the populace, a combination of every description of natural specimens, quick and inert, and perhaps the finest botanical collection in the world. I do not desire to be disloyal to fashion or to science, but I confess I have never been able to join in the enthusiasm of those who rhapsodize over a wilderness of monkeys, or go into ecstasies over cages filled with lions, tigers, leopards, or regard a colossal elephant or awkward hippopotamus with special devotion. To me far more interesting than these curious and savage creatures, were the thousands of French people gathered to rest themselves in these rural retreats, and permitted to enjoy animate and inanimate nature gratuitously by favor of the French Government.

Tell me not of the vice and vulgarity of the Paris million, and of the cruelty of its so-called common people when their wildest passions are let loose. Wherever I have seen them, in their homes, in the streets, at the Exhibition, in their churches, or in places of amusement, they have captured me by their politeness and cleanliness, by their kindness to old people, their love for their children, and their invariable temperance; all of which qualities are as distinctively French as they are distinctly different from the working classes in London.

Much of this contrast arises from the intuitive love of the French from infancy for flowers, pictures, music, dress, comedies, and all that is artistic and graceful. They will detect a false note in an orchestra or a singer, or point out an error in a statue, with a polite shrug, and I have often noticed that the commonest workingman evinces as much genuine delight in high art as the conceited empiric who saunters through the galleries of the Louvre or the Palais Luxembourg.

LETTER XXXVI.

> "Mortality, behold and fear,
> What a change of flesh is here!
> Think how many royal bones
> Sleep within these heaps of stones!
> Here they lie, had realms and lands,
> Who now want strength to stir their hands,
> Where from their pulpits seal'd with dust
> They preach, 'In greatness is no trust.'
> Here's an acre sown indeed
> With the richest, royallest seed
> That the earth did e'er suck in
> Since the first man died for sin;
> Here the bones of birth have cried,
> 'Though gods they were, as men they died!'
> Here are sands, ignoble things,
> Dropt from the ruin'd sides of kings;
> Here's a world of pomp and state
> Buried in dust, once dead by fate."
> Francis Beaumont.

Paris, May, 1878.

I LINGERED in the Place de la Concorde on my way to the Hôtel des Invalides this morning, and as the sun touched the spray of the fountains into radiant prisms and glorified the monolith of Luxor, I thought of the past. The nuptial pageant of Marie Antoinette, terminating in the sad catastrophe of a panic-stricken multitude, followed scarcely more than two decades after by the humiliation and execution of this same beautiful but prodigal queen; the horrors of the Reign of Terror, and the severed heads of Charlotte Corday and Robespierre, trampled under the feet of the *sans culottes;* the demon populace saturating their kerchiefs in the blood of their guillotined king, and the women knitting while they participated in the barbaric carousal; all these crowded into my mental vision almost as vividly as the Egyptian hieroglyphics on the tablets of the Obelisk. The statues of the eight important cities of France: Lyons, Marseilles, Bordeaux, Nantes, Rouen, Brest, Lille, and Strasbourg—the last, alas! French no longer—blazed like shining demigods this brilliant day. To my right, at the top of the Rue Royal, in all its pathetic majesty, were the dark peristyle and hovering angels of the Madelaine, with its patron saint as the central figure of the tympanum, where the Last Judgment has been wrought in stony alto-relievo. She is in an attitude of intercession with Christ for the souls of the condemned. Before me, through the leafy arbor of the Champs Elysées, rose in perspective the Arc de Triomph, the noble monument projected by Napoleon as a cenotaph to the triumphs of the French, and only completed by Louis Philippe in time for the *cortège* bearing the corpse of him whose life's chapters may be read from its walls, to pass under its arches on the way to the resting-place prepared amongst the veterans he loved so well.

Crossing the Pont de la Concorde, I turned towards this magnificent catafalque of the Corsican conqueror. The gilded dome was the first splendor that dazzled me as we came into the fair city, and this was my third attempt, owing to a negligence of the hours of admission, to gain admission to its magnificence.

Napoleon Bonaparte seemed to permeate the very atmosphere of the Hôtel des Invalides; all nature seemed to breathe his name in a hush of reverence. The approach to the glittering tomb is by streets hallowed by the names of Vauban and Varenne, and as you pass through the garden where the veterans are drowsing under branching shade-trees, or planting little plots of flowers, you forget that this haven was not prepared by the first Consul for his scarred and crippled warriors. There is not a thought for Louis XIV, who really founded the hospital for the infirm and aged fighting men of France; every sigh, and every thrill, are for the sorrows and triumphs of the incomparable emperor, general, and statesman. You may say his sad end was only a just retribution for his repudiation of the sweet woman who led him on to fame and empire; but do you not think his dread expiation was continually at work upon him through the interminable line of cormorants who fed and flourished on his power, and finally dragged him down? I was first impressed by the hazy, golden light that veiled the high altar, and hung over the royal crypt in the chapel. It seemed like the holy incense around an ascending spirit. An intense stillness filled the church. Many foreign visitors, toiling men and boys, who had lain down their instruments of labor for a few moments, and *bourgeois* women and children, stood about the throne of the military deity. The men uncovered their heads as they passed the portals of the sanctuary, the boys stepped lightly over the mosaic laurels that wreath the amaranthine tiles of his victories about his bed, a mournful glamour gathered in the eyes of the veteran soldier as he leaned over the urn of porphyry, and instinctive devotion fell upon the whole gazing and voiceless concourse.

Down a broad stairway we passed to the entrance of the vault. Over the doors, supported by caryatides, I saw the last characteristic request of Napoleon, that his "ashes might repose upon the banks of the Seine, in the midst of the people he loved so well." How precisely has his testament been fulfilled! About him are garlanded his conquests; over him wave the banners of the conquered foe; in transept and nave are the remains of general or brother; and guarding the tomb are the sepulchral urns of his loyal Marshals Duroc and Bertrand. There is a constant flow of worshippers about the sarcophagus.

The memory of Louis Napoleon is as cold and dead in the republican capital as if his hands had never held the reins of government; there is no regretful sigh for the fair Eugénie, whose beauty illumined the Tuileries, radiated the boulevards, and shone upon the Bois; whose vaulting ambition hurried Maximilian to his final compt, and imposed the crushing crown upon the brow of the beautiful Carlotta, that holds reason prisoner. The French have even forgotten that the blood of the sleeping hero traversed the veins of the late emperor; all their tears are for the "Little Corporal."

The mourners come from strange lands and the far-off French provinces to revere the great soldier. All around were signs of the Republic; all around were souvenirs of the new liberty, and, within view, the group of Exhibition Palaces designed and completed by the Republic. But still the French masses idolize the "lieutenant of artillery." Other dynasties have risen and faded out of sight; other heroes have had their little day and have been forgotten; but the name and fame of Bonaparte are the unsetting stars in the empyrean of France.

Our next visit was to the celebrated Parisian necropolis. From the Hôtel des Invalides, in the extreme west portion, to the cemetery, on the eastern confines, was a ride of quite an hour, through the Boulevarde St. Germain, washed by the blood of the Bourbons, and past the Rue du Bac, for the gutter of which the diplomate in petticoats had sighed when in exile at Coppet, surrounded by her vice-regal court. Then we crossed the Seine, and looked upon the ruined mass of the Hôtel de Ville. I vainly sought the window at which our friend Lafayette presented Louis Philippe to the people nearly fifty years ago, and the room in which Louis XVI spoke almost a hundred years since, crowned with the cap of liberty, soon to be dragged to an ignominious death. In the Place de la Bastille there was a throng of *ouvriers*. Only the lofty Column of July marks the graves of the victims of the commune of 1830. No stone remains of the old prison to tell the story of the wretched creatures who languished in their living graves, only to be released for their execution; but the quartier is still, apparently, populated by the same elements that devastated their glorious Paris by shot, and shell, and sword, and fire in 1789, 1793, 1830, 1848, and 1871.

From this broad square, covering the ashes of six hundred and fifteen martyrs, we emerged into the most curious of all the fantastic sights in this *sui generis* city, the Rue de la Roquette, where the merchants of the costumes and tributes of the dead maintain their bizarre competition. This street leads directly from the northeastern limit of the Place de la Bastille to the world-renowned Père La Chaise, It is flanked with ateliers or stuccatos of monumental statuary, immortelles, and funeral offerings. This ghostly traffic is peculiar, because so many shops, all selling *facsimile* articles, should be grouped in one block without the alternation and variety found in a thousand other emporiums in other sections, but when I had passed row after row of these stalls and still met not the slightest change in the character of the merchandise, I could not coax myself to believe that this was a business from which men derived remuneration, but a museum for the edification of visitors.

But the Rue de la Roquette was no longer an object of speculation to me after entering the mighty home of the dead. It is one vast collection of mausolea and sarcophagi. There are very few graves, as in our places of burial, and in the chapels, and about the tombs, are strewn wreaths of natural flowers, paper-flowers, and muslin flowers; *immortelles* composed of black and white beads strung upon wire and formed into every description of religious and appropriate device, all of which are constantly renewed from the market in the streets outside. The photographs of entire families bearing loving inscriptions were placed as *souvenirs* upon the altars, and frequently a perpetual light glorified the narrow beds of clay.

I pondered long before one of the countless sanctuaries in the central aisle—it was not the tomb of a celebrity, at least not one of those bright stars of fame whose lustre grows more luminous with added years—peering through the iron door upon the mosaic altar, and silver candelabra, the marble floor and superb purple velvet altar cloth, the paintings, and vases, and manuals, all offerings upon the grave of the departed, evidently a dead Crœsus. Sometimes the bridal wreath, or communion garland, or the broken doll, or the war-sword is laid by the side of its former owner. It was touchingly realistic and full of love for the dead.

Opposite was the tomb of Rossini, of pure white stone, rather unostentatious in the interior. He died only a few years since. In the first avenue, diverging from the right of the broad path, is the tomb of the great Hebrew who thrilled two continents by her almost supernatural portrayal of the dark passions of hatred and revenge, but possessed none of the gentleness that gives woman her greatest charm—Rachel. In the same section was the opulent sepulchre of the princes of Mammon, the golden Rothschilds.

A few steps to the east is the classic cynosure of all the romantic, love-languishing Romeos and Juliets who visit this sweet place of repose—the cenotaph of Abélard and Heloise. And here they stand, and weep, and sigh, and meditate. As I watched these double Niobes, I marvelled if they knew the correct version of the lives they mourned. The pair have been deified by generations. And to what end? Perhaps to incarnate the deceitful precepts of a false philosophy. Ah! it has ever been so. Magdalene is a saint; the thief who repented with his expiring breath, an angel; Abraham, who turned the wronged Hagar and her offspring vagrants upon the world, a holy patriarch; Solomon, with his hundreds of concubines, the scriptural *savant;* Judith, the murderess of Holofernes, a heroine; Catharine, the Russian Faustina, a queen; the incestuous Lucrezia Borgia, the theme of the troubadour; and the names of Robespierre, Nero, Henry VIII, Bloody Mary; flaming meteors upon the historical horizon!

From there we fell into an avenue of graves, planted over with fresh, rank sward, shadowed by weeping willows, and marked only by a white or granite headstone. I liked the solemn, umbrous shadows, and the peaceful hush, and the soft, sighing rustle of the leaves, better than these dazzling tombs and spectacular decorations. And as I sauntered the *otium* and sweetness of the spot enveloped me like an incense. On my path towards the chapel I inadvertently stumbled upon the grave of Ledru Rollin, the

Republican leader of the last empire, who flew to England after failing in an attempt to prevent the Emperor from sending troops to aid in re-establishing the Pope. At the end of twenty years he returned to his native country, and though endeavoring to avoid politics was thrust into the arena, and by a greater constituency than ever was elected to the Assembly, where he took his seat upon the Extreme Left, and pleaded universal suffrage more impressively than formerly. His grave was laden with the offerings of his party, and bound in the tricolors of France.

On the right of the church are the mound and monument of Casimir Périer. The display of monumental splendor was attractive, but there were no democratic offerings from the masses upon the clay that covered the peacemaker, like those cast at the feet of the revolutionist. In this locality are a group of dramatic and musical celebrities, as if seeking congenial companionship in the grave—Bellini, Grétry, Boeildieu, Cherubini, Chopin, and Talma. When I met the name of Constant I involuntarily looked for the next one to be De Staël, but, alas! I recollected how many roods separate these two in death who were so close in life. These lives are ever combined in my mind by the wealth of love and intellect with which this strong woman oppressed her ungrateful lover. She prompted his orations in the Assembly, and wound her arms about his neck until he was satiated by the excess of favor. Marshals Ney, Lefébvre, Massena, Devaust, and Mortier, with the old voluptuary Barras, form a magnificent array. In the extreme north of the cemetery I found Balzac, the naughty novelist, close to the limits of the *fosse communes* or public graves.

There was a procession of Catholic girls clad in white, with long white veils falling over their faces and forms, and borne by six of their companions was a little white coffin, while the others carried candles to light the little soul through the dark path to heaven. Two holy fathers, in sable gowns, carrying rosaries, and repeating the office of the dead, walked at their sides. It was only the burial of a poor little mortal, who had come to rest at last amongst the herd, still how sweet and suggestive it was. Yet in the city so populated by the dead how few were the living persons. But the French are as loving to their dead as they are to the living, and odd enough, if the Commune kills its hecatombs, there is a splendid burial for all.

Much as I had ever loved these cities of the dead at home, my foreign experience was still more affecting. I was loath to quit the sublime rest and beatitude found only here. I wandered amongst graves, and mausolea, and naked mounds; studied the history of great luminaries, whose lustre had been eclipsed, alas! too soon; and though sad with the experience, filled with an ineffaceable memory.

Père La Chaise was converted into an extra-mural cemetery in 1804, and took its name from its former owner, the confessor of Louis XIV, and is of its kind without a peer in Europe, though we have many as beautiful in America, yet none so entirely novel. It is a sanctuary for the quick and the dead, a place of graves, but a source of contrast. We in our country do not follow our departed like those volatile and voluptuous Latins. They are often at the side of their loved ones gone, and many a tomb is a second home, many a vault an altar, many a shrine as familiar as a fireside. Here, as in all cemeteries, you gather the great philosophy of the emptiness of human ambition, and the substantial value of love and literature. The soldier comes here tired of the blood and smoke of battle, too often forgotten by those he has served. The statesman finds in Père La Chaise a panacea for his baffled ambition. As I thought of all these broken hopes and buried fortunes, these failures in love, in money, in station, and in deeds of surprise and empire, I felt again that the happiest and the most enduring of lives, and the sweetest of deaths, came from the tried attachment of devoted friendship, and the enduring solace and holy solitude of books.

LETTER XXXVII.

"Speak low! tread softly through these halls;
  Here Genius lives enshrined;
Here reign, in silent majesty,
  The monarchs of the mind.

A mighty spirit-host they come,
  From every age and clime;
Above the buried wrecks of years,
  They breast the tide of Time."

ANNA C. LYNCH BOTTA.

PARIS, May, 1878.

OF the critics in America who essay to pass judgment upon art, how many possess the actual requisites for the task? One in the thousand has perhaps only truly and conscientiously studied the rise and progress of painting in the great European art centres; yet the dissertations of the whole thousand upon the great theme are loud and pretentious. They talk of tones of shade, gradation of colors, complementary hues, contrasts and combinations, of properly selecting, blending, and balancing pigments, with judicial gravity. Then they drift into discussions of form, and after a technical manipulation of figure the untravelled and untaught reader is forced to believe at the end of the preachment that each critic is a genuine anatomical and chromatic professor. But as we probe the examples we find the professor's vocabulary stereotyped and stinted. The same generic terms, with slight modulation, are applicable in every theory, and with the acquisition of these few scientific phrases the dogmatic connoisseur presumes to become an oracle of art.

Because I have passed several mornings in the Musée du Louvre I shall not assume to classify or censure any of the several schools. It is a vast, bewildering panorama, where the masters of all the nations are grouped into one bouquet of infinite grandeur. I thought I could comprehend it while enveloped in its transcendent glamour, but now, in the seclusion of my *boudoir*, the chaos of ideas warns me to study each picture again and again, before forming even an unspoken conception of its merits.

Having followed the river façade along the Quai du Louvre, and having the window pointed out from which Charles IX fired upon his own people (which I afterwards learned had not been built until long after the perfidious monarch's death!), we turned into the Rue de Rivoli, where the great pile is equally imposing. Begun by Francis I after his return from Italy, burning with the fire of *renaissance*, it became the pretext for royal expenditure in many succeeding reigns, and now, after the addition of wings, and pavilion, and arches, and roofs, this gorgeous toy of the dynasties is one of the grandest aggregates of architecture on the round globe. With such advisers and artists as Titian, Bernini, da Vinci, del Sarto, Cellini, and Romano, with such patrons as the Francises, Henry II and Catharine de Medici, Diane de Poitiers, the luxurious Henry III and IV, Louis XIII and Mazarin, and the great Napoleon, with the frippery of Louis Philippe, and the supplements of the late Emperor, it seems even more complete and glorious because it escaped the perilous crisis of 1871.

For fifteen years Napoleon Bonaparte made of this world's gallery the pride of Paris and the marvel of other nations, by concentrating here from all the public depositories of art in the countries he had ravaged and conquered, their masterpieces in bronzes, marbles, canvas, tapestry, and precious stones. Wherever his victorious banner had floated he sought, and found, and seized the choicest products of human genius, alike those of the Pagans, the Romans, the Greeks, and the Teutons, alike those of the middle eras as of the *renaisssance*, and placed them in the Louvre, which he ostentatiously called the Napoleon Museum. For fifteen years, as I have said, this museum became the lodestar of European admiration, while the plundered capitals of Italy, Germany, Austria, and Russia, mourned the loss of their chiefest treasures. The domination of the all-conquering Corsican seemed to be widespread and eternal. He was the Colossus that bestrode the earth, and when strangers came to look at these foreign *chefs-d'œuvre*, rifled from the dazzling palaces of subdued monarchs, they conceived a new idea of the majesty of the irrepressible soldier, who carried the eagles of France from the Seine to the Tiber, and from the Danube to the frozen frontier of the Muscovite. Yet in a few short months this bright dream had faded. Waterloo ended his meteoric career. The magic fighter became a fugitive, then a guest, and finally a prisoner, who died upon a rock in the sea. Then the rescued kings of the despoiled cities rushed into Paris to demand the restoration of their pilfered treasures, and ransacked the Louvre for the priceless gifts that had been placed there, as the Man of Destiny vainly hoped, forever.

Such were my first sad impressions as I sauntered along the bright and tessellated floors of the Louvre, the theatre of brilliant pageants, dark plots, happy love, and royal license. It is the place to realize equally the power and insignificance of man, the length of his genius, and the shortness of his life. There are said to be five miles of galleries under the roofs of these prodigious palaces of the Louvre, and my immediate and harassing thought was my utter inability to traverse them. The brilliant, deep-toned frescoes of the ceilings, framed in their garlands of *repoussé* and gold, first chained my attention, but as I became accustomed to their garish beauty I could distinguish the various schools and pick out the gems.

Who could pass unnoticed the "Belle Férronière," of da Vinci? Perhaps I lingered longer by it because I knew the story of the last and best-beloved favorite of Francis I, and how the artist had expired in the King's arms, after bequeathing to posterity the chaste and beautiful features of his sweet *amorosa*. Or who neglect the "Belle Jardinière," of Raphael; or the *Ecce Homo* and Magdalen of Guido? With the Venus de Milo, and Jean Goujon's celebrated Diana, an enduring tribute to his celebrated patroness, these are the universal magnets.

The early French art is nothing more than a close transcription of the Italian schools, as the finest specimens of Claude Lorraine, Poussin, Fréminet, and Vernet bear testimony. Poussin, perhaps the greatest of French masters, studied his art in Rome, and his style is strongly imbued with the spirit of renaissance. Le Sueur was the first of this galaxy who circumscribed his duties to Paris, and though he left some fair models of his labor, his star was eclipsed by his aspiring rival, Le Brun, who followed the school of Poussin. Still later the studies of Watteau, Greuze, and David seem to have inaugurated and fixed in permanent fame the present French choice of forms and the mode of treating them.

Certain it is the modern French possess none of the pathos and direful beauty of the early Italians. The latter were possessed with a soul for depicting woful resignation and appealing grief, harrowing lamentations and painful meditations; while the former portray nature in its mature glow of luscious life and loveliness. I had read much of the Spanish type, Valasquez and Murillo, but I confess freely so far in my experience I divine no beauty; the females impressed me as travesties on an eccentric original, and the male figures as fierce, fantastic, and unreal.

In the Rubens gallery I was dazed by the number and size of his works; even with his renowned assistants he seemed a supernatural worker. Fifty or sixty historical, mythological, and scriptural representations, each measuring 10 x 16, were conspicuous for their boldness of outline and radiance of coloring. These alone are self-evident of the indefatigable energies of their creator, to say nothing of the hundreds that grace every gallery and palace, and many private homes throughout Europe. I notice that he was fond of sketching himself, and into all his "Holy Families" were woven the portraits of his kindred. His twenty productions relating to the career of Marie de Medici are regarded as valuable studies for acolytes; this *salon* was thronged by copyists taking miniature models of the great antitype.

The apartments devoted to *faience*, majolica, carved ivories, terra-cotta, and della Robbia bas-reliefs stretch far away in interminable array. But one has not the time to linger here and study fine arts and history; the wealth of the first seems to be continually elbowing the last from its equitable pedestal. As I passed down the steps where Coligny had passed, an honored guest, at a nuptial feast, two days before he was overtaken by traitorous perfidy of the king, the bell of St. Germain l'Auxerrois sent forth a silver music that would have fallen melodiously upon the "hollow of mine ear" had it not been marred with the recollection of the signal for the commencement of the bloody carnival on the appalling St. Bartholomew's day, three hundred years ago.

But now sentinels listlessly patrol their round, and the troops idle upon the square—"the wars are done, the Turks are drown'd."

Directly opposite the Louvre, across the Seine, is the Palace Luxembourg, containing of modern art what its royal neighbor holds of mediæval. The sward was fresh and smoothly cropped, the palace and its parterres alive with visitors, the marble heroines and patron saints, which glisten like white ghosts through the gardens, crude and grossly unsymmetrical, and the luxuriant foliage of the glossy lemon and orange trees in the green tubs skirting the plots, made a most touching drama. The children played while the students parleyed. There was neither sigh nor whisper, recall nor rebuke, of the profligate life of Marie de Medici under these roofs, or her wretchedly penurious ending in Cologne. There is no token of the crafty Richelieu upon the white marble bridge across the stagnant water of the canal below, which he so often trod from the Palais Cardinale. There is no footprint of the Girondins who languished within the walls that had vibrated, and were again destined to resound with the mirth and madness of civil war. Yes, only a little later and the regal halls were filled by the luscious, extravagant, intellectual *houris* of the seraglio of Barras. From her prison Josephine de Beauharnais was transported to this paradise, and from hence her ascendency to queen and empress was steady and speedy. In those troublous days women were more magnanimous to each other than in the calm of a conservative government. The intimacy formed in the dungeon of Carmes, between Madame Tallien and Josephine, resulted in their becoming the unjealous favorites of the Director Barras. It was Tallien who brought the widow of Beauharnais to the ruler, and so sincere was the feminine friendship she entertained for her friend, that she was quite willing that Josephine should share with her the affections and protection of the republican voluptuary. There is no trace now of the debauchery and revels of the beautiful woman in her Greek costume of India muslin embroidered in gold, golden girdle fastening the classic toilet about the waist, and rare cameos upon her shoulders, nor of the witty, racy, yet gentle empress in perspective; nor of Lange of the Comédie Française, except what is restored by memory, often at once trustful and hurtful.

Subsequent to the gay saturnalia, Luxembourg was the seat of the Imperial Senate, and under Louis Philippe the meeting of the Chamber of Peers. Here Louis Blanc congregated the socialists, and now it is the home of the Prefect of the Seine.

An old country like France, with its great benefactors and rulers, its artists and its tyrants in their graves, each leaving behind nothing alive, so to speak, but the enduring memories of bad deeds or the lasting monuments of noble works, is the study of the ages. Over their marble sarcophagi we recall these authors of evil and of good, and so collect from the retrospect at once mournings and hopes. Oddest of all, most of the wrongs of the past were the produce of French kings, and so also were the lovely works of art they encouraged and paid for. Perhaps it seems to have been reserved that as they planted in blood and tears, the harvest in the fulness of time should be gathered by a republican posterity, whose ancestors these tyrants hunted, impoverished, and forced to fight for them.

LETTER XXXVIII.

"VERSAILLES!—Up the chestnut alley,
All in flower, so white and pure,
Strut the red and yellow lacqueys
Of this Madame Pompadour."
THORNBURY.

PARIS, May, 1878.

REFLECTING upon it now, in the sweet French starlight, the whole of my visit to Versailles was a *fiasco*. I found the seat of political government as dull as Goldsmith's "Deserted Village," and what added to the dulness was the unexpected absence of the statesmen from their legislative hall. Yet the railway route was full of interest; the scenery, the habits of the people in the antique villages, the old palaces, the shops, *cafés*, and places of public worship, were all studies.

We passed through a perfect arbor of perfumed flowers and grasses, chateaux gleaming through the dense foliage; the splash of frequent fountains; silent statuary, as if on guard against intruders; white-capped women thronging the streets of the hamlets contrasted with blue-bloused men driving great horses and oxen; females in short petticoats and *sabots*, bending over the gardens where the vegetables of voracious Paris are grown; now and then a priest, in long serge gown and shovel-hat, would cross the scene, like a figure from the seventeenth century, and occasionally a soldier like a Lilliputian image would strut past like an actor in a French farce. It was a moving picture to my American vision, and I had scarcely time to make a note of my fellow-passengers before we swept into the beautiful station, to find ourselves in the political capital of France, the scene of centuries of revolution, luxurious profligacy, joyous events with sorrowful terminations, and the rendezvous in the summer of 1871 of the German invaders.

From St. Lazare station, the first important point we approached was Mount Valerien; from this fort the shell was thrown that fell upon and destroyed the palace at St. Cloud. But in the quiet noonday hush there was not a trace of the fast and furious firing seven years ago. On we rushed through a colonnade of tall, slim poplars, the emblems of equality and liberty, till we paused at St. Cloud, the ancient tribunal of monarchical rule, and the summer residence of the late hapless Napoleon III. I could see the sweet, shady retreats of the wooded park from my seat at the car-window. Thence our route extended through a portion of the *grand parc* to the adjacent town of Sèvres. In the lanes I saw the artisans of the royal manufactory of jewelled porcelain and *patetendre*. This was the toy coaxed by Madame de Pompadour from Louis XV, under whose regal patronage it made a marked advance, and then chemists and artists endeavored to rival one another in the invention of new and exquisite pigments and designs to adorn the gems of clay. The *bleu de roi*, and Pompadour pink, were employed with great effect upon vases and services in compliment to the princely benefactors. After this I fell to studying my companions in the compartment. Opposite was the man of books, with his portfolio and journal, *Le Temps*, and magazine, *Revue des Mondes*, his black silk skull-cap, and small white, delicate hand, and solitaire diamond ring; beside him an elderly lady and a poodle—a sweet woman with a faded face, and an air of rest and calm that seemed a foil to the elegant valet, who stood ready to aid her from the train; next was a flashingly beautiful girl, whose pet was not a lap-dog, but a handsome officer in blue uniform, with silver cording and epaulettes; he evidently required greater *aplomb* and diplomacy to manage than the elder lady's companion, but she was full of the electricity of youth and health, and capable of the task. They took us to be English strangers, as I could understand by the conversation, but when I chatted a little French of my own, there was a sudden well-bred silence, and then a confusing smile; they accepted my challenge as a fair Roland for their Oliver.

Needless that I should recount the story of Versailles, with its illustrious neighbors in a near circle, St. Denis, St. Cloud, St. Germain, Malmaison, Sèvres, Vincennes, and Sceaux; nor extol luxurious fields, massive forests, gray castles, bright cascades, sequestered promenades, and the superb Seine winding like a silver scarf round centuried towers, and towns; nor of the three grand avenues, Paris, St. Cloud, and Sceaux; nor of the great churches, St. Louis, the Prefecture, and the Chancery; nor beyond all the palaces, with their storied picture galleries, parks, lakes, orangery, private theatre, chapel, fountains, statues, colleges, schools, literary and public edifices.

Yes! The incense of favored women hangs about the spot; not one of them without a poison in her story. Maintenon, the ruler of France, and mistress of Grande Trianon, had never touched the soft hand of Fortune until Louis XIV was subdued by the importunities and acumen of the "widow Scarron;" as her biographer says, "she was born in a prison, bred in poverty, the widow of a cripple, and wife of a king." Le Petit Trianon was erected for Madame de Pompadour, who carried more than one stain upon her vice-regal page of life. Here the luxurious daughter of Marie Theresa amused herself with the extravagant toy, the miniature Swiss village, regardless of her approaching fate at the guillotine; and where do we find sadder anecdotes than the narrative of the last days of Josephine and Eugénie? so that the Lares and Penates of Versailles seem to be executing some dread decree upon the fair and unfortunate occupants of her double palaces.

But of all this we can read in history, and our day seems to be in sympathy with the past. *Cocher* was rather an intelligent *bourgeoise*, with the faculty of conversation largely developed, and a fair appreciation of the beauties of nature and art. Versailles is not a pretty town, but *cocher* addressed himself to the task of pleasing, and drove us through dark and leafy avenues, closed in on either side by heavy walls of foliage, where the trees had been trimmed and garlanded in the most novel and fantastic manner; he extolled the Empire, and denounced the Republic, and glorified the Napoleonic dynasties; and finding us complaissant and chatty, he demanded his *pour boire* before we dismissed him, and having enjoyed it on the way volunteered to conduct us to an excellent *café* for lunch. While I was indulging an ecstasy of praise of the obliging Frenchman, we were driven to what looked very like a "beer shop." Undaunted by appearances, we ordered lunch, and oh! what a disenchantment. But *cocher* had taken French leave, and when there we began to investigate our bargain. The wily driver had guided us to a fourth-class restaurant, the proprietor evidently his confederate. I saw it all too late, when the unsavory repast was spread before us. What were we to do? To dispute was vain; to partake impossible. The fowl was old and tough, the butter too strong for its weight, and the wine like raspberry vinegar. Our only alternative was to pay and leave the den. We hastened to Paris oppressed with the hunger and thirst; but as the poet says, "there is no cloud however black but what has its silver lining," and if the poet did not say it, it is an inspiration of my own. In the Café Durand, under the sacred shadow of the Madelaine, and close to the noble and monumental Rue Royal, we forgot our grief and forgave our deceiver.

To this restaurant, and the Café Riche, are ascribed the finest *cuisines* in Paris by epicures.

I believe when I first opened my diary to chronicle the pleasures and disappointments of the day, I said I meditated upon the day as a *fiasco;* but the remark must be frankly discounted by the fact that I had not quite recovered my temper. No! let me be just, and state the dinner at Voisin's was no *faux pas!*

LETTER XXXIX.

"I love no land so well as that of France,
Land of Napoleon and Charlemagne,
Renowned for valor, women, wit, and dance,
For racy Burgundy and bright Champagne,
Whose only word in battle is Advance."

CLASON.

PARIS, May, 1878.

ON the Champs Elysées legions of wraithlike memories continually elbow the *dramatis personæ* of to-day from their equitable dominion.

Once upon the broad avenue, it is not the gay holiday-makers, filling the sidewalks, the *voitures*, and the little iron chairs, a sou apiece, that surprise and please so much, as the brilliant and famous characters and events that seem to reappear from the realm of history and romance. Life on the "Elysian Fields" is always entrancing, but to realize it to the full you must mingle with the joyous multitude on Sunday. Nothing in Paris attains such a variety of pleasure as this multitude on the Sabbath. It is the *day* of the opera and the oratories; the church and the concerts; the players and the priests; the unity of sin and sacrament.

Yes! there are the student and his fair, fat *grisette*, sitting under the chestnuts, eating peanuts and *bon-bons;* the good *bourgeoise* women with their large, white hands, resting extended upon their ample knees, around their skirts clinging three or four little ones chattering French, with a fluency and dainty accent that bring to my cheek a blush of my own inefficiency; then troops of other happy children—the progeny of the uppertendom—with their white-capped attendants; the city *voitures* and cabs for the democracy; the glittering equipages and jewelled trappings of the English and American money kings, and the lumbering vehicles bearing upon their panels the heraldry of the royalists of St. Germain. But it is not only these that throng the mental vision; there are the ghosts of Marie de Médicis, the Louises, the savages of the Directory, the ladies of the first Empire, and the recollections of its later travestie, that rouse us to the contrast between this bright to-day and the long-vanished yesterdays.

And surely the Elysées, the Arc de Triomphe, Column of Luxor, and Bois du Boulogne, are magical combinations, and on this glorious day, more lovely and more bewildering than even my exulting expectation had painted. "A mighty maze! but not without a plan." To enhance these attractions, Nature appeared in her richest robe and sweetest mood. The air was an elixir, the flowers heavy with their own aroma, the luxuriance of the foliage seemed forced, and the sun, though brilliant, was not oppressive.

Along the superb avenue—much broader than our Broad Street—with deep pavements for pedestrians, and the centre drive devoted to horses and vehicles, extending nearly three miles to the gates of the Bois, we wandered and wondered. Advancing toward the Arc de l'Etoile, the left is flanked by stately palaces, while upon the right, through the branching shade, gleams the *Palais d'Elysée*, the home of the Marshal President, and the summer-gardens. As the summit of the grand allée is reached, there sits the triumphal arch to receive you under its massive portals, overlooking the surrounding vicinage, the nucleus of a radius of fine streets, like beams from a central star, whose names perpetuate the trophies of Napoleon, and whose viceregal edifices are the homes of the American colony; it is one brilliant paradise of history, art, diplomacy, and wealth.

This vast, yet symmetrical Dome of Victory, under whose dark arches have marched the royal processions that swept away and succeeded the Napoleonic dynasty, is a daguerreotype in marble of the salient episodes in the career of the conquering hero. It was projected by the chief as a monument of bravery to the *Grande Armée*. It is a marvellous combination of shields, standards, colossal figures, military medallions, and allegorical representations, a frozen parable of the Consulate and the First Empire. Upon every side and by every group we are taught the one lesson, the Heroism of war and the Glory of victory. But in those days all men were brave, and all men battled for empire and power.

Here the Genius of War seems to be omnipotent. We see it inciting the chivalric Mars to motion; we see it cheering the young warrior on to the salvation of his country, while he tears himself from the restraining arms of his father, and turns from his grief-stricken young wife, who holds forth appealingly the body of their dead child; and we see it in the confusion of battle and carnage. Then as the reward of all his sacrifices comes Victory with the crown of laurels, and History with her stylus and scroll, chronicling his heroic deeds. Over all is the emblem of gentle, gracious Peace, with the sword sheathed, " for he and his sword did earn his *chronicle*." At his side Agriculture, with the harvest of fruit and grain, and the sweet domestic sway of wife and children.

The faces upon the Arch are all portraits, and the trumpets of Fame are proclaiming to the whole world that France has conquered her foes. I saw the marvellous conceits with breathless delight. It is a consummation of art, a memorable tribute to valor, a proud cenotaph of a people's gratitude. Yet under this massive monument of French genius to French bravery, the stolid and resistless Germans marched in 1871, after they had conquered Napoleon III. This to the French must have seemed the severest satire of Fate. The Emperor a fugitive (like his great uncle), the Empress flying from and fearing her own subjects, homeless and friendless, while the grim Teuton triumphed over all.

But for philosophy I had little time, and dashed on towards the Bois. Our *fiacre* was one among thousands. Far more extensive and intricate the maze than at Fairmount or Central Park, or even Hyde Park, London, where, on the ultra-fashionable drives one meets nothing but wealth and titles, where the police keep out the plebeians, and the mass are too poor and oppressed to venture in.

Here is a rare combination of royal livery and republican harness. At present, Equality is Emperor in France, and the *ouvrier* and Bourbon ride side by side, to the infinite aversion of the latter, and the ineffable satisfaction of the former. So, as the human ocean poured through the Arc, glittering with all the fashions and peoples of the world, it was a myriad masquerade, where human passions, intrigues, schemes, hates, loves, envies, and ambitions, were concealed under the guise of frivolity and frolic.

Once past the *Arc de l'Etoile*, you stand upon the very confines of the American quarter. The large, flaunting residence across the way is the *sylvan* retreat of the Princess Bonanza, who empties many sequins from her purse for the decoration of her house upon republican fête nights. Though the display is ample and costly, the effect produced is not always sufficient unto the desires of the Princess; there is a murmur of complaint against the "horrid arch" which obstructs the brilliant scene. It was sheer ingratitude—nay, cruelty—for the municipal authorities to refuse to remove or to sell that "horrid thing" at the solicitation of the exacting Princess. Our Minister resides upon the Avenue Josephine; our Commissioner-General to the Exposition upon Avenue d'Eylau; Dr. Thomas Evans, proprietor of the *American Register*, in a palatial home upon the Avenue du Bois de Boulogne; and, indeed, there is not an avenue of the famous radius but what is odorous with Americans. My compatriots seem to flock thither from intuition, as do the pigeons of St. Mark to the Piazza in Venice, or the Jews to their wailing place.

Paris soldiers and Paris horses resemble each other closely. The same process seems to have produced both, and both indifferently. There was not enough to complete a full-sized soldier or a full-sized horse, and I did not wonder when I heard the tall Germans and their big steeds contrasted with these little people. Their legs are too short, and their bodies too long, and the same pecularities are pronouncedly observable in the animal and the man. The famous Centaur has really found a claim to my credulity since I have studied these two Gallic creations; surely this quadruped, to all appearances, was produced as a component part of the soldier, and not to draw the awkward, clumsy, graceless carriages of the Imperialists. I remember how the choice specimens of conveyances on exhibition at the Centennial of French manufacture, impressed me by their ponderous size and loosely-jointed hinges, and even here in the very midst of these inelegant establishments my American eye refuses to become reconciled. They look like great *Black Marias*, conveying common offenders to jail.

The Bois swams with humankind between 4 and 6 P. M.; it is the hour to meet Dame Fashion, and at 7 it is as tenantless as the lone desert; a solitude suggestive of spectres, banditti, poniards, a futile struggle, and a dark death. And yet this is the sweetest and most seductive hour at the Bois, when the garish flare of the *mode* has passed away, leaving soft, twinkling stars and deepening shadows, for your companions.

When I first saw the great French park, it was in the mellow glow of the setting sun's last rays, that were touching the mazarine blue and golden clouds into a glory of color; when its radiance played among the fountain-spray, and sank to rest in opal splendor on the breast of the lake. Again, when the angels had unfurled the curtains of the night, and Nature's gas-jets were all aglow, I rode between the bronze foliage and lingered in the aromatic influences, until Nymphs and Satyrs seemed to whisper around me. In the lusty glare of noon, I penetrated the wood again, as far as the *grand cascade* and *Pré Catelan*, where we dined upon the dainties of a Parisian repast, surrounded by delicious flowers and trees of every clime.

The Bois de Boulogne is not a park of Nature's handicraft alone, but wealth and art have conspired to render it a fitting abode for the gods. Though dolefully damaged by the siege of 1871, artisans and landscape gardeners are constantly repairing the work of the Fire fiend.

Through the Allée de Longchamps the Hippodrome de Longchamps is reached, the race-course of the Jockey Club, where the thoroughbreds are trotted upon the full, fresh sward. The course resembles a royal village in the beauty of its ornate rural architecture, the Emperor's pavilion and the noble Rothschild's villa.

Within sight of the course is the craggy mound of Longchamps, the rush of water ever flowing into the basin below and drifting away in two winding streams. All about the paths are graded and curved with an infinite grace, and ornamented by bowers, and arbors, and stretches of dense forest land.

Further on we have the Théâtre des Fleurs, whose scenery is not the painted canvas of artists, but the shrubbery, and grottos, and stream, and firmament of Nature, beautified by modern skill.

History and romance have garlanded the Bois with a whole wreath of legends, where the amaranth of immortality and the poppy of death are entwined upon one stem; where the olive of peace and the wheat of prosperity are grouped with the rose of York and Lancaster proclaiming war; where the houstonia of content rests upon the very breast of the hollyhock of ambition; where the cypress of despair has coiled its tendrils in inextricable mockery about the hawthorn of hope; and where the marigold of cruelty, with its twin sister lotus, revenge, are couched with the balm of sympathy upon a bed of fir—time.

LETTER XL.

> "The looks of ye, ma'am, rather suits me,
>   The wages you offer will do,
> But then I can't enter your service
>   Without a condition or two;
> And now to begin is the kitchen,
>   Commodious, with plenty of light,
> And fit, you know, for entertainin'
>   Such friends as I like to invite."
>
> ANONYMOUS.

PARIS, May, 1878.

I HAVE been newly interested in the eternal question of servant-girlism. Not on the point of wages, but on the larger subject of dress. And I think I have gathered a few comparative items that will be interesting at home. Nothing has given me more mental concern than the very great difference between the girls out at service in Europe and their sisters in the United States. I am not speaking of those who are retained through generations in wealthy and aristrocratic houses, and have become an integral part of these titled establishments, but of the vast army of females who earn a livelihood in hotels and ordinary families. In London and Paris the usual domestic is almost a slave, receiving little remuneration except from guests, and in nearly all cases far better educated and better behaved than the corresponding class in America. The civility and subordination of the foreign servant-girls resemble the docility and sprightliness of the colored women of the South, only the Europeans are more thoroughly trained by their associations, and contrast painfully with the insolence of too many of the importations from the Emerald Isle in our American households.

Industry and a practical knowledge of the fine as well as the useful arts is the primal ambition of the Frenchwoman. Her struggle is to become worthy of her place, and eventually to ascend in the social scale. On the other hand, assumption is the chief virtue of her Celtic sister. Her first taste of America does not prompt her to acquire understanding and skill, but to copy expensive fashions. While Elise is wandering through the Louvre gaining a knowledge of paintings and ceramics, Bridget only sees the follies of the American lady of society. If Madame is a leader of the *mode*, Bridget must be equally exquisite in the choice of her own toilets, and in this passion she often neglects the duties for which she has been employed. She forgets that she has been duplicating her mistress's style, and frequently so far oversteps her prescribed orbit as to advise the head of the house how to dress.

I have already told you how many chambers our poor *femme-de-chambre*, Jeanne, must arrange and how many pails of water she must carry to the fifth and sixth stories in a day, and she is a fair type of a system; one of millions in Europe. In addition to her vernacular German, she speaks French admirably, English well, and is a woman of considerable information. Yet this poor creature has no leisure to devote to gewgaws and frippery; very rarely does she enjoy God's pure air and the thousand pleasing inventions of modern life When she lays down brush and broom at eleven o'clock, it is to retire to rest.

There are legions as poor as Jeanne in these great centres of population, that to retain their situations must drudge and obey silently. The moment a murmur of complaint escapes them they are mercilessly ejected, and the vacancy supplied by another hungry one.

On duty, the French girls are at all times neat and orderly. When taking their outing, a plain dress minus frills and furbelows, an amplitude of white apron, and a crisp white cap carefully crimped, is the universal uniform.

In London the average girl is called "slavie," and her laboring regalia is invariably a smudge on her nose, a soiled, tattered dress, slipshod shoes, and hair as frowsy as a bird's nest. Off duty, she appears in light calico dress, straw bonnet, and cloth sacque or faded shawl in midwinter.

Upon my own dear enfranchised shores, our ministers plenipotentiary of the culinary department copy the mistress of the house, even to the details of shapes and colors. When my friend purchased a sage-hued silk, her nursemaid copied it in an alpaca of the same color; when my chambermaid expressed her intense admiration for the cut of my black silk princess robe and mantle, it did not strike me that three weeks afterward I should behold her clad in its model of cashmere, and still greater was my amazement when she dazzled my vision in pink lawn after seeing my French organdy of the same shade. This practice is wholly unknown amongst the girls out at service in Europe. With us the passion extends not only to blonde Bridget, but to dusky Dinah. Of course there are exceptions in the sensible, striving girls who place their earnings in the building associations and trust companies, but the rule is those who expend their weekly wages upon costly paraphernalia.

If you will call at any of the great establishments in Philadelphia, like Wanamaker's, where all varieties of women's wear are sold at all prices, you will be surprised at the vast sums laid out on the decoration of the persons of our female help. They may not buy the best, but they spend enormously in silks, laces, hose, bonnets, gloves, and underwear, and when you see them on Sundays or holidays, you are astounded at the expensive elegance of many of their outfits. I do not speak of this habit to complain of it so much as to make a note of it. A Boston lady, now here, says that the *furor* for dress amongst these classes in the New England towns often leads to evil, and has given great pain to humane women who desire to see the servant class improved and elevated. It is a phase of society peculiar to the United States, and is a result of our freedom, an inevitable outgrowth of our emancipated form of government, that what one woman may do all can try to follow; nor am I disposed to dwell upon the bad effects this insane appetite for dress must have upon the discipline of the household and the future of those who manage it. That is the right of the servant as it is of the mistress. But surely a word on a subject that all of us feel can do no harm. Both sides may learn and unlearn from each other. Nor can the example of the Old World servant-girl be held up here for imitation any more than our own luxurious ways should be displayed to mislead our Milesian sisters. Are we ourselves guiltless? Bridget is no longer Irish when she comes to settle in America. She is a citizen of the great Republic, and if she is insolent, extravagant, and dangerous as an imitator, we must even bear with her and try to lead her into better manners by our moderation and humanity. She comes here to the great school, and we are at once her teacher and her friend. An American lady is, therefore, a true missionary.

LETTER XLI.

"When shall I begin with the endless delights
Of this Eden of millinery, monkeys and sights,
This dear busy place where there's nothing transacting
But dressing and dinnering, dancing and acting?"
                                             TOM MOORE.

PARIS, May, 1878.

To the average American the theatres of Paris are the superior cynosure, and they are all so attractive and interesting I scarcely know at which to begin. The New Opera perhaps? Yes! there is surely much to be said of that transcendent edifice. Although I have been lingering in the vicinity a month, it is a constant study and delight. I am charmed by its elaborate grandeur, by its florid capitals, convolved ornaments, crowning Corinthian columns, its multudinous figures, protoplasts in bronze on the niches of the *façade*, its frozen *immortelles* of lyric and dramatic *savants*. There are adverse opinions of the merit of its architecture, many insisting that the prodigality of ornamentation is oppressive; but then it is a masterpiece of French magnificence, and every one gazes upon it with rapture.

The whole auditorium has 1790 places. The seats in the orchestra and *baignoires*—small boxes or tubs under the first loges, to which only men are admitted—sell for twelve and ten francs apiece. The first balcony of boxes is the property of the nobility and the part owners of the

Academie; then we, of the plebeian mass, are permitted a place in any of the other tiers or boxes by paying seven, ten, fifteen, or twenty-two francs each. Upon grand festas, when the kings and queens of the profession appear, seats are sold at a premium, and handsome sums are realized by their titled possessors.

The wealth expended upon the lobby, grand stairway, and *foyer* is fabulous. The stairway is a combination of all the marbles and agates of the chalcedonic plains of Europe and the East. Egyptian alabaster, verde antique, lapis lazuli, carnelian, and a hundred other species of onyx are grouped into stony radiance. From the vaulted dome angels, chubby cupids, muses, and gods look down upon the luxurious, lavish, sacrilegious throngs trampling the precious mosaics underfoot. I walked into one of the third-story balconies overhanging the *grand escalier*, to drink in the essence of royal wealth and sinful extravagance on every side. But the *salle de promenade* is the loadstar of the interior. It is a wildering aggregate of the glitter of gold and the brilliancy of frescoes, one prismatic lustre of glass and lights, a vast sheen of mirrors, the saliency of *repoussé*, glittering colonnades, and lofty ceiling, and here it is that the vast audience make a rendezvous during the *entre-acts*, a Vanity Fair unequalled in the universe.

Representations take place three times a week at the Grand Opera, Mondays, Wednesdays, and Fridays, and these performances are also unsurpassed by any in the world. The scholars from the Conservatoire de Musique constitute the choruses, and the ballet is composed of the famous dancers of Europe. In addition to the eleven millions paid out of the national treasury for this regal gewgaw, a subsidy is granted by the government of 800,000 francs annually, and during the empire it received 100,000 francs from its progenitor, Napoleon III. The Republicans are almost as generous to art and music as the kings.

We secured our places for "Les Huguenots," and though the repertoire was cast with excellence, and the music unsurpassed that ushers in that direful 24th of August, 1572, it seemed to me a little profane that so light and volatile a people should render a creation more in harmony with the mournful Italians or the ponderous Germans.

My greatest regret is that I was not in Paris before the lenten season, during the epoch of mad folly and riotous *insouciance*, when the *Nouvel Opéra* reaches the height of French brilliancy and drollery in the frantic *bals masqués* of the carnival. The present costly edifice is only in the fœtus of its saturnalian experience, but what instances of frolic and fun, intrigue and equivoque, sin and scandal, could be revealed by every stick and stone of the old Opéra on the Rue Lépelletier! These divertisements are always specially organized by the favorites of the principal theatres of Paris, and hugely enjoyed by all Paris. The advocates of pleasure mingle in the wild whirl, and officiate as vestals at the altars of Bacchus, while the more circumspect *connoisseur* gratifies his sated palate behind the shadow of the impenetrable foliage sheltering his palace in the Quartier St. Germain, and only rarely comes to the Bal de l'Opéra to enjoy the orgies of his less patrician contemporaries.

The Comédie Française, on the Rue Richelieu, in the Palais Royal, the scene of the triumphs of Duchenois, Mars, Rachel, Talma,—father and daughter,—Delaunay, Got, and Bernhardt, who is now portraying *Dona Sol* in Victor Hugo's *Hernani*, is really the outgrowth of the Hôtel Bourgoyne, purchased by the then only organized company in Paris, the Troupe Royal, three centuries ago. It was in this primitive play-house that the masterpieces of Racine, the sublime and pathetic delineator of womanly passion, and Corneille, who is called the father of French tragedy and the Gallic Euripides, were first represented and won the laurels of their authors. Three-quarters of a century subsequently Molière entered the litearte-dramatic arena, and Louis XIII was so much more delighted with his efforts as a theatrical zealot than royal *valet de chambre*, that he vouchsafed him a theatre in the Palais du Louvre, where, having attracted the attention of the ecclesiastical premier, Cardinal Richelieu, the aspiring dramatist was granted another stage of action in the regal-clerical Palais Royal.

Though Molière was preceded and succeeded by many famous men, yet he is the presiding genius of the Théâtre Français, and in the vicinity I daily pass the fountain and street dedicated to the dead poet, and the house where he breathed his last in sight of the court of his amaranthine glories.

We are told that the drama is retrograding, and that more attention is paid to the effect and mannerism than to exquisite finish and intensity of action. They tell us that the omnipotent Bernhardt does not wear gracefuly the mantle of her illustrious countrywoman, Rachel, although she nightly holds here audiences breathless by her weird grace, painful beauty, and anguished emotions in *Phedra*, the *Cid*, the *Sphynx*, and *Athalie;* they tell us that Got and Mounet-Sully are raw and lack polish in comparison with Delaunay and Coquelin; yet we read in history that Molière's dramatic enterprise was commenced by only three fiddles at the wings of the stage, and Corneille's *Le Cid* was produced with only "a room with four doors," and other plays with as ridiculous a dearth of appointments; some being equipped with only two daggers and others with three papers. We know that Molière had not reached the topmost round in the ladder of fame until Mars came to strengthen his inspired lines by her genius and power, and that neither she nor Rachel attained the apogee of renown by one unbroken line of progress. But Bernhardt dead, will wield a far more potential wand than Bernhardt alive, though even now not only Paris, but all the world have knelt at her shrine to offer her adoration and gold. When the sage philosopher Hugo returns from a rehearsal at the Française after Bernhardt has rendered a true ideal of his creation, he exclaims in a glow of French beatitude, "I have just kissed the hand of a queen."

The Théâtre Français has a seating capacity of 1405 places; those of the best location commanding thirteen francs. Single fauteuils in the first boxes may be procured for nine francs, and if you do not object to a sofa in the third gallery you may enjoy the vagaries of the inimitable Sara for the vulgar sum of four francs. This house appears to enjoy all the blessings vouchsafed to the profession. It not only has exclusive license to produce tragedy, but a claim on every scholar of the Conservatoire, which right it does not neglect to exercise, and is so enabled to secure every student with the promise of a fair future. Its annual subsidy from the Government is $48,000.

At the Opéra Comique in the Place Boieldieu, where Giraudet is singing *Peter* in *L'Etoile du Nord*, the prices of admission are somewhat more reasonable, though the cast of character is not so fine as I have seen at home.

The Varieties on the Boulevard Montmartre is the palace of vaudeville, where the fair and fat Judic indulges her antics to the delectation of her countless admirers, in the naughty character of *Niniche* or *La Comtesse de Corniska*.

She plays her dual rôle of prude and coquette as only a Frenchwoman "to the manner born" can. When we see her at Dauville, with the count, her husband, she is the quintessence of discretion and deliberation, even to the commendable fawn-colored silk gown and reputable brown hair *à la grécque;* but when she comes to Paris on a rampage, accompanied by one of her old associates, to whom she is known as *Niniche,* the stately, stilted toga of circumspection has evaporated, and we gaze upon her in all the ravishing and half-naked radiance of yellow hair, pale-blue silk, and arch little feet encased in satin slippers, and through the apartment and about its mistress there is an aroma of dash and dare sufficiently eloquent to need no interpretation. Madame Judic is a woman of at least thirty-eight, with the gift of appearing twenty or forty according to caprice. She has the sweet, playful, pathetic voice peculiar to the French; never great, ever gratifying. The Varieties has ever been the cradle of representations bordering on the limitation of decency; yet who does not patronize it? and simply because all who go indulge in a hearty, harmless laugh.

The Odéon, in the Place l'Odéon, the second Française and the favorite resort of the students, has 1500 places, that vary in price from ten to three francs, and is the home of legitimate drama. The "Danichefs," so well remembered in America, is now enjoying an unprecedented run there.

At the Porte St. Martin, on the Boulevard St. Martin, Victor Hugo's horrible and realistic *Les Misérables* is drawing vast multitudes. The audiences of this house have craved food of thrilling cruelty ever since the days when Mademoiselle Georges presented "Lucrece Borgia" to that public, and fed the home-life of the Palais Tuileries with the bones of contention and gossip.

The French are an exacting, laughter-loving clan, and at many of the playhouses three or four separate performances are given in one evening, all attractive and worthy of a distinct chronicle in my diary if I had room.

Despite the naturally impulsive incontinent French character, the audiences do not yield to the spirit of demonstration like the Americans and English. The applause is conducted upon a more systematic plan. The actors and playwrights do not hazard their reputations upon the capricious appetites of a promiscuous mass; they employ their *claqueurs* to lead and educate their houses, to anticipate the worthy points in the drama, to hint at the meritorious renditions of the author, and to temper the popular emotion to the strength of the sentiment. These *claqueurs* are a component element of the *corps dramatique*, and disciplined to their duties by their patronizing artists. The Bernhardt, Croizette, and Got pay them well, and drill them as acclaimers on to glory as they play. They are not allowed to permit the vulgar mass to interrupt *une grande passion* when Bernhardt is plunged into a whirlwind of agony; with their aid she holds the tension of every nerve in the tightest coil until the final lines, and then she is wafted to heaven with her hearers in a French craze of enthusiasm. Besides infusing the artist with the fire of success, this custom serves as a pioneer to the playgoer; it teaches him a virtuous pause, and makes him wait for the echo as his own watchword. The *claque* is the product of centuries. Years ago, when tragedies of intense emotion were to be enacted, females of the same profession were employed to do the crying and fainting; of course I looked for these feminine automata, and failing in my search am lead to believe that that branch of hired Niobes has passed away.

Everywhere we have the female ushers, as in London. At the Grand Opera they seem to be all over forty-eight, many approaching seventy, looking like an antiquated brigade in uniform—a black gown, white apron, white cap, and an amplitude of flaunting pink ribbon. I am told that all these excessively conservative-looking old ladies have agitating romances attached to their earlier lives; many of them have gladdened the heart of a student in their *grisette* days. The heyday of their youth has long melted into gray and grim November, and they have billeted themselves upon the dramatic organizations for the remainder of their days. They are the veterans of the naughty past.

The inevitable footstool that they carry about and insist upon shoving under every pair of female shoes seems to constitute their utmost duty. It was only after I learned that an acceptance of this article meant a fee, that I realized the secret income of this faded fraternity.

It would seem that all these official or licensed amusements would surfeit the French, but nearly every alternate house in Paris is a factory of pleasure. Perhaps in so saying I have unwittingly overstepped the margin; but certainly I shall be safer in the hint that the business of enjoyment is here the chief object of many lives. Religion is a mere source of idle leisure, in a word, a luxury. While many French take the cream from the surface of pleasure themselves, all through this magic city there are thousands toiling to make life entrancing to others, by catering to human appetites and vices. They constantly prove the Shakespearian maxim "All the world's a stage," for they are an artificial show-people, ever in attitudes, and masks, and poses, and colors, and music, and trinkets. They seem to have been born to the travestie, and never reach the *finale* until Death comes, and with his icy hand stills their vagaries. Even then, in the Morgue or Père La Chaise, the corpse is made a joke or a jollity, the funeral an excuse for a fanfaronade, and the tomb a pretext for a playful or grotesque memory.

LETTER XLII.

"Now is there then no earthly place
  Where we can rest in dream Elysian,
Without some curved, round English face
  Popping up near to break the vision?
Who knows, if to the West we roam,
But we may find some blue at home
  Among the blacks of Carolina;
Or flying to the eastward sea,
Some Mrs. Hopkins taking tea
  And toast upon the wall of China."
                                ANONYMOUS.

PARIS, May, 1878.

I CONFESS I do not like to leave Paris, and I say it with a faint heart and write it with a faltering hand. Fain would I linger at the banquet. "Time cannot wither nor custom stale her infinite variety."

There is so much that is weird and old, fresh and startling, in the habits and customs of these people, that each distinguishing characteristic demands and deserves record. And still I do not doubt that the French would be equally amused by what they call our equivalent follies.

We are a domestic nation; they are a community of players. It is the first and chiefest aspiration of Americans, and especially of Philadelphians, to possess a comfortable —a luxurious—home; the family circle is the sanctuary of bliss with us, and all endeavors look eagerly to that goal. The Frenchman's home is the Tuileries, the Champs Élysées, the Parc Monceaux, the *places*, the café, or his little iron chair and table on the sidewalk. We embellish the interior of our houses, because we are more there, and derive greater happiness from that altar of the affections; they decorate the street, the church, the bench of the boulevard, the fountain and the shrine. Every industrious man and woman amongst us must aspire to a flower-garden, bronzes, and fine furniture in the house, because this is where they come when the toil of the day is over, and all that is beautiful must be congregated into this haven of rest. The French enjoy their parterres, and fountains, and monuments in the squares and at the corners of the boulevards; art, sculpture, and regal appointments in the Louvre, the palaces, and the museums. There are one hundred and eighty or one hundred and twenty-eight fountains in the city of Paris,—I have really forgotten which,—and these are invariably accompanied by flowering trees, historic memorials, and comfortable seats. All classes throng these open places and gardens, regardless of station. There, in the garden of the Luxembourg, where once lingered Madame Roland by the side of the Girondists, in the days of cabal and conspiracy, is one of the musty professors from the Collége de France, École de Médecine, Palais des Beaux-Arts, Musée d'Histoire Naturelle, Amphitheatre d'Anatomie, or one of the many other magazines of lore with which this quarter is teeming, he is now shifted "the lean and slippered pantaloon," and though there is much in the busy life around him, he is absorbed in his little book, and does not heed and appears not to see, the pretty, liquid-eyed girls selling violets, the boys with their hoops, and tops, and skipping-ropes,—for childhood is childhood, in romantic, picturesque Paris, and indulges in the same sports as in artless Philadelphia,—nor truant scholars, and roisterers, linked arm-in-arm, airing their idle thoughts. He goes on reading his book and preparing his recitations.

But to the gardens! Later in the day come the nurses and their charges; the lofty dames from their Legitimistic homes, and the queens of the ambiguous circles, who appear in order to fulfil their appointments. Here they mingle, and are permitted to follow the bent of their own impulses so long as they are decorous. With us it is not so; broad public acres and city squares, if not left to questionable classes, are not sought by the better orders, and even a visit to Fairmount Park should be properly made in a carriage. The one dismal feature of the numerous Paris pleasances is the dearth of sward. Other elements conspire to make them beautiful; the gleam of statuary, the refreshing spray, the harmonious fall of fountains, and the luxuriance of foliage. But the French seem to regard grass-plots with antipathy, and prefer vast stretches of arid gravel.

The restaurants and cafés are as interesting as the squares, and the life in them as varied. On the Rive Gauche the *bouillis* are an organized system, and their patrons are the students, professors, and merchants doing business in the *quartier*. I believe they are considered the most remunerative class of restaurants; their prices are moderate, but their ceaseless support is a sure profit. The food is savory, be it only boiled meat or broth. The French are the cooks *par excellence* of the world, and deserve the palm. I would never swear to what I was eating at a Parisian table. It is charmingly palatable, but there are none of the original characteristics of fish, flesh, or fowl left after the process of a French *cuisine*. Many and curious are the anecdotes of *chefs* of the culinary kingdom. We read in history of a certain cook who hanged himself because one of the courses was not done at the proper hour for the royal board. After the fall of Napoleon, Monsieur Véry attended the allied monarchs at three thousand francs a day, and Louis Philippe's "Purveyor of Fish" received twenty-six thousand dollars per annum.

If one wishes to dine with the uppertendom, one must needs repair to Voisin's, Riche, Anglais, Maison Dorée, or one of the epicurean palaces in the Palais Royal; Véry's, Véfour's, Trois Frères Provenceau. At each is a cosmopolitan throng, their respective nationalities distinguished at a glance. The slim, slippery old gentleman opposite, who is eating his dainties in selfish solitude, and sipping his champagne, pouring only enough into his glass at once for a single swallow, is an Englishman, and if I mistake not, he is also a scholar. Near him is a group of his country people, ladies and gentlemen, of the predominent type; large, stalwart, sandy-haired men, "in fair, round belly with good capon lined," and robust women arrayed in uncomplementary colors. There is nothing ephemeral about these ladies. At times they speak French, and at others English, all in a sweet voice, like the tones of a muffled silver bell, and although they are of the upper class their aphæresis and prosthesis with *h* are distinctly audible. Those two raw, crude boys, just of age, accompanied by their male *chaperon* of forty, are my Western brethren; if any one should make inquiries regarding them I would be wicked enough to deny their nativity. The eldest is arduously endeavoring to diffuse his whole body over the table, while the youths are importuning the *garçon* in very boisterous fashion for roast chicken or lamb and plenty of it, and not these *vol-au-vents* and *champignons*, and delicate tidbits. Near by there is an exquisite young lady and her distinguished father. He is a Boston barrister, and these I am proud to claim as my compatriots. Her cultivation may be heard in her pure English accent, and her refined fostering in the harmony of her rich costume and polished manner. When she addresses the waiter it is in his own tongue, with nice emphasis, that emulates his own; while chatting with her father there is a naive unconsciousness of self that is charming. The two young ladies with their dashing cavaliers over in the corner are descendants of Charlemagne, of course. Who would doubt it? To me there is something far more alluring about a Frenchwoman than my American or English sisters. They are a combination of grace and wit, that in other females would seem disreputable daring *insouciance*. They are enjoying all the daintiest morsels of the *ménu*, and demolishing copious draughts of *Château Larose*.

In most of the French restaurants of the better order, and at the theatre-lobby bars, attractive girls are in attendance at the desks; hardened and polished by the steel and ice of flirtation, as beautiful as they are reckless, as dazzling as they are desperate.

The Palais Royal, with its variety of expensive shops and palatial restaurants, is still a hot-bed of faro, though the very wealthy classes frequent the gambling clubs on the boulevards. Most of the cafés have their gambling *salons*, and it is a rare thing to pass in even the choicest of these restaurants, without the flash gentleman at the door interrogating "*une cabinet particulier?*" There is no attempt to screen these vices. They are spread before the public in all their attractions. Gambling is legalized throughout the Continent, and encouraged by the Republic, while the favorite pastime of the plebeians is attending lotteries, where millions are lost and only thousands won.

These people have a way of giving proper names to their leading shops as we do to hôtels, and many of them are supremely ridiculous. The "Bon Marché" is a reasonable appellation for the establishment it dignifies, as all the goods are moderate in price, and upon entering the shop one is incontinently enveloped in the essence of cheapness.

It is the first and last resort of Americans. "Old England" is a shop of homespun woollens and serges on the Boulevarde des Italiens. Its name is compatible with its stock and attendants. It is chiefly valuable to English ladies going over to the Continent, as they may here secure a linen duster, an ugly plaid ulster, made of convict's material, and Turkish towelling, and green barege veiling to tie round their hats. Then the "Carnival of Venice," in which I can discover nothing consistent. The "Good Devil," ah! this to my woman's wit reveals its significance —there will be the devil of a row when the bill comes home. The "Infant Jesus" baffles my powers of discernment, unless through this omnipotent medium all blessings may be obtained. "The Great House of Peace," yes, here are unctions that physic all pains. But for me, "Les grandes Magasins du Louvre!" Here not only all that adorns a woman, but all that beautifies her home is procurable, in the choicest and most ravishing designs.

What a contrast the Paris streets form to-day with their deplorable condition forty years ago! Then when the ladies went on the promenade they were obliged to escape dead cats and putrescent matter of divers species; in many of the smaller byways the garbage floated in the middle of the street. Now they are swept and scoured into ultra-cleanliness. Walk where you will, the same universal purity is pre-eminent, even to the confines of the town at the Porte Maillot, where the *octroi* is collected from the vegetable and fruit vendors, bringing the produce of their little gardens beyond the bastions of the city, to find purchasers within.

When one arrives in this dazzling metropolis, there is a supreme superficial glitter, that one believes may very soon be exhausted; but as we linger new and more profound attractions burst upon us. When we are sated by the parks and palaces, the operas and art galleries, the monuments and the museums, the flowers and fountains; then the great public works of education, charity, and civic government engage us even after these social attractions are powerless. They have hospitals for the treatment of cutaneous diseases exclusively, as the Saint Louis, and the Hôtel Dieu where all afflicted by contagious eruptions are denied admittance; Hôpital du Midi, unexceptionally for males and their *malades impropre;* the Hôpital de Lourcine is the female branch of this peculiar charity; almshouses innumerable for the old and the young, the halt and the blind, and a visit to the Hospice pour les infants través, in the Rue d'Enfer, creates a regret in one's heart for legitimate *gamins* who have no good nun to care for them, and are perhaps starving for bread and rolicking in defilement, while these little *inconnus* are nurtured with tenderness, and stimulated by purity.

LETTER XLIII.

"When, from the sacred garden driven,
    Man fled before his Maker's wrath,
An angel left her place in Heaven,
    And cross'd the wanderer's sunless path.
'Twas Art! sweet Art! new radiance broke
    Where her light foot flew o'er the ground,
And thus with seraph voice she spoke:
    'The curse a blessing shall be found.'"
                                        CHARLES SPRAGUE.

PARIS, May, 1878.

I HAVE visited the palaces clustered on the Champs de Mars, within shadow of the exquisite suburbs,—Passy and Lamuers,—and the Moresque Trocadéro, crowning the historical heights of Chaillot, again and again in the hope of seeing them in a state of completion, and I have half-fearfully sought in their equipments splendor surpassing our display of 1876. Surely I have not found it upon the open territory surrounding the buildings. While the esplanade is broad, and the grassy knolls and gay parterres bordering the main exposition hall are models of harmony and grace, they have no fitting expanse. While the structures are spacious, there is a general appearance of crampedness prevailing throughout, and this feature is attributable to the absence of the vistas in which our glorious Centennial was so fortunate.

In the main hall there are no series of long lines of perspective stretching from end to end, such as gave our building its magnificent expression of distance. But I believe the manner of dissecting streets and spaces by rigid plumb line is pre-eminently Philadelphian, and our adherence to it has won for us the stigma of *conventionalists*. However, the jutting arms of sections, and the abrupt blockading of avenues in the French exhibition, have stripped the *coup d'œil* of all the magnitude of area and symmetry of contour that we had so completely.

Lengthy passages drawn out in seemingly endless extension, serving as a telescope by which to anticipate distant glories, are as a rule more appetizing than a dazzling constellation suddenly thrust upon you after being obscured by a cloud of obstructions. We are more deeply impressed by a grandiose display of pyrotechnics, or a luminous meteor that radiates the firmament from zenith to horizon with empyrean effulgence, than by a series of Roman-candle explosions or a succession of *ignes fatui*. So in the interior construction of the French exhibition the *tout ensemble* of the display is much depreciated, at least to my eyes.

The British department exhibits more geometry in the division of its aisles and the distribution of its cases than any of the other sections, and here I have experienced more real pleasure than even in our American section. Not only have the English been most vigilant in the rectilinear system of the arrangement, but the cases are all so built as to add to the value of their contents.

The buildings themselves are more ornate and artistic than ours of 1876. The prodigality of gay Gallic colors and decorations is very effective. But the whole exposition is as pallid in contrast with the Centennial as the sweet light of the moon—outdazzled by the lusty exuberance of the noonday sun.

In passing from gallery to gallery the rude, brilliant frescoes adorning the *façades* impart to the scene an Oriental glow. Once upon the avenue intersecting the main hall with its bulwark of national architecture, and its many detachments for the reception of *beaux-arts*, the eye is gratified by an infinity of bizarre and entrancing effects. Perhaps it is the rare combination of *sui generis* edifices, domed and shady palisades draped by antique tapestry, or crimson and golden Moorish arras intervening and throwing into bolder relief the opposite method of national erection; or perhaps the many curious foreign representatives, in their variegated costumes and the Babel of mixed vernaculars, that produce these effects; but they are very novel.

Passing between the art gallery and these types of universal national symbols, where the minarets and cupolas of the Mahometan, the lacy fretwork of the Swiss *chalet*, the dismal, austere model of early English, the ease and elegance of modern French and Italian, and the flaunting, yet practical, red brick of American architecture, are blended into one panorama of harmonious variety, we came upon the Prince of Wales's pavilion. Possessing a testimonial of admittance from Governor McCormick, the door was opened instantly, and the favor denied to many was granted unto us. The Prince and his royal spouse were not at home, so the attendant said, but were expected during the afternoon, to remain overnight in their miniature palace on the Champs de Mars, so we were allowed to roam over the apartments at will. Through a broad, tessellated corridor, flanked by small antechambers, we directly entered the dining-hall, where the table was already laid for its princely guests, though the day was young. A long table it was, with places laid for twelve. Though the linen was the heaviest and softest, and shone with the lustre of satin, there were no embroidery nor crestings. Though the glassware was the purest and most sparkling crystal, the brilliancy was unmarred by intricate wreaths of engraving. They were undefiled by the stylus of the artisan, with the exception of a modest armorial device, encircled by a delicate garland of immortelles. An embossed gold flower-urn and corresponding candelabras furnished the centre, while about the sides and corners of the table a golden dinner-service, elaborately wrought in curious designs of *repoussé* and frosted-workmanship, was spread, ready to receive the viands of the sybaritic feast. The four walls were hung with tapestries made at the Queen's castle in the little town of Windsor, and the representations from the scenes in Shakespeare's "Merry Wives." These are the present theme of fashionable criticism in society and the papers. From the ponderous and pompous upholstering and gold plate of the *salle à manger* to the fairy brilliancy of the Princess's boudoir was, indeed, a transformation scene in a holiday pantomime. All that the adjacent chamber contained of the oppressive sumptuousness this one had in the delicate splendor of blue and gilt appointments. In a side alcove there was built an artificial grotto, where the waters of a fountain fall in melodious tinkle upon the exotics, whose bronze foliage acted as a foil to the stony scintillations of gods and goddesses it struggled to hide, and contrasted vividly with the confused tones—brickdust and saffron—of the majolica vases. Farther on we came to dressing-rooms and business bureaus, all characterized by a lavish expenditure in English and French luxuries. The extravagance of princes was forcibly portrayed in the marquétrie mantels and doors, fashioned in the rarest designs from the woods of India—costly additions, that may be useless in a few months, when the pavilion is razed.

Continuing down this avenue we emerge into the broad esplanade of the main hall which strikes me as being much handsomer than our hall in Fairmount Park. The building of itself is a mere shell, but so richly is it colored and columned, so radiant with stained glass windows, so to speak, forming the upper two-thirds of the *façade*, that I felt its influence long afterwards. I hear it nevertheless denounced as *tawdry*, with its crude and showy colossal statues resting against ostentatious pillars far above whose heads float their banners and pennons; but I did not agree with the verdict. A sloping sward closely shaven, planted with flowering plots and freshened by fountains, gravitates to a microcosm of restaurants, kiosks, and foreign bureaus. Through the entrance of the *Quai d'Orsay*, guarded by its gigantic bronzes, you rest upon the *Pont de Jena* to watch the little steamers puffing to and fro on the placid Seine, some conveying a freight of visitors to the Exhibition Palaces, and others moored to the stone wharves, depositing their stores of stone and wood, to complete the temples of art, science, and industry. Many aquatic sportsmen in otiose mood are pulling themselves in little canoes over the still and silent stream, while other riotous parties of bacchantes are filling the air with shout and jest. Upon the bridge are the votaries of fashion and frolic, who have come to see and be seen; the artist with palette and brush, and the architect inspecting with critical eye every curve and capital, base and bend, that make up the colonnades of the Trocadéro; the correspondent who is interviewing the integral parts of the picture *en masse* and jotting down airy nothing from which he will weave several columns of the most substantial material; the fair round churchman with missal and rosary, adding savor, as it were, to this human *olla podrida*.

To view the Trocadéro from the base of the mound is scarcely satisfactory. In this position an accurate prospect of the whole may be obtained, but to enjoy and study the building proper, one must linger about the *parc*, take a seat at one of the little café tables so numerous in the grounds, and while lunching, dwell upon this vast loadstar enthroned upon the verdured summit which a century ago was destined as the site of the regal home of the future

King of Rome. Mark well its many attractive points. It is a vast semicircular edifice; a huge rotunda forming the centre, flanked by square wings with lofty towers, and projecting from these wings, extending from the northeast to the southwest, are sky-lighted galleries modelled after the peristyles of Campanian towns. This canopied and colonnaded promenade stretches from one extremity to the other of the palace with the Spanish name, encompassing the music hall, and connecting at each of the open vestibules of the wings, and reached by spacious stone stairways, or, as a correspondent calls them, stoops from the several footpaths. There is no sterility of decoration, as flags float in an endless array of colors along the margins of the roofs, and statues perfect each pilaster of the superb colonnade. Issuing from the centre of this building, and as if rushing from the columns, is a cascade of foaming water, that takes one plunge to the ground level, and then over a series of gravitating steps until it drifts into the great circular basin; through this volume of crested foam *jets d'eaux* eject their spray aloft, and fountains at opposite angles cast their waters to each other in playful motion. The beds of tulips and early spring flowers are more beautiful by their slight inclination toward the horizon, nestling upon the gentle acclivity, and the four great brazen beasts —the horse, the bull, the elephant, and rhinoceros—at the corners of the basin, though magnificent works of art, seem sadly inharmonious. However, they contribute toward a construction that is most fantastic and unconventional, from the Alpha to the Omega.

The Chaillot Heights, like many of the Parisian suburbs were discovered to be thoroughly alveolated by ancient quarries, rendering it absolutely necessary to form a new and solid foundation for the Palais du Trocadéro, but from this circular condition of the hillside, the curious freshwater aquarium sprang. These aquaria are formed by the natural old quarry cavities, and though presenting the appearance of a succession of small ponds upon the grounds, the water descends gently through the ichthyological retreats.

When the interior of the Trocadéro is quite completed, the long wings will be the depository of art, while the rotunda will be the hall of festas and ceremonials. When I first looked upon the disordered mass, I scarcely hoped to see it in its present glorious state, but the French seem to economize time and weather; they level streets in a night and compass impossibilities in a day. It is a modern version of Aladdin's lamp and the Prince's palace. And it is ever the one story, either in work or in war; they overrun kingdoms and establish republics as rapidly as they forget their beloved dead and forgive the tyrannical living.

To-day the Exposition is a flower and poem, and though I recall the emotions incited by the Centennial in these Paris parterres and palaces spread over the Champs de Mars and hills of Passy, never again can I thrill with the feelings that made me at once so proud and so happy at the celebration of my country's enfranchisement.

LETTER XLIV.

"Turn to the world—its curious dwellers view,
 Like Paul's Athenians, seeking something new.
 Be it a bonfire's or a city's blaze,
 The gibbet's victim, or the nation's gaze,
 A female atheist, or a learned dog,
 A monstrous pumpkin, or a mammoth hog,
 A murder, or a muster, 'tis the same,
 Life's follies, glories, griefs, all feed the flame."
 CHARLES SPRAGUE.

PARIS, May, 1878.

To chronicle the Exhibition Universelle in detail would be the wildest sort of enterprise; still I must record some contrasts and comparisons that made the most impression on me before I say good-bye.

But how to begin and where? At the American section, that is closest my heart, or at the English, French, or Italian, that please my eye? From the chief exhibition entrance, the sea of glory opens with the Indian presents of the Prince of Wales. They glitter under the rich canopy of Oriental design and coloring, called the "India House." To enumerate the jewelled swords, snuff-boxes, medals, royal decorations, shawls, and laces, duplicated again and again, would craze a mathematician. The deeper philosophy taught by all this superabundance of useless gifts is the obeisance equally of the commoners and the nobility to the crown. All day throngs cluster about these India cases, to count over and memorize the honors bestowed upon the Prince, so that they may tell them to others. I join the ocean of humanity, but only to admire and study these sinfully costly gewgaws, just as I linger at the ceramic display of the Minton and Doulton clays, the Copeland and Worcester Parian, the Chelsea porcelain, and the Wedgwood Jasper. Royalty has its uses in the encouragement of genius, and the distribution of the antique models; but it is painful to see how many millions are given to feed the overfed kings of the world, and to decorate those who are already overweighted with their chains of gold. I believe it is generally conceded that the present exhibition of the products of the British potteries outdazzles their specimens at the Centennial display in 1876. It seems only reasonable that it should, in consideration of the difficulties of the voyage, but it does not strike me so. Perhaps I am a patriotic bigot who sees all copies of our national display only to their disparagement, but I never can repeat the first joy of our own universal American banquet. This is the national excuse for depreciation; if so, it is the familiar simile of the little child with the gingerbread horse, the sense of first pleasure lasts through the after years. I still taste that early gingercake. There is nothing to take the place of the Centennial.

Bronzes, tapestries, statuary, and pictures are sources of endless enjoyment at a great fair. Among the most bizarre gems of the English pottery department were the Greek vases in imitation of red granite, from the factories of Wedgwood & Sons, at Etruria, Stoke-on-Trent, Staffordshire. I bent long over a choice collection of clocks, time-pieces, etc., adorned with original plaques of faience, from James Howell, Regent Street, London. Fascinating as many of the modern services are, the most persistent efforts seem to be lavished upon certain panels. These are entrancing beyond description. Many sacred subjects, representations from the early Greek and Roman epics, and themes of feudal troubadours, are faithful, with a delicacy of pigment and exactness of outline that are the perfection of ceramic art. "The Infant Saviour in the arms of Simeon," "Gethsemane," "The Walk from Emmaus," "The Resurrection," "Elaine," and many other equally familiar objects, are treated with almost articulate pathos.

Staffordshire is, so to speak, a priceless mine of clay fields, as one soon learns by walking through the Paris Exposition. It is almost visiting the district of the "Potteries," which extends along the course of the Trent, where the only occupation of the population is the manufacture of this precious earthenware, and though Burslem sends many fine productions, Stoke-upon-Trent, a town of lesser inhabitants, and two hundred factories, transmits the lion's share. Have we not in our country the same earths, and the same skill to mix, mould, and poetize them?

I noticed a case of exquisite ladies' shoes, bearing a close similitude to the same with which our English friends favored the Centennial; surely no French *cordonnier* ever infused greater finish and delicacy into his inspiration, yet the English are the illest-shod females on the two hemispheres. They invent exquisite shoes, but have few feet among their own people to fit them.

The cutlery of Sheffield and Birmingham can no longer claim a place alone, no more can the Manchester prints, since our Yankee steel and cotton are sold upon English counters; another disenchantment began at the Centennial and repeated in Paris. It is upon this platform that the United States stands pre-eminent. I find here other facts for thought. Our agricultural and steam-propelling machines, our pianos, and sewing machines, are everywhere unsurpassed, and let it be said our exhibits of this kind were not only creditable to our inventors, but to our taste in the useful arts. This last feature is also noticeable in our surgical and dental instruments, our carriages, and the exquisite gold and silverware of Tiffany. But, where was the great "Corliss" that impelled our country's industrial and mechanical representatives? How I missed the colossus. It would have made the Frenchmen stare, and compensated for other deficiences.

The Japanese and Chinese departments are interesting, as these almond-eyed people ever are in all their enterprises. But there is a sweet familiarity about all that I see. The carved ivory beds and painted silk canopies are just as wonderful if not quite as fresh as when I saw them in Philadelphia. Still even those Americans who are so indignant because we are not strong enough in the American department in Paris, and scold Congress for not giving Governor McCormick half a million to make a respectable show in this great world's carnival and jewel-house,—even these take comfort because the Japanese showed their most lovely productions first to the world through our spectacles in Fairmount Park. The Centennial is a great comforter, I assure you, away over here.

The crown jewels of Great Britain have been conveyed

hither from the Tower, and here is a splendid treat for the French masses that we were unable to offer in Philadelphia. After that, very naturally, I strayed into the jewel department of the French section, and found this part of the pageant sparkling with diamonds and gold far beyond conception. I wish I had the ability to paint this dazzling scene. It is so, indeed, that a great gem is never lost! It may be stolen, but all the thieves feel a special property in its preservation. It cannot be imitated, and so carries its own protection in its scarcity. A great jewel is like the special discovery of an island, once found all are solicitous to keep it, and a continent cannot be counterfeited. The Russian jewel department, though perhaps not finer than in 1876, is more extensive. It embraces a wider sphere of female decorations, and the Russian manner of giving tone and color to gold is wholly unique. A medallion has upon its upper face the protoplast of a pear and the leaves; the fruit is a *fac simile* pearl of a delicate pink and yellow shade; the leaves are of the metal, presented in frostwork, combining the green, yellow, russet, and brown of autumnal tints. Ear-drops, symbolical of fuchsias, of this same colored gold, having the petals tipped sometimes with coral and sometimes with pearls; ornaments figurative of the rose, shaded from pale-saffron to pink, are only the more simple of these elegant designs. The Muscovite is master in his own school of art, and is strong in his silver and malachite conceits, even beyond the French.

In the French annex of ladies' costumes we find the grandest achievements of Worth's and Pingat's skill. Here are dresses that would create an insurrection if carried into a Philadelphia saloon. I will not attempt to sketch these fantastic anatomies. But then their vagaries were produced to glorify the inventor's name, and though they are the excessive poetry of female attire, it is doubtful if they will remunerate the contriver.

An English lady of considerable cultivation insists that the display of statuary falls in point of merit far beneath our collection in 1876, and not only so, but declares that after visiting all the important galleries of Europe she found none so rich *en masse* as that gathered into our art aggregation in Fairmount Park. I listened but was not convinced, and so took her compliment in silent surprise. To compare our Exhibition, even with all that was loaned from abroad, to the depositories of ancient art, is scarcely just. One is the schoolroom of present study, the other the temple of bygone splendor. We do not look for a Phidias, a Praxiteles, a Milo, or Marble Faun. These are the uncontested and often unknown masters. I see much that pleases me, not so much it is true as I saw at home, but then I look through my patriotic glasses, and I cannot forget original tastes, as I said.

The French disciples of the brush are all here, in the Beaux Arts, in holiday regalia; Jules Breton, in his realistic pencillings of peasant life; Diaz in forest scenes, where the mellow yet brilliant blending of tones is his chief merit; Bouguereau in saintly portrayals; and Messonier in his characteristic little gems. I hear that quite a number of Corots are yet to be hung, but there is some discussion about giving them a place, and I shall have bidden adieu to sweet Paris before the issue can be settled. Many of our old Centennial pictures smile on me a homelike welcome, and among these Frith's Railroad Station and Queen Victoria's Marriage.

In my saunterings, this thought comes: Human intellect is undoubtedly more worshipped and has better chances in France than in England; and there is no more patent display of this fact than in this French Exposition. In Great Britain there is still a large royal family, with only their azure blood to consecrate their titles, and there a higher court must be paid to those whose crowns are worn on their heads than to those whose great thoughts are the gold and jewels hidden in the casket of the brain. The mere snob gives his homage to the sovereign invented by law, but is quite as likely to sneer at the French monarchs of the mind, Louis Blanc, Victor Hugo, Emile de Girardin, and Laboulaye; he never heard or cared to hear of the dead kings of literature and art, Chateaubriand, Scarron, Guizot, Thiers, Voltaire, Molière, Racine, and Sismondi; but this noble show is suggestive of them all, the dead and the living. The face of the Prince of Wales has very much the appearance of a jolly country squire, with his bold forehead and Hanoverian cast of countenance. The old King of Spain looks like a faded *roué*. The Princess of Wales has a plain, refined face, but void of beauty, and a hundred others of these people may be classed in the same category. But there is a presence about Gambetta, with his one eye, that gives him the look of a fierce Cyclops; Girardin seems a polished courtier of seventy, in whose face reason holds the highest throne; Edmund About, a bronze giant; Laboulaye, the statesman and the philosopher; and Victor Hugo, an inspired Dervish. I do not know anybody in the Royal House of England that ever showed any special brains; none of the Princes or Princesses; while over here in France the Orleans and Bourbon pretenders are some of them very able men. Most of the great writers, artists, painters, and sculptors, are Republicans, and have been for years, long before the fall of the last Empire. Most of the philosophers and scientists are on the same side. Of course there are plenty of other men against the Republic, and for reaction; but I look in vain for a man on the Republican side in England who has any special status as a great poet, painter, sculptor, speaker, or essayist. The best Republican in that great country is a woman, and her name is George Eliot.

LETTER XLV.

> "In orange-groves and myrtle bowers,
>   That breathe a gale of fragrance round,
> I charm the fairy-footed hours
>   With my loved lute's romantic sound;
> Or crowns of living laurel weave
> For those that run the race at eve."
>
> ROGERS.

LYONS, May, 1878.

NEVER was Paris more glorious than when I passed through its shining boulevards and open squares toward the Embarcadere de Lyon yesterday. The spires and domes of the marvellous city were sparkling in the sunlight, the flowers blooming at the corners, and the Tricolor of France and the Stars and Stripes of her sister republic, America, blending and floating in the breeze. Perhaps it was this sweet fraternity, and perhaps my own affection for home, that caused the ineffable sadness at my heart as I rode away. There has been an essence of home about this place ever since I came into it one shining Sabbath four weeks ago. Peradventure, you may say, I loved it because it is gay and dazzling, because I caught all the smiles and none of the sighs, because I had seen only the beautiful and none of the bestial, because I was thoughtful only of the charms and thoughtless of the crosses; or, it may be, you will say that I revelled in the wild enchantment, and had no conception of its sins and its sorrows. But eager as I am for fresh territories, the regret at leaving this sweet foreign habitation, as I had grown to regard it, was quite sincere.

As I passed the *cabarets*, hotels, and shops I met occasionally Italian, English, and even German flags, but French and American constantly. We were passing through the *Pays Latin*, where liberty is dearly cherished, and these twin republican symbols were far more frequent than on the opposite border of the Seine amongst the representatives of the ancient *régime*.

Numbers of students were clustered about the libraries that flank the Seine in this portion of the city, where books by famous authors, of whom I never heard, may be purchased from two sous to a Louis d'or.

As we drew near the dépôt, upon the confines of Bercy, we found the streets straggling, and the workmen in their blouses; now and then one in *sabots* would clatter over the stones, a fruit-seller or flower-girl in blue petticoat and white *coiffe*, and arms as bare and as brown as polished porphyry, crossed the white streets that increase in dazzling lustre, with their little stores upon their heads from their homes about Charenton beyond the bastions; great logs and rafts were drifting in the silent flow of the river, or heaped upon the stone quays. Everywhere there was content and thrift, but none of the glitter and crush of the city. We had already crossed the threshold of the Palace of Enchantment.

We took tickets for Lyons, a ride of nine and a quarter hours through the Burgundy vineyards of France. It seemed like a long ride, but I knew it would not prove tedious, lying through this golden district, that presented a new and entrancing picture at each step; but I was not prepared for the burst of glory that greeted me upon leaving Paris, and did not desert me until night came and hid it from my ardent gaze

We rapidly penetrated into the richest sections of France, though not the most picturesque; for it had none of the wild romance of rugged mountains, sharp defiles, dark gorges, and foaming waters; but all the calm, domestic beauty of rich farmlands, cultivated hillsides, and happy homes. I met with no starvation and squalor; all was peaceful and flourishing, and all were at work; no one despised or scorned labor, and therefore all were prosperous.

This absence of the woes of intemperance is the prevailing characteristic of the Valley of the Marne, that stretches far away to the left, in one unbroken plain of fertility. After crossing the waters from which this luxuriant region derives its name, near their confluence with the Seine, guarded on the west by Fort Ivry, and the east by Charenton, our companionship with it ceased, and through Seine et Marne, along the green slopes of the Yéres, a territory of verdure-clad hills, we saw here and there an artistic dwelling set down in a dale of flowers, and the smoke from thriving mills curling over the landscape.

Entering the forest of Fontainebleau the trees seem as if they had been uprooted and replaced in long straight lines by a surveyor. The vegetable gardens are rich in produce for the great city. We have already passed many white-stone quarries, the wealth of which is so extensively utilized in the noble edifices we have left behind us—perhaps forever. I had believed the glistening Paris houses to be composite, and a portion of the city certainly is, but here before me and around me are vast blocks of creamy stone, newly cut from chalky beds beyond. These deposits lie close along the railway, and laborers are busy digging and hewing the material for builders.

And now there are vines everywhere; they are drawn out far ahead as a wayside border of our route. The grapes are grown upon the terraced hillsides, and trained to little sticks not more than two feet high, and women are to be seen everywhere upon the blooming acclivities tending their crops for the approaching vintage. Where are the men? I involuntarily ask; the women are doing all the drudgery. One fertile valley succeeds another, and another, and another, until I am prone to believe there is not an acre of *Yonne* and the *Côté d'or* which is not devoted to the grape and the olive. Behind the hillocks are plateaux of sward and neat little cottages; tall poplars shorn of foliage, until the effect is that of a forest of flagstaffs or telegraph poles, one of the principal features of the French landscape. Hamlets as white as a seagull's wing are couched against gentle inclinations, and feudal chateaux and abbeys crown the summits, where many a revel, and many a secret, and many an exile were hidden in the long ago, when convent was only a euphuism for carousal, and chateau for confinement. The turrets and the spires gleam still and solemn against the intensely blue sky, the land is as full of mediæval history as of present prosperity; perhaps when it rang with wilder revelry, more triumphant victories, and the glory of greater names, it felt the lash of a more tyrannical rule.

As we neared Dijon our line lay through a series of tunnels, cuttings, and viaducts, and as we emerged the dusky gray of the olive was seen in more frequent patches of light, to which the vine-clad hills served as a background. Here and there in vales to our right we saw the golden glisten of orange groves between the glossy foliage; and I realized that I was in a strange country. Ruins, pointing out the spots where time has placed his despoiling finger, were crumbling around where feudal sovereigns dwelt and died. Ah! yes, the Côté d'or is very beautiful and luscious in its green and purple robes, and delights the eye as much as it gratifies the palate.

The peasants were clustered in little groups at the stations, and in the white roads sparkling with silica they looked like moving bouquets of ruddy autumn dahlias. Their costumes were modelled after the picturesque Swiss type, doubtless the dress of their alpine neighbors. These fair maids of France do not fulfil the *fair* conception we had formed of them from romances and traveller's tales. They are almost unexceptionably dwarfed and ungraceful; but a better educational system seems now to prevail in these districts of France. The daughters of the vintage-owners assist in the cultivation of the vine, and no part of mental discipline is neglected to render them proficient. Those we met were merry; not intoxicated by the juice of the grapes, but drunk with the delight of their new liberty.

We were very near to Haute-Saône, and the magnificent forests, with their caverns of coal and iron, branching off from the Vosges, close in the valley like great walls of pine and poplar.

It was 4.30 or 5 P.M. when we stopped at Dijon, and with all the transcendent glory of the Burgundian hillsides, the prosaic name of dinner was not unwelcome. Nothing could be more delightful than the viands spread before us at the station buffet, the wine of the vicinage included, for four francs. A dinner of seven courses, comprising a delicious soup, fish, roast beef, vegetables, spring chicken and lettuce, compote, pudding, fruits, nuts, cheese, and coffee, had the effect of returning the passengers to the train in the most vivacious mood.

Dijon is a zigzag old town, at the confluence of the Ouche and the Souzon, of about 40,000 inhabitants. In earlier days, when France was under the dominion of a number of petty feudal officers, it was the capital of Burgundy, and the home of the reigning duke until the sixteenth century. Now, shining under the sun of the allodial system, we find it the metropolis of the department of the Côte d'or and the heart of the wine trade. A friend told me I had lost much by not remaining overnight and dipping into the curious sights and customs of this provincial town, such as I shall never enjoy by visiting only large cities. Being anxious to sleep in Lyons, womanlike, I follow the dictates of my own desire, and drive on to my intended destination.

Then, as we whirled through soft, green valleys, from which the fruit-burdened hills diverge on every side, and crossed crystal streams whose meagre waters ripple over stony beds, where women sit at the margin dipping their linen in the lucid current and beating it on the stones; on the white roads, winding around the acclivities into the dales, and ascending the dark mountain arms in the far distance again, we saw the grape-wagons drawn by oxen clumsily yet gayly caparisoned, and heard the silver tinkle of their bells vibrating through the sweet evening; the sun threw his last warm radiance over the earth, and the voluptuous hush of eventide was made musical by the dreamy jingling chimes of convent towers.

Now we were in the heart of Haute Bourgogne, and we bade adieu to the famous vineyards of the Clos Vougeot, only to greet those of Gevrey, and lose sight of the yellow and purple heights of Nuits, Volney, or Pomard, to gain the prospect of the slopes of Beaune.

Yes! Night with her owls and bats and starry veil had come to dwell with us. The coach-lamps were lighted, closing all communication with the outer world, and I essayed to read my novel. With the dying gleam of day I saw the misty shadows of the Jura in the east, and my guide tells me in clear weather the icy iridescence of Mont Blanc is perceptible.

When I emerged from the courtyard into the Rue Bellecour this morning, with my first sight of the ramparts or sectional heights of the city of Lyons I wished for the power of a Millet or a Daubigny. It combines all the variety and fascination of pastoral and metropolitan beauty. Before me mounted ridge above ridge of garlanded heights, and rows of tall houses distinctly visible border the rocky ledges. I wanted to ascend the fortifications, but how?

Behind me lay the tongue of the city lapped by the Rhone and Saône, and I turned to the shops and City Hall through the new and beautiful Place de Bellecour. Not so many, it is true, but all around me are shops and streets as beautiful as those of the feverish capital. Not such an endless display of silks and velvets as I anticipated; black laces and fine linens are conspicuous, as though envious of the silkworm's reputation. After tiring of the municipal sights, I engaged *cocher* to open unto me the rural splendor of the Parc de la Tête d'Or, for this community, though scarcely more than a third as large as Philadelphia, must have their Fairmount Park on the left of the Rhone. Starting from the converging point of the two streams, all along the quays on either side are the floating laundries, where the washerwomen come to perform their duties, which seem to be the chief source of emolument amongst the lower classes. The boulevard leading to the Parc is dry and level, planted on either margin with prolific shade trees, and the river is spanned by frequent bridges. One of the great charms of these foreign cities are the rivers that glide through the centre, with their handsome embankments and white-stone wharves.

In the park we find the Zoological and Botanical gardens, a lake where little skiffs are dancing, vast parterres of gay flowers, cultivated by the husbandmen, and a *vacherie* where fresh milk is offered to the pleasure-seekers. To our right a great checkered counterpane of yellow and pink and white and green appears to have been spread. As we approach this gaudy coverlet we find it woven of tall, graceful, waving grain, drooping its golden head as if in modest sense of its mature wealth, blended with patches of pink and white clover, and young crisp verdure.

Toward the silk factories, traversing the heights of Croix-Rousse, we ascended in an infractuous coil, that often proved an arduous pull to our poor old horse. The inclinations are dangerous, the streets narrow, the houses rearing to the height of six and seven stories, and permeating the atmosphere are the moisture of steam and the whirr of looms. The diminutive stature and hunted faces of the silk-weavers are visible, a cogent proof of the seditious sentiments of this sinuous section. I may call almost every house a silk factory, as manufacturers furnish the raw material to the laborers and they transform it into sheeny fabric in their homes.

Mounting ten or twelve pairs of steep steps through

dingy corridors and dismal chambers, we reached one of the leading establishments ; a large room filled with looms, of which only a few were in active operation, and we hear the murmer of "hard times." The looms that were in motion contained the warp of gold and white damask ordered by President MacMahon to upholster a new suit of furniture. The proprietor of this great establishment escorted us to a room adorned with silk pictures, the products of the Jacquard looms ;—"he and his family received by the Emperor and Empress," "Washington," "Lincoln," and many illustrative of French history, all capital portraits. We disdained offering a fee to this pompous silk man, who had been in the presence of royalty, believing profuse thanks to be our only mode of grateful demonstration. I summoned my entire vocabulary of French courtesy and lavished it upon him; but even this did not appease the old vampire's cringing soul. He beckoned us into a small room, and I, believing he was about to reward my ultra civility by a display of further glories, thanked him again and again. At length I yielded to his importunities, and there scattered over a table were a shoal of other woven adornments. I expressed my admiration for the wonderful work in my strongest language, and still not a glimmer of the old man's design dawned upon me until he enumerated the prices of them. Then, and then only, the sun of Wisdom broke through my cloudy perception in a perfect exuberance of light. I comprehended the situation; I was the fly in the spider's web, and my escape could only be purchased by the price of several of these pictures, the cheapest valued at ten francs! So through life one must pay for his ignorance, and though the school of experience exacts the most bitter lessons, they are always the most chastening and enduring.

Lyons presents no appearance of neglect. Its streets are new, its squares adorned with statues, its gardens and plots carefully planted; yet there is ever apparent a simmering insurrection, that with a breath may be fanned into a broil. It is more the city of successful manufactures and weary proletaires, than of costly pleasures. It is a community of toilers and merchants, not poets and statesmen.

LETTER XLVI.

"The cheapness of *wine* seems to be a great cause, not of drunkenness, but of sobriety. The inhabitants of the *wine* countries are in general the soberest people of Europe; witness the Spaniards, the Italians, and the inhabitants of the Southern provinces of France."
      SMITH. *Wealth of Nations.*

"And sound again, bold Melody,
 For baffled millions raise
The last victorious rallying cry,
 The nation's Marseillaise.
Once more advance in the vanguard, France,
 To the roar of the Marseillaise!"

MARSEILLES, May, 1878.

WHEN I rode away from Lyons I was convinced that excellent cooking was not confined to the gilded Capital. The dinners—*vin ordinaire* inclusive—were poems, and I freely confess the chief charm of a foreign hotel to voyagers is an unexceptionable *cuisine.*

From Lyons to Marseilles our route lay through that portion of Transalpine Gaul, rich in the luscious warmth of the grape, the golden glow of the orange, the hectic flush of the poppy, all lending an Oriental hue to the picture that was tempered into harmony by the puritanical robes of the dusky olive; and sumptuous in its numberless relics of Roman occupation. The authenticity of many of these remains and their accompanying legends is undoubted, as the Romans conquered and held tenure in Gaul, which they in those early days overran and appropriated, as they did the other kingdoms of Europe. They sequestered their Cæsars as the Bonapartes did in later times. This immortal garland of history has encouraged romancists to weave many wayside weeds and spurious reminiscences into their fanciful wreaths. As we passed over the Alpine ledges, and through the granite excavations, and by the numerous arrowy streams, tributaries of the Rhone and fed by mountain springs, not only each city and town, but almost every village deserves a special record. Here are vineyards yielding the same delicious "Hermitage" through all these centuries, from the little slips of vine planted between the interstices of rock by the recluse who made his retreat upon the hill, to the hireling of the local duke who inserted saplings that have been the favorite cup of the castle. This exquisite product of white and red wine scarcely ever passes out of France; at least none of the first quality. It is monopolized by the millionaires and native royalists, and when exported the lower grades are invoiced as the prime original. Before touching the conical declivity of the Hermitage, we had passed the Château de Ponsas on the right bank of the Rhone, and in the distance we caught a glimpse of mountain peaks, from which, tradition tells us, Pontius Pilate committed suicide. The tale, however questionable, seems to have become roothound. The group of lofty summits still bear the name of *Mont Pilat*. For a few moments one is in the beautiful valley of the turbulent Isère, only to cross it, and then its swift tide and rocky eminences are left in the northeast as we dash on in our southerly route. We gradually leave the course of the Rhone, though we continue in a parallel line for some distance.

Avignon, once a Roman colony, and in the fourteenth century the seat of the pontifical throne, if containing no magnets of present power, is at least interesting as the theatre of the melodramatic phase in the lives of Petrarch and Laura. This melancholy, love-languishing poet-laureate, crowned in the Roman capital, conceived his immortal passion for Laura de Noves when he was scarcely past boyhood, and though his importunities were repelled with determined purpose,—so the story runs,—throughout this young lady's virginity and wifehood, the faithful Romeo continued to sing his love sonnets until the cold earth shrouded his constant and tempestuous heart forever. It was a woful day when the young Italian poet was first enthralled by the "nymph at her orisons" in the nunnery of St. Claire. The historian forgets to relate whether Laura's passion for her husband, Hugues de Sade, equalled Petrarch's ardent affection. While the lover was travelling through Italy, France, Spain, and Germany, gaining rich laurels alike from the volatile Gaul and grim Teuton, preserving classical manuscripts and pouring out the perennial fountains of a love that were destined to carry his fame down through the unfathomable abysses of time, Laura remained in Avignon, going through the maternal routine of domestic life, and when he returned to the hallowed spot after an absence of nearly a decade, found his idol oppressed by domestic grievances and a prolific offspring. Oh! what a prosaic planet is this earth! We are prone to believe we are living in an age from which all the chivalry and grace, and poetry have departed. But such lessons teach us to wish no longer for the lyrical days when Cupid was just as capricious as now. Poor Petrarch! his passion for Laura was one of those pleasing fancies that serve to point a moral and to hang a tale.

And then Rienzi—Rienzi who was transformed from a poetic dreamer into a political reformer. This wild revolutionist is another sanctifying memory of Avignon. Rienzi, the companion of Petrarch, who languished in prison while the latter luxuriated in palaces. Rienzi, who perished on the Capitol steps at the hands of the infuriated populace,—the same wild populace that had gathered here to dignify Petrarch with the diadem of fame. Yes! One is fascinated with the profound historical reflections of the vicinity, and longs to linger by the way to visit the haunts of the poets. With these close associations, and the southern flush and hush of the landscape, one is inclined to believe he has already crossed the boundaries of the Cisalpine Gaul of the ancients. The gradual transition into Italy is at once distinguishable in the soft pronunciation and dulcet tones of the peasants, the frequent appearance of holy fathers from the cloisters, mountain goats on the rocky passes, and little donkeys bearing weighty burdens over perilous crags. Mountain springs plunge from their dizzy heights to feed the great wells of irrigation that are turned through vast tracks of arable land. Tunnels are becoming frequent now, and we issue from these subterranean cells, sometimes to find ourselves perched upon lofty ledges overhanging the flowering dale or sharp defile, and sometimes at the base of a sterile promontory rearing its summit skywards. Skirting the *Etang de Barre*, an inland lake, a vast sheet of water bluer than heaven, and as silent as death, we entered the longest mountain cavern in France, from which we emerged to greet the mystic Mediterranean, where the little boats with their lateen sails were gliding over the azure ripples like butterflies pausing upon flowers, with gay wings elevated, not outspread; where Marseilles lay in her extensive sandbeds, caressed by the blue surge, protected by the isolated pile of *Château d'If*, and the long pier and blinding bastions of Fort St. Jean, and sheltered by the stony apex of Nôtre Dame de la Garde.

Coming into Marseilles I was impressed by its Moorish appearance and Southern aroma. It is wholly Oriental. There is the smell and the moisture of the sea, the luxuriant foliage of graceful palms, and a miasmatic, stifling atmosphere. The windows are shaded by gaudy awnings of the Turkish type; a flaming combination of orange and blue, green and maroon, pink and purple material in stripes broader than my two hands. Over the shops these showy caparisons extend in variegated ostentation; and all along the margin of the sidewalk orange and lemon trees, and waving palms exhale their fragrance. Women selling fish and fruit stand at the corners under the branching shade, in short, flashy petticoats, low-cut velvet bodices, and crimson or yellow kerchiefs knotted over their bosoms; they have swarthy, carnal faces, framed in a massive coil of raven hair. They are interesting creatures, but essentially earthy. The galley-slaves, chained in long lines, work on the stone harbor and on the pier of St. Jean. They toil in painful silence, and the strains of the *Marseillaise* are suppressed in their agony.

As we drove into the courtyard of the hotel it looked like a scene in a fairy palace. There was a cosmopolitan throng clustered about the tables under the feathery palms, and by the golden fruit-trees; canary birds twittered in brazen cages, while invalid ladies, who had been ordered by physicians to the salubrity of a soft Southern climate, dozed in the sleepy atmosphere, and florid Englishmen equipped for an Alpine or Tyrolese tour, in wash-basin hat and Turkish towel drapery, drank their *Stout* and read their *Times*. A canopy of colored glass overhangs the octagonal rotunda of the court, and as I pass to my left over the great marble stairway an icy chill shivers through me, and I pity the valetudinarian who comes here for health. The hotel is palatial, an extravagance of marbles, frescoes, and gilding, as all such French constructions are; the chambers airy, and the casements draped with lace and crimson satin. Opposite my door I espied several luxuriously appointed bath-rooms; not large tin-tubs to be filled and carried into the apartments, but really American baths. My soul exulted at the revelation, and I determined to occupy one of the welcome novelties. It was like meeting an old and appreciated friend in a foreign land. The maid, upon inquiry, replied they were all vacant, and she would prepare one for my revel immediately.

Now "preparing a bath" in Europe, being interpreted, means placing a Turkish towel, as large as a sheet, on the lower level of the tub, which is an excessively uncomfortable process, and not providing soap, which is quite as inconvenient. I have already learned to carry away my candles, but charging for soap is a phase of hotel extortions I had neglected to note. The Englishman who runs over the Continent generally once a year to escape the dismal season at home, becomes an *habitué* in these meridian regions, and, knowing their customs, invariably travels with his soap. Americans are expected to do likewise, and, failing, they inevitably pay for their neglect. Now when I was wholly immersed I made a direful discovery, —the absence of soap,—and, ringing for the attendant to supply the need, who seemed amazed that I was unfurnished with the article, went in search of it. It was quite half an hour before she made her appearance. Several times in the interim I had rung the bell in the hope of tidings, and was informed that the commissioner had been sent out to purchase it. When I read Mark Twain's anecdote in *Innocents Abroad*, being unsophisticated, and appreciating the wit's facetiæ, I could not credit his story of a similar circumstance. Now I am convinced his book is a work of facts, satirized by this ridiculing genius. And yet the guidebook says "Marseilles is noted for its manufacture of *soaps* and oils."

The wider my journey extends, more fixed becomes the conviction that these Latin nations, with all their centuried wisdom and experience, do not comprehend the luxury of living as we do.

There are some points of comparison between Lyons and Marseilles, but the contrasts overrule, alike in their topographical and commercial features. While the populace of Lyons toils at the looms, the populace of Marseilles labors in the docks; the wealth of Lyons is in its marvellous quantity and quality of cocoons, and the opulence of Marseilles in its valuable exports; if Lyons gave Gambetta to the French Republic, Marseilles furnished Thiers; Lyons manufactures while Marseilles traffics, and Lyons reposes peacefully in a community of her own, while Marseilles gathers within her walls the travelling and trading throngs from the four quarters of the globe.

Lotteries seem to be the prevailing pleasure and vice of the lower classes. When night falls, and the patrician element are riding through the Prado toward home, and the great lamps swing over the doors and throw the dark foliage and flashy awnings into vivid contrast, then the laborers from the quays and the sailors from the vessels, the poor women carrying babies and the meretricious beauties occupying the tall tenant-houses overlooking the mazarine waters of the Mediterranean, throng to these houses of chance and risk their purses upon a dress, a hat, a watch, a bed, a set of jewely, or a broken mirror, which are all gathered into a motley heap. I even saw birds from the Levant and Maltese kittens gambled for in the same breath with an old teakettle. There was a fascination in the strata of life gathered about these Faros, and I loitered in them to study the passion which flattered some with success and happiness, while others were sent home wretched by their disasters and disappointments. Even the fruit-woman must leave her tray at the corner, where the flaming torch casts a more luscious glamour over her sparse store, to enjoy the wild hazard. The peanut-boy and the ragged *gamin* from the docks blend in the excited rivalry, and peril their few coppers—earned, or begged, or stolen, Heaven and themselves alone know best—for the false glitter of some empty bagatelle. And here they flock, night after night, to feed this unhealthy and insatiable passion.

LETTER XLVII.

"In the ages of faith, before the day
When men were too proud to weep or pray,
There stood in a red-roofed Breton town,
Snugly nestled 'twixt sea and down,
A chapel for simple souls to meet
Nightly, and sing with voices sweet,
Ave Maria."

MARSEILLES, May, 1878.

A VISIT to the docks of Marseilles, if not so hazardous, is certainly more interesting than to adventure the crest of Notre Dame de la Garde. This church, perched upon the Alpine vertex sheltering the old port, is regarded by the Marseillaise as their pillars of Hercules; therefore, not to have risked its perillous paths, is not to have seen the city; so I determined upon doing Notre Dame de la Garde, without a suspicion of its situation, its merits, or the mode of access. I had not proceeded far over the hilly streets leading to the plinth of the eminence, before I was terror-stricken, and I would have abandoned the undertaking, had it not been a confession of my pusillanimity. It was a tedious pull over rocky slopes and furrowed coils, until the inclination became a straight oblique plane, and the driver dismounted to guide the horse over the precipitous ridge. At times the road contracted into a mere stony ledge, scarcely wide enough to allow the wheels of our conveyance to pass, frequently rolling and bouncing over fragments of bowlders that bestrewed the way; then, upon the brink of the precipice the gravel crushed and yielded, and we often heard it rattling among the flinty crags below. These repetitions of the earth crumbling away from under our feet, as it were, transformed my journey from one of pleasure, as I had contemplated, into one of pain. From vast granite vaults where rough-hewn walls closed in on every side, only the sky visible, we turned abrupt corners to find ourselves upon sharp spurs, with the blue waves tossing far away to the left, the busy life of the city in dizzy confusion below. Yet still far ahead stood Notre Dame de la Garde, in clear outline against the horizon. The coachman manifested some solicitude for my pleasure by stopping upon every giddy height, and pointing to Marseilles, exclaimed "*regardez, c'est trop grande*," but I was not intrepid enough to take his advice. He could not comprehend my fear, and repeated his importunities until I entreated him to pass on. It was thrilling in its grandeur, but it was not a picture I cared to dwell upon.

It was a religious festa, and the peasants in their fantastic costumes and broad brows, many from the hamlet of Catalans, were scaling the rocky altitudes to offer their waxen tributes at the shrine of their Holy Patroness. Many of the children carried gay chaplets of paper flowers, while their elders bore tapers of every size, varying from the ordinary tallow to spermaceti five feet long and six inches in circumference. Frequently these men and women in holiday attire, on their way to their Virgin Goddess, offerings in their hands and orisons on their lips, paused at our carriage to beg *centimes*, and so pertinacious were they that they often forgot their religious mission. Upon reaching the crest where the sacred fortress is enthroned, an ocean of childhood literally overflowed the long flight of steps leading to the goal; a handsome structure, but not so effective as I had a right to expect, as a reward for my travail; but the view of the city, obtained from this vantage-ground, which expanded over the entire valley, the galaxy of shining villas couched upon the encircling hillsides, the sterile base of Château d'If and Ratonneau, caressed by the azure waves, and the forest of shipping with the colors of many nations floating over the harbor, as if to welcome travellers from every zone, was an entrancing compensation. The coachman led his poor beast over the declivity with an empty *voiture*, while I passed on with bruised feet and agitated limbs over the rocky pathway only to be beset by photograph, cake, lemonade, and souvenir venders; blind beggars, halt beggars, scarred beggars, and mendicant friars, who, in their lusty manhood, seemed counterfeit beggars, assuming the wail of woe upon the appearance of any one who appeared to have two sous to give away. If we refused to sow our coppers broadcast, double-distilled curses, uttered with vehemence, and thrice repeated, hurled our souls down to the depths of perdition. Many of the peasant men we met had crimson or gaudy-striped snoods knotted about their heads; these I instinctively avoided at first fearing they were *banditti*, but upon further acquaintance, discovered them to be of that element known as the Catalans or Spanish gypsies, inhabiting the delta at the southeast of Marseilles, and stretching into the Mediterranean,—the community from which young Edmond Dantés, afterwards Count Monte Cristo, Dumas's hero, chose his bride. This population that I passed on the mountain are the offspring of the Spanish colony who perched like penguins upon the promontory many centuries ago, and in their short beaded and broidered jackets, and flaunting kerchiefs wound about their heads, we traced their Moorish origin. The colors and trinkets of their heteroclite costume have degenerated with the years, but still the principle of the dress of their ancestors is preserved.

To the citadel *Nicolas*, and thence over the quays of the oblong old port, there was a different life from that we left, crawling up and down the rough, religious ladder that led to the heavenward shrine. Beggars! Oh, yes, there were a hundredfold more beggars and swaggerers among the docks than upon the granite mount, but there was too much diversion to heed the tricks of sharpers in the crush of the myriad craft and the throngs of sailors on duty on the merchantmen, the hordes of poor panting human toilers loading and unloading the trading vessels locked in the basins, and the care-free troops of seamen off duty, with full pockets and light hearts, whose gold was soon to vanish in the seduction of the glittening casinos and their black-eyed sweethearts.

Then, in great storehouses of grain, spices, and provisions bordering the wharves, there is very much the same wild life and secret habits common in the great rendezvous of foreign traffic in New York, Baltimore, and Philadelphia. As we rode, we seemed to diffuse an American air, and were several times hailed in our course, and informed that there was an American vessel in port; we were requested to visit the sea-bird from our native land; but we persistently refused all these pertinacious civilities. As we travel we learn that to accept attentions means an expected reward. And so we turned the square of the Ancient Port, and there, upon the opposite quay, we found the shops where the ship mechanics were at work repairing Spanish galleons, Turkish feluccas, broad-bottomed Dutch steam barges, black British cruisers, American brigs that had brought cargoes of tobacco, petroleum, and cotton, and Chinese junks with packages of opium.

Out upon the glaring pier of Fort St. Jean, I overlooked the motionless sea, all along this Southern shore—as motionless and as blue as the cerulean canopy—and then watched the great ships freighted with their treasures of oil, fruits, wines, and perfumes, bound some for the Levant, and others for the Occident, quietly vanishing over the horizon. There is an ineffable charm about these foreign seaports, and to me Marseilles is more wonderful because far more varied than Liverpool. It may have been the salubrity of the French climate and the poetry of the azure Mediterranean, in striking contrast with foggy dingy England, and the muddy Mersey, and it may have been my own mood, but to day the scene upon the wharves was strangely Oriental.

The Ancient Port was the only haven Marseilles owned until within the last thirty years; now the entire facing of the maritime metropolis glistens with the outer walls of the basins. Though it might scarcely be deemed necessary to construct wet docks where the ebb and flow of the tide is so moderate as in the Gulf of Lyons, still not only is the city hemmed by these mammoth inclosures, but there is a demand for increased accommodations owing to the tremendous accession of trade with foreign powers.

In this fair city I enjoyed the broad boulevard of La Cannebière, with its fine shops and garish awnings, and cosmopolitan multitudes; and the Rue de la Republique, which I take to be one of recent birth from its name, where the houses are as tall and white as in pearly Paris; through the Prado I have lolled in dreamy mood under the shadows of leafy avenues that stretch behind and before in unbroken colonnades of green, and even in the Boulevard de Longchamp, with the transcendent fountain and statuesque front of the Palais in the perspective; all these beauties and fascinations, together with the hundred other attractions of a great city, are still inferior to the solemn majesty of the environs.

Starting from the careening naval basin on the eastern extremity of the old port, we continued over a contracted path bordering the sea that winds about the tongue of land that forms the Creek de la Reserve, then to the northeast we met the broad white level Corniche, the pride of Southern France and Italy, which extends from Marseilles down to the toe of Italy along the border of the Mediterranean. In the village des Catalans we found the homes of the community we met upon the Alpine passes. Little whitewashed nests that seemed falling to decay, some holes hewn in the side of rocks, apparently constructed of earth, crumbling to a fine powder certain to evaporate with the first breath of the hyperborean *Mistral* that sweeps over Provence in scourging velocity. Squalor and poverty reigned supreme, yet about all there was a picturesque *phasis* at least pleasing. It may have been the luxuriant arbors of roses, the towering heights, the zigzag titled paths, where these hovels reposed sleepily, the brilliant dress of the inhabitants upon the glaring alleys, or the mystic *lapis lazuli* of the sea.

On the left of this scene we had all the beauty of a rugged, sublime landscape with its pastoral and even gypsy life. On the right were the blue waters laving the Corniche, and dashing upon the base of the sterile islands, with the glamour of romance and peril hanging over them. Far ahead the *chemin de Corniche* coils about the border of the land like a silver ribbon.

In reaching the Rest Roubion we passed the "Valley of the Shepherds," and the Vallon de l'Oriol, that lay like slumbering twins cradled between the heights of Notre Dame de la Garde and the marine ridges.

The Rest Roubion stands upon a plateau above the sea. Entering the grounds of the hotel we climbed sloping paths and groups of little steps until the scene below increased in beauty with every view. Exquisite parterres, and vases burdened by an exuberance of blooming rose vines, and closely-cropped sward, gave the spot a mythological air, resembling the haunts of the Grecian gods and Neapolitan fairies.

The rain fell, but the sea lost none of its wonderful color, and a sharp penetrating wind greeted us even here on this southern shore and in these declining days of May.

LETTER XLVIII.

"O! The earth is fair in plain and glade,
 In valley and mountain range,
But it changes as the ages fade.
 While the brave sea knows no change:
Along the shore, as in ages past,
 His noisy footsteps fall,
And the gray rock melts to his touch at last,
 For the sea rules all!
 Yea! the sea rules all!"

NICE, May, 1878.

MY task should be reserved for the poet. It is not in sober black and white prose that the splendors of the Riviera should be calendared. They demand the glowing harmony of Byron and the inspired pencil of Raphael. Around this Mediterranean nest there is just now an ineffable beatitude in the air and a glorious springtide of color.

"Ah me! what hand can pencil guide, or pen,
 To follow half on which the eye dilates,
Through views more dazzling unto mortal ken
 Than those whereof such things the bard relates,
 Who to the awe-struck world unlocked Elysium's gates?"

Following the line of the Corniche along the brim of sea from Marseilles one realizes the Frenchman's patriotic aphorism, "La belle France." To determine just what beauties are included in this compliment is an insoluble problem, as the boundaries of France are shifted twice in a generation, in conformity with the revolutions of the political axis. Despite stereotyped eulogy, the English landscape never kindled in me much ecstasy, but here God hands us such a perfect chrysolite, that man's genius cannot divine nor describe its peerless radiance. It is not municipal taste nor municipal government, religious sentiment nor political equipoise, not moral dogmas, nor social discipline, that masters the stranger beholding this lovely region for the first time. It is the chaos of enchantment that covers this whole route of travel. Even the toppling towers of the white convents, floating 'twixt sky and sea, seemed to me nature's crown to the whole panorama, just as if she had "snatched a grace beyond the rules of art."

There was a cloud overshadowing Marseilles when I left it, not a political nor commercial cloud, but a dense atmospheric frown that was severed into shreds by the shining scimitar of the sun before we came in sight of Toulon, the war harbor of France, where human beasts of burden toil in long files, manacled by the galley-chain; where the sybaritic sharper, the delicate perfumed lover, who in a frenzy of jealousy had killed his fair one, and the double-distilled felon, suffer side by side.

From the heights beyond Toulon there is a view of earth, sky, and water, that stamps it as one of nature's *chefs-d'œuvre*. Through the tunnels, and over the ledges, we turned an angle, and yonder, nestled on the slopes of Des Maures, we saw what looked to be a great white cathedral, or cloister. It proved to be the town of Hyères, rapidly expanding into a great sanitarium, though perched upon too lofty a ridge to be sheltered from the scourging blasts of the *mistral*. In another curve the town is lost, but we get a full view of its islands, lying off in the Mediterranean, their sterile foundations and fortified capitals blended with a heap of sparkling rugged rock.

For almost seventy miles we skirted the base of the Maritime Alps, nature's eternal monuments, piled ridge upon ridge, finally fading away in the clouds, ungarnished by a blade of verdure. They extended close to our car, until each projection would seem about to dash the windows to splinters; then by an abrupt evolution we were whisked into the black bowels of the tunnelled Colossus.

At the little harbor of St. Raphael, about half an hour from Cannes, Napoleon landed when he came from Egypt, bathed in the glory of transcendent victory. Fourteen years after, crushed by his own reverses, and followed by the scorn of his people, he again weighed anchor from the same port upon his ostracism to Elba, and within the year returned and landed not many miles from the same spot. What more cogent example of the irony of fate than these unforgotten lessons in the meteoric career of the Corsican Corporal?

At Cannes, the Cape May of France, we only rested to deposit our freight of invalid English and rich French, who came to find a haven in its salubrious air and perfumed flowers. Hedges of pink and crimson rose-vines, twisted and woven into one exuberance of bloom, now replaced the glossy, vigorous myrtle. Great groves of blossoming orange-trees stretched around us, and the glow of the cactus and oleander cast the purity of the former into painful pallor. May and June are the harvest months of roses and orange-blossoms in the Midi, and the peasants were embowered in fragrant wreaths, plucking them for the perfume distillers. The peculiarity of the soil in this region seems to be favorable to the cultivation of aromatic plants, as the grape is indigenous to the Burgundy and Bordeaux districts. The English have done much to enhance the value of a section that God has burdened with fruits of splendor, by erecting luxurious homes on the hills and dales, and so attracting the best society from their own bleak island and the French cities and provinces. Perhaps Lord Brougham, by making Cannes his winter home, gave the impetus and impelled the annual tide of visitors to this Mediterranean resort.

These seaside cities of the Latins have none of the ephemeral features of our ocean resorts. They are of marble and granite, and strong in metropolitan splendor and solidity. True, they have existed for centuries, and were temples of art and sanctuaries of learning before we were even struggling in the womb of the past.

But the devotees of fashion and of the golden calf have fled, and Nice is as voiceless as the great Sahara, though as I came upon her to-day she was arrayed like "Solomon in all his glory." The mountain torrents leap from cliff to dale beyond the city gates, and yet the waters of the Paillon which bisect the town scarcely cover the stones of its broad bed. The sparkling city reposes in an amphitheatre, guarded from the northern blasts by the mountains that close around the inland border, with only the blue sea and the drifting boats as a stage scene.

The city is a vast Eden of deserted hotels and vacant villas. Along the principal boulevards and Promenade des Anglais cards of "to let" stare in undaunted succession from portal and shutter. The beat of hoofs, sounds of revelry, and the loud ostentation of foreign nabobs and American millionaires are dead on the parade by the sea, where a few months ago sky, ocean, and air resounded with their saturnalia.

Following the course of the waters, the ramparts seem ablaze in a white column of sunlight, capped by an odorous and fervid blush of cactus and crimson cypress, glowing oleander and golden oranges, the tropical plumose palms waving over the aureate fruit and flaming flowers. The atmosphere seems asleep in an agony of sweetness, and life is as morbid in the streets and gardens as it is in the environs, where we meet only the goatherd or the blossom-gatherers, and see only the monastic towers of convent or cloister. Mounting the apex of Cimiés and St. Pons, we hear only the rippling laugh of a little child, a sign of solitude. There is over the hills and through the dales a religious hush, an odor of sanctity, a beauty of holiness, in marked contrast with the whirl of the capital and the thrift of the provinces, and I am prone to believe I am already within the spiritual sovereignty of Holy Mother Church. We see none of the traditional squalor of Italy, but all its silent comfort. Rough wooden crosses, uncouth crucifixes, and graceless shrines, protect the crops and hallow the roadsides. Who can enjoy such a country but those born upon its soil, and who have mingled in its customs? Surely not those who endeavor to gain an idea of its beauty from canvas, and much less readers of novels and travels. You may figure a steep hillside clad in royal purple and emerald, lighted by the crimson dress of the peasant girl, and a little white cottage home in an arbor of aloe and cypress; a rude ascending path, over which vintagers are drawing grape wagons to which they themselves are harnessed, while their wives or daughters push the wheels; a garden wall, behind which fallow fruit glistens; a village priest counting his Ave Marias and Paternosters; and the hoary ruins of cathedral or château as a sacred coronal upon the mountain brow. You may even see the scene vitalized by broad acres of wheat and timber; but no brush can paint or quill describe the soft laugh of the maiden, the tender lowing of the kine, the perfume of garlands, the marvellous maze of color, and the sublime influences of atmosphere; they must be inhaled and felt to be realized. It is not so much perception as emotion.

The world would tell me I have lost much by finding this siren's nest stripped of its gay audience and their gayer pursuits and tastes. But if it was rife with frolic, music, receptions, baccarat saloons, and the riot of human life, would this *spirituelle* element be potential? No! I have viewed the fair goddess of the sea in all the sweet purity of nakedness, and find her one of the sacred creatures that the flash of jewels and the glitter of gold would carnalize.

There are fine boulevards of shops, extending from one extremity of the town to the other, but, with few exceptions, they exhibit only the extract of the grape and the olive, and these appear in great profusion. The streets seem to have been swept and the gardens garnished for Sunday; the denizens have donned their Sabbath garb, the white roads, white houses, honey-laden atmosphere, the fervent clearness of the sky, each man and woman taking shelter from the noonday heat under a crimson, blue, pink, green, or yellow umbrella; the whole place looks like the opening scene in an opera bouffe. Nature is in a swoon and the people are in a holiday.

Although a city of the sea, there is none of its moisture in the climate; the mountain air is volatile; the May season is full of peace; Harlequin is in his bed; the fiddle is at rest; all the fun of the place is pantomime; and nothing seems alive but the sweet melody of a distant chime and the sad call of a solitary robin.

LETTER XLIX.

"O Christ! it is a goodly sight to see
  What Heaven hath done for this delicious land!
What fruits of fragrance blush on every tree!
  What goodly prospects o'er the hills expand!
  But man would mar them with an impious hand,
And when the Almighty lifts his fiercest scourge
  'Gainst those who must transgress his high command,
With treble vengeance will his hot shafts urge,
Gaul's locust host, and earth from fellest foeman purge."
                                       CHILDE HAROLD.

MONACO, May, 1878.

MONACO is the Principality, but Monte Carlo is the Casino, and Casino is king. Monaco sits upon a lofty promontory overhanging the sea, looking like the ruins of a great cathedral. But there are no architectural or geographical ruins at Monte Carlo, only an incalculable wreck of lives, and these are not exhibited to the seeking stranger like crumbling mounds and decaying castles, but hidden under the gayety and glitter of seductive vices and costly adornments. Few stop at Monaco; all go to Monte Carlo, and when I left Nice on my further south-bound route along the Riviera, passing away from its pure, restful, religious atmosphere,—enhanced by the sweet Sabbath,—I felt as if I was taking one stupendous leap from heaven to—— well no, for Monte Carlo is a strange and fascinating hybrid of heaven and hell.

The same beauty of feature and outline prevails through the short ridge that leads from Nice to Monte Carlo. Perhaps the roses are in closer clusters, the cactuses in a greater blaze of fire, the sea bluer, the sky more intense, and the heights more dizzy; but the characteristics are exactly like those of this Franco-Italian region since I left Marseilles. Admiral Le Roy's vessel lay in the bay of Villafranca at the corner of Nice, which I only glanced at from a natural louver window in the rocks. The line was now wholly subterranean, except at the stations or a rent in the mountain, where we welcomed daylight only for a second, to be again whisked into utter darkness.

Around a great projecting curve Monaco bursts upon you! It seems detached from the mainland, and hangs 'twixt earth and sea like a great swinging garden. Novels and tracts, Murray or Baedeker had painted the Arcadia to which I was hastening; although none have succeeded in extolling. nor even justifying its attractions, as its most pronounced influences are a sense, not perception. The Corniche coils about it, and the railway traverses the Principality from one extremity to the other, where the Maritime Alps project in bold spurs into the Mediterranean. It is the star of the most luxuriant and charming district of the Riviera, though the view obtained from the car is greatly disparaged by the irrepressible granite monuments. Monaco crests the culminating point of the road, though it and Monte Carlo and the environs are overlooked by the towered pediment of Turbia.

The history of the *petit* principality is cloudy, but it has been under the sovereignty of the Grimaldi since the tenth century, of which the reigning prince, Charles Honoré III, is a direct descendant. He is a man of sixty, sensitive of all the delicious beauty and beguiling pleasures of his monarchy, and a voluptuary in costly Paris, where he passes six months of the year. Tired of entertaining and gambling at home, he goes to the capital, that is only more of a metropolis in latitude and population, there to be entertained and gambled with. Within his own contracted walls he has all that Paris may unfold except miles and peoples,—churches, cloisters, colleges, palaces, gardens, *cafés*, and casinos, and the addition of nature's handicraft in the wild supernal landscape.

There is a *dogano* (custom-house), with the escutcheon of the Grimaldi, at the station, but there is no overhauling of merchandise nor duties to be paid. There are no formulas, nor irritating detention at the gates; we passed the golden portals as jauntily as so many deadheads into the gamesters heaven. We required no passport, no credentials of character, and our tempers were not ruffled by the tedium of the red-tape process with our baggage. We all felt a mutual ownership in the elysium. Of course we pushed forward to the casino station, Monte Carlo, a short mile from the principality throne. Why stop at Monaco? All its sweets I had fed upon *ad nauseam;* pictures, statuary, flowers, birds, palaces, antiquities. Oh, yes! I was very fond of all, but I had already enjoyed them in lavish loveliness, and if not exactly surfeited—for there are *comfits* of which I am never *blasé*—I knew their colors, flavors, and effects; but in the casino I had a *bonbonnier* from which I had not torn the shining tinsel wrapper.

Monte Carlo is the lovely hill of sin and swindling, if I may be permitted to use two synonyms to express one thought. There is no concealment, all is open. The luxurious railway carriage stops at a station that looks like a piece of highly polished furniture. I ascended the money paradise by a road as easy as a velvet walk, flanked by urns and wreaths of flowers, and as I reached the top I was enveloped in perfume, and fairly speechless with surprise. Everything is regardless of cost, and regardful of harmony. Bazaars are open on all sides; carriages, as gayly dressed as Cinderella's equipages drawn by fairies, glide by laden with flashily dressed women, and liveried attendants with gold and silver lace gleaming in the sunlight, pass along the cultivated walks; magnificent châteaux and hotels, and conversation halls of yellow stone; exotics embowered the lace-draped windows, and framed the ledges; throngs of people flocking into a lovely saloon, from which exquisite strains of music float in a sort of eloquent radiance upon the startled senses,—all this I saw in a dazed way as I hurried to the hotel. One's first thought is to join the glittering procession and take in the points of the organized spectacle. How superb the landscape here in the loveliest part of old Italy and new France, where the purple hills I have so often seen in foreign pictures close about me. There is a golden glow in the atmosphere, and these strange yet fascinating colors exceed in mystic radiance the copies I once thought impossibly artificial. Monte Carlo is a rock polished into a sort of devil's elysium, and the purple hills, often veiled in a sadder mist, rise about it as if they had been placed by some mechanical invention, and add rather to the prepared beauty; small delicate houses of white stone, and Catholic churches in snowy purity, set off the darker hues, like seagulls floating in a black tempest on the deep ocean.

The Monte Carlo faro is upon the plateau of rock hovering over the station. Great flights of marble steps and glowing terraces, glistening parapets and sparkling balustrades, lead to the fair Circe. A rumbling little coach carried us over a steep narrow road, flanked by beautiful cottages and gardens, to the Hôtel de Paris, within the Casino grounds. I saw it was a silvery place upon entering by the vast marble vestibules, spacious stairways, and costly appointments; not so refreshing and calm as the hotel at Nice, with the shady palms waving through the stone corridors, and the little beds draped with their fleecy bobinet curtains. The smallest and simplest double chamber in this castle of a hotel was two dollars a day, rates that would exceed ours at home, when the table and extras were included. Although we are out of season, the halls are rife with the hum and jargon of foreign voices and hurrying footsteps. Here at least there is none of the painful silence pervading the English hotels. Every one seems selfishly heedful of his own desires and pleasures, and bent upon his own pursuits. There is a continual tide of gamblers drifting between the hotel and the Temple of Faro, only a few yards apart.

The last strains of the afternoon concert have died upon the air, but still the votaries of this strange and seductive worship come and go. The plot in front of the piazza and the broad steps of the sanctuary of sin are ever full and ever changing. The whirl of human flies looks like the evolutions of moats in a spot of noonday sunlight. The steep gray rocks and loftier mountains close in the Casino arena on the north, the east, and the west, and the white palisades overhang the blue sea on the south. From where I sit and gaze about me, I discover no visible egress for the poor unfortunate neophyte who realizes an ill-chosen vocation and too arduous a rubric in the Holy of Holies, except to plunge from the snowy parapet into the surging eternity below. But could any one ever grow heartsore or *ennuied* in so beautiful and well-attuned a section? Surely, they must be ingrates. It is an enchanted region, and the insurmountable walls of granite close about us, not to impress us with a sense of imprisonment, but only as a sweet retreat from the vulgar world. This is the innocent visitor's first impression. Little kiosks, cafés, and pavilions, dazzling in Oriental frescoes, border the coast and are scattered over the gardens; fountains cast their playful waters to and from vases toppling under their weight of luxuriance and perfume, and marble gods and goddesses glance between the foliage of pines, aloes, palms, and oleanders, around whose roots, and over the earth, great black gutta-percha water-pipes coil like vitalizing serpents. A Dominican friar, in black gown and calotte, flanked by his acolytes, crosses the white square, but persistently ignores the colonnades and disciples of the Palace of Chance. With the gathering shadows a chill air blows off the northeastern peaks, that chastens the atmosphere of all its saline moisture, and the sound of the dinner-gong disturbs the devotees. There they come, flocking out from the solemnity of Vespers to the flesh-pots.

Dinner at the Hôtel de Paris is one of the most novel and characteristic processes of this gaming city. The *salon* differs from any of the others I have seen along the southern shore, and contrasts vividly with the one at the Hôtel de Louvre et de la Paix at Marseilles, where my eye sought vainly for rest upon one square inch of lath and plaster, that was not blinding in a glare of white, gold repoussé, and frescoes; even the doors were china gloss, frescoed panels, and gilt beading. Here all decorations are equally elaborate, but in dark velvety tones of Pompeiian red, olive, green, dun shades, walnut and ebony woods and plate-glass; no crystal and gilt chandeliers, but bronze metal. The room is an extensive oblong with a lofty dome, and long windows set in deep embrasures, gorgeously upholstered, and looks like the hall where Apicius might have held his banquets. Columns separate it into two sections; the first furnished with small tables, where viands are ordered *à la carte*; the latter assigned to the *table d'hôte*. The *à la carte* department was thronged by those whose faith was their mistress, and here the female element prevailed. Ah! it gladdened my very soul to gain so potential a proof of the unselfishness and constancy of my sex; even if manifested in behalf of an impure cause, it proclaimed a loftier cast of character than that shown by the male cormorants by whom I was surrounded. Their wedded wife was forgotten in their appetites. They had two goddesses, *Hazard* and *Glutony*; which was the most despotic I am unable to say. Is it not George Eliot who says, "The passion of jealousy makes fiends, and the passion of hunger makes beasts of men?" The latter species were all around me at the table. They are the sustaining element of this glittering palace, and have bribed all the waiters into their slaves. They were the first to be served with every course, and if a lady intervened she was omitted for the next gambler in the line. If the supply of food was unequal for the number of guests, a lady would be denied the delicacy, while a mysterious wink or sign to a waiter from the gambler next her commanded a replenished dish of the luxury she had been told was quite exhausted. I ordered ice-cream. As I was about to help myself one of the individuals near gave the cue, the cream and servant were transported as if by electricity, and when I collected my disbanded faculties I had the pleasure of seeing my fellow-diner enjoying my dessert after having disposed of his own. Need I dwell or moralize upon this gross vulgarity? Need I say that men with these base manners have baser morals, and that to be robbed of one's ice-cream was not so flagrant an indecency as to be robbed of one's amiability by the leering gaze of these heartless ghouls? But we were here as others were, even the best of our kind, to gratify a natural curiosity; and true safety was to get out of it, quickly and quietly as possible. To remonstrate would be as great a folly as a proposition to purchase the bank. Such monsters are the foundation upon which the great temple rests, the fulcrum which supports it, the girder that binds it, the pillar that strengthens it, the stanchion that upholds it, the axis upon which it revolves. These creatures are the Atlantes, Caryatides, and Hercules that carry it. They are the elect children, the faithful believers, the clergy, the propagandists, and the society of the Tabernacle of Fortune.

The gambling-hall in the hotel is *en déshabille;* being garnished for the winter frolic; the green-baize tables with the chalked numerals are turned upside down, and the frescoers' trestles are conspicuous in their stead. Although this *green-room*, if I may use the term, is entered from an octagonal conservatory, where stained glass, frescoes, exotics, divans, and other superb embellishments reign supreme, there is a chill about it as of a sepulchre. It is not the dismal solitude of the "banquet-hall deserted," depressing by the gayer memory of happy hearts and light feet, but the ghastly grandeur of the murder-chamber in Elsinore Castle; it is like a palatial judgment-hall, where thousands of souls have received their death-warrant, and the haunting, terrifying memory hangs in cloudy oppression. It is a Golgotha.

The first melodious notes of the evening concert came floating from the crowded, stuffy chambers of the Casino upon the sweet evening. I crossed the broad, white, macadamized square, and climbing the marble stairway, paused beneath the portals, and turned to gaze once more upon the entrancing landscape, before plunging into the abyss of Risk, the great lure of lucre. The adornments were rich, but not meretricious; *outre* decorum was paramount; foreign servants and well-dressed gentlemen were hurrying through the corridors. It had rather the appearance of a nobleman's palace prepared for a ball than a gaming-house. One is not compelled to gamble or even enter the *slaughterhouse* of souls because he comes here. There is the concert, free to all, and to it I resorted to iron out the wrinkles of prudery from my conscience with the soothing harmonies of Rossini, Strauss, Meyerbeer, and Mozart. The hall was crowded when I entered; many ladies and gentlemen, immature misses of fifteen or sixteen, and some of my delectable companions of the *table d'hôte*, but this stratum I at once discovered to be restive—only listening to a couple of bars of the music, and then vanishing for perhaps a half or three-quarters of an hour. There floated in young ladies, unattended by gentlemen, from time to time, who disappeared as rapidly and mysteriously as the men. These were the vestals, and I followed them to the shrine of their devotion. The roulette tables were surrounded by double and treble rows, the greater number females not past the meridian of life. The wheels were in motion, and the croupiers sat on either side of the centre of the long board, armed with their little money-rakes, and sixty times in an hour they command in sepulchral tones the "gentlemen to make their game." It is as silent as death within these walls, while thousands of dollars are changing hands, the bank winning every eight of ten games. The ladies were the most successful, risking very little at a time, but invariably adding to it. The men are of two classes; the young and brainless fops of fortune, who are here cutting their social eye-teeth, perhaps with less pain to themselves than to their parents, upon the brilliants of Monte Carlo, and the burly, bullying *roués* and sharpers I have already spoken of. The women are of every age, station, and nation under the sun, the younger tossing down their stakes with the playful recklessness of children, and the elder ones seated at the table, brows furrowed with thought and anxiety, as if they were solving the problem of their fate. I studied the game long. The more I lingered the more interested I became. Several times I thought I had unravelled the warp of its progress and penetrated its darkest secrets, when by some new law of success I became aware of my utter helplessness to disentangle the skein.

The amusement is absorbing and seductive, and as I looked I too felt its peculiar influence. It is the charming expectancy of luck that enchants, and we are beguiled into the machination by an ecstasy of anticipation. Several times I found my hand upon my *porte-monnaie*, for I confess my evil genius was busy, particularly as I watched a young lady who never staked more than a five franc piece, and yet whose star was ever propitious. Besides here, in the presence of the delusive evil, we do not think of the printed admonitions of the moralists.

All is peaceful and luxurious, and with the exception of now and then a broken-hearted-looking old woman or a haggard man leaving the table in despair, we see none of the misery we had expected would stare at us like wretched deaths'-heads from every corner. There are many eager candidates for the vacant chair of the unfortunate one, and our budding sympathy for him is soon forgotten in the risks and triumphs of his successor. I ceased to recollect the whole category of painful affections, the inevitable outgrowth of this passion; I forgot the attending sins and sorrows, and saw only the lottery wheel of a church fair. Surely, I then said, there can be no wrong in this, since it is only the machine employed to fulfil a purely religious and charitable end. The sin is so highly veneered by glistening prosperity and artifice that the hideous fact is lost, and a sedulous mental review of the thousand tragic scenes enacted on the spot is necessary to withhold one's self away from the vampire's talons. Roulette seemed nothing more than a mere innocent child's game of chance, or fair raffle, with its revolving wheel and balls, dropping into the alternate red and black sockets, but *trente et quarante*, to which one apartment is devoted, is much more serious. It is played with cards, and nothing but gold coin is staked. It is not so exciting as the roulette, fewer indulge, and of these mostly women are seated at the tables; a most deathly silence reigns, and the gamers devote their most subtle intellect to the work. Vast rouleaux of Napoleons and heaps of Bank of France notes lay on the tables, and after the cards are dealt around twice, the game declared, the money is raked in by the croupier and distributed amongst the winners. I saw fifty dollars staked, and by some trick of betting on the first card dealt, the winner received fifteen hundred.

The Casino is not the only gambling *salon* of Monaco; indeed, there are numbers of assemblies or circles in all the towns and hamlets of the Riviera where baccarat is played all day long. Almost every private house and hotel has its roulette tables, as they are for sale in the shops as plenty as peanuts at our corners. Gambling is the miasma in the air, and to remain in the atmosphere you can no more hope to escape the infection than the yellow fever in Memphis, or the malaria upon the Pontine marshes.

Gambling is not the only vice of this chosen district. The business of pleasure—and ruin—is studied in its most minute details and abstract phases, and all that may contribute to the enjoyment of man is congregated here. I have heard loathsome tales of loose morals and free life here; the lamias, who sweep down in hordes upon unsuspecting youths, and of frequent murders and suicides. Of course my limited stay prevented me from seeing any of this, but where so much sin exists retribution is inevitable. Nemesis is as certain as Satan.

When Emperor William ostracized Monsieur Blanc and his nefarious comrades from Baden Baden, it was here, in the corner of Prince Monaco's paradise, that he found a sanitary refuge under the French Tri-color. I call the occupation nefarious; still is it any more guilty than railway, stock, commercial, and political speculations? It is bolder, but before the Eternal Judge it will not be more severely punished than the systematic villany that is practised daily by those who make the food, the comfort, and the peace of nations the sport of great corners, the excuse for living in luxury upon property not their own, and the opportunity to ruin those who invest in their false speculations. Human law justly chastises the gambler, and the chief of Monte Carlo has massed millions upon millions by his organized vice; but there is no human law for the rulers who gamble with the lives of their people, and slaughter millions in great and useless wars.

LETTER L.

"Heroic guide! whose wings are never furl'd,
By thee Spain's voyager sought another world;
What but poetic impulse could sustain
That dauntless pilgrim on the dreary main?
Day after day his mariners protest,
And gaze with dread along the pathless west;
Beyond that realm of waves, untrack'd before,
Thy fairy pencil traced the promised shore.
Through weary storms and faction's fiercer rage,
The scoffs of ingrates and the chills of age,
Thy voice renewed his earnestness of aim,
And whisper'd pledges of eternal fame;
Thy cheering smile atoned for fortunes's frown,
And made his fetters garlands of renown."
                                                TUCKERMAN.

GENOA, June, 1878.

I WOULD not dare to apply the threadbare and hackneyed boast of "La Superba" upon Monte Carlo, and yet it might be justly applied to that glittering pageant, and not to Genoa. Genoa is dirty, dismal, and dilapidated, and though the beauties of Monaco still linger in my mind like the pomp of some gorgeous pageant, the first picture that met my gaze here as I threw open my casement window, made a sad and lasting impress; a manacled defile of convicts passing over the railway embankment under my lattice, from their toil upon the quays, as the Angelus bell chimed the evening hour.

For some miles after leaving Monte Carlo, we had the fair French landscape about us, and the peddling peasants of French Savoy pushing their little wagons of carved wooden ornaments and cuckoo clocks over the white mountain paths, but after passing the line of the custom station, Ventimiglia, Italy was apparent in a general aspect of untidiness, squalor, and decay, which we saw only in the intervals we were upon *terra firma*, as our route was almost wholly subterranean, emerging from one tunnel only to encounter another. The guide-books say there are forty-one tunnels between Monte Carlo and Genoa, but it seemed like four hundred to me. As we approached many of the Italian towns grape-vines formed the walls and canopy of arbors that stretched through green fields; but so close as to disparage this beautiful view were crumbling houses, whose fortunes and lineage had expired together; manufactories, now only decaying shells, and schoolhouses tottering and dismantled. The once ruddy frescoes, now defaced by time, appearing frequently upon the *façades* of buildings, and Virgin shrines at the street corners, told me I was near Genoa, dearly and clearly associated with his own country in the mind of every American. Of course, the first object I looked for was something referring to Columbus, and found it in the *Piazza Acquaverde* adjoining the station. The monument of *Christoforo Columbo* is pointed out by every *vetturino* and *cicerone* to Americans as the loadstar.

To me Genoa is depressing in its decline; it seems like a beautiful woman reduced to a skeleton—a master intellect worn to a thread,—a monarch nodding to his fall; and memory reverts with a tinge of sadness to the time when this colossal wreck was a sovereign of the sea, powerful in her domestic wealth, and strong in her foreign possessions; when victories over the Saracens, conquests of the Pisans, and prolific trade in the Levant gave her a supremacy that even Venice envied; when the great names of Doria, Grimaldi, Spinola, and Fieschi shed a halo over the oligarchy, that in the present shines with spectral lustre upon the withering city.

I was not only impressed by its utter dilapidation—partly the work of the scythe of time—but by the mouldering, festering foulness universally met with, and as a strong effluvium of putrescent vegetable matter, maggoty garbage, bilge-water from the vessels, rancid oil from locomotives, the musty rag-shops, and the naked and offensive *chiffonniers*, floated in upon my susceptible senses, I prayed the merciful gods to rain a powerful antiseptic down upon this fetid city.

Through the crooked, labyrinthine, narrow streets—so narrow and the buildings so tall that never a ray of sunlight penetrates—we came upon the quays, where the arches are crumbling to powder. Under these the Italians sell macaroni and pick rags; but under these same colonnades we pushed open a door and ascended the marble stairway of the Hotel Trombetta, formerly the Palace of the Admiralty. Spacious dining halls, vast marble corridors, and luxurious chambers, formed a striking contrast to the exterior filth and decay. Through zigzag passages, and dark, damp, slimy alleys, where the antique palaces of the alternate black and white stone blocks rear their heads heavenward, I found the Doria estate, and entering met not even a symptom of the outside pollution, but a mansion crowned with the glories of *Perino del Vaga*, one of Raphael's pupils. The church of the *Annunziata*, though the bricks and mortar appear moth-eaten, is as superbly finished inside as a mosaic picture or a lady's enamelled gewgaw, and to me more beautiful than the Madelaine in Paris. Hours could be passed in this highly embellished sanctuary, and gladly would I have lingered longer with the young Italian acolyte as guide, feasting upon the beauties of the superb temple, had not time beckoned me away. This is my initial day in the religious tournament of Italy. It is a country of churches and a church-going community; every one who comes here immediately launches upon the peaceful sea of sanctity; holiness is the infection, and we can no more escape it than the gambling contagion at Monte Carlo. I do not know whether the Catholic custom of keeping their churches open all day and every day fosters a moral and powerful population, but it certainly has its merits. It is the only proper way for the house of God to be conducted. I never approved the system by which supplication and repentance are condensed into one conglomerate mass during six days, to be hurled, a pious projectile, upon the seventh. Religion should, like love, be an emotion of the heart—an ecstasy; and we should seek our God as our sweetheart, at the moment irresistible impulse prompts us to sweet communication. Worshipping God by routine and wooing by rule are for austere bigots only. If we sin on the first day of the week, and upon the second or third our soul cries *Peccavi*, we must bear the stings of the still small voice within four more days before we may cast our contrite hearts upon the altar of the Great Confessor, and it would demand a very tender conscience to bleed with the same remorse after this lapse of time. And so when Sunday morning shines, the ardor of our penitence has cooled; our heart-scourgings have been seared by time and the worldly work; we veneer one part of our guilt and forget another, and go our way with only a partial forgiveness. There is a prologue of penitence, but the wounds are only cauterized, the poison still festering at the core.

If my proclivities are Romish, let it be attributed to the fact, I entered a convent school at the age of eleven, and though my sentiments are far too liberal ever to adopt all the precepts of the Church, yet at so early an age the mind is placable, quick to receive and slow to remove, and the surroundings and teachings have left their vivid and enduring colors.

Genoa is built upon altitudes, and the streets coil round and round, until the first, the easiest, and the most frequent thing a stranger is guilty of is, to lose himself. There are spacious squares and fine stores, but they are the exception. The new *Mazzini Gallery*, christened in honor of the fierce and inspired Italian republican, is the pride of the Genoese. It is an exquisite glass-covered avenue, lined by fresh and costly establishments, while the half of one side is occupied by the new hotel.

I had heard much of Campo Santo, the picturesque cemetery of Genoa, and my first steps were turned towards it. I found almost as much food for reflection upon my route as in the *sui generis* necropolis. And of all I saw and all I studied, dirt and donkeys were the most affecting. All along the quays rag hovels—Genoa is the great rag mart of the world—were plenteous. Dark, foul, half-naked men were assorting their tattered merchandise, and baling it upon the numberless drays that were to convey it to the vessels. The air was permeated with the fumes of bad tobacco and garlic. By a mysterious turn we found ourselves in the broad Via Nuova, where the sunlight seemed to pour down with treble effulgence upon the white square by being debarred by narrow byways; where the Palazzo del Municipio reposes upon an inclination adorned by the eternal story of Doge Grimaldi in fresco, and guarded by Mazzini in marble. The stairway from the court is one of those costly and masterly works that, alas, sadly recall to us the art of bygone days, now a soiled vestige of former loveliness. In the Council Chamber Columbus and Marco Polo are blazoned in gaudy mosaics, and in a room adjoining is preserved the violin into which Paganini breathed the melodious life that electrified the world. This and two autograph letters from Columbus were the only objects of interest in the municipal palace.

The ladies of Genoa are, as a class, elegant and fantastic. They have ever been noted for the signal grace of their step. Add to this most eloquent beauty of woman, a prematurely developed, yet shapely form, clear olive complexion, large luminous eyes, and a wealth of raven hair, that seems a burden to the wearer, in its multiplied coils, and you have a model of this attractive province. Then their costume is so *bizarre* and romantic, they look like the antique females stepped from the canvas of a Spanish or Italian picture, in their rich, brilliant colors, with only a filmy scarf of black lace draped about the head and throat, and their large Oriental fans. There seem to be fewer visitors upon the streets than in any of the other foreign cities. I cannot account for this dearth of strangers, but I can point out every alien female by her bonnet. The upper classes of the natives' *coiffure* is only the veil, fastened on one side by a luscious damask rose or gilt ornament.

The shop windows display but one character of jewelry —the filagree. There are three species manufactured: the pure gold, the pure silver, and the silver with gold facing; and every description of bauble for which the female heart longs may be found in confused superfluity. These, with velvet, are the chief staples, and the prices, compared to those at home, are excessively moderate. An exquisite set of ear-rings and pin of the pure gold, are sold for eight American dollars, a bracelet for twelve, a necklace for sixteen,—ranging higher, according to the intricacy of the work and weight of metal, while the lower grades depreciate with the value of the silver.

Toward the Porta Romana we passed through streets in which I feared we might be wedged. Certainly some calamity would have occurred had a mule, a man, or even a mouse, been encountered. Fortunately neither conveyance nor animal was met. Where either would have sought refuge from the contact is still a sealed problem, as there were only here and there holes beaten into the hedging walls where blacksmiths, tinkers, cobblers, and rag-pickers ply their meagre trade. Once outside the gates we breathe the fresh air and try to force from our lungs the noxious gases that have all but strangled us in our ride through the cramped town. Laundresses are beating their linen on stones in the Bisagno, whose waters seem insufficient for the process. It is a peculiar way these Italian rivers have, yielding more pebbles than water. The flow is always scanty, and rolls in its stony bed like the ebbing life of some torpid creature. The poor, pathetic little mules trot over the hills and steep passes, their pannier baskets laden with every sort of household or personal furniture, vegetables for market, and frequently carrying whole families. These beasts, with their hunted, mournful faces, if subjected to a phrenological examination, would be found to possess the faculty of location in the highest stage of development. They take their own route; their master sleeps upon their back in the happy consciousness of perfect faith. At first I believed some poor man to be the possessor of a donkey who had acquired this wonderful endowment, perhaps from the habit that becomes second nature, and perhaps a hereditary gift from father and grandfather who had travelled the path before him; but as I passed on I learned it was a characteristic attribute. All these patient quadrupeds went unfaltering over their way; all the drivers were asleep.

The Campo Santo was a surprise and a pleasure. It differs *toto cœlo* from any city of the dead I have delighted in; as I have, in truth, an infirmity for cemeteries. Great marble corridors or galleries of shelves, reaching from floor to ceiling, contain the coffins of the dead, square marble tablets, bearing the name and date of birth and death, hide the unsightly mural caskets. Long palisades of monuments skirt the outer walls, and rising with the terraces on the hill are costly tombs and chapels. There seems to be enough funeral statuary upon this burial hill to exhaust all the marble quarries of Italy, and offer employment to every disciple of Phidias and Praxiteles in the Old World. Only the lower classes are buried under the earth, over each grave a black stick bearing a little black lantern.

Here in this lovely white and silent city, modern Italy shows its inherited genius. The dead are as recent as the artists; and among the first are soldiers and statesmen of conceded local fame, while among the last are proved masters of sculpture. Many, indeed most of these carved effigies have names unknown to Americans, and so also of most of those who moulded and finished their forms and features. Only Mazzini on his hill, recalled the fiery Democrat, whose life was a great agony for liberty, and whose soul breathed its incense over all the world—only he was familiar to me.

21*

LETTER LI.

"O Rome! my country! city of my soul!
　The orphans of the heart must turn to thee
Lone mother of dead empires! and control
In their shut breasts their petty misery.
What are our woes and sufferance? Come and see
　The cypress, hear the owl, and plod your way
O'er steps of broken thrones and temples, Ye!
　Whose agonies are evils of a day—
　A world is at our feet as fragile as our clay."
　　　　　　　　　　　　　　　BYRON.

ROME, June, 1878.

THE impoverished condition of Italy is painfully apparent in the tottering habitations, decaying stations, crumbling aqueducts, and broad stretches of barren moorland. Last night I passed through some forty tunnels, but thanks to Somnus, he folded his peaceful wings about me, and I dreamed of triple-action springs and luxurious mattresses in these dark caverns, only to waken with the dawn, and find my cramped limbs and aching head painfully real in comparison with my happy delusions.

Pisa was the first station I saw in the early morning, and I thought if I could catch the least sight of the Leaning Tower I should go on my way contented and satisfied that I had not vainly climbed its apex, traversed the winding ways of the town, and witnessed the reputed sensuality of the populace. But not a line of its columns nor a scroll of its fretwork gladdened my expectant gaze. A group of dusky Italian boys lounged about the platform, and I beckoned one to the carriage window. Handing him a towel, I asked him in French to dip it in water; the boy's eyes wandered alternately between the towel and my face in blank amazement; then, interrogating me in Italian, I comprehended he had not the slightest idea of the language in which I was addressing him. I made this discovery with some surprise, as it was the first peasant or native I had met on the continent not able to speak the polite and really standard language of Europe,—and I could not master one word of Italian. After a few moments' annoying hesitation and silence filled with pantomimic gestures, I made an endeavor upon him with the Latin word *aqua*, which was the magic key to his understanding. For my breakfast I purchased a small flagon of wine for ten cents, and a sandwich made of bologna sausage so impregnated with garlic that the atmosphere was redolent at once, and had it not been for a cold fowl tucked away in one corner of my lunch basket, at Genoa, I should have been obliged to go fasting to Rome.

The Italian railway stations are frequently separated by extended stretches of country, utterly houseless and godforsaken. The train often makes a run of three or four hours without cessation, and, unlike America, there are no luxuries, nor even conveniences; if you are suffering from hunger or thirst you must bear it until your necessities grow into agony. Then at the first stopping-place, which is frequently a little mouldering town, with an offensive railway *bouffet*, there is a general outpouring of passengers, and the slightest succor or relief must be paid for. How I recalled the splendid comforts of the railways of my own country!

I thought I should be made aware of my approach to the Eternal City by certain signs of sanctity, which would at once transform me into a *devotée* of his Reverence Leo XIII. Surely this could not be the city of Cæsar and Brutus, of Augustus and Trajan, and the great Constantine. Surely this is not the Rome of Romulus and the See of St. Peter, revealed to me in the crumbling aqueducts and white cattle knee deep in the lush grass of the Campagnian marshes. Where is the glory of the Gracchi, the glamour of Michael Angelo, Raphael, and Canova, the grandeur of Trajan, and the cruelty of Nero? Oh where, where are all these influences and elements that really make the sublimity of Rome? I asked myself again and again as I came through the new quarter of the city, where the façades are as fresh and glaring, and life as *insouçiant* and youthful as in Paris. I vainly looked for some sign by which the consciousness of the sacred city might take possession of me. Perhaps I sought an emperor in crimson-bordered toga and sandalled feet. Perhaps a legion of gladiators, or the early disciples of Jesus. There were scores of Capucini and Dominican friars upon the streets; but these were familiar objects, and then they were all either too dirty or too corpulent and carnal to summon the ghosts of the past; they were pre-eminently of the present.

And so my *entrée* into this Etrurian capital was disappointing. I had expected its splendor to burst upon me like some great meteor of a southern sky. I was premature; much that was magnificent, and much that was anomalous, awaited me, but it is not the order of grandeur that overpowers by one glory of effulgence. It is all so uniform in its magnitude that you must grow into and slowly absorb it.

My first steps were not turned toward St. Peter's. It was too late in the day; another reason, I always "save the best wine until the last." So after dining sumptuously upon robin, artichokes, macaroni, prawns, and *Lacrima Christi*, in the sweet glow of the dying day, I joined in the glittering line of equipages slowly mounting Monte Pincio. I should have preferred to walk; then I could have studied the curious street corners, sparkling with the spray of fountains, and sacred with the Virgin shrines, but I did not know the way, and must submit to *vetturino*. The life I met was as much a vanity fair as Paris, and only a repetition of a ride to the Bois de Boulogne. There was no fragrance of antiquity, nor chime of holiness, nor gloss of imperialism. No *Angelus* bells made sweet and solemn music; no orisons floated upon the air, no prayerful hush upon the place, no peaceful benediction to balsam a bleeding soul, no *Te Deum* of praise, no genuflexion of worship to tell me I was in the city of God. Long parades of costly turnouts, with high-stepping steeds and liveried attendants, ostentatious crests, and dark, gaudily-dressed women, chaperoning their infantile progeny and nurses through the procession. The nurses, as gay as peacocks in their garish plumes, I at first mistook for ladies of some high degree of nobility, and while I did not admire their pomposity of paraphernalia and streaming pink head ribbons,—I think the pink pennons are the universal indice of this order,—I did regard the republicanism and maternal pride with which these *grand duchesses* bore their own children—as I then supposed.

The Roman matrons do not seek to alleviate nor even to spiritualize their essentially earthy faces and forms by their mode of dress. Many among the showy community in which I mingled last night—only the upper-tendom—were magnificently beautiful women, but with sensual faces. Their charms lie in massive coils of dusky hair, eyes that are luminous with the dew of unshed tears, and creamy luscious throats.

We entered Monte Pincio from the Piazza del Popolo, where the obelisk of Ramses, with its quartette of guarding beasts and dancing fountains, crowns the centre of the great oblong circle, while the monumental churches, great fonts of leaping water, the gate of the piazza, and lofty columns and walls, surmounted by colossal statues of Rome, Neptune, Spring, Summer, Autumn, and Winter, form an unforgotten coronal.

Passing under the portal, where the seasons blend in glorious harmony, we were among the cypress and box, ilex and palms, cedars and oleanders, stretches of sward and mounds of prodigal bloom. Gods and goddesses, heroes of war and conquerors of science, masters of verse and victors of art, glance from between the pines and behind corners of bronze foliage in a state of pitiable decay. The strains of the musicians assisted in dispersing any gathering shade of sublimity in this twilight retreat of stony celebrities; for they were all silent,—the marble effigies bordering the paths not more so than the flashy groups of fashion upon the avenues. I left the glittering Roman crowd, and again passing the broad piazza entered the Villa Borghese beyond the city walls that hedge the park. Here there was no pageant of money, nor titles, nor fashion; no dead emperors nor slaughtered generals gazing in marble dignity; but shady avenues, great forests of dense herbage, the sweet odor of earth, and a stifled air of purity that chastened the spot of all the profligacy of its Corsican Princess, and left only the memory of her beauty and grace as a hallowing reflection. Still there remains, in one of the upper chambers of the palace, the celebrated Venus Victrix of Canova, modelled from Pauline Bonaparte, Princess Borghese.

The original seven hills upon which ancient Rome rested like so many pediments, have now multiplied into as many more. Upon any one of these altitudes we see the city, with its domes, and spires, and monuments, and ruins, rise and fall like the breast of the ocean. This undulating belt forms an entire girdle to the city, and each summit has a special monumental crown: St. Peter's and the Holy Prison (?) of the Pope upon Vaticanas; the Franciscan's Gardens and a group of villas upon Janiculum, in the district of Trastevere; the Palace of the Cæsars upon Palatinus; the Palace of King Humbert upon the Quirinalis; Santana Sabina and several other churches upon Aventinus; the Basilica of Santa Maria Maggiore and the Baths of Titus upon Esquilinus; the Baths of Diocletian upon Viminalis; and St. John in Lateran at the base of Cælian; and the Mamertine Prison, the archæological institution with arches, temples, and columns innumerable to mythical deities and dead emperors.

LETTER LII.

> "Or turning to the Vatican, go see
>   Laocoon's torture dignifying pain—
> A father's love and mortal's agony
>   With an immortal's patience blending :—Vain
>   The struggle ; vain, against the coiling strain
> And gripe, and deepening of the dragon's grasp,
>   The old man's clench ; the long evenom'd chain
> Rivets the living links,—the enormous asp
> Enforces pang on pang, and stifles gasp on gasp."
>   BYRON.

ROME, June, 1878.

As I rode home from Monte Pincio and the Villa Borghese, a few evenings since, the little lamps shone like stars in front of virgin shrines at the street corners and over the doors, while the great celestial lamps swung in the broad dome above, casting more of a carnival than a religious glow over the Catholic capital. When I woke next morning, with the dazzling Italian sun flooding the chamber, and throwing the rude highly-colored frescoes into blinding brilliancy, the troops of King Humbert were drilling in the great square beyond, while the tinkling of church chimes made festive the early day. And this double parade of soldiers and saintly worship was on the Sabbath! I could not realize that it was in Rome I had slept.

It is a city for reflection! "Rome was not built in a day;" this idea flashes upon one through every step of experience. Neither can it be seen nor studied in a day, and one must meditate, whether he will or not. Every moment some aged relic or mouldering ruin rouses a vivid recollection; anything modern in this venerable shadow seems a profanation. While I feel old in the presence of these crumbling centuries, yet it is what I sought in Rome. The broad streets, bright new houses, and unfinished Protestant church, are unanticipated pleasures in Rome, yet the only real sublimity, the only inspiration in this capital of the centuries, is the mould, and rust, and dampness of the antique. Still how lovely the aged city in its ancient *noblesse* and tattered lazzaroni; with its souvenirs of greatness and evidences of decay; with the memory of myrrh, frankincense, and all the aromatic spices of the East, and the too offensive odors of the present; with its wealth of mediæval art and hordes of modern disciples.

Here only do I falter in my strong proclivities for the primigenious. The great names that form a circling halo to Roman history are here portrayed, not in the freshness and fashion of their day, but with all the impression of the fifteenth and sixteenth centuries upon them. Our eye, not inured to primeval art, even at the rugged height of its glory, wanders to the modern copies and back to the originals, while the treasonous thought creeps in: Would these immortal names shine with the same lustre if they were of the present epoch, and if they were the product of the genius of this magnificent era of scientific discoveries, philosophical demonstration; artistic cultivation, and archæological explorations—in *our* day, when human life and human brains, wealth, and invention are devoted to the education and elevation of the masses; when the world's battle-cry is *advance?* Is it not only the legendary cloud of age that hangs in transcendent mystery around the *chefs d'œuvre* of earlier days? Time, to the untaught mind, has robbed the canvas and marble of their expectant charms. Are we disappointed because we behold art touched by the despoiling finger of age, because, as he passes on from year to year, he adds a brighter tone to the names they bear? The fame that to-day shines only with a wan and pallid light, sufficient to illuminate a city, may, in the next century, when death has claimed and seasons have hallowed it, burst forth a meteor to dazzle and bewilder worlds. What a volume to read! What monuments to study! What relics to gather, to decipher, and to organize!

Come through the Piazza di Spagna, where we find great libraries of English books, cafés, photograph shops, and windows laden with the gaudy scarfs of Roman silk; where the picturesque but soiled models (soiled body and soul) recline in artistic costumes upon the great rows of steps that lead to Trinità de Monti. From dawn till the sinking sun throws his rosy mantle over the hills of Albano, these beautiful, luscious, unwashed Roman women swarm in this quarter, waiting to be chosen by one of the hundreds of students of the vicinity. Glance at them as you pass, then come with me to St. Peter's. It is not a temple to be visited, but a sanctuary in which to linger; where we may return again and again, and the oftener we come the more we shall find to feast upon. It is the one spot to resort when the heart is oppressed and the soul craves a balsam, there to remain until these holy shadows fold you in their sweet embrace. Do not look in when you are hastening toward another monument. That annihilates the entire splendors of the effect. Your mind first absorbs enough of the great cathedral to be enthralled by its sovereignty; then, when sufficiently filled with its majesty, you are safe from the influence of subordinate charms.

Now come and drink deeply of its imperishable mosaics that are as brilliant to-day as they were centuries ago. Come linger at the tombs where all the horror of the decaying bones within is lost in admiration of the statuary on the top. In truth the place is a purified charnel-house, and we are surrounded by the sarcophagi of mouldering saints and vanished popes; but we see only the deeds of great heroes, and the fasting, prayer, and castigations of devotees in classic marble. It is not a vault of the dead, but a temple of art to keep their memories fresh forever.

The Piazza of St. Peter's rests upon the inclination of the hill. In the centre an Egyptian obelisk, with fountains on either side, is dwarfed in the shadow of the great basilica. Semicircular wings of the temple, in the form of peristyles, a perfect labyrinth of Doric columns and massive pilasters, surmounted by colossal statues of saints and popes, inclose the square. The interior seems to boast a peculiar atmosphere of its own. When the malarial sun is scorching all Rome in the porticos beyond, here it is calm and cool, even chilly, though never damp. Far up the nave men appear like mice, and the wonderful Confession of St. Peter, the cynosure of the interior, where one hundred and forty-two bronze lamps shed perpetual immortality upon the Christ-elected pope, seems only a twinkling star. In the crypt beneath rest the ashes of the apostle, directly under the broad gilded canopy. If you would descend and be in the holy presence of the anointed dead you must pay. Such favors are not for the impecunious. "Put money in your purse," as Iago tells Roderigo, and all paths do lie open. Chapels adorn every nook and nave, chapels whose mosaics and monuments apotheosize the names of Michael Angelo, Canova, Bernini, Guido, and Sacchi, and under whose garlanded and carved arcades, aliens, such as Christina of Sweden, who abdicated the throne before she was thirty, the Stuarts, and the Countess Matilda, have found their last sleep far from the country of their fathers.

Alas! the mosaics that we regard as works of artistic delicacy in the dome, hanging like a great balloon at a dizzy height above us, are rude enough upon closer examination. But the precious marbles of the altar, the porphyry steps, the lapis lazuli, malachite, and Egyptian alabaster are in themselves an El Dorado of wealth.

May I say that I enjoyed the Vatican Palace, or papal prisons, as the holy occupant chooses to term it, still more than St. Peter's, or shall I say the pleasure it afforded me was more ecstatic than reverential? First came the gigantic cartoons and frescoes of Raphael, over which we are expected to rhapsodize because they are from the mystic pencil of the peerless magician, and the Loggiè of Raphael, that extends in portico about the upper stories of the southeastern wing of the palace. They consist of fifty-two biblical themes drawn from Raphael's cartoons, executed, with very few exceptions, by his pupils. The pictures of the Loggie are not characterized by the same boldness of outline and eccentricity of attitude as the great frescoes of Jurisprudence, the School of Athens, and Mount Parnassus, but they are more brilliant in hue, and conventional in construction.

In the halls of sculpture we have such a feast that it becomes a burden, and we are wont to wish we had not dined so profoundly upon the other good things spread before us. Much that is fine, and much that is fragmentary; each has its story, and many are the relics of vanished ages of which we have nothing authentic. Such grand conceptions as Apollo Belvidere, the Laocoon of Rhodes, the Nile, which to me is a still more marvellous piece of art than the Laocoon, the recumbent Ariadne on the Isle of Naxos, the wonderful Faun, a copy of Praxiteles,—these are lessons to be remembered; who, indeed, once having viewed them, could forget? Yet in these halls there are multiplied statues, sans eyes, sans noses, sans arms, sans legs, sans everything—gods and heroes who lost their physiognomic members in the pagan era. Torsos and hermæ that would require the inspiration of a Phidias to invest with any of their original symmetry, yet these are invaluable to show the antiquity of art in this vast world of art. Days have I passed amongst these marbles, until they became the companions of my life, and when at last compelled to leave them I felt indescribable sadness and solitude. Then I could discern the enthusiasm of the sculptor for his stony creations, rather than for his living models. As he moulds and chisels, he invests his offspring with all the fire of his soul, the cunning of his hand, the genius of his brain, and the majesty of his ambition. Being finished he loves it and shuns parting with it, because there is more of his life in the cold marble than in the vital frame.

As I pass up the royal stairs of Bernini, the equestrian archetype of Constantine seems to frown me down; and why? It must be that I passed him so often with only a glance, ever hastening on to other gods. Now the tapestries, then the pictures, again the Last Judgment, and then back to the statuary or the papal library.

The Last Judgment of Angelo in the Sistine Chapel is considered the masterpiece of his life. The fresco is in his vigorous contortionate style, but the conception is an avenging Judge, not a merciful Saviour. Christ upon the celestial throne seems to be hurling the offending souls into eternal damnation in confused multitudes; his eye is aflame, scorching even his mother, who trembles at his side, while Mary Magdalene is in an equivocal position of supplication, half fearful of farther exciting her Master's wrath; you almost hear the unuttered prayer for the condemned die in a stifled sob. The upper part of the fresco is filled in with soaring figures—the blessed, who have received their testament of virtue and are ascending to the golden tribunal in happy indifference. The artist has woven a silhouette of his life into the picture: the angels have the faces of his friends, whilst the sinners are portraits of his enemies, with him to whom he bore the greatest hatred as Judas in the depths of hell.

The Vatican library teaches us the opulence, royalty, power, and world-wide influence of Catholicism. Not in the 80,000 volumes and 24,000 MSS. alone do we read this profound truth, but in the sumptuous saloons and costly gifts of foreign potentates. Sèvres vases from Napoleon, malachite timepieces and ornaments from the Czar, Egyptian alabaster from Mehemet Ali; buhl cabinets and tables of rarest Grecian and Italian stones line the great hall, where frescoes and gold repoussé seem to have had their finishing touches overnight. In fact, I fancied I could smell the paint, and stood aloof from the pillars and walls; and this is only one of the cells in the sacred prisoner's dungeon.

Then the gardens, where his reverence may ventilate his ever pious plans, are not a dark and slimy cavern where toads do procreate and serpents crawl, but inclosures as beautiful and bright as a Parisian pleasance. They extend along the declivity of the hill, and manifest all the splendor of natural and artificial embellishment; the shrubbery is exquisitely trimmed; pedestals and bronzes stand here and there; even curious and ingenious water-works surprise the stranger, by issuing from invisible apertures beneath his feet as he pauses to admire the huge pine cone from the mausoleum of Adrian, or passes on from terrace to terrace.

The manufactory of mosaics within the Vatican walls is a catchpenny. I do not intend to intimate that it is unworthy a visit, for to see it is the only way to gain an idea of these Catholic workmen and adepts. Even the coarsest of their products require pains and time to finish. Thousands of boxes of the enamelled stone, of every hue and shade, are arranged upon the shelves that surround the long rooms from floor to ceiling. They are at present employed upon the medallion portraits of the Popes for St. Paul's in Lateran, or beyond the walls. Each executor has an oil picture of the subject before him as a model, and watching the process we discover it requires some skill to perfect the copy. Now, I called this manufactory a catchpenny, because our guide, who is, as I think, even an exaggeration of the importunate boring and falsifying traditional guide, told us it was free to strangers. True, there was no charge to enter, but the ransom of deliverance was heavy; every one who opened a door, or turned a picture, or handed you a specimen of stone, expected and demanded some of the small coin of the kingdom.

Though not inspired with the same hush of solitude and healing rest in the private palace galleries, perhaps I gained a more instructive idea of art than in the holy museums. Of course, I went to the Barbarini to hunt out the original Beatrice Cenci by Guido, of which they say all the copies that float the universe as thick as flies upon the shambles are shameful travesties. I found it amongst a whole family of Cencis, and that was a disappointment. Surely this brave, fanatic girl deserves a place alone, as the suffering heroine of her line, instead of being grouped with stepmother, aunt, sister-in-law, and a host of other relatives, of whom the world never heard. Perhaps it was done that her kin might shine in the reflection of her lustre; but the glory of a self-created martyr should not be sacrificed to the vanity of a family. There are those whom this sad face, lighted by the great pathetic eyes, have haunted a lifetime, but I freely confess, and let it be attributed to my ignorance of art or dearth of intelligence, that it did not impress me as deeply, viewing it from the protoplast I had in mind, as a little painting I have at home, by no very eminent master. Sorrow and suffering are admirably depicted, but there are cold lines about the mouth and nose, and even eyes, that Beatrice, as I conceive the character, never had. There is fixed purpose and strong determination upon the canvas, and these were her ruling attributes.

Raphael's Fornarina glows with all the magic of her lover's brush. It is not a beautiful face, neither is it a face of a patrician, but one to be loved; a face of Southern warmth and passion and youthful freshness. But all enchantment faded when I heard she was a baker-girl, and existed in one of the thousand dark, dirty little holes of Rome, where "*forno*" appears over the door in large text. "*Forno*" is the oven, and Fornarina was the young lady who kneaded and baked the black bread in yard measures for the Italian mass. Yet, through the love of the artist, she is immortalized in oil from zone to zone.

Del Sarto's Virgin more completely fills my conception of Mary, at the birth of Christ, than any I have looked upon amongst the thousands here. Sacred painting was paramount in the halcyon days of art; what else had these early masters as subjects but the Bible and mythology? There are some few illustrative of their own lives, but such scenes labor under a disadvantage that biblical ones never can contend with; the former often need an interpreter, the latter are read at once. Now Del Sarto draws the Madonna as a luscious, radiant young female, with the infant Saviour upon her lap; all other artists represent the woman with the infant, and the woman clinging to the cross upon Mount Calvary, thirty-three years afterward, of the same age, cast of feature, and with the same expression of weight and care; a physical impossibility.

But there is a small picture, I know not by whom, that made an ineffaceable impress. So long as life lasts I shall see it as I saw it then. Mark it well; it hangs in a small *salon* at the rear of the gallery. No diary nor guide will ever be necessary to recall it, for it lingers in my memory like strains of unforgotten music—"Orpheus Charming Birds and Beasts;" very odd, touching, and grotesque,—the listening air and attitude of the captivated cow, the hearkening horse, the absorbed owl, the mesmerized monkey, the silenced magpie, the surprised fox, the tickled fish, the arrested eagle, the terrified tiger, the languishing lion, and even the whale called out from the ocean by the dulcet music; the birds stilled in their flight, and the very air listing among the branches of the trees. When you visit Rome seek it, and see and hear this enraptured animal world in the Palazzo of the Barbarini.

LETTER LIII.

> "In the breathless gloom
> I sought the Coliseum, for I felt
> The spirits of a manlier age were forth;
> And there against the mossy wall I leaned,
> And thought upon my country. Why was I
> Idle, and she in chains? The storm now answered:
> It broke as heaven's high masonry were crumbling:
> And the wide vault, in one unpausing peal,
> Throbbed with the angry pulse of Deity!"
>
> JACK CADE.

ROME, June, 1878.

I FOUND the Rome I sought upon the Palatine and Capitoline. Not the holy Rome of Vaticanus, nor the political Rome of Quirinalus, but the antique pagan Rome of the Cæsars. I had thought a visit to the palaces of the Cæsars was to be the culminating ecstasy of my Italian experience. But while I found the mound full of the glory of the past, life in the vicinity was lusty with the pleasures of the present. The foul, contracted byways of old Rome were thronged with men, women, and children. Dark, dirty drowsy beings seemed to be in a slow putrefaction by dint of their own sloth and squalor. Their only employment is the animal functions of life, including the exhalation of their noxious garlic breath upon the stifling atmosphere. The females are beautiful. Though an intense admirer of womanly grace, my frenzy is not sufficient to excuse unclean persons and soiled gowns; but these voluptuous Roman women possess a fascination of face and form that almost cancels their contempt for purity.

In this southern climate nature matures earlier than in our slower north. The same sun that causes the orange to glow, the cypress and oleander to blaze, and the grape to ripen, kisses the human buds into a precocious exuberance of bloom. At the age of fourteen we find these girls in the full flush of adolescence, but at twenty-five, when the flower of life should be most aromatic, they have declined into middle-aged, toiling, wasted wrecks. Where do we discover one trace of the radiant, luxuriant maid, of the sweet, soft shadows about the dusky throat, of the luminous eyes and dewy complexion, ten years after in the hard face and obdurate lines of the matron, the saffron skin, angular form, dull or glaring eye, and furrowed cheek?

Their wealth of hair, black as a raven's wing and lustrous as satin, is the only enduring attribute of former beauty. And then the babies! The superfluity of babies is one of the most impressive features of Italian life. Every woman has an infant upon her arm, and two scarcely older clinging to her skirts or wallowing at her feet in the gutter; a woman minus the infantile appendage would be as great a curiosity as the fabled Centaur, Minotaur, or Cyclops. A very usual picture in these Latin cities is a scanty doorstep, upon which two youthful scions of a plebeian family are at work; the second is perched at an altitude overlooking the former's crown, which he manipulates in the most sedulous manner; so I was at first nonplussed to which I should apply the term of "industrious fleas," the hunted or the hunters. These urchins seem to be universally skilled artisans in this, the only trade they are taught. And thus the soil procreates pollution. In no other country are the conventionalities of social laws so completely abandoned. All that is sweet and sacred in the ties of nature is utterly ignored. I have read much of the classic dignity of the Roman women, but certainly in this community it is an unknown quantity. The august chastity of Cornelia, the innocence of the youthful Metella, seem to have vanished with the unforgotten dead, and only the saturnalias of Faustina, the cupidity of Danae, and the licentiousness of Messalina, remain as a code and a principle to these modern Laidis. Yet, let me say, in this whirlpool of profligacy the inherent delicacy of woman stood forth pre-eminent to the disparagement of the opposite sex. Never had I such a rare opportunity to read the potent parable: A woman's vices may be most offensive and flagrant, but there is a something that her Creator has placed in her soul—a common endowment of the sex—which deters her from sinking to the same degree of brutality and vulgarity with her burly brothers.

Such were the life-pictures I saw, and the life-lessons I studied. But what of the palaces of the Cæsars, the home of Caligula, and the house of Cicero? What of the Roman Forum, where great Cæsar fell; of the formidable Tarpeian Rock, from which Cassius—not the "lean and hungry" conspirator against Cæsar, but of the same lineage —was hurled? Ruins all; a mouldering mass of shattered grandeur;—these baths where the voluptuary was wont to pass his hours; these temples of false gods where the great pagans worshipped; these triumphal arches under which the conquerors rode; these theatres where the consuls and prætors enjoyed the wild cruelty of the early sports; and these prisons where the adherents of Cataline perished, and St. Peter languished under the tyranny of the savage Nero.

The remains of the mansions of these Etrurian poets, potentates, and philosophers are tiresome, and though the durability of the early masonry is marvellously real in the foundations of these structures, where time seems to have added to the immutability of the bricks and the fixedness of the mortar, the high art and enduring pigments of the ancients potentially significant in the remnants of mosaic pavements and the brilliant hues of frescoes, yet it requires the fancy of the poet to supply the departed beauty and missing members that once gave the scene its sublimity. The chambers of Cæsar's palace are mere sleeping cribs, not so spacious as the bathrooms of our moderate-sized houses, and while the artistic adornments in the courts and ground-floors were costly, if not chaste, these ancient kings had none of the common and continuous luxuries of our day. A stroll amongst the fragments of Roman luxury is tedious and perilous. The memory of great names and intrepid exploits, the classic odor and empyrean lustre of other eras, is shadowed in the heavy pall of death. Ah! pitiable the dilapidation of the crumbling, moss-grown, mutilated statues, once the embodied virtues and vices of a now dead religion! What are they now? Nor man, nor woman, nor thing. Here we find a human trunk, there a bodiless head, again a headless face, or a faceless head, and so we go searching about the gardens for members that might complete one perfect man, where wandered the pleading Calphurnia upon the fated ides of March, when her lord unheeding went forth to fall at Pompey's statue.

The awe-inspiring Tarpeian Rock, which history in the schoolroom, and Byron in the Parlor, taught us was steep and

> "Fittest goal of Treason's race,
> The promontory whence the Traitor's leap
> Cured all ambition"——

is another sad delusion. Instead of a lofty and rugged vertex, with a raging torrent below, I found a gentle mound, against which dwellings recline, the Archæological Institute, and Prussian Embassy gardens stretch around in pleasant perspective, with a very dirty, sluggish stream drowsing at the base, and a vast quantity of broken soil, partly the accumulation of time, and the exhumations of the vicinity, filling the surrounding ditch and levelling the mighty altitude to an indifferent hillock.

Rome, so overcrowded with the dead is, nevertheless, often suffocatingly full of the living, and it has been well said of this pagan-Christian capital that although owned by the Latins and populated by their descendants, it is more thoroughly enjoyed and improved by the French, the Germans, the English, and the Americans.

In strolling through the Palatine, the Coliseum, the Pantheon, St. Peter's, the various amphitheatres and circuses, I met crowds and coteries of these strangers, some with guides and others with guide-books, tracing the inscriptions on the monuments, the old frescoes, and the discovered and recovered secrets of the long gone centuries. Among these foreigners were *savants*, priests, artists, princes, and even monarchs, called to Rome by the unceasing wonders of the sacred city. The two Napoleons—I and III—spent enormous sums in the excavations, even out-rivalling the great Popes, who from the beginning have also given time and money to the revelation and improvement of ancient Rome. The Coliseum, about which I had read and thought so much, was one of those things that transcended imagination; it has been painted and photographed and engraved, so runs the record, more than any other human habitation or edifice, and it has attracted the attention of princes and kings and potentates since it was projected by Vespasian, and to this day, covered as it is with the dust of over nineteen hundred Christian years, is still a fresh wonder of civilization. It was a superb June day, but a Roman day with all the drowsy oppressive miasma of the Campagna in the atmosphere, when I passed through the front court or vestibule of the colossal ruin, where the legendary insurgent Thracian refused to meet his brother in gladiatorial combat, and where now vendors of cheap jewelry stand with great trays of rough mosaic ornaments of the ruined hills.

Although the city was bare of visitors, and the hotels preparing to close for the summer, I had an opportunity to see the majestic ruin under exceptional advantages. There is something awful in this mighty space, and even if you are not familiar with the history of the ages, you are forced to stop and study it for very shame sake. It is so vast that although two-thirds of the original edifice have disappeared, the materials to build the palaces of the Roman nobility having been taken for two hundred years from its colossal walls, the almost perfect circle that is left standing gives you a fair idea of the stupendous whole.

Nearly every excursionist or traveller who visits these ancient massive structures recites Byron. Poor Byron! he is the compelled decorator of most of the guide-books, and is sung by the verdant pilgrim from the St. Lawrence at home, who makes a vehicle of his poetry when he describes Niagara, to the Rhine in Germany, where he expresses his ecstasy over that vaunted stream, and when he gets to Rome and enters St. Peter's, and the Vatican, and the Coliseum, he becomes the involuntary echo of the poetic pictures of the British bard.

Upon the Appian Way we see the supposititious spot blessed by the footprints of Christ, the Monarch of Heaven, and glorified by Constantine and the Cæsars, conquerors of the world, over which they led their puissant armies. We see the baths of Caracalla, where the early sybarites lounged amid pungent scents and spicy opiates, when perfumes were more alluring to the natives than they are to their posterity, discussing politics or the latest scandal in a prætor's or a consul's family; so the *thermæ* were to the ancients what the beer saloon and cigar shop is to the Scipios, Diomeds, and Claudii of the present. The Catacombs, that completely seton the Campagna, and even extend as far as Ostia, are another wicked fallacy practised upon the unsophisticated stranger. No doubt they were the retreats of the early persecuted followers of Faith when Rome was rife with the religious cabals of the first century, and no doubt much of the virus rising from the great sterile moors is only the poison of these long-hoarded bones in the subterranean sepulchres. From the Porta San Sebastiano to the right are the great Christian cemeteries; and to the left the Jewish, hedged in by walls, marked by a series of interstices resembling pigeon-holes. To grovel through these narrow, dirty, labyrinthine dungeons, preceded by a cadavarous-looking friar, with only the ghostly gleam of a puny tallow candle to add horror to the spectral scene, is not calculated to inspire poetry or safety. The martyrdom, scourging, and dire flagellations of these Christian standard-bearers is forgotten in their own fraud and the fright of their guests. Winding about uneven paths, stumbling up and down crumbling clay steps, peering into little holes that *once*, perhaps, contained dry and whited bones, but, alas! have been sacrilegiously rifled by visitors in search of souvenirs; occasionally having a little incision in the wall, near a coffin-shelf covered by glass, pointed out as the casket that contains the blood of a saint, caught from his wounds while dying, and preserved through the centuries, and while you search for the vital fluid and discover only a smear like a soiled finger-mark upon the glass, your canonical guide tells you the rest has evaporated, and then vanishes around a corner, some corner, there are so many corners you are undecided which one to turn. To follow the wrong path will be death; to hesitate will be death. In another moment our holy friend, curtailed of his fair proportions, will have swept another curve, and then the wan glimmer is lost forever. We follow in a state of unpleasant and eager expectancy, and heave a sob of relief when we see the ghastly flame and grim visage. All this and more is not the most delectable entertainment, and yet this "is seeing the Catacombs." We tell our anointed brethren we have had sufficient of the repulsive repast, and beg to be excused from tasting it further. But we are informed there can be no retraction; hungry or satiated the spectral banquet-hall has been entered; to stop at the *entrées* is not permissible; we must agonize through the succeeding courses of blood and bones, dust and darkness and clay, to the tail-end of the *menu*. With these unpleasant reflections we are asked to pay for the murderous and cankerous meal, which we do unresistingly, glad to escape the further hospitalities of the grim host. He is obsequious upon rolling our silver in his grimy palm, and importunes us to gaze upon a splinter from the Holy Cross and one of the Crown of Thorns as a sort of receipt for our pains!

I have touched the stone that contains the sacred footprints of Christ when he met St. Peter on the Appian Way, but I had to pay for it; and to see the original nail that pierced one of his hands at the crucifixion also requires some *liras;* these things are not preserved for the sanctification of souls, but as so much stock in trade.

Far out along this ancient bridle path are lines of mouldering tombs—these and the broken aqueducts the only features of the barren, desolate Campagna. Tombs of heroes and royal families, where the humanity interred has long since faded into air, but the sculptured figures and stone foundations remain to proclaim the immortality of art.

All along the road the workmen of King Humbert were

building new ramparts, and I asked why the youthful monarch was taking this precaution. If Italy be endangered, I saw no sign of it. I presume it is the papal power he fears, that everflowing font of omnipotence and bigotry. The whole society here savors of the Catholic Church. The masses proper are adherents of the Vatican. Catholicism is so much capital, and the result is, even other religions partake of the odor of the Holy Mother. Protestantism is a very feeble affair, and as the Roman nobility and cardinals hold the keys of the social Sesame, it only opens to obedient worshippers, or generous givers.

The laborers had ceased work to take their noonday meal, as we turned toward a dilapidated farm inn, to take a piece of black bread and a flagon of sour wine, under the shadow of great trees and upon the greensward, where dogs and babies lay sleeping in each other's embrace, and Roman women were picking and making their dinner from raw peas. The proletaires out upon the road were feasting upon their "hard tack" and raw onions, that cast their aroma—stronger, though not so sweet as new-mown hay, orange blossoms, or tangerines—upon the atmosphere for miles. This cepivorous race, patrician and plebeian, feed upon the bulb pungent, and subject it to all the intricacies of their culinary art.

An attempt to epitomize the churches of Rome, with their thrilling pictures and appending stories, would be a wild enterprise. Long I studied the beautiful fresh adornments of St. Paul beyond the gates, and St. John, where crawl repentant sinners over the Scala Santa, said to have been the steps of Pilate's house, over which the suffering Saviour descended after judgment. Here the contrite pilgrims cringe and creep and go through their genuflexions upon each of the twenty-eight steps, and every step grants eight hundred years' indulgence—so I was told. Oh! what a convenient and elastic creed!

And St. Paul's, apart from the tomb of the body of St. Paul,—his head lies side by side with his brother evangelist, Peter, in the Lateran,—is of singular beauty, with an unusual abundance of precious decoration, yet fresh and untarnished from the hand of the artisans, the basilica having been reduced to ruins by fire in the summer of 1823. If not so vast, it is certainly more compact than St. Peter's, and by most travellers considered the gem of Roman churches.

LETTER LIV.

"There is a new Rome upon the ruined site,
A bright and modern metropole,
Where telegraphs and all their kindred light
Assert the presence of the monopole.
Low down the Corso will the horse car fly,
Already newsboys fill the ambient air
With the wild clamor of their hourly cry,
And now the bycicle awakes the dusky fair.
Imperial Rome is rushing to its doom.
The democratic age is hammering at the door.
Cæsar and Rienzi are in deserted gloom,
Beatrice Cenci is an ecstasy no more."

ANONYMOUS.

ROME, June, 1878.

WAS it not Cicero who said, every fragment of stone upon a Roman roadside had its history? and this was two thousand years ago, before the Pagan ravages and the Christian innovations.

To ride along the Appian Way now is like a journey through the remembered or written ages. That still splendid avenue is eloquent of the long-gone past, and the Pagan and Christian time-marks may be easily defined. Alas! if the iconoclasts had been one-tenth less busy in destroying the vestiges of the dead than the moderns have been in restoring them, the Appian Way would now be full of the marble effigies of the vanished generations. For what is left, let us thank the era of the printing press, telegraph, and railroad. Till they came to rule the world and arrest the ruin, Rome was becoming more and more the ghastly graveyard of the ages. Other capitals have felt the presence of the salt that saves the carrion, and Rome has been saved to the future by the new-born energy of the nations. With one hand this resistless energy has lifted the sinking body of the Imperial city, and with the other imparted new life into the desolation of death. The Roman Government is now vital, active, and full of the fire of enfranchisement. The press is free, speech is loud, and Italy has found a new call to reform. Even the Catholic Church has gone a little into the fashion, and if Rome pervades all Paris, Paris makes the clothes and modern architecture of Rome.

To be in Rome, where Te Deums and anthems float about us; where the Great St. Peter hallows us and carnivals intoxicate us; where the story of the Gracchi thrills us and the treachery that killed Rienzi oppresses us; where the greatest fantasies of greatest men are painted on canvas and walls and chiselled in marble; where we may invoke the blessing and forgiveness of the Virgin at each corner for our daily sins, and rove conscience free; where the fountains splash and the water-pails clank, and the miserable old tinkers mend pots, hats, umbrellas, and shoes, in their little dark holes beaten into the sides of the wall; where the art of Phidias, Raphael, and Canova joins hands with the work of Story, Rogers, and Miss Hosmer; where we may walk the silent sublimity of the palaces where the voices of dead gods speak to us from the choice legacy they have left—all this is what thousands before me have enjoyed as a sort of matchless ecstasy. But to be in Rome as an artist is something more; it is the supreme content of double possession and participation. The artist has, therefore, more than an equal ownership in all these marbles and jewels with King Humbert or Pope Leo XIII. He does more than either; he contributes of his life to the great treasure.

There are whole streets of art ateliers here, such as are to be found nowhere else. The Via Margutta is a model beehive, and here their gods and idols are worshipped in oil, clay, bronze, and marble. There are other headquarters, such as the passage di Ripetta and the Via Babuino, but the first is the quarter in which the genii cluster. Entering it from the Piazza di Spagna, it is known by the efflorescence of its shrubbery; clay powder and marble-filings make the portals and leaves as white as the statues they hide. The numbers of the residences are cut into the gate pillars, and frequently there are four or five of the same number in the same street with only the distinguishing addition of St. 8., or 7 B., or 6ª, or 7 A. 4° P°.; what the meaning of this very peculiar mode of designation is, except to rob one of his time and amiability, I have not discovered. We were in search of Randolph Rogers—did you ever hear of an American who visited Rome and did not call at the studio of our courteous countryman? After much talk and pantomime, and a few French words to the Italian hackman, and many windings, we found Rogers amongst his stony offspring. He greeted us in the front court, where Illyria's sun burnt the rank grass to its roots and the insects droned, and led us into the cool recesses of his celestial arbor. Surely celestial! for who were here but the pure and the brave? Nydia, the blind girl of

Pompeii, a bust of a New York belle, a bust of his own little daughter, and the Lost Pleiad, are his proudest achievements. The latter is represented in her descent from the golden throne, after having fallen in love with a mortal; her limbs float upon air as she turns to gaze backward and upward upon her six sisters in their heavenly zone, while her little hand is raised to shade her eyes from the lustre of their virtuous effulgence. I rhapsodized upon the graceful curves, purity of tone, and the ethereal expression of her wondrous eyes, almost as potent and speaking as mortality. Looking at this fair vision again and again, the exquisite personation of an enchanting fable, the master smiled at my enthusiasm, and in his own *naïve* way he spoke of her as "the young lady who left her old maid sisters in Elysium to follow her hubby." My dream was dispelled, the haze of romance faded, and I saw only the satire in marble. Thus in life do our sweetest delusions vanish; our gods are dashed from their pedestals by the jest of the minute, and we find the clay hollow and filled with vermin.

I repeat, who would not be a sculptor and live in Rome, and pass his life in one of those cool, quiet, shady sanctums, among his own creations? And though the reward be worldly, have the remuneration of gold, as well as glory.

But where do the nobility reside? This has been my constant self-interrogation. I do not mean the Corsini, Doria, Borghese, Barberini, and other noted palace-owners; if they have left an opulent posterity, they inhabit a portion of the old castle, and magnanimously open the galleries to the public. If their fortunes have decayed, or the family is extinct, the property becomes the home of one of the foreign ambassadors, or wealthy English or Americans. Nor do I refer to the royal residences in the district of Trastevere, Palestrina, nor upon the Sabine hills. I never dreamed that these lofty, spacious structures, with the jail-like grated windows, and cow or mule stables occupying the ground floor, were the mansions of Italian *noblesse*. Yet so they are. Once having made the discovery I rapidly grew familiar with the sight, and learned to look beyond the stalls of animals, and heaps of decayed vegetables, into the cool shade of palace-courts, where crystal fountains drip, and greensward and gay flowers light the picture; while ilex and palms wave through the atrium, in the perspective. The Romans, while perfectly insensible to noxious odors, are keenly alive to aromatic essences; they live in stench below, and glory in perfume above!

The Mole of Adrian, long the papal stronghold, is only interesting to me as the prison of the youthful Beatrice Cenci. It is a great circular citadel, entered from the bridge of St. Angelo, guarded by archangels, and has served as a fortress for St. Peter's, a tomb for ancient emperors, a seclusion for ecclesiastical insurgents, an appendage of royalty, a retreat for the popes, the scene of many a saturnalia in the tenth century, and, in fact, an epitome of Roman history from the second Christian period to the present. To visit such a tower teaches us that the title of ruler in the ancient monarchies was often a brevet. These Italian dukes were many of them, tyrants fearful of their subjects. The walls of this fort are forty-five feet thick, while here and there along the stairway narrow windows pierce the depth of stone, through which the light struggles. And this precaution the Emperor Adrian took to protect his body, living or dead, from his foes. But the romantic and hallowing influence is that of Beatrice Cenci, who languished in one of these cells. We yield our sympathy to the murderess, not the murdered. Who, with those haunting eyes upon them, and the fresh memory of her sweet girl's strength and wrongs, could class her as a parricide? There are some tragedies better than some texts; some sins cancelled by a holy logic, and hers was of them. The sluggish stream that washes the base of the Mole is the same that our school books describe as the turbulent Tiber. The river is a corresponding link in the chain of ancient Roman reminiscences. Like the community of the Palatine and Capitoline it crawls in its putrescent bed foul as the rotten shambles on its slant shores. Commerce repudiates it, infection rises from it, and dogs make it their grave. Oh! spirit of the great Galileo, inspire these instructors of the youthful mind in our academies, and let the truth be told of these Roman ruins! And this is the fierce rolling Tiber!

Near to the Castle St. Angelo is the house where Raphael's presence still hangs a sanctifying influence; not the grander residence where he died, nor the walls that tell the story of his love-life in the suburbs, but the casket with which he invested the chapel of his sarcophagus in the Pantheon! At whose tomb I bartered for spicy pinks with a dusky Roman boy, and then looked upon the altar where rests the late soldier monarch, Victor Emanuel. The marvellous canopy of the Pantheon is a sort of one-eyed giant, through which the dews of heaven fell for centuries upon pagan idolators and Christian worshippers, and the sun of God penetrated as if to light the way for the Saviour of the world.

St. Marie Maggiore, sacred crown to the Esquiline summit, is the most beautiful of all the Virginal dedications of Rome. You ascend the height from the street of the Four Fountains. If the day be torrid, as it was when I attempted it, stop at an intervening *café* and get some *granite* (Roman ice-cream), then continue your way along the dusty eminence. You will meet a number of very pretty girls, who have been at their orisons, with excessively dirty men, who exhale a cogent decoction of perspiration and garlic. An aged woman, crippled and indigent, debars your entrance, with a flaming tongue—not sword—and extended arms, until she drops her knitting and hobbles to the portals to hold aside the great swinging curtain of Canton matting. If you are not in a remunerative mood as you pass in, a shade of disappointment appears in her old eyes; that is all. You enter to find a temple of precious gems and holy marbles, pontifical tombs, saintly shrines, and royal chapels, of which the one bearing the Borghese arms is the radiant star, and you gaze at the mosaic pavement beneath, and the brilliant adornments above, until you yield to the holy peace of the hour, and kneel to pray with the laborers in their noonday prayers. I am impressed by the wealth of the Catholic Church, the sincerity of its devotees, and its increasing power. There can be no such thing as permanent Protestantism in Italy. But what touches me most is the equality of their discipline. The countess, in her silks and jewels, kneels side by side with the dirty *lazzaroni*, and dips her dainty hand into the same chalice of holy water where he plunges his filthy fingers. The scrub-girl comes in with her bucket and brush to thank her Holy Mother for her kilo of black bread, and miladi supplicates forgiveness for her *petite faute*.

As you make your exit there stands the female St. Peter, guarding the holy entrance; she scrambles from her haunches and again makes a plunge for the curtain, which she snatches, and throws obsequious genuflexions around you in a circle; then, if you be still of an uncompensating turn, or if small coin does not fall like a shower into her leather palm, the flaming tongue hurls scathing curses upon your offending soul, and scorches your charity into a cinder.

LETTER LV.

"Of sackcloth was thy wedding garment made;
Thy bridal's fruit is ashes."
BYRON.

ROME, June, 1878.

YE who have not lived in Rome know nothing of popery; the power, the magnificence, the processions, the societies, and the troops of black cloth filling the streets. They are either medicants or opulent churchmen, the former dirty and unshaven, the others well dressed and supremely well fed. A beaming smile of courteous familiarity greets me wherever I meet one; none present an appearance of severe deprivation, unless of soap and water in the case of the first. The brown hair-cloth gown and cowl, sandalled feet, and huge rosaries of the Capucini, the black frocks of other orders, the gayer dress of papal dignitaries, and the fantastic costume of His Holiness's Swiss Guard, look like a scene from one of the early passion or mystery plays. The Catholic religion in Italy, especially in the capital, is a great trade, a system of profit for the priests, a world-wide drama, a direful delusion for the poor. Of the tens of thousands of ecclesiasts how few do any work beyond what they call worship, and how much they demand of the fold in matters of faith, charity, and doctrine! Whenever we meet one of these he is eternally counting his beads or murmuring his *aves*, and though he gracefully salutes his comrades, and smiles upon the stranger, the sacred hum is uninterrupted as he seems to have transcended the point where foreign elements may prove a distraction. All religious celebrations and festas are frolics. Ostentation and fun transform sacred ovations into saturnalias and jubilees. And though the kingdom is now divided into two great powers, the Pope in the palace of the Vatican, and young King Humbert in the palace of the Quirinal, each having his own court, still there is a potential and pervading incense of the former, and to-day the intrigues of the Church exceed those of the State.

The city is at present floating in a sea of glory in honor of the political triumph of united Italy; but in this ceremony the Pope and the cardinals will take no part. While the Castle of St. Angelo will be bathed in a phosphorescence of splendor and victory, the church dignitaries will hide their holy heads under their blessed togas for fear of being contaminated by a glimpse of the lustre. But the Pope has a hundred jollifications to every one of the king's, thus strengthening himself so much per cent. in the hearts of the masses. The community is fond of merry-making, and no community so much as the Catholics. Therefore he who offers or affords them the most amusement is monarch, if not nominally, in reality he is the worshipped god.

The more I linger amongst the papists so much more readily do I comprehend their world-wide influence. Their ceremonies are impressive and dramatic, their temples soothing, their religious rites venerated more by spectacle than by study, and the masses are universally ruled through the medium of the senses.

Certainly the Catholics have many ways of conquering converts. They lay all manner of customs under tribute, and they excel in the glory, the gory, and the ghastly. They deal in blood and thunder; they flourish in robes of crimson and gold, and literally revel in bones. The *boniest* repast offered in Rome is the Capucini Convent, a collection of petrified corpses, and a vast crypt of centuried dead. Fancy your ancestors laid out in their cerements on the cellar shelves; their bones only remaining, all flesh and former resemblance fled, and each man labelled with his proper name. There are the grim and grinning skeletons ticketed and standing in their places just like a chemist's bottles or a student's books, and you have only to inquire to discover whether the dried anatomy at your side was a Roman republican or imperialist; a man of the town or of the ton; or at least I so thought till I was quietly informed that many of these bony gentlemen had been cured for several hundred years, and their names had died or dried out with their flesh. There is ever something hideous in death, and I endeavored to be as nonchalant amongst these well-ordered and silent vertebræ as the priest beside me, but I confess I had just a scintilla of poor Juliet's emotion when she conjures up the ghosts of her forefathers in their festering shrouds all about her in the tomb of the Capulets.

Several attempts were made before gaining admission to the Capucini Convent, cresting the undulated mound of the Piazza Barberini. We had been advised never to leave Rome until we had walked the Bone Gallery. The name inspired horror, and though I had passed the ordeal of the Catacombs with considerable trepidation, I went undaunted up to "old rawhead and bloody bones." I hesitated at which door I should knock, as they all seemed to be barred in a hermetically significant manner. I mounted the main flight of steps ascending from the piazza; after a prolonged and arduous encounter with the bell-handle and brass rapper which I attacked alternately, one of the friars made his appearance behind the great door and communicated with us through the shifting panel. I demanded entrance in French, and he answering in Italian, consternation ensued; from what words I imagined I understood, and his expressive gestures, I felt assured he was endeavoring to convey that one of the rules in their code was to admit males only. And so we parted, he seeming relieved by my taking my shadow from off his door, and I indignantly murmuring contracted misogynist, as I walked over the broad square and stopped to chat with one of the vegetable huckters who had her sparse store spread upon the arid, dusty ground of the piazza, where market was being held; and what a market! No stalls, no counters, no covering; the sun pouring all the flood of his fire down upon stock and traders; withering the vegetables, melting the fish, wearying buyers and sellers, and stupefying the poor old mules that were hitched to the garden wall of Barberini Palace. My dusky communicant of doubtful erudition, told me ladies were admitted; however, my patience exhausted and temper ruffled, I supplicated no further that day.

Next morning I consulted the clerk at the hotel, and relying upon his information, started upon the visitation of skulls and skeletons again. I went to the same great door at which I had played one of the characters in the pantomime before. I was now greeted by a younger, more accomplished, and placable brother, who directed me in the Gallic vernacular to apply at a side door, where I was received by one of the holy order, who addreesed me in surprisingly clever English, but was a walking personation of uncleanliness. This confederacy is regardless of the old aphorism, "cleanliness is next to godliness." They have acquired the chiefest virtue and pay no heed to subordinate ones.

It was a wonderful and ghastly spectacle, this gallery of bones, where over six thousand skeletons of the monks of the fraternity are arranged in curious devices and emblems to ornament floor, ceiling, and side walls. Mantel-shelves of bones sustain crosses and other sacred designs made from the smaller parts of the human anatomy. Hanging-baskets and swinging-lamps in every variety of fantastic shape are suspended from the ceiling, which is frescoed and stuccoed in the most ingenious patterns with the bones of this sickening sepulchre. Many of the dead were laid upon shelves in their grave-clothes, the shrivelled skin on their bony hands, and the beard still clinging to their fleshless chins, while others peered at me from the corners, where they stood stark upright; some posed against columns or brackets, and some were still in their narrow beds of clay. The last of these strange interments has taken place for the last time. No more will a Capuchin transform his unoffending brother into a lamp, jardinier, shield, anchor, or star. No more will one poor old friar be exhumed from his cold bed of earth for a brother usurper to rest in his couch, while the former undergoes the embalming process, only to appear after a time in some grotesque shape. By a wise decree of Victor Emanuel the horrible and inhuman practice was forever prohibited in 1870. This charnel-house was as clean and sweet as a lady's boudoir, and I inquired what deodorizer or acid they made use of, and marvelled at the answer, "none." I discovered my condemnation of these good men as misogynists was unjust, as our courteous guide told us they had entertained a few months previous several nuns from America, who were visiting Europe. This led to a pleasant little confab of my experience with the *religeuses* of my schooldays, and when I left the tabernacle of death I felt nearer to the dirty cloisterer, who looked as if the use of water had been tabooed in the monastery. As we were about to make our adieu the monk quietly repeated, they were absolute mendicants, and lived only by the charity of visitors and alms begged on the streets of the Imperial City. This language needed no interpretation, so we filled his palm with pennies.

A *sui generis* pageant certainly, and one to be remembered long after the more romantic have faded into oblivion. I lingered here, arrested as it were, by a fascinating awe, not with the ecstasy I had dwelt upon the graceful shapes of the marble galleries, the very names of whose authors have been obliterated from the memory of man, and into whose dreamy eyes I have gazed until I wished their stony lips would open and reveal the lost story of their origin.

But the streets of Rome! Here indeed are food and refreshment for the student. I had thought the libidinous customs of these people, so unequivocally laid down in the pagan classics, a fable, or, if not, so ambiguous that at least the degradation had evaporated with idolatry. Not so. The manners of the masses to-day on the public highways are little better than the narrative of Petronius in the *Satyricon*, whose lines lose all the fascination of equivoque in their disgusting details.

LETTER LVI.

"In the fair land o'erwatched by Ischia's mountains,
    Across the charmèd bay,
Whose blue waves keep with Capri's silver fountains
    Perpetual holiday."
                    JOHN GREENLEAF WHITTIER.

NAPLES, June, 1879.

IRRESISTIBLE as the impulse may be for an enthusiast to repeat the melodious lay of our sweetest singer, the lamented Buchanan Read, when looking upon Vesuvius, Naples, its azure bay, and still more mystic islands, I am quite determined not to impose the harmonious measure and topographical exactness of these musical lines upon my unoffending friends, though it is the song of my heart. Not alone do I refrain from public declamation because the theme is hackneyed, but to me a more humiliating reason: with all the assumption of ignorance I read the exquisite verses of "Drifting" once to a *maestro* of English, and so bitterly did he criticise my elocution that I made a grave for my favorite deep in my heart, where it still remains.

Who would not feel sad at leaving Rome; and who would not thrill with pleasure at beholding Naples? The crumbling disjointed arches of the aqueducts, straddling over the Pontine Marshes, and the white cattle knee-deep in the rank herbage upon these death-breathing swamps, is a picture nowhere else to be found; and while we linger upon the archaic and Oriental scene we mourn over the decay and desolation of this wide waste of uninhabitable country. Vast stretches of pestilential soil, where not a human abode is seen nor a mortal voice is heard, are the ghastly features of the landscape for many miles after quitting the Holy See. To the left the peaks of the Volcian range are often crested by convent turrets, while at the base sweet vales and luxuriant vineyards blossom; far away to the right the infectious moors extend to the sea, within whose islands we find all the romance of history and mythology. The approach to Naples is indicated by the groves of fiery pomegranates, contrasting with the lighter and darker aureate tones of the orange and lemon; and the opulent plantations where the dusty olive trees are garlanded by the coils and wreaths of the purple grape. When the day is fine the waving plume of Vesuvius may be seen long before the train traverses the fertile district of Capua. What you at first mistake for a cloud gradually reveals itself as the graceful feather upon the mountain brow; couched as it is upon the dome of heaven, you can barely decide whether it is a visitor of the upper or lower realms. Out in the Mediterranean are the haunts of banditti and the legendary rendezvous of the nymphs. The elysium to which Circe allured her victims is not the only weird influence of the shores of southern Italy. There are the caves where the sirens sang; the strongholds where convicts are prisoned to-day; and the isolated isles where outraged fathers and husbands banished their wives and daughters, some to seek repentance, others to find repentant deaths; the plains over which Fra Diavolo roamed, and, indeed, there seems to be little either authentic or legendary in the story of Illyria but what adds new beauties to the garland that hangs over this maze of islands. We seem to have transcended the limits of earth and live amidst fabulous charms, with the memoirs of deities floating about us in a sea of song, and a glory of blue waves and crystal grottos, over which white-winged skiffs drift and dip; where the golden glow of sunlight plays upon high rocks and finds its image in the almighty mirror below; where a riotous magnificence of color blends in a marvellous mist of incense from shore to shore; where the wild heights of Ischia, the rocky coasts and watchfires of Capri, and the chimes of Ave Maria are heard through the rocked-ribbed galleries of Amalfi, who would not yield to the *dolce far niente* of the place and time? The nestling isles, rocked in the caressing seas and protected by the filmy coronal of haughty Vesuvius, need no Bourbon empire nor omnipotent church, no universal commerce, not even the classic art of early times, to gild their natural splendor. Here in the rags of lazzaroni and the wild fisher's odorous skirts, the rot of ages and the darkness of poverty and ignorance, the Immortal Architect has painted and illuminated the great picture with his own eternal pigments.

Naples is a genuine seaport. Every description of man throngs the depot; the Turk with his long tinselled toga and crimson cap is there, so that not only a cosmopolitan but an Oriental odor pervades the town. As I rode to the hotel great loads of wilting vegetables were heaped upon the quay, where vessels were depositing their varied stores; bordering the parapets of the Chiaja are parterres of gay flowers of ruddy southern cultivation; half-nude men and boys lounge indolently in the public roads, over which the heights of quaint houses throw their shadows,—houses that seem jammed up, one against the other, and one on top of the other, without any regard to comfort or appearance, with great curtains of gaudily painted matting floating from the windows, from which are stretched clotheslines, adorned with the motley apparel of the family. So tattered were these habiliments that it was an impossibility to distinguish the original shape or sex of the garments. I marvelled how they stood the abluting process, and how they were to be worn, and who wore them? The foreigners are the only well-dressed people I see, excepting the cabmen and priests; the nobility I do not see at all; and the masses upon the streets seem to have donned a costume many years ago, how long I could not say, as the greasy, clinging fragments seem never to have quitted the body that claims them since first the work of decline began; the dress has grown old and soiled with the individual; they are part of one another, and once isolated, like parted lovers, never again could enjoy graceful and melting adherence. The poor little donkeys are as shaggy as their masters; and so with the overwrought beasts and slothful attendants, there is an air of sadness and laziness all round.

The Neapolitans all ride. Perhaps carriage-hire is slightly lower in Rome, but in Naples it is a confession of shameful penury not to patronize the hackmen, and a very frequent sight is the little one-horse public calash laden with young women and men, bonnetless and hatless, on a holiday frolic. The country people possess a weird little donkey to carry their produce to market, and often harness an ox and a horse with their surefooted quadruped, or debasingly yoke the mother of the family with the beast of burden, while a great, torpid, lazy husband stretches his larded length upon the wagon. I noticed female car-conductors were universal, and ladies promenade the Strada di Roma (the Neapolitan Chestnut Street) without head-covering, their bosoms quite bare, and while this is the prevailing mode it has a startling appearance to the circumspect American, who never crosses her threshold unless her charms be hidden almost as sedulously as the Turkish dame.

The greatest expense and most nefarious extortions in Italy arise from the transfer of baggage. All must be paid extra for, as no appurtenances are conveyed with the passenger or included in his fare of transportation. Every package is weighed at the station and a heavy duty levied. Upon no consideration whatever allow your baggage to be expressed in advance. When we tried this plan from Nice to Rome we were sadly swindled. After having stopped at several intermediate cities we arrived in Rome, found no trunk, and after telegraphing for three days, living in anxiety, going through an endless red-tape process, and paying *fifteen dollars*, we obtained our *one* trunk. The question in my mind was, had it not been more comfortable and economical to buy a new equipment?

Our hotel on the Strada Chiatamone is one of those new palatial structures that looks as if it had been placed by some enterprising Yankee to teach old Italy a lesson of cleanliness. Exquisite reception-rooms, garnished in blue and gold frescoes and furniture, with just a dash of Pompeian drawing to glorify them. A dining-room that seems to have had the plasters and pigments of the buried city transported *toto cœlo*. An apartment that might have proudly dined Agamemnon, had it not been debased by the discordant voices of travelling magpies, at *table d'hote*. Those who have never suffered the plague can neither sympathize with nor conceive the affliction of those mortals who have waded through the trying and seemingly endless slough of *table d'hote*. I am not going to assail my own countrywomen in this paragraph for their shrill loquacity, the usual wail of such a chapter. While I often shrink from the wordy and empty babble in which they indulge, seemingly more for the parrotlike pleasure of hearing their own chatter and regaling others by a display of their ignorance than because they have something in their hearts clamoring for utterance, yet, let it be said, the most indecent manners at table I have noticed have been those of foreigners. I think some of the Italian and German Hebrews are the worst. If an American girl laughs too often, or has not toned her voice to the low sweet contralto, these at the worst are slight imperfections; but women who extend their bodies half over the board in pursuit of food, or who ask you to pass them the ice you have ordered (ice is a luxury here) and do not return it, or who freeze your marrow in your bones by using a toothquill at table, such people deserve expulsion from delicate society. The levity of the Yankee may be condoned; gross indecency never! But this *table d'hote*, with the high-sounding name and bombastic bill-of-fare, is a horrible delusion, a bitter snare. A glimpse at the hall previously, assures you that the tables are laid in their candelabras and crystals, flowers and fine linen for a banquet; the head waiter, who does nothing but superintend the laying, is importunate to know if you will dine *table d'hote;* he exhibits the *menu*, and you at once yield to the ostentatious showing. The dinner generally lasts an hour and a half; it is served in courses, each course being separated into limited portions, so that the sparse supply meets the end of the circle; no individual is permitted a second instalment of the food he prefers, but must continue in the routine of the programme, whether the succeeding dish be palatable or not. This then is the first direful disappointment,—the meagre supply and variety of dishes,—but not the worst for me as I enjoy a diversity and am content on little, but the gross humanity around me gives no Apician flavor to the feast. There are occasions when delightful little symposiæ may be enjoyed in this manner, but such cases are the exception.

Night approaches, and I sit upon the piazza projecting from my window, where the placid Vesuvian bay expands far away to meet the horizon; pale Cynthia sheds her silver rays in a band of jewelled splendor to my right, where dance the little cutters and brigs upon the star-lit phosphoric ripples. The lights are coming out one by one in the white fishing cottages on the delta of Posilipo, jutting far out into the bay. The equipages of the Italian nobility drawn by high-stepping mountain-trained chestnuts are returning from their evening jaunt to the Villa Nazionalle along the Chiaja, while the shadows deepen and the column of white smoke on the volcano fades into night. Under my window the natives lounge, some threadbare, more ragged, and many stript of clothing, such a scene as I never beheld in any other city; yet no note is made of these vulgar customs. The boys play marbles and spin their tops, as ours do at home, clothed in only Nature's apparel; the men—dirty, brawny, disgusting men—pitch pennies, a sort of mild gambling, upon the wharves; the priests, in long black cloaks and shovel-hats, guarding their acolytes, enjoy the beauty of land and climate vouchsafed to them, heedless of the despoiling morals of the inhabitants; then comes a mendicant Capucini over the scene as the last light of day fades and the white feather of the fiery monster is now a lurid flame. Our ardent friend on the opposite curve of the horseshoe manifests signs of uncontrollable irritation; whether he is preparing to belch forth new worlds and destroy old ones, or whether this deep growl is only one of his playful antics, I am all anxiety to learn. The natives expect an exhibition of dangerous temper from the fervent symptoms of their good friend, and I hear the liquid Italian tongue weaving a prayerful solicitation for the happy event into the evening Ave. Happy, indeed, to this penurious, speculating community, as such a grand *dénouement* would attract myriads of strangers to their city, and thus offer a fresh and extended field for plunder, from which the professional beggars and sharpers always garner rich harvests.

A crimson column of flame is issuing from the crater, accompanied by bursts of stone in intermittent periods, when the whole mountain assumes a turbulent, angry aspect, while the glare blazons upon the purple peaks of rock far out in the bay. Vesuvius is not so large, neither in height nor circumference, as I expected, yet it stands a conspicuous and distinct feature against the clear sky. I deem it indeed a special dispensation of nature that this supreme incendiary should *fête* me while in Naples with one of his magnificent pyrotechnical solemnities. I may visit and revisit the spot, but will I ever see this petroleuse disgorging fire and ashes and lava as I have seen it spit forth to-night? so vivid is it all I fancy I hear the retch of ejection as the flaming food is vomited from the tempestuous stomach.

As dawn spreads her rosy wings over earth the agonies of the burning mountain subside; the meteoric ravings have died with the parting night, and the white feather waves in the gentle breeze of the new-born day. The celestial curtain is gradually furling behind the crater, where the background is a scarf of delicate variegated hues as soft as silk and as fleecy as Indian tissues, with here and there the sparkle of a tinsel thread; such a mantle as Cupid folds about his victims while leading them in ecstasy on to the engulfing stream of fire and frenzy.

LETTER LVII.

"With Pompeii itself at the distance of a few miles—the sea that once bore her commerce, and received her fugitives at his feet—and the fatal mountain of Vesuvius, still breathing forth smoke and fire, constantly before his eyes!" BULWER.

NAPLES, June, 1878.

THE old aphorism runs "See Naples and die." My advice is, having gotten to Naples, do not die until you see Pompeii; that is, if it be possible to survive a night in the city with those pestiferous bedfellows vulgarly known as fleas. They drained the venom through my veins, until I believed the adage was indeed to be verified. I, however, struggled with my adversaries, and when day rescued me from their clutches I still lived. I was thoroughly resolved not to risk another night amongst them before walking the city of the dead, and so started on my Pompeian excursion at once.

The entire scene seemed the tableaux of a romance. From the initial, where the little dusky Nubian boy, in his Eastern garb and polyglot tongue, assisted me into the carriage with its gayly comparisoned horses and little tinkling bells, and clapped his slender Ethiopian hands and gabbled his jargon as we dashed off, to the return in the golden twilight over the white roads sacred with the footprints of Sallust and Glaucus, it was as quaint as a picture two thousand years old.

Saturday is market-day here in the land of the gods, as it is in adolescent America; and though I was disposed to believe that provision for the creature comforts was an unknown vulgarity in a section apotheosized by the splendor of classical deities, I found the georgical supplies in more abundant masses than at home. A caravan of donkey-carts filled the streets. Poor little beasts, how oppressed they looked hauling their heavy loads, or burdened by two great pannier-baskets entirely concealing the animal; all I saw was a succession of wailing faces, with great nodding ears, and spindle legs trotting, trotting, trotting, over the lava paths. Two great brass horns project from either side the plaintive eyes, from which are suspended on a yoke three bells—bells that re-echo each other's melody. Owing to the salubrity of the Neapolitan climate every variety of trade is carried on in the open air. The cobbler and carpenter, tinker and tailor, hatter and hosier, work at the street corners, their stock spread about them on the pavement; here they sew and saw, sweat and solder, paint and polish, and bawl for *centisimi* when they spy a stranger. But these are not the professional mumpers, whose stock in trade is in advertising nameless deformities and novel maladies, ill-shapen monsters, Calibans, each a Lazarus of the lazzaroni.

The street merchants only try their luck as momentary mendicants, but the official beggars are an organized national nuisance, the remnants of an ancient system born in these districts, when the wealth of centuries was controlled by such houses as the Medici and Borgia. Though banditti are erroneously supposed to be different from the old evils, the present eleemosynary classes look like brigands —reckless and wicked, daring and repulsive. These beggars seem to move in battalions, that spring out from the walls in certain neighborhoods where they are indigenous, and these localities multiply as Pompeii is approached, till the numbers increase into a small army.

All along the route were the macaroni and Italian paste manufactories. The unclothed men and boys were at work in the dough, while others were spreading the wheaten blankets upon the pavement, over racks, and upon roofs to dry; dark and dingy establishments, that not even the amplitude of flour-dust has power to chasten. Every couple of steps were vendors of earthen jugs of the early Roman form—large round bodies, long narrow necks, a handle on either side. Travellers purchase them to take home as relics; the natives still use them as household utensils. The road was dusty as it is ever in the dry season, and the inhabitants seemed crumbling into earth. Here paupers and princes cluster together. The filthiest people live and carry on their trade in the first stories of the palaces, while above them and behind them are ineffable extravagance and beauty. The high-road is the empire of the unwashed, uncombed, and unkempt classes, a very sink of corruption, while through iron-barred courts I caught exquisite views of the magnificence beyond, where the palace lawns slope down to the margin of the blue bay and the hoary pallor of the marbles casts the vivid Italian hues of nature into a richer color. Here the old apothegm is transposed, foul without and fair within.

As we rode on, the eternal crater,—cloud by day and fire at night,—kept us company. Sometimes we seemed to be scaling his very base, at another he was receding, and again he was upright by our side. Great bowlders of lava bestrewed the way, and served as supports to the wretched shanties; and here they were, just as the molten fire rolled down the mountain-side, and accumulated, and grew solid, eighteen hundred years ago. What with the scorching sun and the pumice-stone powder from the highway, the plants were as arid and white as the wall by which they drooped. It was a warm disagreeable ride of two and a half hours, with no fresh patches of glowing scenery to relieve the squalor of the road; all was as doleful and dirty as if Sorrento's orange-groves, Capri's sapphire caves, and Ischia's purple rocky heights were not glistening off in the bay like "jewels in the Ethiop's ear." The sunshine was there, but there was no green nature to temper its rays; it fell fierce and blinding upon all around. I was glad when we came to our journey's end, curious as all of it was to my stranger gaze.

The Diomed Inn, a dirty miserable hostelry at the gates of Pompeii, is the rest for tourists while waiting for the guide of the unearthed city: and here we tarried long before a *cicerone* appeared; they were either dining or engaged with earlier patrons, and while I lingered I noted the incongruities of the place. In a back chamber of the shanty immortalized by the title of the opulent Pompeian merchant, was a Singer sewing machine, operated by a modern Julia, perhaps more beautiful though not so rich nor so petted as her centuried-buried progenitor, as her robe was plain and at her side a baby pawed. In the atrium a troubadour in Spanish costume, thumbing a guitar suspended over his shoulder by a crimson riband, begged coin for the music. He had a vile look, the olive skin and black beard, and bad habits of his class, who would sing or stab as opportunity served. The beggars and cripples are annoying; the minstrels dangerous. The house of the wealthy trader was not famed for its modern larder, despite the tradition of his luxurious feasts in the long ago; the tastes of this portion of the family must have degenerated with their fortunes. A good bottle of red wine you are ever certain of in Italy —a wine that refreshes and strengthens without intoxicating; but I fear as there was no French *chef* in the household economy, the culinary department fell below par. Still as I gazed upon the surrounding district from the second story of the inn, the vicinage was lovely; it was a study for poet and artist. The luxuriant still-life in sight of the frowning volcano was almost startling. The varied brilliancy of the vegetation grew to the very crown of the crater in the softest and most dazzling garments. It is the internal and all-consuming fire in the womb of the mother, that gives the hectic flush to the face, and the feverish delirium to the blood of her prolific offspring. And this is the entrance to Euthanasia! This the Stygian shore flowering in the lusty beauty of the fabled gods. Vesuvius is death robed in the gaudy raiment of a gala-day; jocund Jove throws his shining mantle o'er the hills above the tomb of centuries! The jaws of death are fringed by the lotus flowers; the strains of the *chant du sygne* are smothered by the note of the lark; the woful death-rattle is drowned by the playful dashing of the wanton sea, the last gasp is stifled by the trail and tangle of vines, and the hum of myriad insect creation; a *bravura* of life at the throat of the fiery sepulchre.

Need I mar the harmonious chant of Pliny, Bulwer, Dumas, or Nicolini by a discordant repetition? They have bequeathed to the world the religion, the sports, and the romance of this early Roman Newport. They have added an account of the moral diseases, gnawing like cankerworms at the heart of society, when poor Pompeii was overtaken by the triple storm of fire, ashes, and lava, on that dark and dreadful August day of 79 A. D., when wives sought husbands, mothers their children, and lovers cried aloud in vain for each other, finding peace only in eternity. I had read the stories of that eventful day, with the same wonder and awe as I had read of the Creation, the Flood, the Crucifixion; perhaps with some of the vague bewilderment with which I read Revelations, and a seasoning of the romantic skepticism with which I read the *Arabian Nights*, *Robinson Crusoe*, or *Gulliver's Travels*. There, in the museum, I sought the exhumed proofs of the existence that was choked so long ago as scarcely to have a lineal connection with our world. I found eight human bodies perfectly petrified in their ashen sheaths; in these I read the encouraging lesson that Cicero, Pompey, or Marcus Antoninus, Glaucus or Clodius, were not men of greater physical stature than our present poets, statesmen, and orators. The skeleton of a dog, a bird, a bone of roast-beef, a loaf of bread, a dish of barley, a napkin (the warp still preserved), bronze-lamps, household luxuries, earrings, bracelets, and necklaces, teach us that the work of creation, the human appetite, the preparation of food, the habits and cravings of females for gewgaws, were the same in the classic ages as they are to-day. It is a cold, stern fact that the life we found in the streets of Naples is very much the life that was stilled in the street of Tombs eighteen centuries ago, where the front and lower story of the palaces were let to merchants, while the ædile supped in the atrium with his lordly guests, upon lampreys, pistachio, figs, and Vesuvio wine. We saw that the baths, the theatre, the temple, and the forum were the loadstars of men and women then as now. Luxuriously as these Sybarites lived in their houses, sparkling with all the glory of fresco, mosaic statuary, rich in their retinues of slaves, lulled by the fall of fountains, charmed by the beauty of Greek female loveliness, still the most opulent homes were comparatively small, while vast spaces were devoted to the public buildings, where the populace met to discuss statecraft in the forum, social scandal at the baths, to worship the false gods, and be duped by the charlatanry of such false priests as Arbaces in the temples, and enjoy the bestial sports of the amphitheatre. Here the masterpieces of Greek and Roman princes of the chisel and the brush were exhibited; here the song of the poet and voice of the declaimer rang through column and archway, from foundation to capital; here the patricians felicitated in a transport of oil and aromatic ointment; here the contrite matron and maid repaired to solicit pardon for the old sin, and sign a contract with her absolver for a new one.

The streets are narrow, the carriage-way scarcely broad enough to admit one of our two-wheeled vehicles of to-day, sinking more than a foot below the sidewalk, in the centre of which are stepping-stones, retaining the print of horses' hoofs. The ruts of wheels and the worn and rounded curbs are evidences of the superannuation of the city before its destruction, or, as I have heard it termed, its preservation. Would we have Pompeii in so perfect a state of conservation to-day had not the ashes from Vesuvius embalmed it, and protected it from the decay and corruption of ages? The fountain-basins at the street corners are worn into hollows by the press of weary human hands upon the brim, while the water filled the pail, or by lazy indolent hands that lolled here while their owners chatted the hours away. The stone steps are worn into grooves by the tramp of many feet, but the word of welcome, *salve*, or *cave canem* (beware of the dog) are still in perfect black and white mosaic in the pavements. Shafts are gone, columns broken, and altars defiled, but the colors and forms of the frescoes are marvellously unmarred. Walking the streets we exclaimed at the limited dimensions of the town: How much sleeps still under yonder hills of pumice-stone?

Come with me to the house of Diomed. Every one goes to the house of Diomed! Of course, is that a just reason I should neglect it? It is slightly out of town and elevated from the road. A flight of steps lead to the peristyle, from which we entered the baths, the atrium, the eating rooms, the gardens, the library; another flight of steps descend to the cellar, to the scullery offices of the house, and where the amphoræ of wine were kept; the vault that gave forth the dead that sought shelter in it with their stores of oil and food; the subterranean retreat to which the vain Julia came with her jewels and frail life, eighteen hundred years ago, hoping to foil the insatiate avenger. Here are the chambers where Julia writhed in an agony of envy when she heard the fair Ione had won the heart of Glaucus; here the halls where vulgar wealth entertained and flattered genius; here the libraries of charred and blackened papyri scrolls, from which the master assumed to cultivate a love of Greek literature; here the cabinets of gems, intaglio and cameo, that formed the pride of the rich man's ambition; here the spot where the skeleton arm was found bearing still upon the whited bone the golden circlet with the name "Julia," a false charm that endured how many hundred years after the decay of nature's; here the doorposts at which Diomed was transfixed in a preserve of ashes and steam as a sample and a text to posterity.

Come then to the house of the tragic poet, sanctified by the pure adoration of the Thessalian slave-girl, who loved her master for the charms her sightless eyes could not behold; ah! I can see her now, sitting in the shadow of broken columns, weaving a garland to crown her god, and singing away his hours of ennui and her own heart; I fancy I hear the echo of their mutual prayer to their pagan deities for one gleam of light to break through the closed windows of her soul,—her prayer that she might gaze upon the radiance of her king; his, that she might see the beauty of his Ione. Oh! what a satirist is Love!

Come to the wine shops, where the counters are groined and dented by the arms of loungers, where the great casks still stand as if the proprietor had just stepped out to discuss the new prætorship with a neighbor-politician. Come to the shrine of the Cyprian goddess, where you find curious inscriptions on the walls which I could not read, and peculiar emblems or beacons of trade that I could decipher. If these people were lewd and their art wanton, remember they were only in the embryo of civilization.

I am not here to preach a sermon upon their lives nor to moralize upon their vices, only to record what I saw, yet objects that are pointed out as those of chiefest interest I dare not expound. Who has not listened to a moral harangue upon this text, the point of which was the corruption of the populace, and that God in his wrath had swept off this community not an hour too soon, as their crimes exceeded those of Sodom and Gomorrah? Is this doctrine a true one? Have *we* reformed? I fear not; go into any of the great capitals of Europe or America to-day, and you will find vice existing in as many forms and colors and of course more frequent in proportion to the population, as at the annihilation of Pompeii. If these gross iniquities do not stare us into horror and shame, it is because of the prescribed orbit in which we revolve, or because the record of our time has not been written, and not because the base infection is not raging and inoculating in our homes and highways, like a subtle poison or the fierce fire of petroleum.

After visiting the town theatre, a neat, moderate-sized playhouse, where the tragedies of Euripides, Sophocles, and Æschylus won the applause of listening crowds, we trudged over the dusty country paths, out to the amphitheatre where the gladiatorial sports were enacted, an edifice not only for the accommodation of the Pompeian commonwealth, but for such voluptuaries as should come from Naples and the neighboring towns at the time of the grand pageants. The noble patrons drove into the theatre in their chariots, and entered their boxes by a concealed passage extending around the arena in an irregular circle. The interior arrangement is much like the Coliseum at Rome, and not unlike the theatres of our day, tiers of stalls and galleries being the chief features. Here, perched upon some cruel emperor's box, with the memories of wild beasts tearing, limb from limb, early Christians, and lapping the human blood from off their nether jaw, while the audiences turned their thumbs for death, with Castellamare across the bay burning me to blindness with the sparkle of its silver and jewelled heights, I drank the fiery blood of Vesuvius,—a franc and a half a bottle, from an adjacent vineyard,—drank to the pagan deities, that have left us such a sweet legacy of hallowing sublimities and beguiling romances; to the Greek dramatists and sculptors for the benefaction of their literature and art, and to the flaming scourge waving his graceful plume over the complete demolition of the city of sin and debauchery.

The guide was one of those incorruptible officials who cannot be feed with two francs, but who does conduct you to a photograph shed, where you are requested to buy an album for eight, ten, or twenty francs, which he divides with the proprietor of the atelier.

Back to Naples through the valley sacred with the thundering eloquence of Cicero, or the song of Virgil, and the praise of Tacitus, or the kisses of Johannas Secundas, and the panegyrics of Sallust, where the little asses were returning from the busy city rid of their burden of provisions, but carrying their dreamy masters to their suburban homes, where the most grotesque forms were beaten with black pebbles into white walls, and lamps were lighted to honor curious dwarfed Virgins, that resembled jointing-dolls of the last century.

In the Museum Borbonico a perfect feast of inscriptions, whole quarters of walls, with the frescoes preserved, taken from the exhumed city, and mosaics, statuary, paintings, gems, antiquities, and papyri is spread for the antiquarians. Of the Pompeian frescoes we note strong colors, fine lines, and considerable grace of treatment.

The one valuable text of this wonderful sermon of Pompeii is that infidels who doubt the wonders and the miracles of the Scriptures, and others who laugh at *Robinson Crusoe* and *Pilgrim's Progress*, and *Arabian Nights*, will find the romance of reality and the fiction of fact in this unearthed city.

LETTER LVIII.

"We gaze and turn away, and know not where,
   Dazzled and drunk with beauty, till the heart
Reels with its fulness; there—for ever there—
   Chain'd to the chariot of triumphale Art,
We stand as captives, and would not depart."
                                    BYRON.

FLORENCE, June, 1878.

AT Rome I remained overnight *en route* to this lovely city where I am now writing. The papal capital is in torpor and its hotels are dismantled, but it is ever fascinating to me. I believe the Costanzi was the only startling experience of that night in Rome, and the staggering blow was its hotel bill. Envious friends may say it was a just retribution for my choice of such ostentatious lodgings. It was not pretension that prompted me to the costly *albergo* where American sovereigns dine foreign princes, but the rational motive of a modest traveller, who found the Costanzi near the depot. Possessing a keen appreciation of the luxuries of life, I revelled, of course, in the palatial apartments assigned me, dined in the royal basement dining-hall, amongst Pompeian and Egyptian frescoes, and congratulated myself on all the landlord's excess of courtesy. Alas! when the account came to be settled the sweet delusion vanished; every blue sphinx and crimson dragon on the wall, every block of marble in the floor, and every antique brazier or lamp that had so delighted me the previous evening, had to be bravely paid for. There is no pleasure equal to that of the travel-stained tourist as he recruits his strength in a regal hall hung with costly tapestries and laces, but you who have had to square such debts in gold painfully realize how rapidly the sheen of the satin and the fleeciness of lace fade under these circumstances, and how soon remorse comes to enforce a stern economy. But there is some compensation for one such thoughtless extravagance. It was a healthy reaction, and as I reflected upon the Roman epicure Apicius, who lived in the time of Augustus and Tiberius, and spent one hundred millions of sesterces (about $3,600,000) on his kitchen alone, and poisoned himself because he had only $360,000 left, I felt that I might be pardoned this folly of a night at the Costanzi.

The entrance to Florence is a continuous flower-garden of quite twenty miles. The more extended my travel in Italy the more marvellous become the variety and wealth of vegetation. The spontaneity of still nature is the uninterrupted delight of the voyager. The Tuscans worship the emblem of life as the protector of their crops as devoutly as the Calabrians, and very curious are the huge personations appearing in the fields and at the roadsides of their tutelary god. The blue heavens, the golden grain waving under the shadow of the gray mountains, the white roads, the emerald turf, and the olive-bronze foliage of the trees, make up the colors of the picture in the exquisite suburbs of the sweet city of art. The colors were rendered more living by the vision of two mules carrying their burdens up the steep mountain-path that winds in snakelike coils to the summit, which is crowned by a monastery.

Florence is perhaps the most aristocratic city in Italy, considered in relation to its ancient families and art, its recent improvements, and the influence of the English concentrated here, though at present it is under the ban of national poverty, and feels the exigencies of the times no less than America. Its garniture is, however, much more threadbare than the young republic's, but this is more attributable to age than present indigence. Here history and romance have combined, here the past and the present have been newly married, and if we have no flaming Vesuvius, nor Castello de l'Ovo frowning grimly from the bay, no cracking of whips, and shouts of hawkers, no smell of fish, nor traffic of a seaport, as at Naples, we are more than compensated by the half-vague, religious, studious hush of the art emporium, the noble palaces, and the gentle Arno bathed in the silver beams of the lovely moonlight; its flow is so calm and its murmur so melodious that it seems some animated phantom beneath my window.

I first saw Florence by moonlight, or by moonlight and gaslight, as the gas lighted up the piazza of the Cathedral and the adjacent streets; where street merchants were holding little fairs, their tawdry stock glorified by glaring pitch torches, while the moonlight chastened the statues upon the Ponte Trinita and in the open squares, and I think that memory will linger longer than any other. Where can one turn here without encountering a fresh revelation? and each new one seems to elbow the preceding from its pedestal. It is quite impossible to forget the sanctifying genii of Florence, as they speak to you from every corner, square, portico, and church.

Dante in the piazza Santa Croce recalls the "Inferno," the "Vita Nuovo," and his idealic love of the youthful Beatrice; and how many ghosts of former glory rise before us in the Church of Santa Croce? It seems to be the treasure-house of immortal memories: tombs and mausolea that are consecrated by the bones they cover, marbles that tell long life-stories of toil and triumph, monuments that speak of love's suffering and devotion, dust that mingles in death as the spirits blended in life; yet here the scathing tongue of calumny has lost its fatal sting. Go look upon the prince of artists' sanctuary guarded by the sister arts, Painting, Sculpture, and Architecture. Go to the tomb of him who hails you in the piazza. Go to the catafalque of the crafty "Florentine secretary," and ponder the life of the subtle statesman and student, yet public benefactor. Go to the resting-places of the mad but sincere lovers, Alfieri and the Countess of Albany, and tell me if there is not a holy atmosphere about their ashes despite their irreverent passion?

Come, then, to the S. Lorenzo; you will not tarry in the old sacristy amongst the rattling bones of the sons of Cosmo de' Medici, but wend your way to the Medician Chapel, where evidences of the family wealth and piety are portrayed in precious marbles, paintings, statuary, and golden-bronze effigies of the former monarchs of this house. The fac similes of Julian and Lawrence de' Medici upon their sarcophagi are the cynosures of the sacristy, not so much by the immaculate drawing of the representative figures as by the hovering sovereignty of the personifications of Day and Night, Twilight and Dawn. The supernatural significance yet vital lineaments of these emblematic figures is something so inimitable, and the end so devoutly to be attained, that I was almost about to advise the young aspirant to study every curve and expression of these allegorical mentors for three years, as the immortal Malibran acquired the elements of music from a card, and then apply the combinations to whatever subject they may treat.

Yet there were no copyists here, while the Pitti and Uffizi galleries were swarming with young ambitious devotees. Long I watched these students, and often preferred the new and obscure duplicate to the honored original.

The Pitti and Uffizi Palace galleries are connected by a corridor-bridge across the Arno, and very peculiar the sensation to be suddenly aware of your novel situation, with only the deeply flowing waters beneath, while pictures and tapestries are on all sides. I should say the distinguishing features of this thesaurus of art are the furlongs of tapestry that embellish the walls of the passage girding the galleries on either shore of the classic stream. They are the manufactures of the establishment inaugurated by Cosmo de' Medici over three centuries ago and while the cabinets of gems, woodcuts, and national schools of art are here in magnificent profusion, it is a dose oft repeated, while the woven representations of eminent masters shine forth in salient splendor. There is a marked contrast between these museums of Florence and the Borbonico at Naples. Pitti is opulent in the number and schools of painting; Borbonico in its gems, antique marbles, and Pompeian preserves. Not having enjoyed the archaic intaglios and their cameo obverse,—jewels from the collections of Sallust and Pansa,—those in the Uffizi would have been a gratifying treat; but the graceful grouping, allegorical and mythological combinations, and minutiæ of execution, shadow the rivalling collection into comparative obscurity.

Then the marbles! Does the Florentine quarry contain anything as startling in their style of manipulation as the Farnese Bull and the Diana of Ephesus, or that insinuating little Bacchus,—whose I cannot say, but he cannot be mistaken, though standing amongst a legion of brother gods? And where does there exist another so bizarre a treasury as contained in the barred rooms of the Neapolitan Museum. I allude to the apartments from which the visitor is warned by a flaming Italian inscription, which may be read by one of almost any nationality; where the exhumed illustrations of pagan vitiation are spread in unblushing effrontery; designs that proclaim each step of moral philosophy through the era of idolatry. Yet only the favored few, the archæological students, are permitted access to this depository, and if a priestess of the sanctum of Clio enter with all the aplomb of one of the elect she is hurled out as a firebrand from a powder magazine. The awful and sad lesson taught by these remains I must dwell upon just for a moment. Never do I refer to the destroyed city, but some new and terrible evidence of God's implacable vengeance suggests itself to my mind. Not content to pour down the liquid fire of His wrath upon these malefactors while plunged in the very summer of their sin, He preserved every symbol and epigraph of their iniquity as a declaration of their shame to all succeeding ages, while there remains hardly a trace of whatever virtuous or chivalric tendencies may have graced them. In the Pitti all that is great in government, ennobling in art, pure in religion, and sweet in domesticity is presented. In each *salon* the deification—either pagan or Christian—of one of the early patrons of the gallery is portrayed in fresco; it may be termed by the Stoic a romantic conception, but does it not inspire a spirit of public benefaction? Then, in the hall of portraits of painters—is it not an incentive to young ambition that he may in the future fill a place in one of these panels?

In Florence one need not go to public hall or private palace to enjoy the fairest flowers of art that ever bloomed upon the plant of human genius, nor the rarest jewels coined in the crucible of the human mind. Every piazza is crowned by its shining coronal of marble gems; every street is bordered by a zone of beautiful conceits and precious devices. Art is as plenty as chestnut cakes at the corners; Venus, Cupid, Mars, Juno, or Adonis, sparkling in all the symmetry of inspiration, fresh from hands that toiled in unison to the purest promptings of the soul, are sold in shops, which are as frequent as drygoods stores on Chestnut Street.

On the Ponte Vecchio is a marvellous street of jewelry shops. How long have they stood? Ah! since the days Fra Angelico prayed and painted at Fiesole, or Savonarola's voice thundered through the streets in zealous and crude eloquence against the corruption of the de Medicis. Perhaps the Florentine demimonde decked themselves in turquoise and pearls from these dark, low-roofed stores upon the bridge. Pearls befitting the purity of Desdemona; pearls hanging in great hanks in the windows, in such amplitudes as we display wax beads at home; pearls for which my woman's heart yearned, yet from which I was obliged to turn, without even venturing to price.

All these Italian towns, certainly since the accession of Victor Emanuel and the dazzling triumphs of Garibaldi, have added to their old art treasures in the public and private palaces, beautiful galleries, or, as they call them, piazzas, as also fine parks, and walks, and drives; and the genius of United Italy is seen everywhere in abundant statuary to Cavour, Garibaldi, Mazzini, and the later leaders of thought and action. You mark the healthy difference between ancient kings and favorites and the recent republican innovators, by the money spent upon these latter, and although many of the worshippers of the past will tearfully tell you of the great loss sustained by the dismantling of the palaces heretofore belonging to the crown, and to the discrowned dukes and nobility of such falsely-called republics as Genoa, Venice, Florence, Milan, and Naples, I hail the better time when the money of the state is rather given to the state for popular education, than lavished upon the luxuries of princes. Among these beautiful, popular places let me rank the Cascine or park of Florence, called, from a farm to which it once belonged, casino or dairy. Bounded by the rivers Arno and Mugnone, the road rises to a striking "open" about two miles in length, approached by broad highways, leading to a large circle, where the military band plays several times a week. As we stood listening to the music, carriages, filled with the nobility, drawn by spirited horses, came up, the occupants pausing also to hear, and to see the soldiers flirting with the girls in the shade; we next started off through the unique avenues radiating to the monument of the Rajah of Holapore, a young Indian prince who died at Florence in 1870 on his way home from England, and whose body was cremated on the spot, his attendants making the whole neighborhood resound with their strange and melancholy worship. These avenues were singularly wild and picturesque, the tall and venerable trees by which they were lined recalling some of the natural arcades in our Fairmount Park.

But older and more interesting than this fashionable retreat are the Boboli Gardens, which are approached through the Pitti Palace, and whose history takes you back to its origin 350 years ago. From its height there is a charming view of Florence, with its palaces and churches, and as I stand and gaze upon the ample landscape below, and enjoy the mass of shrubbery, and statuary, and fountains, with their swans and other water-fowl immediately around me, I think my gaze never drank in a more enrapturing sight. The evening was so mild, the air so balmy and so heavy with the incense of the spicy odors of cedar and of palm, that I did not wonder at the pride of the Florentines in this exquisite and elaborate conservatory.

Florence lay drowsing sweetly in the valley of the Arno, with the golden mists of heaven falling between the rigid palace walls and in the narrow streets where chilling damps strike to the soul, while the piazza beyond is in one blaze of white fire. Such heat that even the wretched beasts in the hacks droop until they fall dead in their harness; the stranger hurries into the raw shuddering by-streets, and the natives loll along unconscious of the caloric. The brothers of the Misericordia are in the streets and upon the bridges in their long black gowns and hoods and black masks, some bearing a bier upon their shoulders, others returning from their visits to the sick. The calm silver waters flow gently in their course, and to my right and to my left and beyond are the villas of illustrious American sculptors, English painters, and wealthy authoresses, near the roads glorified by the names of Michael Angelo, Galileo, Machiavelli, and Dante.

Fair Florence indeed! fitting home of the great masters, seat of art, science, and bravery, favorite of Angelo and Raphael, Leonardo da Vinci, and their scholars and contemporaries, and at a later date the capital of the kingdom; it seemed a thousand pities that the urgency of the government and the historic logic of Italian unity demanded the removal of central authority to the great capital founded by the Cæsars, consecrated by the sublime sacrifice of Rienzi, and the later statesmanship of Cavour and his illustrious red-shirted co-worker, the hero of Caprera.

LETTER LIX.

"You may remember, scarce five years are past,
Since in your brigantine you sailed to see
The Adriatic wedded by our duke."
OTWAY'S VENICE PRESERVED.

VENICE, June, 1878.

BETWEEN Naples and Florence there are pronounced points of contrast and comparison. Venice has no parallel nor approximate. If it were an animal I might call it mongrel; a plant, heterogenous; a fish amphibious; a language, hybrid; a human being, hermaphrodite. Be there a word in the queen's English, in the whole category of tongues upon which to couch it? *Sui generis* is too weak; *outré* too vague a term. Anomalous would suit the rhetorician, while nonpareil would be the chosen phrase of the printer. I might call it an eccentricity of nature, an aberration of earth, a prodigy of the cosmical sphere, an incongruity of the universe; and so richly clothed in parlance, yet no picture of this fair Aphrodite would be presented, rocked in her briny cradle, whose hues have as many changes as the chameleon—now azure, then emerald, and again a pale opaline rose.

It was eight in the evening when I left Florence, and as arid and breathless a night as one might expect in the torrid zone. Emanuletta, the celebrated flower-girl of Italy,—who has, alas! long since shed her youthful and brilliant plumage,—was at the station, tossing her nosegays into the ladies' laps, and presenting them to the gentlemen with all the beguiling coquetry of eighteen. I had heard much of this girl, who had reigned queen of her clan for decades, sometimes appearing in one Italian capital, then in another, floating and dipping into all the saturnalias these southern cities afford, now the pet of a duke, then the protégé of a countess, always the favorite of the community. She is now a woman of quite sixty, but her natural graces and artificial personal perquisites make her look at least twenty years younger. Her full figure and fantastic costume are her characteristic advantages. With her, life has been one uninterrupted drama from the cradle; all the natural incidents and tastes of the several epochs of a woman's existence have been given to the winds, and the play has gone on day after day in a succession of tableaux. To-day she wears the same crimson petticoat, the same velvet bodice, the same lace kerchief, neatly folded over her bosom, that she did forty-three years ago; even the same smile curves her lips, the same *naïve* sparkle brightens her eyes, the same *bon-mots* drop from her tongue, and the same quick repartee. Her life-chain of adventure has not dulled with time, but rather brightened with its attritions. As she has lived so will she live on to the end. The deep night rapidly growing through the twilight has not deadened any of her gay dress nor effervescing spirits, and when life has been eclipsed by death she will be remembered as Emanuletta the flower-girl.

As we left the gentle valley of the Arno far behind, the clouds burst into a flood of water, and the atmosphere became more endurable; but as tunnels were frequent, and my fellow-travellers in the carriage, one a British daughter of nobility,—the Lady Louisa and her companion,—were excessively fidgety regarding the adjustment of the windows, the blessed oblivion of sleep was not the portion of any of the occupants until our titled Englisher changed cars for the Tyrol; then we poor republican mortals resigned ourselves to the seductions of the sweet soother, and dreamed the hours away until morning.

The approach to Venice is marked by the swamps that dot the landscape, where vegetation is prolific and thrusts its glowing life through the brackish estuaries, and an infinity of vegetable color glows in the shallow water of the blue lagoons. These marshes increase and extend until the great bridge is crossed that carries travellers directly into the station on one of the large islands washed by the Grand Canal. As I stood in the dawn looking out upon the city of the sea from the depot quay the dank atmosphere enveloped land and water in a misty cloak, the weeds clung to the door-posts and foundation stones, and a saline odor and taste filled the air. The lines of Rogers came to me then, and not those of Byron, which is the acknowledgment of an undisciplined mind; surely the "Childe" should take precedence, and yet there is a theory afloat attaching school-girl romance to these poems, and if we would be considered past our tyronism we must keep our mental cells well swept of these vagrant verses. But who, with the sentiment of a mud-turtle, could cross the Bridge of Sighs, pass the palace of the Foscari, ascend the Giant's Stairway, or linger in the piazza of San Marco without recalling the lordly English bard? Who drift under the Rialto without recollecting Shakespeare? Or who gaze upon the widowed Adriatic and forget Otway? Some say these are the influences of the past, but they are the powers which will endure, and be they hackneyed or having the odor of a young lady's manual, they are popular because they are permanent.

There is a decided flavor of the Orient about Venice. It may lie chiefly in historical associations, and certainly the traders from the Levant, the decaying glory, and prevailing moresque style of architecture, revive the legends of the Turkish wars centuries ago.

Riding to the hotel in a gondola, through a street of water, and driven by two sailor-boys in white shirts and blue ribbons, was a peculiar experience, and not a pleasant one to me. I had contemplated a delirium of ecstasy floating through the canals where Desdemona had drifted, and swimming in the boats that had carried Belvidera and

Portia. The old halo vanished in the depression of the present. The decaying magnificence of other centuries is the grim-visaged phantom that stares one into revery; from the crumbling art the mind reverts to the degenerate populace, the waning commerce, the buried doges; then the intense silence of the streets, where no sound of horse's hoof nor rumble of wheel is heard, nought save the solitary dip of the gondolier's oar, and his weird salute to his fellow-oarsman as he whirls his black barge around the acute corners of the watery pathways. It was all very oppressing to me; indeed, I felt more as if I were exploring a city of the dead than I did at Pompeii. The entombed glory of ages seemed to underlie the waters, and the sombre boats—which are entirely black by order of law—appeared the sailing hearses of expired majesty.

The hotels as a rule are not any more fascinating at the entrance than the sea, from which they seem to rise. The atrium, as the Roman would say, is damp, dark, and presents very much the appearance of a boathouse, or ship-chandlery. Ascending a spacious stairway there are second, third, fourth, and fifth floors, abounding in all the charming equipments of a Parisian house; the chambers luxurious, the floors mosaic, and the inevitable porcelain stove, the conspicuous feature that baffled my imagination long before I discovered its use. In every hall and chamber I saw a great, white, fluted, cylindrical apparatus, and I walked round and round them, turning every screw and crank, and at length divined their purpose, and although it is June their warmth is not unwelcome in the salt climate and the chilling rain.

The formation of this strange product of the pirates of 2000 years ago puzzled and interested me. How came it here? was my continual mental interrogation. It is indeed mountain debris and drifting alpine currents that fashioned this floating city? While it is declining in power it is growing in latitude. Every year earth is added to the sand islands covered by the lagoons, and some day these fœtus worlds will have completed their gestation and spring into existence, glorious and beautiful spheres. Children of the sea, may I call them? and Venice the regent, though hoary and superannuated, is augmenting her progeny each year. And a healthy offspring it is; rich in its capabilities, affluent in its growth of fruits, vegetables, flowers, and animal life.

These lagoons, so lusty with life, would be sinks of infection were it not for the chastening saline ingredients; and where all glows with vitality death would exhale its venomous breath. The ragged weeds coursing in the stream and the green scum that marks the flow and ebb of the tide upon the marble foundations, are its true conservators of life, and teach us God's ubiquitous providence.

"Hast ever swum in a gondola at Venice?" Ah, yes! and a very emotional swim it was. The magnificence of the grand canal coiling far beyond like a great S of sapphire crystal losing itself in the curve, spanned by its bridges and bordered by its palaces, is the first impression; then as the barge moves onward with measured sweep, the custom-house, a long narrow edifice at the entrance of the canal upon the left shore, recalls the extended traffic of the past; the churches, with their variety of schools and eras of art; the palaces, with their storied recollections of dukes and demigods, of pampered favorites and oppressed genius, and after all the abode of poets; piles that still echo the names of Othello and Shylock, Antonio, Pierre, and Jaffier; stones that suggest the base of tragedies, and façades that portray the art of the Saracens, the austerity of the Decadence, and the resplendence of the Renaissance. Here a regal home, grim in the rigid splendor of mediæval days; there an illuminated front, glowing in its gold and frescoes, awnings, and jutting balconies; farther on an exterior of white, elaborated in black marble; and again the most brilliant pictures in mosaic, vaguely hidden by canopies, arches, and columned porticos.

The Rialto, where the Christians were wont to rate the Jews about their moneys and spit upon them; where the traders sell their gay beads from their stalls upon the bridge, and the venders of hot boiled potatoes supply their customers with the Irish vegetable in their bursting jackets, while the varied populace drift under the dark arches beneath, was one of my chosen rendezvous. Farther on, the Grand Canal curves the delta of the Camps di Marte,—a large grassy island, a sort of suburban retreat of the ultramarine city,—and loses itself in the Guidecca, that separates the city proper from the island where the laborers and factory employés have their homes; the district of Guidecca is to Venice what Manayunk is to Philadelphia. Its channel is broad and deep enough to pass large craft, and is the thoroughfare of traffic for the manufactories and exporting houses. Here the romantic delight of the Grand Canal faded into an emotion akin to fear as the clouds lowered, the riotous winds came sweeping over the broad bosom of the ocean, creeping amongst the sand reefs, swelling the waves into foam-crested billows, that broke into tempestuous eddies, and rocked the frail skiff fore and aft with the growing storm. The gondolier's sharp cries grew louder, and as I rode around this wilderness of water I thought if I were careened in the brine it would be an easy and soon forgotten sleep.

The city may be traversed through the contracted alley-ways, and by the bridges that serve as stepping-stones over the mammoth gutters of sea-water. This is a tedious mode of transit, but the only method by which to get an idea of the construction of Venice. A ride in a gondola to the piazza of St. Mark condenses all the beauty and romance of the situation; but to thread the labyrinthine sinuosities of the footpath a picture of lowly Venetian life is best obtained. Narrow avenues, that seem only arcades, flanked by prosperous shops, whose doorsteps almost touch in the centre of the passage. Wandering through these curtailed inflexions of the town, I found myself in the noble square of San Marco. I cannot relate by what route I came, suffice it, I got there; my saunterings brought me face to face with the temple of the tutelary saint guarded by the winged lions of the Apocalypse. Indeed, where may the eyes turn in Venice and not rest upon these prophetic monsters? They are in the immediate piazza of the tabernacle in a countless variety and multitude. They are gaudy in fresco, rude in mosaic, glowering in bronze, mounted upon columns at a dizzy altitude; they hover in the court of the doges, they crouch at the tomb of Canova, and crown the cenotaph of Titian; they hail you from common and court, ornament portal and pediment, symbolize saint and sinner, the crest of prince and pauper, and are the genii of the Queen of the Adriatic.

The piazza of St. Mark is the focus of municipal power. It has an opening quay toward the sea on the west, and a fencing of palace, shop, and church, upon the three other checks. The devotees come to their matins and vespers, the fashions come to enjoy the gayety and *sorbetta*, the traveller to see, the ladies to be seen, the trader to fulfil his mission, the Jew to barter, the seamen to sport, and the flower-girl to sell her bouquets and receive the glances of admiration from the throng. Truly, a scene of fair witchery when the glowing lamps throw their mellow, golden light over the square and its gossiping occupants, and find a triple reflection in the blue waves, which are lighted into a phosphorescence by the moon, and the sweet strains of the dulcet Italian band float over all a surge of melody.

The Venetian flower-girl is the most conspicuous object of the picture; she circulates between the cafés and the little tables under the arches. They are most decidedly the youngest, best-dressed, and best-looking women of this school I have seen, and are also the most importunate canvassers for personal favor. I watched the subtlety and cajolery of one of these fair ones as she endeavored to decoy the male fish into the net she wove—the woof of smiles and blushes; she courtsied, winked, blinked, smiled archly, wafted kisses from her aromatic finger-tips, and, as a binding favor, fastened the flowers upon the cavaliers' coats.

The Cathedral is a flashingly ornate structure, with low mosque or minaret domes. Blackened by time, it stands a majestic relic of the past. The coarse, garish mosaics in the façade that overarch the doors are rendered more flaunting by contrast with the sombre pile and its poor surroundings. Inside there is none of the characteristic cleanliness of the basilicas in Rome and Florence. The mosaic blocks of the pavement are lacerated and dislocated by the scythe of Time, grimed by the dust he carries with him, and unwashed by friendly hands. The jewels and precious marbles of the altar have alone defied the almighty despoiler, standing forth the stars of the withering sanctuary.

The Palace of the Doges is a dream of wonder to the stranger. Its great rows of cloisters or columned galleries are of architecture so graceful as to appear the poetry and music of masonry, and yet so enduring as to last through the eternity. Such elaboration of base and capital I had yet not beheld; curves, loopholes, and entablatures that seemed the inspiration of the troubadour. A great stairway—the Giant's Staircase—down which Marino Faliero's head is said to have rolled at his execution, though it was not erected until after he was guillotined, leads from the court to the colonnades above. A gaping wound in the wall marks the spot where conspirators dropped the poisonous billets against their enemies into the lion's mouth, in the dead watches of the night. Next day the unsuspecting, pitiable wretches were tried by the Council of Ten or the Council of Three, and condemned to death or a dungeon—guilty ever, as the tribunal chose to find them. Here are the chambers where the inquisitors judged the innocent, lined by a wealth of cunning marbles—beauty that enraptures the soul of the gazer by its sublimity one moment, only to make the despair still more dark into which it is plunged the next, by the frowning Bridge of Sighs, that spans the narrow canal and connects palace and prison, and the tenebrious cells for the convicted, where no ray of hope or sunlight entered; a rough-hewn hole in the upper portion of the cell-wall served as an aperture through which food was handed to the prisoner. There was a mysterious glamour and an awful silence about these subterranean dens that carried me back to the days of shadowy confessors, secret doors, and sliding panels; I expected to see the four walls contract and crush me, or a threatening firebrand appear in the darkness and vibrate over my unoffending head, or seas of molten fire to flood the cave and swallow me in their lurid depths, or the ground upon which I stood to yawn and reveal hungry beasts ready to devour me. It was not until I had shaken off the damp and must in the outer air of heaven that I felt fairly rid of the ghastly phantom.

The illustrious paintings of the palace relate the great story of the ancient Venetian Republic. Recollections of big ships and glorious victories are all about us. On wall and ceiling are the noble achievements of Tintoretto and Paul Veronese, works that proclaim the dignity of the doges as well as the immortality of the artists. The palace was a pronounced contrast to the prison, but even here there was an aroma of arbitrary grandeur or autocratic lustre that did not please my republican tastes, and cast a sad reflection through the vivid pigments of fresco. The poverty and thraldom of the masses were deplorably apparent in contrast with lavish wealth and obtrusive pomp.

I had often read and listened to the anecdote of the "Pigeons of St. Mark." I will not say I disbelieved its authenticity, but I thought there was some insidious humbug or *suggestio falsi*, so to speak, about the story; and I determined to convince myself of its truth, like Thomas, by seeing with my own eyes and demonstrating with my own hands. I was in one of the legion of photograph shops of the piazza, overhauling the Italian Hebrew's stock of *blue* pictures—three tones bluer than I ever saw the main and sky. In the pictures everything is of the same tint, cathedral, palace, custom-house, men, water, and boats; in nature each object has a distinct color of its own, and the representations that draw nearest to fact are those floating in a pale, rosy haze or incense. However, to revert to our *moutons;* as I was in the shop I noticed a vast number of these birds flitting about the square and on the porches, but then, said I, the community are feeding them, and it is only natural that they should gather; but, at the tolling of two from the clock-tower, a dense cloud of them hovered over the piazza, and made the ground, the eaves of the Campanile, and every sill, buttress, projection, and capital, black as they fluttered down, and army after army crowded upon the others so closely that I could not escape gratifying conviction.

Venice has less attraction in its churches, perhaps, than any other Italian capital. Its topographical paradoxes are the cynosure, and, being a seaport town, it loses all drowsy religious odor in the bustle of its traders. *St. John and St. Paul* is worthy of consideration, as it served as the Westminster of Venice, inasmuch as the vaults of the doges are here, and here their funeral service was ever solemnized. The Frari is attractive as containing the mausolea of Titian and Canova, and, indeed, every temple of divine worship in the noiseless city is a treasure-house of art. But what have I to do with art and architecture here in the presence of the Bride of the Adriatic, where the sea flows all around?—the sea, that was wedded by the duke nine centuries ago, and yet continues in its joyous current, no older, no feebler; the sea, that crawls about the churches, and palaces, and prisons, leaving the saliva of its salty tongue upon their foundation-stones; the sea, that floats one into dreams and nurses sweet memory in its murmur.

LETTER LX.

> On Como's lake the sunset fell,
>   Then passed away in golden flame,
> And fair o'er vine and olive dell
>   The star through purple shadows came,
> While far o'er leagues of twilight gloom,
>   The Alps still burned in rosy glow,
> And mirrored back, like scattered bloom,
>   Lay, shining in the wave below."

MILAN. CADENABBIA ON LAKE COMO, June, 1878.

I do not say that there is nothing interesting in Milan save the Cathedral; but that it is my only vivid impression. I saw it first at the twilight hour, when the shadows of night had softened every line of its thousands of statues (some authorities say over 2000, others 8000, I did not pause to count them), mellowed each Gothic turret that crowns the roof, and cast a gauze of tenderness over the entire structure as it couched against the witching blue sky, where its graceful lineaments were traced in a fretwork of stone as airy and delicate as the finest lace. I rode round and round to gratify the passion its ethereal beauties had kindled into life, and at every wing and buttress the marvel grew. The myriads of marble angels, saints, soldiers, and statesmen, also popes, painters, and sculptors mingled amongst its many folds and interweaving lines, seemed the work of celestial art. Its many piercing spires looked the ephemeral pinnacles of some fairy palace. In the holy dusk and sombre decline of day it resembled a frozen poem, an anthem, or a drama in marble. The exterior had reduced me to a state of revery, so my mood was in harmony with the religious glamour and haze of incense within, when I pushed back the great doors, and found myself incontinently yielding to the bewildering influence. While it lacks all of the ostentatious adornment of the great St. Peter's in Rome, it is this very chastity that lends the grace of sanctity that the greatest Roman cathedral can never claim with its garish glory. The one is a gorgeous palace, where art and wealth have been exhausted, the other a classic temple that inspires prayer. I no longer wonder at the armies of papal devotees in this Catholic country; the religion is so pleasing, calm, and restful. As I stood a few feet within the portals, upon the rich mosaic floor, the lofty vaulted roof above and the regal banners and paintings hanging upon every pillar of grouped columns, I was spellbound by the spirit of holiness enthroned in my bosom, and as I unconsciously obeyed the promptings of my heart and knelt, I could have sighed my soul away in one eternal apostrophe to my God.

There are no jewelled shrines nor frescoed panels, no Russian marbles nor Eastern alabaster here. The arches of the roof, the altar, and capitals of the pillars, from which start hundreds of statues, are wrought in an interminable filigree of stone, so pure, so cold, so hoary, that the golden light that falls in semitones through the great colored glass window over the entrance euphonizes all into one oratorio. I said, "This must be the mansion of the All-merciful, the peace and rest of Heaven is upon me." The cause of my supreme content seemed something palpable, and inadvertently I groped the air for a tangible influence; a maze of holy incense was absorbing and bearing off my earthiness in its mesmerism, when I was aroused to a sense of chill and darkness. As I passed out I longed for the morrow when I might return.

But with the dawn came Corpus Domini. High solemnities were to be celebrated, the city was in gala-day garb, and thousands of every class thronged the streets. There were military and ecclesiastical parades, crowds of people, bands of music, clouds of incense; the shops were closed and a general spirit of frolic prevailed. The Cathedral did not seem the holy of holies in which I had meditated the night before; the crowd desecrated it, and so fearing the subtleties of the yesterday might be quite undone by the impending ceremonies and thickening throng, I hurried away.

Milan is so pure and clean and elegant one might readily be persuaded he had passed out of Italy, proverbial for dirt. The white houses and gay shops lend to it a Parisian appearance. But there are ample recollections of Italy in the Victor Emanuel Gallery, the statue of Cavour, and the many monuments to local celebrities.

This gallery is a palatial arcade of shops in the form of a Latin cross, connecting the Cathedral piazza with the La Scala opera-house. The façades of the stores are florid with scrolls and jalousies and caryatides, the overarching canopy of glass admits the light of day, and by night the dome looms out like some southern meteor, dazzling in its two thousand gas-jets, casting a resplendence over the great frescoes of the rotunda, and a radiance over the archetypes of the presiding artistic and political genii. The great services of the late Emperor, Garibaldi, and Cavour, are commemorated throughout Italy by statues, galleries, paintings, and edifices. As I write Cavour is looking at me with his bronze face from his pedestal of granite, where Fame sits carving his name with an indelible stylus.

The La Scala is closed for the summer, but I went to enjoy its vast proportions, the majesty of the Emperor's box, and the stage where Adelina Patti has achieved her greatest triumphs. The immense auditorium, and stage as large as a circus arena, somewhat modifies the oppressive ornamentation of the tiers and boxes. Directly opposite the stage, situated in what we call the balcony, is the royal loge, bearing the crown and princely crimson hangings; in the vestibule are statues of Malibran, Rossini, and Donizetti. But it was at the La Verme that I passed such a delightful evening with "La Sonnambula," and though a second-class opera house was exceedingly capacious. It is evidently a summer establishment, where all the gentlemen smoke, and the ladies attend in ordinary street costume. After the opera proper came a protracted ballet,—the opera in Italy is generally succeeded by a ballet,—I may call it a pantomime ballet, "Discovery of America by Columbo." Very unique, interesting, and instructive. The dancing was the poetry of motion, and the dumb show the eloquence of graceful silence. Without the aid of speech their gestures were so intelligible as to make a language by itself.

All the Italian cities boast of fine parks and drives. That of Milan is very beautiful, the course for the carriages and horsemen being over the ramparts; the top of the original military wall that hemmed in the desirable city from foraging despoilers. Here the nobility and gentry come to ventilate their regality in the soft Italian gloaming. To vie with each other's crests and liveries seems their heaven, and as the dimensions are limited, they ride round and round the park like puppets in a toy circus. The Milanese may dress plainly, he may live economically, he may even dine without macaroni, but not to own an equipage and drive upon the bastions is a sign of shameful impecuniosity.

I dreaded visiting other churches in the fear of dispelling the enthusiastic thraldom of the Cathedral, but I could not leave Milan without seeing Leonardo da Vinci in his most inspired work. My only errand to the S. Marie delle

Grazie was to this end. I cannot rhapsodize here, as the noted fresco of the Last Supper is so vilely defaced as almost to obliterate all original lines. I have heard of travellers being lost in admiration of the master-touches of this glorious composition, and transported by grief at the passion portrayed. I freely confess I saw only the dust and ashes of a once noble monument, and if there were a shade of sad regret, it was for the shameful purpose to which the apartment had been devoted by Napoleon, and the ravages perpetrated by the monks. There were copyits there by the dozen, seemingly to portray the conception of the great master with pleasing skill. As I quitted its presence, children who could scarcely articulate their first syllables had been taught to ask charity at the very church door, and to glorify your soul in choice Italian if you refused them largess.

But the episode to be most earnestly remembered was my experience at St. Ambrose, originally a heathen temple of Bacchus; old in history, Oriental in form, and odorous of incense. There was a strange combination of pagan and Christian antiquities. It was a festa day, and the faithful worshippers were gathered about a glittering casket behind the high altar, extending their rosaries, prayer-books, bandannas, and other articles to a priest, who passed the objects over the sides of the glass and brass bindings, returned them to their owners, and received pennies for polishing off the sacred cabinet with the handkerchiefs of the children of Light. I dropped three coppers into the plate, and had my Protestant linen rubbed over the holy brass, and now I am afraid to have it washed, as I am not sure but the process will destroy the odor of sanctity, so it must be enshrined amongst my sacred relics.

It seems incongruous to emerge from such a ceremony in a temple hung with ancient tapestry, to a street where American tramways are as familiar as signs of Singer's and Howe's sewing machines; and these are whizzing from the Seine to the Tiber, and from the Ural Mountains in White Russia to the Jura Hills in Switzerland.

At the northwest marginal line of the city stands the Arch of Peace, proud trophy of Napoleon's occupation. The marked contrast of the springing bronze horses mounting the snowy arc, on the one side, to typify the glory of the Great Captain of his age, with the modern trophy in honor of his successor, the last emperor's Italian campaigns, was suggestive and painful.

* * * * * * *

The town of Como, distant from Milan by rail about one hour and three-quarters on one of the most beautiful lakes in the north of Italy, was extolled by Virgil before the birth of Christ. Passing up the lake it is one succession of transcendent panoramas. The mountains rise to a height of seven thousand feet from the extreme margin of the lake, which is kept constantly full in summer by the melted snows from the various altitudes by which it is hemmed in, and abounds in fish. The trout have none of the delicacy of the American or English fish; the immense size to which they grow frequently equals twenty pounds, rendering them tough and tasteless.

It is a declining manufacturing town, dusty and smoky, where the industrious inhabitants are engaged at the silk-loom.

Como is the Newport of Milan, and lying on both banks of the lake are the luxurious residences of the Milanese aristocracy. They look like fairy abodes, swinging between the olive heights and azure mirror, embowered in densest pine and wreathing vines. There is a spiritual existence about all these southern French and Italian towns; the air, the water, the sky, the stars, the vegetation, and the flowers are all sacred or semi-tropical. The hamlets of the Lake of Como are to me the last expression of this thought. It is an *olla podrida* of aristocratic villas, gardens, vineyards, mountains, and defiles, and seated by its waters I find myself unconsciously murmuring the words of Melnotte in the "Lady of Lyons," when he pictures Como to his sweetheart as his earthly paradise.

My first impressions of Como left me destitute of power to describe them. I saw the lake first in the twilight hush of June, from the iron balcony of the Belle View on the western side in the exquisite town of Cadenabbia. Sailing up the lake from the dirty capital of the province on a crowded local steamer, if you were apt to believe Bulwer's rhapsody of the inland water supply an innocent falsehood, his entrancing picture would be sublimated into a sublime reality upon locating at one of the many beguiling settlements. I can easily conceive his exact emotions writing as I do now in the sweet subjection of this transcendent spot.

The lake seems mountain-bound on four sides without any visible outlet. The day in Milan was as hot as Africa; the evening at Cadenabbia as mild as the close of an American autumn day. It is like a painted picture in a glowing melodrama; and so perfect is it in all the minutiæ of scenic effect, that it seems to have been rehearsed for my special delectation. Below me a picturesque pageant; the lake lies as still and waveless as a baby in its earliest softest slumber, save the starting and flashing oars of the tiny boats sent out at intervals with their gayly dressed freight. One of these little shells has for its oarsman a beautiful girl, carrying out her aged, white-haired mother on the tranquil water; another floated from its prow the emblem of my own dear country, with its bright red stripes and its sparkling stars; another has a company of English people, the women in their heavy ulsters, the men suffocating under the Turkish towel veils wound about their hats. A mile across the lake is a cluster of white cottages, where the starry lights, coming out one by one, and trebled in the glassy waters of the lake, are touching in their silent beauty, while across the old hills sound the audible throbbings of distant church chimes. It is a scene of pensive and soothing and consoling majesty, and if any influence were needed to make it more impressive it is furnished by the alternate changes of the mountains as the afternoon sobers into evening, and as the evening darkens into night. First the golden glow of the sinking sun, then the violet of the departed god of day and the looming shadows of the hills in the water, then the gray shroud over the more distant Alps, and finally night, with its ebon veil, gradually studded with the same stars that have shone for ten thousand thousand years; and now nothing is seen except the flash of the light in the boats like crimson and yellow fire-flies dancing in the waves.

The hotel is evidently an old castle. Stone stairs, marble and mosaic floors, frescoed salons, and a marvellously lovely garden around it. Ultra neatness and elegance of style pervade the establishment. Adjacent is the Villa Carlotta, now the property of Duke George of Saxe Meiningen, filled with magnificent statues by Thorwaldsen and Canova, and adorned with costly objects of *virtu*.

To describe Cadenabbia and the Villa Carlotta is to picture all the other hotels and villas bordering the lovely expanse of water for thirty miles. All the lakes of Northern Italy are sources of wealth to the great cities in their neighborhood, and Maggiore and Lugano have the same peculiar seductions of atmosphere, colors, foliage, and architecture.

To these miniature inland seas flock the culture and art

of all the word; and I met many of the Bonanza kings of my own country in the trains and boats travelling in this lovely region. All the shores of these mirrored waters are gemmed with the places of titled and untitled millionaires, and these are so beautiful and so finished, that if nature were not herself still more so, one would take the whole panorama for a painted and polished medallion; but as it is, though man excels himself in his inventions and his expenditures, God is the real master, because His works are not only more lovely, but more lasting.

LETTER LXI.

"'T was late,—the sun had almost shone
  His last and best, when I ran on,
Anxious to reach that splendid view
  Before the daybeams quite withdrew;
'T was at this instant—while there glowed
  This last, intensest gleam of light—
Suddenly, through the opening road,
  The valley burst upon my sight!
That glorious valley, with its lake,
  And Alps on Alps in clusters swelling
Mighty and pure and fit to make
  The ramparts of a Godhead's dwelling!"
                                TOM MOORE.

GENEVA, June, 1878.

THE ride from Milan to Turin, the capital of Piedmont, is through an exquisite territory of rice plantations, where the fresh beryl stiletto-shaped leaf rises like a world of miniature church spires above its bed of water—the Alpine streams that are turned through the fields to irrigate and flood them. I enjoyed the beautiful vegetable more in the fields than I did on the table, where it appeared in every disguise.

There are many historical monuments and memories by the way, as Piedmont seems to have been the destined arena of warlike action, and the focus of the struggles of the nation with almost every power and in every epoch. But these events appear to lose prestige in sight of the lovely maize and rice of the plains, and the vines and cocooneries of the hills, guarded by the uncouth crucifixes and heathen symbols which still hold a conspicuous place on the Italian farms.

Turin is only a fraction smaller than Milan, but has none of her gayety, lightness, nor delicacy. It is a dull city, and had it not been for the pageant of St. John the Baptist would have seemed a slow and slothful town. What impressed me most were the number and excruciating attitudes of the statues. With one or two exceptions these marble and bronze monsters seem to have been taken at a moment when they had been either too intimately associated with Bacchus or writhing in an agony of mortal pain. Their faces are contorted, and their forms distorted and their postures to my mind most awkward and ungainly.

There are fine shops under the arcades in the Via di Po, but they have a gloomy appearance and even in the Piazza Victor Emanuel and the Piazza Castello life seemed to be constrained and cold.

The ecclesiastical parade on the feast of the nativity of John the Evangelist was the reigning religious festa. A long file of nuns, monks, cardinals, bishops, old women, boys chanting Latin verses and carrying lighted candles, completed the demonstrating concourse, while thousands of every denomination thronged the sidewalk, and as the consecrated wafer passed the faithful Catholics prostrated themselves in the dust. Down went the ladies in their silks and laces on the pavements, curbs, and even in the gutters; men followed their example regardless of their paraphernalia, devotees to the mandate of the church. The excess of these exhibitions has somewhat moderated since the reforms of Victor Emanuel; previously, the credulous flung themselves before the holy image whether in alley or ditch, with the servility of the benighted Hindoo, who threw himself under the wheels of his Juggernaut. The Italian asks if unalloyed faith should pick nice occasions and pleasing places for its worship?

To ride through the pensive paths of the public gardens and cross the long bridge that spans the Po, or ascend the heights crowned by the Capucini monastery, from which an extended view is gained of the winding waters and city beneath, and its Alpine background, where the ancient giants lean their snowy caps against the soft blue dome, was the only sweet divertisement I enjoyed in Turin.

All that might be remembered of Turin is dwarfed by the memorable journey between that city and Geneva, the passage of the Mont Cenis tunnel being the chief object of interest There was a long succession of tunnels, with here and there a glimpse of wild, rugged landscape from the start. The Valley of the Dora lay sweetly peaceful amongst its vine-clad hills, over-frowned by its lofty mountains, where the goats and donkeys were skipping the crags and trudging the rugged hills.

At the little village of Bardonchia the ascent of the terrible height of the Alps began. It was over these hitherto inaccessible mountain ranges that Napoleon seventy years ago carried his armies and poured them down into the plains of Piedmont and Lombardy, thus making himself master of all Italy;—these altitudes, through which I was to penetrate in a few minutes, aided by the mighty modern work by which these unattainable heights are pierced. Higher and still higher we mounted, sometimes skimming along the sharp ledge of a spur of rock, then hanging upon a thread of straight oblique granite, and again perched upon what seemed the culminating pinnacle of the stupendous range, while, beyond, swift mountain streams wound their waters like satin ribbons about the gray rocks. At my side foaming torrents gushed and leaped like angry monsters, carrying everything in their course; the little white cities of the plains seeming toy towns from the airy height, while beneath, great chasms yawned, black and bottomless as eternity.

The experience of passing through the tunnel was new and unexpected. The former tunnels had been close, noisome, and dark, and in this most formidable of all I anticipated awful possibilities; a collision, a caving in of roof, perhaps suffocation. But this almost supernatural construction, eight miles long, was so light and well ventilated that the atmosphere was as pure as the air of a lady's boudoir. Great windows were cut here and there in the rocks, and large lanterns cast a pleasant glow through the long cavern. We entered from the south, 4163 feet above sea level, and maintained this height until we gradually descended on the right at a level of 3802, so that our mean average was 4093 feet below the surface of the mountain. The amazing feature of this wonderful excavation is the admirable manner in which it is ligthed, ventilated, and drained. The engineers started at opposite sides, and so accurate was their survey that the workmen with their diamond-pointed drill met plumb in the middle. It was the inspiration of genius defying time and nature.

Immediately upon emerging from the heart of the eternal Alps we halted at Modane, the frontier town between Italy and France, to submit to the annoying examination of passports. Perhaps those who rave against our country have not considered all these unecccessary vexations abroad. While between our respective States we are one people from zone to zone, and may travel from the Atlantic shore to the Pacific slope without question or stoppage by government official or change of coin; here there are official customs and sentinels at every frontier, and as many coins or currency as dialects.

Now we were in France again, and Gallic cleanliness, sanctifying convent, and castle battlements were mingled with the wild sublimity of Alpine scenery, luxurious vineyards, and fashionable resorts, such as Aix les Bains; and the azure crystal lake, along the border of which the train rushed rapidly for twelve miles, following the blue flow of the placid water. A short, heavenly ride in France; then, yielding to another frontier pause, we were whisked into Switzerland, the old curiosity shop of the Almighty Creator. About fifty miles off lay Geneva, chief of the republic, city of John Calvin, Rousseau, and Voltaire, whose environs are memorable for many interesting souvenirs. As we approached, in the sweet, odorous sunset of June, I had my first glimpse of Mont Blanc. The fading beams of the sun gave to the distant snowpeaks first a glowing pink, mellowing into a deep violet, and finally sobering into gray. Nature's mysterious machinery was profoundly touching by its awful manifestations.

I found Geneva in a glow of preparation for the celebration of the centenary of the death of its great social reformer, Jean Jacques Rousseau. The city was in a regalia of flags of the nations; wreaths were suspended from street to street, and triumphal arches in every square; surging crowds hustled each other in the highways and on the quays. The pageant, which I viewed from my window on Sunday, was conspicuous only for the absence of military of any description; a few of the bands were good, but the long parade of trudging citizens was monotonous. Three days were devoted to the festival, and evidently the whole population joined in the demonstration. Rousseau had none of the genius or courage of Voltaire, neither was he a republican like the sage of Ferney; but what recked the people of Geneva, so they could extract a frolic from the memory of the man who was born in their town the greater part of two centuries ago? What did they know of him? As little as they cared. The first day of jollity the town swam in a sea of glory—speeches, cannons, music, and everything that was wild and exciting, nothing really classic or good. The women danced quadrilles and waltzes in the streets to public music, and the country dames strutted in the line with the men, while at night there was a tolerable illumination of the city; the varied colors of the lights, red, green, blue, and yellow, in long rows upon the bridge, and shining from the boats upon the lake, contrived to make a dazzling spectacle. Before midnight a pandemonium of drunken Swiss choruses began that continued till next morning, and, as I lay in my disturbed demi-slumber, I thought of their inevitable retribution for this foolish dissipation, and then marvelled how many of these wild bacchantes thought of Jean Jacques Rousseau.

I fear the good Switzers are not as graceful and successful in art as the volatile French. Geneva, as a rule, I should say, was a quiet town of manufactories—a town of musical-boxes and watches. These greet us at every corner and window, and demand attention. It has many of the French and Italian characteristics of architecture and topography, very little of the purely Swiss; even the market-women speak good French. There are many fine hotels and cafés, rows of noble shops, and broad streets, but the chief interest of the Swiss capital lies, not in the city, but in its surroundings—its odorous wayside paths and wildering waters.

On an eminence a few miles from the city I looked down upon a lovely freak of nature,—the marriage of the blue, arrowy Rhone and the gray, ashen Arve. The city itself lay mapped out before me, a lovely queen seated in a lap of hills, crowned with her snowy diadem of Mont Blanc, while all around was green and peaceful. At the end of the lake the two streams mingle and flow on in one course, sleep in the same bed, and yet each preserving its own peculiar color and character for many miles. I had witnessed the amalgamation of other great streams where they blent naturally into one, but here the unexplained phenomenon of two great tributaries of the ocean, flowing from the same mountain sources, joining. yet forcibly two currents, set me to moralizing and making personal applications. It was nothing more than a symbol of the marriage of man, where bodies, not souls, are united. A little village occupied the delta of land between the two waters, where large heaps of stone and sand lay on the banks, seeming to have been taken from the basin of the Arve, and on the extreme shore sat an artist amidst the handiwork of God. The memory of the picture would be complete had not a girl demanded a franc for the simple privilege for looking at one of the municipal attractions of Geneva. It seemed very like exacting a fee from a stranger for the right to enjoy Fairmount Park.

Through a few miles of aromatic lanes we came to the gates of Adolph Rothschild's imposing chateau at Pieghny, but it was closed against visitors, so we could not even peep over the great, granite fortifications that surrounded the estate. In building these grim stone walls the object is to exclude obtruders, and the effect is to create a depression and contempt in the minds of travellers. Such feudal selfishness is particularly disgraceful in the towns of England and the Continent. I have ever been of the opinion that the dull stone walls around Girard College are an insult to the people and to the memory of the illustrious Frenchman; these barriers are only for prisons and madhouses. So where I anticipated a revel amongst art and wealth I met a dark disappointment, and obtained not a glimpse of the many delicacies I had read of in books and magazines.

We proceeded to Coppet, the home of the celebrated Madame De Staël; the home where her childhood was passed when her father was a Parisian banker; the home to which she retreated with her confidant, Benjamin Constant, and here maintained a court of her own when Napoleon banished her from her paradise in Paris, after having been the nucleus of the highest diplomatic and intellectual circles, while her father was Minister of Finance to Louis XVI. The estate is now the property of her grandson, Duc de Broglie, present reactionary member of the French Senate, but in a little chapel hidden by a grove the body of the French Pythoness is buried by the side of her father.

The vestibule of the house is pure white marble. A spacious flight of glistening steps led to the entresol, where a statue of M. Necker, with cynical nose and receding chin, stands guard. The family portraits were hung in the main sitting room. The fine painting, by David, of this goddess of love, from which all the photographs and engravings are struck that float the hemispheres, is three-quarter length. Her hair is arranged in numerous little curls, lifted from her neck and forehead by a band; her dress white, embellished with gold embroidery, and a gaudy scarf carelessly thrown over her shoulders; in her hand she bears the inevitable and significant myrtle sprig. There are various other models of her scattered through the apartments, in curious guises and character; this bright constellation of intellect had the fatal vice of her sex, vanity. Her husband and son hang side by side; the first, though a man of rank, was allowed to figure very little in her destiny. Her daughter, afterward the Duchess de Broglie, was a superbly beautiful woman, as shown by her statuette and portrait. The library, containing few of the old books, is interesting on account of its associations, and the portraits of herself as Corinne; Raphael, a copy of the original painted by himself; Jean Jacques Rousseau, and the German poet Schlegel, who acted as her good friend, adviser, and preceptor of her children. Adjoining her library was her chamber. The walls were upholstered in the old tapestries embroidered for her in her time. Her bed, desk, and other furniture are used by the present duchess when she comes from Paris to the lovely Swiss hamlet on the northern bank of Lake Leman.

How many times have these ancestral halls sparkled with the wit and beauty of the eighteenth century! How many of life's romances and tragedies have been enacted in sport and reality, no living tongue can relate! How many times has the beautiful Recamier swayed in the poetry of motion in these salons! How many times have the voices of Constant, Talleyrand, and Schlegel vibrated in this retreat! How many times have the powerful oratory and dazzling energies of this woman turned to tears and moans in these very halls!

The beautiful borders of the lake, and the sweet shady roads that intersect the neighborhood are punctuated by historical chateaux and baronial estates. Far more interesting to me was Ferney, the home of the cynic Voltaire, than Nyon, where the celebrated adherents of Napoleon I found a refuge, and the chateau formerly the property of Joseph Bonaparte, and that belonging to Prince Jerome Napoleon. Through a bridle-path, where the wreathing vines of France bordered our left, while the golden grain of Switzerland waved on our right, we found Ferney, a village on the Swiss frontier, in French territory; a beautiful hamlet full of French habits, and although only divorced from its Swiss consort by a narrow bar of highway, marked by all the Gallic peculiarities.

Need I say Voltaire was a radical, an extreme republican, a non-conformist, a deist, a free-thinker, and a special friend of Washington and Franklin? On the 30th of May he was dead one hundred years, and the Liberals of the Continent rose to do him honor, to the utter disgust of the Catholics. Besides, to worship him was to protest against Rousseau

The grounds of the *savant's* estate are preserved in all their original beauty. Rose vines clamber over arbors and form fairy retreats, separated from vast parterres of gaudy flowers, planted in symbolic devices, by well-rolled gravel walks. Voltaire's famous arched bower is a masterwork of botanical art, where the evergreens interlace and form a canopy roof, while at intervals windows are cut in the walls of foliage to admit the light to this strange man's loved snuggery. The rooms shown to visitors face a noble terrace, while there is an immediate plateau of small flowers and box edging. Away off lies the city of Geneva, the frosted-silver peak of Mont Blanc, and a circular range of rude hills.

Rooms burdened with luxuries, still there was the same weird, mysterious spirit pervading them that always was the grotesque expression of his features and life. In the first apartment was the fac-simile of his mausoleum, finely executed, a spectral ornament; also a colossal bronze bust of himself, with keen French face, and the walls were rich with the originals of eminent artists. In his chamber were gathered his literary favorites and contemporaries. Over his bed within shadow of the curtains, was a fine head of LeKain, the celebrated actor. Above the mantel hung a large allegorical subject by Du Reissy, of Melpomene—muse of Tragedy—leading Voltaire from the temple of Fame to present him to Apollo. At the base Humanity, Liberty, all the virtues and graces paid court to the illustrious French poet, while still lower Tyranny, Priestcraft, Bigotry, and Hypocrisy were flying in terror before his scathing denunciations. Republican though he was, Catharine of Russia and Frederick of Prussia were his nearest friends, whose pictures are hanging above his bed, presented by themselves. But greater powers than kings or queens were there,—Washington presented by Lafayette, Franklin painted in Paris, Isaac Newton, Milton, Racine, D'Alembert, Diderot, and an embroidery executed by the honorary maids of Queen Catharine, and presented by her. On the side of the wall opposite the door hung a proof engraving of the coronation of Voltaire in the Théâtre Française, March 30th, 1778, upon the occasion of the production of one of his immortal tragedies. I must not be understood as speaking of his religion, which was doubtful, nor of his virtues which were disputed; I only recall his eccentric and dazzling genius.

LETTER LXII.

"I had a dream, which was not all a dream."

*   *   *   *   *   *

"And dreams in their development have breath,
And tears, and tortures, and the touch of joy;
They leave a weight upon our waking thoughts,
They take a weight from off our waking toils,
They do divide our being; they become
A portion of ourselves as of our time,
And look like heralds of eternity."

BYRON.

LAUSANNE, July, 1878.

NATURE makes amends to Switzerland for the stern severity of her winters by the magnificent lakes which she sets like so many emeralds among her luxuriant and gigantic mountains and mysterious glaciers. With these words upon my lips I stepped upon the deck of the clean and graceful steamer *Mont Blanc* that was to carry me from Geneva over the placid waters of Leman. I think that was last week, but it seems ages ago; in the interval I have had a strange dream that appeared to cover centuries.

The day was perfect; perhaps slightly cool for the season, but so brilliantly transparent that life was a luxury with the double attractions of earth and sky. I was just as keenly sensible of all these beauties as I had ever been, and when the unexplained lethargy overtook me, and I fell asleep, I remember a little prancing greyhound at my side, and its elongated shadow reflected in the sunshine on the quay. My dream was not a fancy where all is deliciously incoherent; nor a fine frenzy, where all is wildly romantic; neither was it one of those flimsy somnambulistic vagaries where scores of incidents and objects are thrust out of sight—even the most attractive—to make place for equally shadowy successors. It was not one of those ecstatic jumbles where phantom forms appear and vanish in a will-o'-the-wisp sort of way, and when we waken nothing remains but a vague sensation akin to the memory of a haunting conscience. Every episode of my strange trance was natural and permanent, the only abnormal phase was the continual growth of the past into the present and the retrograde of the present into the past. There was a conglomerate of eras that would have puzzled an ancient Egyptian magician.

I remember blue-bloused porters wheeling baggage along the banks of the beautiful quay under the shadow of the chestnut trees, passengers coming on board, a clatter of French tongues bidding *adieu* and *au revoir*, and two handsome Frenchwomen in black and white striped silk dresses, who tramped the deck like halberdiers. In my sweetly drifting unconsciousness the striped dresses, martial tread, and loud air of these women annoyed me. Just as oblivion was wrapping about me and bearing me off to Elysium, those dreadful linear robes that had grown into checkers in my weakening vision, and the stalk of those recurring four legs, interrupted the *dolce far niente* like some horrible phantom of disordered reason. But my most vivid recollection of this drowsy period was of a French family seated near me, the proprietors of the little dancing greyhound.

At last all confusion seemed to cease, and as the whistle blew and the boat dropped off the quay, I floated with it into the peaceful waters of Lethe. For a short time all was blank, but as I slept I dreamed,—dreamed of gliding easily over a great blue breast of crystal water, bordered by lofty banks, terraced and planted with vines of changing purple and emerald. Pomegranates, figs, and laurel trees grew as luxuriously as I had seen them in Italy, and great ridges of pine added the element of strength to all this brilliant and romantic beauty. Here and there, in little dales of tender sward, white cottages nestled like buds hidden from the rude world by their hoods of moss, trains of steam cars seemed to follow the course of our boat along the land's edge, mountain goats and fantastically arrayed shepherds trudged the ascending and winding paths over the rugged hills. Large white stone hotels, standing upon the very water's brink, blinding in the sun's bright rays, were duplicated in the crystal world over which I seemed to be travelling; everything—boats, people, mountains—was reflected in this odd azure cave over which I soared, until they appeared sounding the very depths with their mighty shadows. The heaven above and the water below were of a shade so marvellously harmonious that I wondered from which each had borrowed its beauty. To add awe to this enrapturing picture there was in the far background a chain of snow-white mountains, and one peak loomed like a mammoth iceberg, far above its compeers. Everybody's attention was attracted to it, and in my dream I viewed it through a lorgnette. There he stood, the hoary monarch, wrapped in the unwrinkled folds of his snowy mantle. Said I, is this the giant of the hills, or the evil genii of the spot? So majestically cold and despotic did he look, that I turned from him with a chilling sadness, for as I gazed I traced upon the glacier's polished hips phantom skeletons, grinning skulls, and ghostly forms of mortals who had been shrouded in the folds of the icy drapery. In their spectral hands they held scrolls whereon were written in wierd characters sad tales of widowed wives and fatherless orphans, and others bore extinguished torches of youthful ambition; horrible chasms yawned grim and frigid, and in their depths I seemed to see a mass of fleshless bones, broken ladders, and tangled ropes, chastened by the hoarfrost into a plaiting of silver. These were the remains of philosophers and scientists who had sought to pluck out the secrets of this mysterious creation for intellectual advancement; of aspiring young women who had an infirmity for lofty adventure; of foolhardy travellers and over-trustful guides. It was beguiling, and at the same time forbidding, and I turned from it with a shiver of awe; yet I was tempted to look and look again, and as I passed on I saw on one side, engraven in letters fiercely visible by their ultra whiteness and stoniness upon the ghastly entablature, ' *His Inclement Majesty, Mont Blanc.*"

We were not the only occupants of this beautiful lake; other boats steamed by, laden with passengers, trailing a great column of gray smoke after them; little skiffs holding one or two glided by ruffling the water with their oars, and tiny sails started out from the shore like spotless doves fanning with their wings the wave tops.

On and on we skimmed; chaste bridal towns smiled upon us from every side, ancient and modern poets' names were written upon each hill, and as I leaned over the taffrail I saw down in the mirrored waves the images of those who, through the inspiration of these same scenes in the perished years, have left us their records upon canvas and parchment. We paused at towns that seemed to lie along the lake border and closed in by an amphitheatre of rocks piled one on the other to an immense height. Sometimes a long handsome pier extended far out into the lake to which the boat moored, and again we coursed up to the very mountain side and anchored by a flight of stone steps cut in the rocks, which led to the hotel that seemed to hang to sterile crags and jutting elbows; fairy pavilions standing isolated from the mainland on spurs of rock were in impressive contrast with the formidable towers perched on lofty altitudes, by which they were overlooked. At length, after making many insignificant pauses, we stopped at a live town; the Alpine streets were filled with people, but they all seemed holiday people; there were no signs of occupation, and no proletaires treading the paths; they were all well-dressed, well fed, and fat-pocketed pleasure-seekers, would-be invalids fanned into comparative vitality by the salubrious airs and congenial skies, and picturesque rowers. On a great board suspended over the pier gate I read "Ouchy," and this I heard them say was the lake-port to Lausanne, which lay over a mile farther up in the mountains.

We steamed off again, and passing exquisite hamlets where titled villas fringed the lake I saw old and familiar faces and forms at each and every stoppage. They were not all people I had known, but many only the life copies of well-remembered pictures; each seemed to have some important story in connection with his appearance. French, English, German, Austrian, and Belgian nobility, men of wealth, and men of letters had sought these sylvan retreats as havens of rest or safety. The Bonapartes were all there, from the "Little Corporal" to the young Prince Imperial, and in my dream, it did not seem strange that the exile of St. Helena should be promenading with the dethroned Empress Eugénie, nor that I should pass Madame de Staël and Rousseau within the same hour. All the celebrities of the Old World seemed clustered about these enchanting spots. Byron followed me persistently like some elfin sprite. The others I saw and lost again to meet strange faces as I did their scenic surroundings, but before, behind, above, below, and interweaving all else, was that perpetually recurring poet's face and name. It made of my dream a horrible nightmare by its constant pursuit and my fruitless efforts to escape it. The rocks were girdled by the famous name; on the blue capitals of heaven the minstrel's face was medallioned; as the waves broke under our keel a hundred images shone in the eddies, birds lisped his verses in their song, and the waters murmured his words, while he himself, I thought, appeared in every town following and pointing to his own glory. He seemed defrauding Rousseau of his little wood at Clarens, Voltaire of his residence at Ferney, and Madame de Staël of Coppet.

We stopped at a place called Vevey. This, I saw, was a fashionable summer resort by the host of flounced and ribboned ladies,—Americans too, I could see by their delicate beauty, and was sure of it when I heard one of my fellow-travellers exclaim, "What stylish young girls!" I cannot say why, but even in my sleep I took this phrase as a personal offence, as I knew "stylish" was only applied to my countrywomen by foreigners, and then I vaguely dreaded hearing voices pitched in the highest and thinnest register float out from the shore where the bevy of crisp-ruffled ladies were clustering. Indeed, it seemed as if I were transported to Cape May or Long Branch; still, there was a mingling of foreign elements that made it cosmopolitan, in the slender flying flags, and the great signs of "hotel" and "*pension*," and the well-drilled waiters, with here and there scattered over the sloping sward an invalid English matron or a languishing Russian countess silently ignoring the nonchalent Americans. As we paused here I thought I saw the dancing canine of the French family, after sliding out of the laps of the ladies and capering about the knees of the gentlemen with careless grace, gleefully skip on shore, believing we were to lose our companions, I found to my dismay his owners on board as the boat backed into the water, while the poor little Italian dog stood mournfully measuring the distance between the wharf and the receding steamer. When the French family discovered the melancholy fugitive, the dowager was frozen into dignified and majestic surprise, the young husband of her daughter was transfixed with amazement, while his gentlemen friends gave vent to shrieks of laughter, and last of all the suppressed anger of the young wife, as she flashed rebukes upon her culprit husband for neglecting her pet, and fastened her indignant stare upon the loud merriment of her own friends, while disappearing in the distance was the solitary form and piteous face of the truant quadruped.

All this I dreamed and more;—dreamed that we sailed on and on, until I came to a place called Territet-Chillon. It was a lovely laketown, that reminded me of similar ones I had seen on the stage, with its fresh paint and varnish, and granite hotels with shining floors, glowing frescoes and Parian marbles. There were neat green boats, with green paddles, soft cushions, little flags flying to the fore, gayly-dressed water-men, and sometimes young and handsome women, pulling the little cockle-shells through the purple waters. Surely it could not be all real, I thought; yet nature is as finished as art. Man comes to train the vine, to terrace the hills, to persuade the water down to the land, and to set in uniform the olive; but it is the Almighty that presides in awful dignity on these battlemented mountains, wrapping their crests in the haze of the storm, lighting them with the quivering fire of electricity, and agitating them down to their deep foundations with the thunders of His wrath.

I went ashore and commenced the ascent of an acclivity, while the boat quitted the pier and continued its course. I paused upon the path, for I felt weary, and looked out upon the blue waters. Boats were moored to the shore, and feluccas with gay-striped sails and canvas cabins were carrying fishermen's and peasants' stores over the lake. A large white hotel elevated upon a ridge of rock faced the water, and awnings and matting shades drooped over balconies bordered by branching plants at every story. A neat little summer-house hung on to the last spur of land, and flowers bloomed in profusion. I saw no town, no shops; only a street levelled along the water where the hotel and several Swiss chalets stood, and a little shanty post-office where pens, ink, and paper, pins and thread, were sold. Beyond this there were no visible means of human existence. The well-wooded mountains rose abruptly in rear of the contracted pathway, but slightly higher and farther back workmen were cutting away foliage and reducing sharp granite edges to a foundation level.

This retreat seemed some angel's nest, closed off from the rude world by God's great walls, and I thought, in my dream, what a beatitude to live in such a golden seclusion, where no word of strife nor worldly suffering might obtrude to spoil supreme content and unclouded peace! But looking beyond I saw a strange, dismal pile of building upon an isolated rock in the lake. It had high towers and strong walls; feudal buttresses started out from the angles and hung from the corners of the eaves; little, dingy, deep-set windows I saw too, here and there in the old stony fortress. It inspired me with sorrow, and I turned from it with all my human sympathies welling in my soul. Even this lovely region then was not free from sorrow and shame! I went into the hotel, and they told me there it was a prison; then my heart sank and the world seemed darker, and nature, that had only a moment before been throbbing with the rapture of beauty, was stripped of her glorious plumes. I inquired who languished in the living tomb, but there seemed none to tell the story; then I wondered how long I might remain at this halcyon spot, for even in my dream I had a vague dread of some unseen and uncontrollable power interrupting my happiness.

The hotel had spacious apartments, but the larder must have been scanty, for I remember a gnawing hunger tearing at me that seemed insatiable, not because I was such a prodigious gastronome, but because there was absolutely nothing to eat. Night lowered her sable pall, and still suffering from an unappeased desire I seemed to sleep; then a horrible phantom carried me to a banquet-hall where tables, burdened with delicacies maddened me with their inviting aroma, and increased my ravenous appetite. Sometimes great bowls of terrapin, pyramids of croquettes, ravishing salads, pate-de-fois-gras, caviare, or barbecued robins tempted me, and as I was about to propitiate my persistent enemy by one of these, they magically disappeared; then luscious fruit, for which I reached, receded from my grasp, and as I followed the deceiver it ever kept near enough to beguile me and far enough to escape; last of all I saw a bottle of champagne, from which the cork seemed to be rising spontaneously; "Here," said I, "is the unknown power to alleviate my suffering," and pursing my lips for the life-giving draught, I heard the wine flowing to the ground, and I thought I awakened with frenzy at my heart.

The enervation of hunger and lethargy was upon me, yet I had an imaginary recollection of a grim tower they called prison. It was day again, but veils of mist hung over Jura's heights, and the water was black and foreboding. I looked out upon all this from my window, then went down to follow the rugged Alpine path to the fortress. It was a short walk, and I only passed some wanderers, like myself, and a few mountain peasants. I stood and gazed upon the cruel stronghold—with windows opening only upon the great waste of waters, where even the birds chirped notes of sorrow, and the waves heaved melancholy sighs for the languishing victims—before crossing the crude bridge, the solitary link between the lake-bound rock and the mainland. There were other strangers there paying their francs to the castellan, and buying neat little paintings of the historied precincts from the artist at the door.

I was ushered through a dirty courtyard, where rats and mice and miscellaneous vermin might gambol *ad libitum*. Dungeons, I saw, where human slaves had perished and human wolves had left their ineffaceable footprints; halls where princes of Savoy had lodged, still hung with armor of departed chieftains; arsenals of artillery; halls of justice and columned and arched dining-chambers. At last I came to the subterranean halls that are excavated from the rock, far down under the walls of the stronghold, and yet above the surface of the stream; long narrow windows were cut through the granite that reflected the light upon the water back upon the roof, making an ethereal glamour through the dungeons; little dark holes intersticed the several apartments where, they whispered, prisoners had been executed. In the last of these dismal chambers I saw the form of a man perched upon a foothold in the rocky wall and peering through the grated loophole. He turned, when I entered, and coming forward in a mysterious manner took my hand and said, "Do not fear. I am only a prisoner now, by self-imposed fetters. I have grown to love bondage." I was not frightened, in my dream, at being so familiarly greeted by a *détenu*, but I looked up and saw a man gray, stooped and weary, but not with age, and retaining all the remains of strong physical beauty. He spoke to me in a nebulous tone in consonance with our surroundings, and said, "Come!" I followed him and he conducted me to a small dark room on the ground floor. It contained two other occupants—convict and escort; a trap of planks fixed to the floor by iron hinges was lifted, and my new cicerone gave me the cue to look, but not to venture near the gap; I saw a few steps like the beginning of a contracted oblique stairway, all else was lost in intense obscurity. I said nothing, but stepped back overawed, imagining these steps to lead to a deepseated dungeon; then the condemned walked forward, and as he took his first descending step a supernatural hush seemed to pervade the hall. We all stood breathless, and, in my dream, I felt as if a heavy weight was pressing upon my breast; another he took, then all was still as death; a plunge, a splash of waves, and I knew a burdened soul was being carried out to its submarine grave through the abyss. As my guide led me away he only said "Ninety feet deep;" but I understood. He conducted me back to the hall of seven pillars; he pointed to the fifth, with its cankering, clanging ring and chain, saying, "Here my ancestor, the brave knight-errant Bonivard, languished;" then to the third, where I saw the name Byron, and my eye caught still other names—Eugéne Sue and Victor Hugo—that I had a mystic remembrance were filling the earth with glory. He told me his pedigree and the sufferings of his ancestors for national liberty, and the triumphs of the prior of Saint Victor more than three centuries ago for the abatement of papal tyranny and ecclesiastical degradation, and added, "There should be no slaves of religion or government." No! I shook my head dismally; thinking we were all vassals to some mysterious authority.

I do not know how many hours elapsed, but we walked back through the vistas of time and seemed to see all the episodes and characters that filled these historical halls with fame.

He said, "Before you leave me I must tell you that I am he of whom the poet speaks:—

"'My hair is gray, but not with years,
Nor grew it white——'"

I raised my hand with an expostulatory motion. "Oh, mercy!" I cried; "spare me, allow me to go in peace; that inevitable fame and face and form have been pursuing and preceding me for days." "But," he insisted, "you must hear, for it is the music of *his* melody and the halo of his genius that have glorified this charnelhouse; the romance of poetry has supplanted sober history. Until he poured the light of his intellect upon this prison, Lake Leman was comparatively unknown; *his* poem has given it a priceless value, and like the fabled music of the nymphs attracts thousands of strangers to the island. Now," said he, "it occurs to me that Byron's posterity should have a legal claim to the royalty, just as playwrights or patentees have their poundage. Of our thousands of visitors they all leave a substantial token; now if this is not to prove a portion of the income of *his* descendants it should at least be devoted to a monument to his memory. But what voice have I?" he continued; "I, who am only a poor convict, who have learned to love my cavern home, with the mice and spiders and toads, the smell of dampness, and the graves of my fathers for my bed; they," with a gesture of his head toward the outer door, "will not listen to me, and protest as you may against his haunting influence, *his* inspiration flamed all over Switzerland, as it flamed over Belgium and Italy, and wherever it touched it seemed to transmute everything into gold, not only casting a rosy haze over each spot, but adding to its intrinsic value. When he showered these streams of radiance upon my prison home he little thought he was contributing profit to hotels, steamboats, railways, castellans, and conferring fame upon me. Deemest thou me ungrateful now? Oh, magic mental power! how thou outlivest the bravery of the soldier, and even the sacrifice of the martyr," and as he knelt at the shrine of his immortalizing bard, the spaces grew darker, and the troubadour's image suspended in vacancy shone with the glory of the mounted sun that blinded my vision, filling the dungeon with a golden incense that drowned my senses, and thus I drifted into peaceful oblivion, until waking I found myself in the Hotel Gibbon at Lausanne.

LETTER LXIII.

"The clouds are on the Oberland,
The Jungfrau snows look faint and far;
But bright are those green fields at hand,
And through those fields comes down the Aar."
ARNOLD.

BERNE, July, 1878.

I ROSE on the Fourth to find myself mentally celebrating the anniversary of American independence in the quiet little Protestant Swiss town of Lausanne. Although a cultivated place, with four or five newspapers, a great library, a long history, and the chief centre of one of the provinces of Switzerland, no more account was taken of our national holiday than if the Declaration of Independence had never been proclaimed or America never discovered.

I sat writing in the garden where the great English historian, Gibbon, wrote the concluding portion of his ponderous book, *The Decline and Fall of the Roman Empire*, ninety-one years ago. The Hotel Gibbon deserves a glorious name, for it is a gem of its kind, and worthy of eulogium as well for its unexceptional cuisine as for its moderate prices.

The English were present in full force at the fine house dedicated to their learned countryman. A cold, reticent, exclusive race are they, and while Mrs. John Bull and her gentle heifers are as easily distinguished for their characteristics as Mrs. Brother Jonathan, John Bull is generally more loquacious and companionable than his sister. Just here I am reminded that an American woman generally prefers the sterner sex—an aspersion to which I disdain a reply.

Lausanne is a peaceful, picturesque town, built upon crags and mountain-sides. Wherever a street or villa might be hung, whether upon turret, spur, or pass, we find one. Every road is a hilly path, and every house on an inclined plane. The slopes are rigid and oftentimes circuitous. And while my sisters were broiling at home, I was rolled in a heavy shawl, for the air was colder than an American October. It is a curious town, with pretty shops of wood-carvings, and great hills to climb, and a soothing influence, where one might rest content and forget the world.

Above the city the paths twine about the Alps, over which the peasants trudge in their coarse costumes, bearing their burdens of wood and water upon their backs. Few strong men I saw, mostly women; some shrivelled and bent by the weight of years; others young, but rapidly passing from the springtime of life into the autumn by their double trials. They carry the necessaries of existence up the rugged ascents to their little Alpine huts, tucked under the granite edges. There are no individual hydrants and wood-piles in each of these humble homes, as we have across the water. Here the water must be drawn at the public street-fountains, and carried in great wooden pails strapped upon the back, and the kindling must be gathered in mountain forests from the fallen brushwood.

This part of Switzerland is cultivated in the highest degree. Every rood is utilized. The regions along the lakes are a succession of villas and stone towns, the roads being super-solid, thrift and cleanliness are joined to luxury and taste. This little republic, sandwiched between great kingdoms, flourishes upon travellers. The long and rigorous winters exhaust the garnered gains from the harvest of summer tourists, so each year finds the hotel and shopkeepers feeding upon the unsuspecting strangers like cormorants. The iron-roads are used little by the natives, who are mostly industrious and frugal. Ingenious and simple, they are happy among "their future oils and vines," in the skill of their exquisite wood-sculptures, and pretty little paintings of mountains and lakes. I verily believe every one in Switzerland is master of the brush and chisel; and there they sit upon lake-shore or Alpine ledge, transmuting God's masterpieces into gold.

Nature has been prolific of beauty to Switzerland. To the United States it has vouchsafed the wealth of the world. Our country is a succession of climates and zones. Without passing beyond our own territory we may, with small expense, live in perpetual spring and summer. This new world, with all its gifts, seems a special dispensation of Providence, as the final refuge and salvation of mankind. Here, with comparatively few of these advantages, the long winters and short summers, with the marvellous glaciers, snow mountains only slightly elevated above fields green with verdure, Alps on Alps, the absence of coal and iron, make the people dependent upon their own industries or the bounty of strangers. The whole face of the country is wrinkled, indented, and cut up into rocky mountains of vast height; yet, by the law of compensation, the cavities are translucent lakes, while their narrow shores are exquisitely adorned by public resorts or elegant private residences.

Near Lausanne I saw the first genuine Swisser barns, a combination of dwelling-house, kitchen, stable, and granary, all under one roof, and not an unpleasant accumulation of comforts, if the manure-heap was not invariably before the dining-room window.

In the ride between Lausanne and Berne the Swisser barns began to multiply. French costumes gave way to the short petticoats of broad, awkward women and large-footed men in brogans. Italian art recedes before German industry. Catholic crosses disappear from the roadside. Calvin and Luther push out the Pope and cardinals. The shaven fields, comfortable homes, and broad, genuine faces have a Lancaster or Berks County air. The nauseating garlic of the Italian conductors is lost in the equally strong odor of Limberger cheese and beer. The beggars of Italy are replaced by toiling women in the fields and on the highways.

The railway-carriages of Switzerland are entered from a platform front and rear, like our own; not in parallel seats, however, but divided into small sections, with connecting doors and passages through the centre (the effect of this arrangement is to make less space, and less comfort), and every alternate section is devoted to smoking.

The cold climate of Lausanne has disappeared under a summer sun in Berne, though there is none of the intense heat of an American July.

The first picture I met was a bevy of Swiss peasants at the dépôt, in their picturesque costumes of coarse black petticoat, plaited full at the waist and falling just above the ankles; black velvet corsage, high in the back, cut in a low square on the bosom, exposing a chemisette of crude cotton cloth. Most of these mountain-bred women are short, sturdy, and solid as pine knots. They are as utterly graceless as if they were sexless, and possess all the hardihood of animals of burden.

Berne itself, the political capital of the Republic of Switzerland, is not half so handsome and bright a city as Reading, yet somewhat resembles it by the lofty mountain in the rear. Here there is neither grace in the men, beauty in the women, elegance in the streets, nor perfume in the air. The women saw and split wood, clean highways, pull heavy wagons up steep hills, haul their own moving, and of course bear all the ills entailed by nature upon the sex just as if they were the petted darlings of royalty. But the frame in which this ugly old town is placed is inconceivably lovely; the fields are alternately green and golden; the mountainous Alps are from seven to ten thousand feet in height, covered with snow or shining with vines; while the rivers, bright as jewel-beds, flow round the city, endless streams of health.

My first impressions of Berne were that it was a clean, calm, Dutch town, a striking contrast to France or Italy; after I had seen its public places and streets, that it was a very dull, very dirty, and very Dutch town, with a nomenclature in which Bigler, Baer, Baur, Ritter, Karnhaus and Zugler frequently appear. True there is an amplitude of squalor in Italy, but all is hallowed by their superlative art.

I was about to say they had no art or music in this ancient burgh. Yes, they have the Tyrolese airs, and their photographs, engravings, and paintings are pre-eminently Dutch, with a prominent attempt at something more dilettante, just as their language is a patois. There is a pronounced indisposition of the natives to speak the mother tongue; they aspire to French, which being adulterated makes a perfectly incomprehensible jargon, understood only by the population of the Canton. Should they feel dishonor at the language of Luther, Schiller, Goethe, Liebig, and the great religious, political, and poetical writers of the past?

I walked to the Cathedral terrace, a public resort beautifully situated overlooking the winding river Aar. There were shady walks, bronze statues, and jutting pavilions at the corners overhanging the dismal town below; but it was crowded with old men smoking bad pipes, and coase sauerkraut and pork women drinking beer. How different is all this from the gay throngs along the boulevards of Paris, or the voluptuous Roman maidens in their tawdry but dazzling costumes clustering on the steps that lead from the Piazza di Spagna at the hour of sunset. Even the ruined Cathedral is bare and desolate after the rich fulness of Catholic temples.

There are a number of so-called attractions in Berne which beguile the stranger into a visit. They are all frauds of the most flagrant odor, from the grotesque Kinderfresser, or child-eater, to the bear-pits. This awkward cormorant, in his Oriental costume, is perched upon the lofty height of a street fountain, evidently enjoying his evening meal of youthful progeny that peep out from his pockets in the most appetizing way. Ask a Bernese the attractions of his town, and he will enumerate them, always beginning with the Kinderfresser as the cynosure, and ending with the clock tower, which is a superlative fraud. The former has only the merit of being an oddity, and with its accompanying bears, which are the heraldic emblem of the city, refers to an old tradition.

The savage tribes were proverbial for worshipping animals. The Persians adore the sun; in Pagan eras the white bull was sacred; in scriptural epochs the lamb, sheep, and rams were holy sacrifices. In India the white elephant, in Constantinople the dog, in Venice the picongs and winged lions, and in many climates the serpents have homage done them. In Berne the bear is the ubiquitous symbol. If I desired to make a pun, and a very bad one, I would say, for a decent town it is the *bearest* one I ever saw. The awkward animal is everywhere. Four living bears are kept at the municipal expense in a pit in the very heart of the city, and very offensively kept in addition; to add disgust to the repellant den dirty boys and bloated men overhang the iron railing tossing food to the rank animals. Two granite bears, badly executed, keep guard over the Aberthun—main gate to the city. Others support the shield of the Cornhall; a whole troop of bears go through a series of genuflexions at the clock tower. There are bear photographs innumerable, bears in wood as ornaments, bears in gold and silver as charms or trinkets, bears dancing, bears fighting, bears cooing, bears at billiards, baby bears, mother bears, and father bears, in a word, a community of bears, and for a quiet people a *barefaced* community. Indeed the ancient Egyptians had not a greater reverence for Ibis than these people have for their tutelary emblem.

The clock tower is another hideous curiosity, if I may honor the structure by such an epithet. It was originally erected as a watch-tower in 1191, and renovated in 1770. It is now poorly preserved, as if to perpetuate the habits of the old Bernese. The value of vigilance seems to be the apothegm entailed by its curious mechanism. Three minutes before every hour a wooden cock claps its wings and crows; a minute later the bears march around in a circle; a Dutch clown strikes the hour on a bell as the hands of the clock point to the hour; an old man counts the time by turning a glass and raising a sceptre with each stroke; and a bear on his right accompanies him by inclinations of its head. This silly spectacle attracts a number of visitors hourly, and when I saw it, to add to my discomfort, the entire square was filled by a stifling and nameless odor, that I presume arose from the gutter that flowed through the middle of the street.

Yet Berne may claim a genuine sentiment, as a recent incident which I gathered from a resident here proves. The well-known Jubilee Singers, who have been making a tour of Europe for some months in the interest of the Fisk University at Nashville, Tenn., seven females and four males, gave their first concert at Berne on the evening of the 15th of last May, in the French church. A colored person in Switzerland is as rare as a Turk in America, and so, apart from their talent as musicians, was the excitement created by their bronze faces. True, rumors of their proficiency had preceded them; they had electrified the *savants*, scientists, and artists of Berlin, Leipsic, Magdeburg, Lubeck, Hamburg, Cologne, Frankfort-on-the-Main, and some of the most distinguished professors of schools and colleges yielded to the influence of their sweet, yet weird and sacred melodies. In London, eminent persons, —the Duchess of Sutherland, Mr. Gladstone, the Duke of Devonshire, while the Duke of Argyle paid tribute to their genius by inviting them to his castle. In Holland they roused a perfect enthusiasm. Queen Victoria, the Crown Prince and Princess of Germany, and Emperor of Austria attended their concerts and testified to their extraordinary abilities.

At the close of their first exhibition in Berne, Mr. Van Buren, President of the city, invited them to return for a second concert, and placed the Cathedral at their disposal. To enable those residing at a distance to attend, the concert was fixed for the afternoon, and in the evening they dined with their patron at the "Enge," a celebrated restaurant in the suburbs, to meet such persons as had evinced intense interest in their history. This concert in the Cathedral was a greater success than the former, when they were welcomed to Switzerland by Mr. Van Buren, who spoke of the great sympathy their wonderful genius and their deliverance from slavery had excited among his people. The response was made by Mr. F. J. Loudin, one of the minstrels, with touching eloquence. At the "Enge," the musical Societies of Berne came to honor the Jubilee Singers with Moody and Sankey melodies, and, fatigued as they were, they replied to the eulogistic serenade in their famous song of "The Bells."

An impressive incident shows how these colored artists arouse all nations with their harmonies and their sufferings. An English lady, Madame de Watteville, *née* O'Connor, was so much moved by the thrilling fervor of their music that she invited them to her elegant villa near Thoune to pass a week with her.

Berne preserves more thoroughly its old eccentricities than any other Swiss city. It is true to its ancient liquor and legends—beer and bears, though there is a wine-cellar with hogsheads containing sixty-two thousand quarts of wine. There are a few really imposing public buildings, but the simplicity of republicanism is severely maintained in the city of the Swiss Congress. Yet even here, in the very heart of republicanism, we find a rich and poor aristocracy. The families with a long pedigree are as exclusive as they were a thousand years ago.

While in Rome I heard curious stories of the poverty and pride of titled families. Many of them reside in the cellars of their own palaces and live upon the rentals; while frequently the upper floors of the old castles are occupied by wealthy Americans and English, and the Italian dukes and counts are content to hide their own destitution by sharing the same floor with the pigs and poultry. But it was even more interesting to me, who had not looked for blue blood amongst the German Swiss, to find that there was so much of the miserable pride of ancestry here.

There is some excuse, however, for this foolish arrogance in Europe, and we tolerate it when we remember that these narrow souls were not only born to, but have inherited the belief of their especial superiority; still there is no apology for Americans who are either ashamed of their ancestors or overly fond of boasting of them.

Such a course is ever a confession of personal inferiority. He who has won his own title to nobility never points to his pedigree, whether his grandfather be a saint, a sovereign or a scavenger. His individual patent of royalty is too apparent to need the advertising medium of his progenitor's dust. He never resurrects his grandfather's ghost to heave at you twenty times in an hour as the family crest of heraldry.

On an elevation beyond the botanical gardens stands a beautiful residence, the home of the American Minister, Nicholas Fish, son of the late Secretary of State. The highly-cultivated official and his family reflect grace and credit upon our country, and form the contrasting and redeeming link in the chain of ministers and consuls who force themselves into positions for which they are neither qualified by nature or education by a too elaborate personal canvass, or as the reward for partisan zeal. This intrigue on the part of the politicians, and cowardice on the part of the appointing power at Washington, has merited for our country and some American ambassadors at foreign courts many mortifying slurs.

My task is done, my notes of Berne are taken, and now at the close of the sweet Sabbath I look from my window upon a broad expanse of glorious landscape where nature reigns supreme. God has done so much to embellish this exquisite picture that art seems to have been awed into silence by the stroke of the master-hand. The Aar is flowing swiftly in its course this quiet Sunday afternoon, dashing against the stone piers of a little bridge, while farther on it foams and plunges over a rock into a milky cataract, where the color of the water changes from a pale blue to emerald. The white roads wind through the luxuriant fields of grass and golden grain. The little white farm-houses across the stream, with great crimson roofs, are closed and silent. Dutch peasants are walking in the cool shady lanes, and little boats are moored to the river's brink under the tall poplars that stand motionless in the summer twilight. The picture is vitalized by a tiny black dog standing upon the delta of sandy soil.

How rich and picturesque the grand plateau of land opposite, touched by the afterglow—the peculiar phenomenon of the Bernese Oberland. Phœbus has gone to rest behind the Alps, and pale Cynthia swings her silver crescent overhead, and as the eternal dome gradually changes her robes of vivid orange, intense blue, and dazzling crimson for the sombre hues of gray and slate, I hear the Tyrolese songs of cottagers coming in nebulous strains through the valley, the river tide as it rolls and dashes like the mighty waves of ocean, the screeching of the hawks as they fly round and round in circles on the mountain peaks, and the report of the sportsman's gun in the distance, all blent into one heavenly harmony. A circlet of gold binds the western zone, and a hazy blue-and-white flecked veil hangs overhead as I sit in the mystic afterglow of the Bernese Alps.

LETTER LXIV.

"There is a light in darkness which the soul
 Can seldom know, until the sense have crept
 From height to height across the shadowless peaks
 Which sentinel thy valley; there are deeps
 In thy green hollows, where still thought could lie
 Through summer noons unending, glad with dreams."
                                       ANNIE FIELDS.

INTERLAKEN, July, 1878.

WHEN I was a wee little girl my school-teacher told me to write a composition on Interlaken. I really do not recollect whether I had ever heard of the superb toy Swiss town, with its crystal lakes and ice mountains, until that minute; however, from the name I had a mystic idea that it was somewhere in the East, but this did not hint what I should say of it, as I had not the most ambiguous conception of its geographical situation or its physical aspects. Points were given upon which the class were to elaborate. Now the points of a composition for a class of young children are generally the complete article with the addition of several stilted adjectives interjected here and there to heighten the glow of the scenes. I began to *elaborate*, and described a storm on the lake,—I was told there was a lake,—spoke of tiny skiffs, fantastically dressed peasants, and thundering heights. This composition made an ineffaceable impress on my mind, for the paradoxical reason that I had not the vaguest knowledge of what I was writing. I finished the production and handed it in to our small board of education for inspection, without being sure of the national position of the village in question. Now that I have seen Interlaken, I long for those early sheets that I might insert them just here as a much truer approach to nature than any picture I am now able to draw. The realization of this fact saddens me as I feel that the sense of genuine inspiration—the inspiration that emanates from the muse, not from knowledge—lies buried under the ashes of years.

The district between Berne and Interlaken is like a leaf taken from a story-book. Into a sweet valley of not more than twenty-five miles is crowded a combination of beauties. The ride from Thun is across a level meadow-garden, between two chains of mighty Alpine hills, interspersed with vast Swisser barns, and animated by throngs of men and women laboring in the fields, with the overshadowing presence of the Bernese Oberland, that fragment of Switzerland famous for weird and romantic scenery, dangerous passes, shining lakes, and rivers full of melted snow, that pours and plunges in torrents from the hills.

All this section is controlled by the Protestants, and everywhere the presence of Protestant influence is perceptible. There are about 1,000,000 Catholics in Switzerland, and 1,500,000 Protestants, but in the Cantons of Berne and Zurich the Papists number five to one.

Thun is a dull, uncleanly town, with large and costly hotels. The main street is built in arcades, where the fronts of the houses projecting about ten feet above the ground form magazines. On the roof of these is the pavement for foot-passengers. There are many busy shops, and residences looking as archaic as the hills by which they are inclosed. But in the midst of all this antiquity are almost countless fresh and gorgeous hotels: Hotels whose decorations are something altogether foreign from our American establishments in the mere matter of frescoes, gilding, carving, stucco, statuary, mosaic and parqueterie floors, arbors, walks, fountains, cascades; in a word, of infinite variety and skill. The construction and improvement of these hotels prove two facts: the boundless resources of the capitalists of Europe, and the enormous profits gathered at European summer resorts. They abound in every region. They are not confined to the great cities, but in every little French, Italian, German, Swiss, and Dutch town, on every romantic plateau, or mountain summit, or lake border, and in every nook and corner that history or poetry has immortalized, there are these resplendent temptations to the purses of the wealthy stranger.

Every new hotel is a fresh marvel to me, and a new one rises every year in every available spot; but there is no surprise more startling than the apparent scarcity of guests even in the most successful season. These hotels are never crowded, and just now the superior magnet of the Paris Exposition is drawing away their patrons and exhausting their exchequers. I have wondered that a journalist does not undertake to record the statistics of the expense, income, and ownership of this continental hotel system.

We dined at the Bellevue, just beyond the city boundary, perched on an edge of land overhanging the valley of the Aar. The food was good, plain and inexpensive, but when we attempted to contract for a carriage to drive us to some of the castles and villas on the lake while we tarried for the boat to Interlaken, we discovered that the schedule of prices exceeded those in Philadelphia or New York; so this pleasure was abandoned—reluctantly—as we had no aspirations to become the benefactors of the Thun livery stables.

About one mile from the city proper, at the head of the lake, we took the boat for Interlaken. All along the shore there were enchanting glimpses of Swiss nature and modern art. It was neat and trim, clean and beautiful, yet different from the Lake of Como with its glamour of tradition and romance. The superb scene had a peculiar fascination of grim majestic heights blended with cosy rest and youthful jollity. The banks were studded with picturesque villas and glowing gardens, but everywhere there were chateaux and hotels and home attractions for travellers; everywhere brilliant parterres, emerald terraces, and blooming slopes, little boats dancing on the translucent waves, the jocund voices of tourists, with the ringing laugh of children and young girls mingling like silver bells in the chorus.

As our boat advanced over the path it ploughed for itself in the serene waters, the colossal hills seemed to close overhead in an arch of granite; they bowed their majestic pinnacles before us and barred our way. Just at the moment when all egress was apparently cut off the granite cliffs opened, and we glided through as providentially as the children of Israel crossed the Red Sea when the waters heaved into two great walls on either side of them; and, indeed, our path between the frowning rocks seemed as miraculous. All was so wild, inscrutable, mysterious, and silent, that toil seemed to have died out of the world; yet among these rocks and ravines labor's hands are sore, and woman drudges like a slave while she discharges the double duties of wife and mother.

See yonder she is piling the sheaves of wheat upon the wagon, sweeping the scythe through the bending grain, pulling heavy loads upon the mountain-side; and farther on are four sturdy, muscular peasant women straining at the oars of a boat burdened with hay, and pushing it into the neighboring shore; and over on the roadside is a girl, not more than sixteen, and her aged mother splitting granite with a pick for a turnpike.

Where are the fathers, the brothers, the husbands, or the lovers? Such creatures must exist in this region, else how the wives and the daughters? And these slaves are the creatures to whom men refuse suffrage, because such an act would entail upon them an unsexing servitude, and subject them to degrading positions or hazardous exposure; these are they against whom men bar their university doors, because they are too fragile to bear the travail of arduous study, or too rose-like and beautiful to come in constant contact with a promiscuous crowd of men, or too delicate and fair and chaste to listen to learned discussions on pathology and anatomy. These are the creatures upon whom even the more favored of their own sex say it would be a demoralizing and degenerating influence to allow them to take part in the science of government and the higher professions with their brothers! Let us be logical if we cannot be just. At least in these old countries, if women must work, and men must fight, let the burdens of life be equalized. Do not say that those we call in America the feeblest should here be made to do the heaviest of all human toils.

After leaving the boat, a small line of railway—a ten minutes' ride—took me to the little show town presided over by that callous young lady, arrayed in her glistening, icy garments, Jungfrau. I rode up a long street that seemed to extend itself far beyond my vision, until it was lost in the water or cut off by the rocks. This street was bordered by double rows of walnut trees, and on either hand were shops of wooden sculptures and paintings of Alpine scenery; as I proceeded handsome hotels with ostentatious façades and gaudy flower-gardens took the place of the magazines on one side, and on the other lovely stretches of emerald turf shone in pronounced contrast with the gray rocks and frozen mountains. These hotels seemed to have been erected overnight, so modern in architecture and fresh in paint were they. On and on we rode until I marvelled how many of these sinking funds the town owned. I had settled upon my own hostel, which I found was rather far up-town, having, however, two advantages,—that of being directly opposite the chaste and silent bride, where I might gaze upon her shining robes and feel her frozen smile in return; then, the second benefit was, to reach the business centre I was obliged to pass an infinite variety of rich and picturesque stores. Half way down the long street I turned off to my right and found the Cursaal, where the whey from the mountain goats' milk is sold to complaining invalids. It is a beautiful open garden, situated half on the ground level, and tilted slightly on the mountain ascent, where summer-houses and flower beds framed in odd devices, a restaurant, and a platform for the band are the interesting features. Farther up toward the Lake of Brienz, on the opposite bank of the Aar, I could see the peasants of Unterseen treading the steep paths. It was a sweet picture, and as I stood enraptured the one question pushed itself into prominence: Is the life I see here as fascinating in practice as it is in ideal?

Interlaken is a purely show place,—neat and clean as a young woman dressed for a fair; but how the shopkeepers and landlords subsist is a marvel. Said I to the waiter at table this morning, "You have many hotels here; can you tell me how many?" "Oh, yes," he replied in very bad English, "we have quite five hundred." "What!" I exclaimed in startled amazement; then I added calmly, "Oh, my good man, you are mistaken." But he assured me it was true, so my next question was: " Have you any idea of your population?" For a few moments he had a far-away expression, and then replied " Five hundred." Then said I, " You have as many great hotels as you have people;" and he replied with supreme complaisance, " Yes, just as many." I did not solicit further knowledge from this young person; but as he walked away I thought what a clever hyperbole the poor fellow had unconsciously achieved.

The Victoria is the best filled, has a better *cuisine*, and has equally moderate rates with the others, but I was frightened away from it by the expensive flower-pots, and concluded not to help the landlord defray the florist's bill from my bank account. But there is nothing cheap at Interlaken. The place is too fine, and every stranger is fair game to pluck. Cab hire is just doubled here, and when I attempted to invest in photographs I was astounded at the tariff. But how exhilarating the air, how sweet the flowers, how green the grass, how like mighty fortifications the mountains, and how like a white-robed Goddess of Peace, the Jungfrau looks down from her snowy throne upon the tranquil vale!

And why has this exquisite town to complain of a dearth of patronage? Simply because people are getting tired of imposition, and I predict a speedy downfall for those extortionate proprietors in the near future.

My stay at Interlaken was hallowed by a sweet experience with the old lady in the English library. I do not know what in my face or manner struck the confidential and pathetic cord of her organization; however, she told me her story, which was neither an ordinary nor unromantic one. Said she: " My grandfather established a newspaper in Thun eighty years ago, which is still printed by my family. We have several editions, a daily and three weeklies issued from the same office, and you know," she added, " Thun is a small town fenced in by a rocky and thinly populated neighborhood, but my family have been prosperous printers, and proud am I to say devoted heart and soul to liberalism. My life," she said, " has been an easy, happy one on the whole, though like all others I have had my cross to bear. My little grandson, who was destined to become a printer and so honor and prolong the family name was suddenly called away in the spring. Now I feel as if I had nothing more to hold me to earth." The old lady's library is a rendezvous for intelligent travellers, and she herself a great and deserved favorite.

In Interlaken stands a tree, a great tree, the monarch of the wood, only less majestic than the Alps themselves, with its lordly branches, and great coronal of emerald, and deep cool shade, and as I saw the forest giant hemmed in by small houses my soul cried aloud for room to let the noble mammoth breathe, by making it free and unconfined, instead of suffering it to languish and to die surrounded by stifling limits. Mark it well, stranger. The dear old lady, Mrs. Christian, will point it out to you, and will doubtless tell you how the American prayed with her to ask the authorities to give the lordly monarch air.

Interlaken is the chief centre for wood sculptures and the exquisite little paintings which preserve and perpetuate the lovely Swiss lakes and mountains. These two vocations and keeping hotels seem to fill the winter and summer of the inhabitants. Without these resources hundreds would scarcely know how to exist, and without strangers Switzerland would be almost a solitude. Strike out the Americans, English, Russians, and Germans in the tide of travel that sweeps over the Continent, and the country would become bankrupt. American tourists are much more numerous than other travellers, with the exception of the English, and more generous and appreciative than any other nation. There are more American artists in Rome than French, Russian, or English, and when we come to such places as Abbotsford and Stratford-on-Avon we find more Americans worshipping at the shrines of Shakespeare or Scott than Englishmen. We have great oceans to cross, yet year after year in all seasons we penetrate every cranny of the Old World. Americans are at once the most enterprising, liberal, inquisitive, inventive, and interesting people on the face of the globe. Wherever we turn our steps we meet them, yes! and their contrivances, their dollars, and their books.

LETTER LXV.

> "I've roamed amongst the eternal Alps. I've stood
> And gazed on the diminished world below ;
> Marking, at frightful distance, field and flood,
> And spire and town, like things of pigmy show,
> Shrink into nothing : while those peaks of snow,
> While yet the winds themselves but seldom climb,
> Arose like giants from the void below."
> BRYAN WALLER PROCTER.

LUZERNE, July, 1878.

NATURE has written a wonderful language in the topography of Switzerland ; a language weird, mysterious, and inscrutable. These masses of rock, moulded into vast mountains and hurled into strange shapes ; these vast glaciers, extending continuously eighteen hundred miles, cropping out in perpetual snow, and again sparkling in solid masses of azure and iridescent ice, deep down in the earth ; these indescribable lakes of pure water; and then the abundant and dashing cascades flowing in glittering rivulets from the hills into the valleys, create altogether a region of ceaseless and bewildering fascination. The Supreme ordinance has made of Switzerland an inexhaustible curiosity-shop to baffle modern science; and man has converted the mighty museum into a machine for speculation and show. Everywhere we must render unto man tribute, to enjoy what nature gave us for nothing ; but he is no more an owner in these phenomena than myself.

A short line of rail took me from Interlaken to the boat station on the Lake of Brienz, over which we glided to the Giessbach, the Niagara of Switzerland. This startling fall of water plunges from an altitude of eleven hundred and forty-eight feet into Lake Brienz in a series of seven cascades, bounding from rock to rock, and casting back its rainbow spray in jewels on the brown crags and bowlders. We halted at a rude plank landing, with only a shanty ticket-office, built against a projection of granite. There were many American and British tourists and a host of savage-looking old men with palanquins to carry delicate travellers to the mountain summit,—the only point from which the waterfall could be seen with satisfaction ; and as this was the chief thing to be seen in these wild mountains, those who would not submit to be conveyed by a couple of creatures who looked very like brigands, Alpine banditti, or gypsy blacklegs, must stride up a mountain that seemed to lose its head in the clouds. I preferred the latter course to resigning myself into the care of these *chevaliers·d'industrie*.

The path was good, but steep and narrow, and often dark, where the brown stone crags and walls came so thick and fast that not a fugitive glimmer falls athwart the track ; but there was ever the rush and crash of waters heard in the weird retreat. Sometimes the windings brought me out upon a sharp ledge, where, looking upward, I could see the great height from which the torrent sprang, and below the yawning and rocky chasm into which it plunged. I could feel the force of its flow, and the irresistible whirl of death in its terrible forces. The wind howled about me, and seemed to play with its power to hurl me into eternity. The higher I mounted the more of the light and warmth of God's hospitality shook from heaven into the narrow mountain defiles gladdened my way. I walked along, therefore, charmed by the thundering waters mingling in the wild saturnalia.

Once upon the elevated plateau the scene was ineffably sweet, solemn, sublime, and picturesque; indeed, a divine crystallization of all the beauties I have described.

A flight of steps led to the hotel; of course there was a hotel (where can we escape one?). Seated on its emerald terrace, commanding a complete view of the Giessbach, which is invested with a peculiar interest, as well from the great volume of water that rushes, as it were, from an invisible fountain into the green lake below, as from the rich and variegated foliage in which they are framed; small tables and natty waiters stood ready to accommodate the weary climbers; the gardens were thronged with visitors, and Alpine peasants, and *bonnes;* troubadours, and jugglers, too, joined the *mélee*. A *garçon* asked me if I would remain all night? I turned upon the man with sudden surprise and said, "What! remain here all night to sleep ? Do people ever stay here with that (pointing to the torrent) thundering machine opposite the window ?" "Oh, yes !" he replied, with the provoking nonchalance that only an ignorant foreigner can assume , " the beobles say it make shleep ; or, if you object, we give you a back room ; but, oh ! dat is de glory ;" and then, as he drifted into an apostrophe to the cataract, I told him No! and ordered a slight lunch.

On the left, far below, a lovely Swiss village slept amongst the hills, despite the hellish racket, like a freshly washed baby in its first slumber. It was green, and golden, and white; and over the roads came neat peasants from their cottage homes. It was a scene of mighty majesty and docile domesticity that I rested upon until the veil of night unfurled its first gauzy folds.

After the sharp edge of novelty produced by the crashing and splashing, and gleaming and streaming, and flushing and gushing torrent was dulled, I studied an American family around me. There was the lord supreme,—to be conventional I begin with him,—a man rapidly approaching the vale of years,—and his wife and progeny as distinctive and peculiar as the new civilization from which they came. He was a cotton, a woolen, or a railroad king, for he moved as if he had made his millions with sudden success. I liked him because he had the easy submissive conscious money air that spoke of complete content; he seemed to care no more for Europe than for some impossible story of rabbinical lore. He was a resigned sacrifice on the altar of his wife's ambition and his children's desire, and that is why he had all my sympathy. Then, there was the wife and mother, a plump, pretty little woman about forty-five, arrayed in all the laces and feathers denied her in earlier days; she was now supping bounteously upon the harvest feast of his investments; she must be carried over the steep rough path in a palanquin; how could she walk, and why should she? Having run barefoot over the thorny and stony ways of life, she now soothes away the memory of sharp cuts and weary pulls amid downy cushions. There was the first born,—a daughter of twenty-two,—a prim little person who assumed dilettante ways and tastes, and knew only enough to feel sure that the eldest of a rich house should take on herself much state. Then there was the prince imperial to this noble line, say twenty; he as their heir apparent had been pampered and petted until he was an annoyance to himself; he called for a dozen different dishes and drinks, and with oversated palate and assumed fastidiousness dismissed them almost as rapidly as they were set before him. He was one of those miserable striplings at whose constitution premature disease was gnawing like a canker-worm. Besides the physical indisposition, he had contracted an insufferable *ego*. O physician! is there no vaccine to check the ravages of this hideous malady?

There was the younger daughter, a graceful girl of eighteen. She made her début upon this "mortal coil" just in time to be taught her own insignificance in contrast with her elder sister and brother. The result was beneficial; in place of an inflated pigmy she was a sweet sensible woman with the aroma of the seminary clinging to her skirts and a lingering love of books and nature; she sat apart busily writing a description of the exquisite scene. Her two younger sisters, just at the age when girls do not know what to do with themselves, and nobody knows what to do with them, completed the family party.

And now my eyes fell upon the father, and my pity and tenderness were all his; out of the six dependent upon him, there was only one who was returning an atom of happiness after his long struggle. This is only one picture of thousands of originals.

The terrace seemed to be a rendezvous of the nations, including a band of wretched strolling minstrels, a conglomeration unconsciously photographed. John Bull, always in white towel as a headgear and reading Murray; Mrs. Bull, rubicund and beery; two Miss Bulls in long gray ulsters, "all buttoned down before;" the entire party silent and sour. The French gracefully attired and chattering like magpies. The Germans smoking long pipes and sketching the falls, while their tawny hair fell in "gusty flow." A Swiss family, grandfather, grandmother, sons, daughters, and grandchildren, attended by fancy-costumed peasant women, made a beautiful little group in the rocky platform. Withal, the American family was the most attractive, genteel, and intelligent. But, is it not natural that we should search for the faults of our own children, because we are ambitious they should rise above the ordinary level?

The Giessbach is frequently compared to Niagara, but the simile is as preposterous as likening the Thames to the Mississippi. If Niagara were on the Continent it would be turned into as many sources of profit by speculators as if the Europeans had discovered and brought down between heaven and earth a new celestial world.

At 8 P. M. the falls were to be illuminated, for which I did not wait, as it is a sad fraud, like many other things in this land of natural marvels and hollow artifices. But descending the gray and ghostly paths, followed and flanked by elves and wraiths, to the music of roaring waters and reverberating shouts on the higher heights, I reached the lake, where I was importuned by a brigade of ruffian boatmen to cross in their little skiffs and under their protection, an honor I declined, and waited for the steamer for Brienz, which lay modestly waiting across the lake.

Brienz is a little village of wooden houses stretched along the mountain base, with a quaint hotel—" La Croix Blanche"—where we had a capital supper at 9 P. M. In the twilight the peasants were driving home the goats and mules, while their tinkling bells made silver music between the hills. Some came with their wood sculptures, others laden with food, for the morrow would be Sunday, and little mouths must be fed in these tall, bleak mountains. Ah! what a life it seemed as I gazed upon the broad honest-faced women and burly men, with no thought of the great world beyond. All looked so simple and sweet and arcadian, yet human passion and human vices rage even here. Where there is life there is sin.

A natty femme-de-chambre in the hotel spoke English with such an unmistakable American accent that I was tempted to ask her where she was born, and she answered in the State of Missouri! On account of business reverses her father had returned to his native valley. Now I endeavored to extract philosophy from the story, but I failed. However dark the times, however degenerate and torpid the town, there could be no spot in America so utterly destitute of ways and means of existence as this Alpine dell.

Next morning, bright and early, really too early to promote good temper, I was wakened by the jingling bells of the diligence that was to carry me over the Brunig Pass. Now crossing the Alpine pass in a Federal post was something new, and my sensations were those of ecstasy as I looked down upon the cumbrous establishment fashioned after those of the English system of old-time travelling. Five spirited steeds stood neighing, impatient to be off on their mountainous jaunt, whips cracked and horns blew, while my spirits rose in consonance with the new and joyous sounds about me. So after breakfasting at 6.30 A. M., we started on the hazardous journey. The day was glorious! No dust, no flies, no heat, and the sun as moderate as in September; and though I wrapped a heavy shawl about me as we set off, the advancing day soon equalized the chilly temperature. I must needs have the choice seat at the banquet—on the top of the diligence, so I might miss no mite of the phenomenal panorama.

Thoughts of crossing the Brunig had always excited my

fancy, but I had formed no conception of its singular exorcism. I met nature in her grandest and gentlest moods. I have never seen the Rocky Mountains, but those who have, describe the Brunig and the mighty chain of granite fastnesses of which it is a link, as far more imposing and complicated; not so vast and comprehensive, but closer, more involved, and marvellous. Here even the untrained mind realizes the difficulty of constructing railroads in Switzerland.

We came to little villages amongst the rocks; hamlets that were only a handful of shanties squatted down on nobody's land; and here people lived and were happy. Yet how did they exist? Only through Nature's providence.

The public highway wound like like a petrified serpent along the sides of these primitive formations; as I looked down from the cool heights where the eagle eyries, my brain fairly reeled to see the people dwindling to manikins, and their habitations into tiny black spots. Our chariot hung at times, on the rocky ledges as if held there by some magnetic power. Higher and higher we rose, rougher and steeper the road at each advance, until we attained an altitude of 6581 feet above sea level. Having reached the topmost point of our route we began gradually to descend toward lovely Lucerne.

All along these deserted coils I found Swiss chalets large enough to accommodate two or three families, whose only source of livelihood is wood-carving. Their sheds, attached to the house, were well stocked with the requisites of their art. And so they pass their days in their forest homes. In winter they carve, and in summer they sell in the nearest towns the fragile wares that find their way into every American home. Whenever we passed toy or blackberry venders, with their scanty store spread in an alcove of rock, and overshadowed by great hanging craggy canopies, it was the herald to our approach to a town,—towns where we saw only a hotel that seemed slack of guests and entertainment at the same time, and only a stopping place to gather the mails and water our horses.

In the sweet Sabbath morning the Catholic peasants thronged the paths in vast numbers on their way to Mass; and though rather well dressed, judging by their habitations among the hills they were miserably poor. Nothing could be more deplorable than the most of their homes, and I shuddered as I thought of their privations in this dismal region during the long, cheerless winters. Men, women, and children, like mountain chamois, climbed the rough roads, and greeted the Federal post with passing smiles.

What ghastly and indescribable battlements this rocky region presents to the stranger! At times the coach plunged into deep valleys, from which I looked up to the stony forts, that pierced the very clouds; then we crawled along the crest of a precipice, from which I gazed into an almost unfathomable abyss.

It was a six hours' journey over the hills, and in the interval we passed other lakes, considerable towns, and many beautiful valleys. But of all the dales for sweet salubrity, gentle and thriving domesticity, luxuriant pastures, and glowing orchards, give me the Valley of Sarnen, lying side by side with its azure lake abounding in finny food. Oh, what a wealth of nature was there! Great Phœbus poured his lusty light with double force upon the fair undulations of the sapphire lake by being closed out of the gray crannies beyond, and kissed all about him into a glow of beauty. Sparkling waters lost themselves in the clefts of rocks, while the old groined hillsides shone in girdles of jewels.

In the town I found a better civilization, a higher degree of comfort, and more intelligence was revealed. The peasants of Sarnen have a peculiar and picturesque costume; all the women interlace the plaits of their hair with white ribbons fastened with a unique spoonlike silver buckle. But how few were comely! even the youngest were hard-featured and prematurely wrinkled. Sunday, as it was, everywhere many were working in the fields, and generally not a man to be seen. All this district is under Romish influence; Catholic churchyards, Catholic churches, crosses, and wayside shrines, nuns and children saying their rosaries and *Ave Maria* predominated, and as we approached the Lake of Lucerne, the papal preponderance became more and more apparent; but there was not a beggar on the route.

Descending my lofty throne on the back of the diligence, I stepped upon the pretty steamer at Alpnach and sailed up the lovely lake. Inconceivably grand was the scene as we proceeded along the famous water, with its jutting promontories and vast mounds of alluvial deposit. On our left Rigi, and to the right Pilatus escorted us, both shores indented with handsome villas and antique towns, while many of the heights were crowned with military and medical institutions. The water was a level sheet of emerald, and as I leaned over the taffrail I saw in the little crevices of the hills artificial fountains casting up their silver spray, while pushed out from the coast were wharves which sent forth and received passengers. Neat boats were gracefully gliding over the waveless main, and as if to harmonize with the Sunday panorama a band of Protestant singers blended their voices in the touching sacred melody of the " Sweet-By-and-By." The familiar strains carried my memory to my own dear home, so far away.

I had been among other charming scenes before—in the majestic harbor of New York, Delaware Bay, Boston Bay, the unrivalled ocean home at Martha's Vineyard, Chesapeake Bay, the Potomac at Washington, and I have lingered in the glamour of the Gulf of Genoa, the Gulf of Lyons at Marseilles, the Mediterranean at Nice, the Neapolitan Bay, the beautiful Seine, and the sluggish Thames in its sweetest resting-places, but never was I so affected as by the superlative influences of the quiet Sabbath noon on the waters of Lucerne.

LETTER LXVI.

" E'en now, where Alpine solitudes ascend,
I sit me down a pensive hour to spend ;
And placed on high above the storm's career,
Look downward where an hundred realms appear ;
Lakes, forests, cities, plains extending wide,
The pomp of kings, the shepherd's humbler pride."
OLIVER GOLDSMITH.

LUCERNE, OVER THE RIGI, July, 1878.

APART from the unrivalled position of Lucerne on the lake, lovingly placed in the amphitheatre formed by surrounding mountains, the most impressive feature of the city is its consistent and singular cleanliness and the superexcellence of its hotels. All along the Schweizerhof Quay, fronting the lake, there is such a cordon of these gorgeous palaces, that one wonders how they are supported in this town of 14,500; and as we drove out on the more sequestered roads leading to Kussnacht and the great mountains there were more of these same superb structures. The season is short, but the influx of visitors increases each day from the middle of June until the last of August, when there is a general stagnation. Yet, at Lucerne, the charges are moderate, and the entertainment surpasses most of the other mountain cities.

Lucerne is held in the protecting arms of the strongest Swiss battlements, some rearing their desolate heights in solitary splendor, others bound peak to peak by iron road or bridge; and again, those that stand in all the virginal iciness of purity. Lucerne may truly boast of its position and environs, perhaps of its legendary associations, but in the city there is little of artistic beauty or interest.

The famous Lion of Lucerne, cut in the solid sandstone, in a romantic corner of the town, after a model by the illustrious Danish sculptor Thorwaldsen, in memory of the Swiss officers and soldiers who fell in defence of the expiring French monarchy of Louis XVI., in their noble efforts to save the Tuileries, August, 1792, is only interesting by the story it relates. The art may be marvellous, chiselled as it is from the fixed bowlder of sandstone, but it is illy kept, and a spring above it drips its everlasting trickle into a stagnant pool, which does not represent the picture we sometimes see of the expiring beast reflected in a crystal green lake. The royal lion, while writhing in the agonies of death, protects the French shield and *fleur de lis* with its paw. True, the expression of unuttered suffering of the colossus is effective, and when I first saw it I exclaimed, "Oh, the dying gladiator." This was the first and strongest impression the work made upon me; so has it remained. It seems a curious memento for a republic to hold amongst its choice treasures, but the work is considered a supreme achievement, and it is in this light that it is cherished for posterity, and also to perpetuate the bravery of the Swiss Guard of the unfortunate Louis and his queen.

The "Gladiator" is shown gratis, but as if to express regret for the liberality one franc is charged admittance to the glacier garden adjoining. Now a glacier breathes volumes of wonderful and reverential things to me. So, this so-called phenomenon I must see, if, like Prometheus, I must filch the fire from heaven to obtain entrance. There were no such violent means required, however, and I do not believe I was ever tricked by so poor a cheat. There were no glaciers, some bad statuary—which might have been petrified in ice—a number of inexplicable aerolites, several sickly fountains, a long hysteric stair of rustic logs ascending to a cupola, a catchpenny model of the surrounding lake and mountain system, and a few dilapidated birds. What it all meant I could not conceive; my expectations soared to a glorious height of iridescent hills and azure caves. When these beauties did not burst upon my vision I was disappointed; still, I considered them worth hunting, though I had not thought that would be required of me, but having searched and not found them I went away sore and sorrowing, and consoled myself by trying to extract comfort out of the long scientific account in the guide-book of all that I could not interpret.

Across the Ruesse, whose green waters divide the city, are several superannuated bridges, that are quite as ridiculous as municipal shows. They are profusely decorated with paintings; every crossbeam and arch, every panel and post, is covered with pigments and portraits from startling designs; it seems as if some artist of unappreciated genius had passed his days in this shabby work for the love of it, for certainly no authorities could ever have so disgraced the city property. One contained a hundred and fifty-four paintings, representing events from the lives of the patron saints of Lucerne; the other "the Dance of Death," and here the artist had an open field to indulge his passion for the horrible and hideous. They were bad originally, judging by the sad remains left by the ravages of time. Nevertheless the hotel architecture of Lucerne is superlative. Art seems to have made its best work there.

It is generally and habitually asserted that wherever Catholicism prevails in Switzerland, there is lack of thrift, order, and enterprise; but here the accusation fails. The town and population are models of propriety, gentility, and cleanliness. Mendicity is also charged against the Continental Catholics, and it is fully verified in Southern Italy, but I did not meet a beggar in Lucerne, and impositions were scarce.

To see Altorf and William Tell's chapel, once at Lucerne, was like visiting Versailles from Paris. As we put out from shore *en route* to the spot commemorated by that wonderful feat of archery, so long ago that we begin to doubt the apple story (not but that we know there were apples at the time, for the apple is at the bottom of all mischief, but then you see another apple story, of national fame, has succeeded it in America), we saw brightly painted boats to the memory of Tell and Winkelreid and other Swiss republican heroes. Every point, whether promontory or island, every hill and valley, is planted with trees and flowers, decorated with little white shrines, where wooden virgins pray in gentle peace. The little towns along the lake were crowded with tourists, and gayly dressed strangers thronged about the quays to welcome the incomers, or wave farewell to the departing guests. The scene was full of harmony with the silence of nature and the repose of man. The lake-border seemed in holiday trim, but on the boat humanity was industriously satisfying the inner hunger.

A Swiss lake steamer is a new study of the habits of travellers. Eating and drinking is the universal pastime. It begins early and continues through the entire tour. As soon as the boat drops off the quay the Swiss families who have come for an outing, order the rations, but whether the eating was a labor or a pleasure I could not discern. My first conception was that it was a pleasure; but when it ran through hours I concluded it had grown into a sort of duty. The Swiss are as successful in the practice of eating cheese and drinking beer as the English, who never travel by land or sea without five full meals a day.

Tell's platte at Fluelen was our destination; a very poorly painted, fragile little hut, covered with awkward frescoes, and scrawled over with vulgar pencilled names and designs to keep alive the doubtful tradition of the dramatic patriot of Switzerland, which Schiller and Sheridan Knowles have lauded into enduring fame by their glorious plays. Then why should we cherish these ambiguous memories when Switzerland has a stronger hold on the respect of man in its real poets, heroes, and statesmen? By the names of Winkelreid, Freliegrath, and Zwingle, on the boats and *pensions*, I felt compensated for the disappointment at Tell's chapel and its destitution of historical foundation.

Next day a steamer carried us from Lucerne to Vitznau, a mountain village with a new and elegant station, whence the railway starts over the Rigi, that formidable and hitherto insurmountable granite barrier. I do not know which contemplation had for me the most fascination, crossing the Brunig or ascending and descending the Rigi. The former was invested with all romance and ecstasy but no fear, while Rigi inspired me with horrible forebodings of being suddenly precipitated from a cloudy pinnacle into an abysmal ravine with a mass of broken bones and mangled flesh closing the last struggle for life. The railway that traverses and connects this series of lofty peaks is constructed in imitation of the iron road which brings the White Mountains of New England into communication with the heretofore isolated sky-world of that region.

It is only since 1848 this mysterious and interesting combination of rock and ice, lying between Lakes Lucerne and Zug, arrested the serious attention of men of science and generous governments. Before that period this vast mountain system was only a district of cowherds, pasture-lands, and a colony of degenerate peasants' huts. Before then pilgrims made the tour of these steep, and rugged, and deserted paths with much labor and fatigue. The railway gauge is constructed after the model of the ordinary American road, but it has rails within rails provided with teeth on which a cog-wheel under the locomotive catches with each revolution. The locomotives are of one hundred and twenty horse-power, having upright boilers, and the passenger carriages are placed always above the engine, from which it is disconnected by couplings, and can be stopped instantaneously in case of accidents; and although I perfectly understood the system and was doubly assured of the impossibility of danger, yet as the train began to crawl up the hill backward like a little iron crab, and I felt the car sloping away from me till my sensation was akin to that of hanging on the inclination of the roof of some high building, a thrill of terror convulsed me, which was not decreased as I looked from my starry height into the frightful vacancy below.

Being the height of the season the little station platform was staggering beneath its human freight that surged and scrambled for places as the train came up to our side. Our ascent through the beautiful little pastoral village was gradual, and after passing a few of the loftier altitudes an exquisite view of the green lake, the spires and towers of Lucerne, and then one by one the famous Alpine summits dawned upon us, and lastly, as a frame to the picture, came the undulating yet unbroken wave-line of the Bernese Oberland. A half an hour on our airy tour and we penetrated a tunnel through conglomerate rock as suddenly as a lightning flash, and only emerged to cross a fragile trestle bridge spanning a dark and awful gorge, seventy-five feet deep. At this perilous point in the flight the reckless passengers rushed to the right of the car to gaze into the gap below, and made the air hideous with exclamations about its imposing beauty, while the little car swayed and shook with the overbalancing weight. Step by step we penetrated forest and rocky wastes at an easy gradient, passing peasants and tourists making the journey, some on foot, others astride their braying beast. The sensations may have been something like those experienced in a rising balloon, with this difference, the earth did not recede from us; we gradually seemed to be melting into illimitable space. Despite the possible calamities, it was glorious to rise like a bird in air, and floating among azure clouds and misty mountain-tops gaze into the heart of the valleys below, the shimmering lakes, and mountains of glowing verdure, hemmed in by dazzling ridges of ice, unmelted by the fiery glance and scorching breath of the sun, and to hear the sweet tinkle of cow-bells coming from the deep vales, mellowed and mingling in the nebulous air and perfumes of the sweet July.

The two intermediate stations, Kaltbad and Staffel, were busy scenes of tourist life; but why rest at the gate or vestibule when we might mount to the cupola of the Nymphs and Satyrs' glorious mansion? So we pushed on to Rigi-Kulm, where, pausing on the minaret of the granite temple, I turned my eyes upon the marvellous panorama around me. Various emotions struggled for utterance and choked each other in their rapid succession. First, the boundless power and majesty of God; the daring confidence and ingenuity of man; the sad and benighted story related by the antediluvian homes perched on these inaccessible towers by generations passed away, who trod these paths and knew only of earth what they could see far, far beneath them; like the crows, they had grown old and died in the trees where they were born.

The lower dales lay at our feet with the lines of the farms, and streams, and roads, faint by the distance, greatly resembling a toy miniature of some distant metropolis. Few of the pioneers of the granite hills ever trod the earth at the base of the Rigi, but worshipped God and nature among their own fields and herds. Close by was the more pretentious modern civilization; the outgrowth of the railroad and the course of intelligent travel attracted from all parts of the world. I seemed to be standing on the edge of a great planet, with all the marvels, air, sky, and water and land spread out below and around me. Then again I felt suspended in the atmosphere like the fairy on the great bird in the *Arabian Nights*, when the snow-clad Alps, one hundred and twenty miles in length, burst upon my astonished gaze: the chain began in the far east, and growing nearer and nearer I saw the huge snowy crests of the bleak Glarnisch range, with their long white lines connecting with the other ice giants of the series; then my eyes travelled to the Bernese Alps and their shining peaks, the Wetterhorn and Jungfrau standing out in all the sublimity of silent and solitary majesty. The lakes shone like silver mirrors below, the villages were painted pictures, and the rivers meandered through the green campagna like silken cords. Away beyond were the battlements and towers of Lucerne, of schoolhouse and hospital, dense woodlands of the Black Forest, and the overguarding serrated peaks of sombre, weird Pilatus.

Beyond and above all these glories is the sunrise and sunset seen from the majestic peaks. All that I saw from the car window is exhibited in the dawn in new lights and cooler radiance; as bright day advances the lakes seem to rise near enough that we may see the ripples caused by tossing in a stone, the beauties of the landscape flash upon us in duplicated colors, and the ice, that has a cold stony glitter under the rays of the full-risen sun, is at this hour suffused in warm rosy haze.

The motley groups gathered upon Kulm to watch for the superb coming of the sun make of it a sort of Tower of Babel, a conglomerate of dialects. There is no intimacy between the various elements of this cosmopolitan campmeeting. Strangers they are and strangers they remain. Strangers they come and strangers they go. One bond only have they, that of curiosity, and it evaporates with the dissolving tints of the mountain pageant.

Having risen to the clouds from Lake Lucerne, the entertainment ended, we prepared to reach the mundane sphere over the route leading to Arth, on the opposite side of the great pile from Vitznau. Not nearly so perilous, wild, or lengthy was our line of descent. The district was very much like the Allegheny section of Pennsylvania, and in a fraction more than an hour we found ourselves on the borders of Lake Zug. Very peaceful, and fruitful, and rural is this famous valley. Harvest and haymaking are close neighbors in these mountain solitudes, and pretty valleys are sent like compensations for the sterility of the ravines of the higher latitudes. While Providence sends Alps on Alps to Switzerland, and countless marvels of lakes, it vouchsafes insufficient harvests; neither gold, nor coal, nor silver is among the treasures of these mountains. So, the poor mountaineer must buy his fuel from Germany, his food from the Baltic, and his light from the petroleum of Pennsylvania.

The Valley of Arth, the Lake of Zug, and its city form an elaborate and glowing entry to the city of Zurich.

LETTER LXVII.

"On Zurich's spires, with rosy light,
The mountains smile at morn and eve,
And Zurich's waters, blue and bright,
The glories of those hills receive."
THOMAS BUCHANAN READ.

ZURICH, July, 1878.

ALTHOUGH it was an intensely tropical afternoon when I came into Zurich, yet I marked the absence of dust and insects. Its position at the head of its lake, bisected as it is by several small streams and rivers, may be the antidote to the former pest, while it would be only reasonable to suppose these very causes would prove hotbeds of mosquitos and vermin.

Zurich is fascinating from its resemblance to Venice in the color of sky and water toward sunset, and this impression is enhanced by the rosy haze that hangs from and partly veils the distant mountains, and the expression of the clear perspective of the rushing lake tributaries, that seem drifting far away to some distant ocean. Still, transformed into an almost Italian-looking city by the influences of color and climate, and by its busy life about the quays, the preponderance of German elements weighs down the whole place. There are the heavy, graceless lines of Teutonic art, the broad awkward physique of the women, the stolid bearing of the men. Indeed, the bridges, boats, public institutions, and monuments all speak of a race of beer drinkers and *spec* consumers. There are indeed some modern squares, some glittering shops, and other transcripts of Parisian prototypes, but they are sad hybrids among the heavy crumbling stones of the Sweitzer antiquities.

Even the villas bordering the water-edges seem to have lost their beauty of outline, being neither French nor German; yet here again the wonderful natural points of grace and sublimity in all the vicinage fully compensate for the defects of human creation.

Switzerland lacks entirely the palatial inland steamers of the United States. Indeed, from the Mersey to the Mediterranean, no such superb floating hotels are ever met as adorn our great American rivers. But Switzerland, like Venice, is a marvellous architect of the graceful smaller craft which ply like butterflies up and down her narrow streams.

Zurich being a learned city—a city of schools, seminaries, societies, and libraries—is also a musical city, and every evening in the Tonhalle, a fine open saloon on the lake, are excellent concerts, and sometimes balls, where all classes mingle. Seated around little tables, they eat, drink, and decorously make merry, while out on the glittering starlit water, hundreds of the more exclusive residents or travellers linger in their dancing boats and enjoy the music of one of the finest orchestras I have met since I left Paris. Though our position on the lake was satisfactory, by paying twelve cents admission fee we changed it for a seat in the temple of harmony, where the audience was wholly genteel, consisting for the most part of tradesmen and their families enjoying wine and waltzes in true domestic fashion. Unlike such amusements in America, these concert gardens partake of no feature of the variety show, and are therefore ever the resort of the refined. Curiously, this tabernacle of Erato is transformed every Friday into the scene of a discordant body by the sessions of the Zurich Exchange or Bourse, where hundreds and thousands of cotton dealers, silk manufacturers, railway kings, and expatriated ex-sovereigns, eagerly congregate to risk their fortunes upon the turbulent waters of barter, here frequently most violently agitated, especially among the silk merchants. But the hall of mellifluous cadences will not long be defiled by the money-changers after the new Bourse is completed, now constructing, which is to be not only an imposing adornment to the city, but an epitaph in stone to the generous citizen who bequeathed several millions of francs as a tribute of gratitude to the town in which he accumulated his fortune; and his grand gift pays for the new exchange.

Zurich is the centre of varied and conflicting theories, and I was much surprised to find in this republican centre so many sympathizers with monarchy, and to hear of a succession of discrowned German noblemen among its *habitués*. But disturbers of the peace, enemies of kings and murderers of royalty, like Nobling and his associates, make this a point also of rendezvous and convergence. The community is of pronounced sentiments and strong attachments to republican institutions; and free speech is the motto of the little republic as it is of our greater one. The Zurich hotels are indifferent after enjoying the superiority of those of Lucerne. They are costly, and while the Baur au Lac may boast an unrivalled position at the confluence of the lake and the Limmat, with extensive wooded gardens, that seem to float in the stream, the Bellevue, on the opposite quay, adds poor fare and bad attendance to excessive charges. Carriage hire is double in republican Zurich what it is in imperial Rome. The charming simplicity of the better classes is shown by their willingness to walk in Zurich, while in the southern and sleepy cities of Italy even the lazzaroni must ride.

In the suburbs of Zurich, upon an elevation overlooking the city and a noble stretch of country, there is a charming resort. Weary merchants ride out here in summer afternoons to dine under the shade of great trees, and travellers leave the city without enjoying one of its greatest luxuries unless they have, as we had, resident friends to conduct them thither. Little tables are spread on the brow of the hill in the open air, and all around the grounds are old ladies knitting, young ones reading, with their children playing at their side or rocking in the swings; here and there family parties dining upon frugal cake and red wine. There was no idle curiosity, as is always the case with too many of the hollow pretenders who infest the great hotels; no vulgar staring crowds, and no whispered comment. No sooner does a stranger take a seat than he becomes one of the domestic circle at the lowly Beau Séjour; humble and unostentatious it was, but had it been more aristocratic and costly, it could not have been maintained without the presence of, what is called at home, the fast class. Here the light wines and modest charges repress intoxication, and the meretricious element, even if it were allowed, would not patronize its plain domesticity.

From this lofty seat the city lay compact and smoky beneath; great columns of gray and white steam issued from the chimneys of the factories, while broad avenues of trees gradually insinuated themselves through blocks of houses and old streets, until all circumscribed city line was dissolved in vineyards and orchards, or mazes of shrubbery. The city was divided into two sections, and bordered upon an outer margin by the waters of the Limmat and the Sihl, like roads of shining crystal, until they joined and flowed in one channel. Dark ridges of rock bound the city and its environs, and these were again bound by the succession of snowy crests of the beautiful Glarnisch range, that rested their silver peaks in clear outline against the ever-changing and duplicating colors of the clouds. These perspectives were as lovely as those of the Jungfrau—the presiding divinity of Interlaken.

Although there is no communication between Switzerland and the ocean, yet her fresh-water seas, her crystal lakes, and the blue and arrowy mountain currents, furnish forth a varied feast of fancy and of food; a feast for the imagination in matchless landscape, and endless supplies for the inner man; and eagerly do the Swiss seize these attractions and convert them into wealth. Their best hotels are placed upon the quays. Again we note the strange similarity between these silent streams and the quiet monotony of the Grand Canal at Venice. The pure waters of Lake Zurich and the wedded streams adjacent promote the health of the hordes of stalwart men and women, and are the unconscious contributors to the exquisite quality of its silks, which create the local nabobs and millionaires.

There is no better place to study and satisfy one's self as to the existence of a prehistoric world than in the antiquarian department of the town library at Zurich. If I, with the rest of mankind, fell a victim to the popular fallacy of regarding all we read of the mammoth epoch amusing extravaganzas, coined from an exceedingly fertile but erratic brain, has the fault rested with the community of readers, or with the few who knew or assumed to know of what they wrote? Why should whole lives be passed in scientific experiments or explorations if it be not to enrich and instruct mankind? For years every atom of self-existent matter, relative to the ages preceding written tradition, culled from the earth by the archæologist and cherished by the antiquarian, has been woven into a fairy tale for small boys. These works were not only perused with doubt by the masses, but, literally, with the feeling that there was not a word or line of them that the author had intended to be believed. But these very works set forth some years ago as conglomerates of trash, to-day take fresh hold upon the best minds of the world. It is certainly not to the advancement of mankind to have new discoveries presented as vagaries. The adbare historical facts may serve as a basis to scores of romantic tales, but paradoxical theories treated in a like manner can exert none other than an evil influence.

Now, in this museum, there is abundant proof of the lake dwellings which existed in these territories through the epochs of stone, bronze, and iron, thousands of years before the birth of Christ; here are the relics of the wonderful discovery of a people more or less civilized living in the water valleys between the Alps in houses, or rather huts, erected upon piles driven in the bottom of the lake.

"In the winter of 1853-54 the Swiss streams and lakes were lower than they had ever been known. At Meilin, on Lake Zurich, some workmen took advantage of the receded waters to excavate earth from the lake beds, for the purpose of filling in additional garden spots on the shore; while thus engaged they were astonished by striking their spades into what proved to be the tops of many wooden piles, arranged in clusters and in rows." This is the keynote to the whole amazing revelation.

Before me were spread miniature model plans of the homes of these antique and mysterious people, built upon piles driven in the early lake-beds, until rotting away by the slow progress of time they formed peat, upon which other similar piles were erected, and new villages grew up upon the homes and graves of those who had gone centuries before. Their implements of labor, the ornaments they wore, their cooking utensils, the vestiges of their clothing, and the remains of their food, tell only half the secret of the unravelled mystery. Here are the evidences of cities that were old when Pompeii was in its infancy. Strongest amongst the proofs is the number of cubes of peat formed under the water. The known period it requires to grow this substance being calculated, if we could tell nothing of the era of their existence by the relics of stone and bronze, is the one fact of nature to destroy all incredulity. Those who might have been doubters at home can be so no longer, after such a personal experience as I had in the presence of performed facts.

Science is quietly assuming the ascendency all over the universe, and presently, that is, in the course of a century or two, there will be no mile of sky, no spot of earth, and no rood of water, that will not be probed by the chemist, the astronomer, the geologist, the geographer, the anatomist, or the explorer. What all such processes will do, we can foretell by what they have done. The outlook is very interesting, and we may fondly hope that if man has entered upon so grand a career, he may improve himself as he improves the face of the world in which he lives.

LETTER LXVIII.

> The Temple builders, where are they!
> The worshippers most passed away;
> Who came the first to offer there
> The song of praise, the heart of prayer!
> Man's generation passes soon—
> It comes and changes like the moon.
> He rears the perishable wall,
> But ere it crumble he himself must fall.
> ANONYMOUS.

STRASSBURG, July, 1878.

SWITZERLAND is so small a country in comparison with the rest of Europe, that despite her beautiful lakes, great mountains, and brave people, one is compelled to wonder why she has not been ground to powder by the great nations ranged about her. So, when I left Zurich, bidding farewell to Switzerland, for Constance, a German town in the province of Baden-Baden, it was very like leaving a village for the broader sights of a vast city.

There was the usual array of Alpine heights and glens flush with the fragrant flowers of rural rest until we came in sight of the Rhine Falls, whose foaming flow varied the German-Swiss picture. This cataract, a tame transcript of the white thunders of Niagara, is a cascade of greater volume than any other in Europe. From the car window I could enjoy in quiet dignity the voluminous efflux of the upper waters and the agitation of the lower stream, as the torrent after leaping over three unequal ridges of rock plunged into its channel, fermenting the glassy green surge into a broil of creamy froth, and rushing away down the tide in a variegated foam. There were little skiffs, driven around in the whirlpool by the waves, that seemed about to be rifled of their human freight, while numerous rainbows formed above them in arches of spray. Perhaps it would have been a proof of my own intrepidity had I risked my life in one of these cockle-shells that I might gaze from the pavilion on the summit of the central rock into the whirl below, or traced the many footpaths to the iron platform overhanging the roaring abyss, or mounted the terraces and parapets near the sluices left and right, but I relinquished all these delights in favor of the pleasanter memories of a safe inside situation.

I do not know if one may say he has seen a town by merely riding through its streets and along its wharves, but I feel sure I saw as much of the municipality of Schaffhausen in my desultory rambles as if I had lived there several weeks. I saw that it retained all the deformities and none of the beauties of its mediæval origin. The buildings were, without exception, tall and flat, with a garish showing of rude mosaic façades and flashy frescoes, with florid Dutch cornices and buttresses and rude adornments in startling places. They were dimmed and blackened by age, and seemed falling to decay, while the streets were uncleanly; and the fierce rays of the sun which fell over and among all this moth-eaten, rusty community of drones, only exaggerated the deficiencies. In the tropical summer noon the windows and shutters were all closed, the city was asleep, and the atrocious statuary of the old town stood boldly forth in hideous ugliness.

A boat that would have been a disgrace to a Pennsylvania canal before railroads were dreamed of lay at the crumbling, worm-eaten wharf to carry us up the Rhine, and over Lake Constance. It was little larger than the old-fashioned passenger craft employed between Harrisburg and Williamsport, but without a single convenience of those tortoise conveyances, with one exception: it was propelled by steam. First and second class passengers were carried on the upper and only deck, and indeed, when cattle were brought aboard at some of the lake stations, they too occupied a corner of the same floor. There were long benches of rude slats alternated with spaces, through which the occupants were in imminent danger of falling, if the utmost care was not practised when disposing of the body. Perforated and ventilated backs are in a way a blessing in summer, but upon the comfort of such accommodations I need not dilate. Fortunately, I had my inevitable cushion, which I used as a throttle to the yawning gap beneath. As the boat shoved off the superannuated quay, a begrimed awning was stretched over the heads of the highest price payers, the other poor devils were left to melt in the African temperature. The mercury stood at 95°, and I suffered as much in the fervent glow as I had in the caloric of the famous Centennial summer in Philadelphia. The unfurling of the canvas I hailed, at least, as a humane act, and had just commenced to feel partly compensated for my suffering upon the benches, resembling the tortures of the Inquisition, when our only shelter was deliberately removed, and in the fierce fire of the tropical afternoon we rode and roasted for four hours. Umbrellas and sun-shades were vainly raised to screen the passengers from the white flame. Protests would have been futile; suffering was inexorable and, indeed, the German gentlemen seemed rather to enjoy, or to say the least, they were indifferent to the ordeal, looking clean and cool in their immaculate linen, while I was in a glow of perspiration.

The whole experience was a horror: in the manners of the passengers, in the customs of the attendants, in the suffocating steamer. How many complaints are scored against my countrymen; yet, taking them as a mass, where do we find greater delicacy of conduct? For example: a rather fine-looking German woman, suffering from the common affliction, sprawled herself out at full length regardless of her pedal extremities, and slumbered all through the fabled shores of the Rhine, and upon the lauded bosom of Lake Constance. At every low bridge, and there were many, the smoke-pipe was lowered, belching forth a supplemental volcano upon the unoffending, yet much offended, heads of the barbecued pilgrims; and to complete the outrage, a mammoth steer was lugged on deck amongst the terrified company. Was there ever an American organization that attempted such a studied outrage upon the travelling community? Among the thousands of transatlantic tourists is there no one to censure? Is there not one voice raised in protest from our travelling representative men? Why does not Thomas Cook fulminate against the entire affair; his tickets are used upon the line, and his general system I cannot too honestly commend; but in such a case he should interfere to protect his own interests, if not to secure the comfort of his patrons.

But, despite these wretched drawbacks, both shores were interesting throughout the narrow course of the Rhine.

There was much that was shabby, ragged, and sterile. There was none of the rugged Alpine scenery, and it was not until we drifted into Lake Constance with its blue waters and storied villas, gleaming white through the lofty forests, that something of an Italian glamour surrounded me.

In Germany! The buzz of the broad guttural vernacular, and the demands of custom-house officers to examine baggage, told the potent truth. By the treaty of Presburg in 1805 Constance was adjudged to Baden, and when Germany was unified in 1866 its own local sovereign, together with all the host of little dukes, was swept away by the stern iron arm of Bismarck, and now Germany is like the United States, one harmonious people.

We came into the harbor of the Bay of Constance in the sweet evening, after our day of damnable basting on the water, and as we neared the long curved pier the quaint old German city lay calmly beautiful in the opaline glory of the falling sun on the distant snow peaks. The reflection on the mounds of ice, and their colors duplicated against the sky, had so blended cloud and mountain that where the crystal ridges ended and the ethereal dome began was utterly indiscernible, until as the sun disappeared entirely, the dark rocks drew their own profile against the heavens.

Early the next morning—Sunday—I was awakened by a German military band coming over the bridge, discoursing the march from "Fatinitza;" what with the transcendent music of the brass instruments, the hush of the new day, and the pellucid reverbation of sound as it fell on the water, the whole produced an effect I shall never outlive, and wherever or whenever I hear the same strains again, but one thought will be suggested, one code of events reproduced—Constance and its memories.

The flourish of trumpets and beat of drums meant a parade of the Constance fire brigade. So I looked from my window in the warm Sabbath and saw in the arid streets below a crowd and display very like our own pageants of a similar character, with the one exception of the Sunday frolic. Here again we had Paris. I had been so long amidst the rigid Catholicism of Italy, and so full of the provincialism of Swiss forests, that this saturnalia was very like sacrilege. The streets and broad squares were alive with military melody and surging populace, but shortly after twelve o'clock the revellers retired, sober, subdued, and satisfied. There were no Swiss costumes in the throng; the odd dress of the German burgher and his homely wife is gradually assuming its authority, as is the German silver *mark*. The Helvetian coins and Italian lira are no more, though the French *franc* has been with us from Paris, it too has disappeared and we are to learn a new money table of marks, pfennigs, florins, thalers, and kreutzers. It seems only yesterday since the French currency ruled all; now the hand of this powerful government overspreads its entire domain; the broad German mark and the ubiquitous soldier vindicate the master intellect that dominates the great state through all its borders.

The characteristics of the German in America are typical of them on their native heath. The Sunday noon being fair, the railway carriages were filled by the better classes travelling in family parties on little pastoral jaunts, as well as by third class the same as the working people. In all this broad extent of country there was not a beggar; the poorest were clean and decorous; the higher degrees robed in the Parisian fashions; but there were many strange uniforms amongst the peasantry. In the district of Homberg the women wore black petticoats, scarlet bodices, broad-brimmed straw hat, setting around the face like a nimbus, ornamented with black or red rosettes; while the men trudged by their sides in black coats lined with crimson, and very curious was the effect they produced; as the sun went down on the gray hills they shone like fireflies in the deepening shadows. Sunday as it was, the fields were full of laborers of both sexes. Have I not said enough of the way in which the females are burdened here? With the hauling, and moving, and sawing, and being harnessed with dogs and donkeys, they are so unsexed that all the higher feminine faculties and fascinations seem to have faded, leaving the animal nature paramount. Yet we have been taught, and still there is an effort afoot to sustain the doctrine, that all connection with science, philosophy, and logic, energizes the female mind beyond its circumscribed limits,—once having drifted into the channel of the deeper arts there is an irresistible undercurrent that carries her out and out beyond her delicate status, and eventually makes her virile, prosaic, and unsentimental. But which is to make the most utter devastation with the spiritual and carnal beauty of woman, brutish labor or mental exercise? True, the latter may, in time, deprive her cheek of some of its exquisite contour, or reduce the blooming flesh tints to a tone less dazzling, and the eye may be restless instead of soft and lustrous; but, the light of intellect sheds a glorious halo over all personal deficiencies.

Assuredly, this practice of extreme manual labor must account for the absence of beauty among the lower orders of women in Continental Europe. I scanned the crowds coming and going in the cars, and save that they were clean, sober, and apparently happy, there was not a comely woman in the throng. The men were far better looking as a class; their fresh blonde complexions and hair, and erect bearing, rather indicated that while the women were reared to work the men were educated to war. I had ample opportunity to study the German faces and phases, as there had been an industrial exhibition at Triberg in the very heart of the Black Forest, and here the peasants came in droves from their various little hamlet-homes, where their lives are passed in making watches and clocks, to be sent far out in the great world of which they know so little.

Our way through the Black Forest was marked by many of the impressive features of the borders of the Mediterranean or the Alpine districts; first, in the number of tunnels, and then in the wild scenery and the herculean labor of the forest-workers. Sweeping plains, awful chasms, and flinty mountain-ranges, flew by us like shadows across a brilliant mirror. Yet it was indeed Germany, dark, heavy, impenetrable, and stolid; Germany without excuse or qualification. Very like the riotous luxuriance of southern French or Italian-Swiss landscape, still lacking all of their indescribable charm that is their mysterious fascination. The landscape had a Bismarckian outlook.

The tunnelling of the Black Forest is another revelation in railway science. Until I had seen the Italian lines, my ideas, like most untravelled Americans, were that the railroads of the United States, especially those across the Rocky Mountains, were unparalleled in the difficulties of construction, as they are known to be unequalled in the extent of country they traverse; but all these preconceived notions faded before the over two hundred tunnels of Italy, eight consecutive miles under Mont Cenis, and finally by the nine continuous miles of St. Gothard, now constructing jointly by Italy, Germany, and Switzerland; and the revelation of the Black Forest, seemed to me a more stupendous work than any of the others. Vast mineral treasures lay in the ridges of these granite hills. Timber, coal, and water mingle with incredible varieties of agriculture and a long catalogue of diversified manufactures. In one hundred miles of travel there was a series of tunnels, carriage-roads, bridges, and viaducts that followed each other in marvellous and rapid succession.

All through the Black Forest there are thousands of archaic relics of every description. Old abbeys, castles, and chateaux recall the ancient times when Germany was divided among many princes and priests; and as the train flashes along its iron ways glimpses may be caught of tanneries, factories, wine-presses, sweet villages, and broad fields, which attest the opulence and power of this magnificent German Empire. Ruins are as frequent as in Italy, and the appending tales as weird and romantic. The Chateau of Ortenburg, which occupies an ancient site of a stronghold destroyed in the seventeenth century, cannot fail to attract the attention of the traveller; the vine-clad hills nestled closely about its base, and in the tastefully planted grounds where the patter of little feet and the shout of happy childish voices, ringing as jubilantly on the summer air as if the spot had never been harrowed by bloody faction. Wherever we looked there was scenery as wild and legends as spectral as those of Greece or Egypt, and despite the repulsive guttural dialect of even the best-educated German, I do not marvel at the desire of the English to travel through the Black Forest, with its quaint old towns, its simple-hearted people, its impenetrable wildernesses, its geological formations, all so much at variance with the crowded cities, narrow limits, and dissipated populace of their own boasted kingdom.

Had landscape and tradition alone been the surrounding influences I might have imagined I was in some far-famed land of the gods; but all this fair delusion was dissolved by the continued and curious commotion of travel and the disagreeable twang and jaw-dislocators of the passengers. I picked up these few and then searched a German lexicon for the translation: Donseuschingen, an ancient town; Nibelungenlied, a library; Kilpenstrasse, a street: Ehlenbogenthal, Kinzigthal, Eberstienstrasse, Jugæhweiler, Geicsenkopfchen, Gimmeldingen, Guncenbachthal, Schweppenhausen; now these are proper names, and I have not picked the most abstruse either. As we go into the body of the German speech ordinary terms are apparently more incomprehensible; yet, in this language Luther partly conquered the Catholic Church, Goethe and Schiller electrified the hemispheres by their verse, and to-day it creates a literature of magazines, newspapers, and every variety of books, that even puts the pedantic English publisher to the blush. Then to heap Ossa on Pelion was the shouting, horn-blowing, and bell-ringing at every station, and I longed for the

English silence and the promptitude of our own system, but I remembered that England is a very small and compact kingdom, and that American railways run in straight lines with comparatively few branches, while the continent of Europe is made complex by its various powers, coins, dialects, religions, customs, and laws, and that its railroads receive and discharge every day specimens of nearly all the civilized travellers of the age. It is by these sounds then that necessary communication is held between officials and passengers. My theory was confirmed by the arrival of a heavily laden train of cosmopolitan tourists, and their amusing conflicts with the German *kelners*, guards, cab-drivers, and hotel porters, when they, speaking but one language and the underlings not more than two, expected all their questions to be answered immediately and intelligently, whether applied in Turkish, Greek, English, Chinese, Russian, or Japanese, and then flew into the most turbulent passion, while the Teuton preserved his stolid equanimity.

At the historic town of Kehl—half an hour from Strassburg—I saw for the first time some of the scars left by the war of 1870. This was indeed Germany, or Germany with a French heart. Fortifications stretched all about; as far as the eye could reach, in every direction were those great circular projecting mounds, and I could easily see traces of the advancing columns of the mighty host that swept down upon the French battalions.

Strasburg, the capital of Alsace and German Lorraine, the headquarters of the 15th corps of the Teuton forces, is German in speech, German in dress, and for two hundred years German in the customs of its inhabitants, and yet as thoroughly French, heart and soul, as the occupants of the Rue de Rivoli or the Faubourg St. Honoré in Paris.

Strasburg is a quaint city of many gables, chimneys, red-tiled roofs, and a mingling of French, German, and Swiss architecture. I cannot say that any portion of it impressed me as being pretty. There are some fine shops in the business portion; but the many *platz* of the city, which were intended as adornment, had a scorched arid appearance, and the dust seemed to have penetrated the houses; as was the fact at the hotel, where the cuisine was unexcelled and the floors and furniture grimy, with a general aroma in contradiction of the "sweet south breathing o'er a bank of violets." There is no time spent in the cultivation of taste for municipal embellishments. Structures are colored yellow, or red, or blue, while multitudinous chimneys start out from the most inconceivable points in as great a diversity of shapes as in numbers, and façades and eaves are florid with wood carvings. The building called the Old House in Strasburg is highly ornate with wooden sculptures, capitals and eaves, and gabled roof, and very like an exalted edition of a Swiss châlet. It is the oldest standing house of the city, and though its architecture is weird its looks of preservation belie its years.

One cannot speak of Strasburg and omit its Cathedral with its seven hundred years of history, its mingled architecture,—Romanesque and Gothic,—its numerous sculptures, its beautiful interior, and its dizzy tower, which I did not ascend; I am tired crawling up and down crooked stairways to meet with nothing but aching limbs and unrequited efforts, and peril my life through the stone fretwork of the upper tower. Neither did I look upon the embalmed bodies of a German Prince and his daughter, as I have tasted *ad nauseam* of canonized saints and apotheosized sinners, dead priests raised to the empyrean, and sublimated princes.

I turned away from all these attractive reminiscences of distilled carnality into one of the many cramped crooked streets, and was surprised at the vast quantity of *sabots* for sale at an humble shop door. They were packed in barrels and tubs, and heaped upon the sidewalk, where the peasants were purchasing them at three marks (seventy-five cents) per pair; one pair wears two years. Heavy, awkward, cruel, tortuous inventions, ruder than the rudest brogans, and confessing, as it were, the extreme destitution of the proletaires. The poor toilers who wear these barbarous wooden shoes were working on the highways, and difficult it was to distinguish the sexes; they looked like pictures of a feudal age.

The cynosure of Strasburg is the barracks, which constitutes a series of girdles to the city. One gate after another, guarded by grim Teutons, we passed; one mountain of earth after another we rode over, until I surely thought we must have passed the limitation of fortification, and still again and again the strong outworks loomed before me in the July twilight.. Thirteen ridges of defence, four and five miles from the town, proved not only what the French had constructed to debar the Germans, and built in vain, but what the Germans have since erected as a protection should the French attempt to step in and renew the dance which they so impulsively opened eight years ago.

The driver of the hack was a thorough Alsatian, and the volubility of his German confirmed the sincerity of his French affections. He pointed out the extensive military barracks of the various divisions of the German army corps now quartered at Strasburg; the captured ammunition and valuable bronzes, relics of the conquests of Napoleon I.; designated the portions of the city destroyed by the resistless Germans in their terrific bombardment for five days in August of 1870. There seemed enough confiscated fire-arms and balls to make war on the universe, and as the poor fellow looked at these victorious trophies of the conquerors, he related his story with all the gestures of an excited Parisian, and not with the stolid austerity of the victors. He had convinced himself that the French empire was the only government for the working classes, and I was impressed with the contrast between this plebeian Imperialist and the quiet, strong dignity of the officer in command of the fortifications, indicative, as it were, of the difference between the volatile gasconade of the Alsatian and the silent power of the German.

As we crossed the great bridge of boats over the Rhine we were greeted by a swarm of mosquitos that boarded us with spiteful unanimity, vividly recalling home. We fled from the assault in honest terror, but when we re-entered the city our myriad enemies had retreated; they seemed to confine themselves to the river precincts.

LETTER LXIX.

Noiseless Carlsruhe, grave of Ducal pride!
  Whose silent life is speechless books,
The daily haven of the truant bride,
  Or evening shelter of the noisy rooks.
                                ANONYMOUS.

CARLSRUHE, July, 1878.

IN passing from the mountains, glaciers, and lakes of Switzerland, I miss the congenial climate, wild pictures, and quaint dress of the peasant-women, with the white ribbons wound in the plaits of their brown hair; but in Germany I have found excessive heat, flies, and mosquitos, and these, if not exactly a compensation for the transcendent pleasures of the Alpine Republic, are, at least, sharp reminders of home.

The journey from Strasburg to Carlsruhe was a short, pleasant one, despite the torrid heat. The Grand Duchy of Baden is a lovely agricultural region, redolent of flowers and trees and the fresh earth, and principally interesting by our course through the former gambling town of Baden-Baden. Stripped of its glittering robes of sin, its only attractions are now its healing waters and lovely environs. There was something of a Newport air about the station, the fine hotels, the cosy restaurants, and shady avenues that showed it to be a conservatory of attractions for those of full pockets and aristocratic tastes; yet Baden-Baden has only a local population of 11,000, chiefly Roman Catholic. Now that the sinners have gone since the Emperor William whipped the money-changers from the brilliant temples of Baden-Baden, all the sumptuous palaces erected with the gamester's money are used by the moral multitudes, who seem to have forgotten the pleasure of sin to which they were long dedicated. Baden-Baden, with its groves, waterfalls, theatres, and even churches built by Mr. Benezet, the late king gambler, has a decorous, sedate air, and a fair, healthy appearance, where one might find the calm of rustic refinement and happiness. The old paradise of hazard seems to be given up to what claims to be a newer and better generation.

Carlsruhe, capital of the Grand Duchy of Baden, is rather a new town, a fact readily perceived by the modern and unsoiled architecture, the outgrowth of the miniature town erected by the prince about his hunting-grounds in 1715, since ruled by a succession of local monarchs of one family until 1866, when all these petty feudalities were abolished by order of Bismarck, after the German armies had defeated the Austrians, and the many principalities of Germany became united under one sovereign head. It is a dismal sight to see the splendid palaces of the expatriated provincial kings standing all around in grim solitude; silent among their own highly cultivated grounds, fountains, and statuary, while their former possessors, who lived and revelled in them, are now passing their days in foreign countries, not daring to return to their own. The Grand Duke Frederick William, having married the daughter of Kaiser Wilhelm, was not one of the nobles obliged to flee, through their allegiance to Austria; he still reigns in the palace, from which the town radiates fan-shaded. The uprooting of the host of smaller empires by which Germany was overrun has proven immensely advantageous to the comfort of the masses.

Carlsruhe seems more a town of wealthy burghers and students than of manufactures. It is clean, and has a domestic air not found in any of the Swiss-German cities. It is a city of art schools, libraries, and a vast polytechnic, with seven hundred students. What laborers I saw seemed to be working leisurely on expensive new houses; there is a calm, sleepy, pulseless indolence in the place that invites repose, yet the institutions of learning indicate exceptional prosperity. These attractions and architectural wonders of harmony and style loudly proclaim the difference between the simplicity of republics and the extravagance of monarchies. The American city passenger cars that pass my window, the happy children on their way to school, with their shining, morning faces,—carrying the same description of satchel we see at home, and whistling the same airs we hear there,—and the well-dressed wayfarers recall keenly similar sights in Philadelphia. There is less character in dress and habits here than in Italy or Switzerland, yet human costumes and customs are very much alike everywhere. Germany differs from France, as Berks County differs from Philadelphia; as, indeed, plain people differ from polished ones; yet for all this disparity there is infinite grandeur in the palaces and parks of the old dismantled nobility, and in the great public edifices they erected when they were lords and masters of the multiplicity of German duchies and towns.

The estates of the present Grand Duke, that is the palace and parks, may be said to occupy the acropolis or central point of a district from which the city diverges in front, while the hunting-grounds of Hardwald spread out to the rear. The castle and its appendages,—dining, banqueting, and reception halls,—sumptuously appointed, form a semicircle, with the stables on the east and the court theatre on the right, which is still used for public amusements. Here is another of those monuments of regal folly in a town of limited population, with a highly finished exterior; the pediment containing reliefs of Goethe, Schiller, Mozart, Beethoven, and Gluck, while the interior is only a repetition of all those highly embellished public structures so abundant on the Continent. The palace gardens are as exquisite in fountains, statues, gay flower-plots, palm-houses, and orangeries as a freshly painted scene in a glowing play. The flag was flying from the turret to indicate the duke's presence; a detachment of German soldiers was at the main gate as we entered, and the sovereign's three hundred servants at their many vocations, yet with all there was a pronounced air of indolence about the palace as we sauntered through the halls and art gallery enjoying the gems of the modern German school. Most of the paintings are from the pencil of the former and present director of the Carlsruhe Academy, though there are some few by the older Dutch artists, Jan Steen and Rembrandt. But Carlsruhe being an art city with an art quarter, and a galaxy of studios gathered in one corner of the town, patronizes and encourages principally the modern school and the rising aspirants. Rhenish art is progressing rapidly now in all the larger German cities, as we notice in the architecture as well as in painting.

Military guards were stationed all about the vast palace grounds, still there were no signs of activity, no guests, and no evidences of a family. At length I came across one of the young scions of the noble house playing with a ball on a back porch, yet playing in a restrained way, as if he had been imbued, by long and thorough instruction, with the thought that to surrender himself to his impulses and sportive desires would be to degrade his dignity; and so the boy grows up never to know what true, blithe, heedless, unambitious childhood is; childhood with mud and mire, patched breeches and tops, scuffed boots and scarred hands. The absence of all life and hilarity seemed to be the normal condition of the regal home; yet there were other evidences of high and luxurious living in the presence of the paper-capped French *chef* and his corps. As the son-in-law of the Emperor of Germany, and the descendant of the Grand Dukes of Baden, he is perhaps entitled to exceptional advantages, but the visit made rather a sad impression. Here was the throne-room of the Kaiser, when he came to his daughter's palace, with a suite of luxurious apartments, yet all deserted and silent, waiting as it were for the visit that is not paid but once a year. The Duke is fortunate in his near relation to the reigning family of the empire, and in his fidelity to the German cause which made its many principalities one in the struggle twelve years ago. Others fled to the side of Austria, or faltered, and suffered in consequence of their defection, but the Grand Duke of Baden remained true, and is now rewarded by the confidence of his king and the love of his people.

What with his servants, and hundred carriages, and eighty horses, and contingent of invited guests, the Duke must spend every year a large fortune. When we reflect how many such establishments exist throughout the Continent and the British Isles, do we longer doubt there is justice in the wail of those who demand a redistribution of the accumulated wealth of the world?

LETTER LXX.

> A blended glory spread around—
> The workshop of imperial mind—
> Goethe has made it holy ground,
> And Luther sacred to mankind.
> ANONYMOUS.

FRANKFORT-ON-MAIN, July, 1878.

OUR route from Carlsruhe to Frankfort carried us through a country closely connected with the history of American independence. And though Heidelberg was the first and chief feature, the Grand Duchy of Hesse holds a dearer place in the heart of my nation. They are both pregnant of history. Heidelberg through its illustrious university; Darmstadt, capital of Hesse, has a different claim upon our regard: the one has given us great scholars, lights to science and art; the other sustained an equivocal relation to the American struggle for equality and independence.

Heidelberg is no longer an exclusive nursery of *savants;* it has been modernized by a brisk commerce, and has lost much of its precious literary character. The aged dust of centuried learning has been swept away by the besom of trade, the clouds of golden lore have evaporated, musty professors have been pushed aside by bustling merchants, and the odor of books has been replaced by the variety of other manufactures. The University, though still enjoying an attendance of seven hundred students, is bereft of its former prestige. The castle, a monument of the thirteenth century, is like Kenilworth, a vast ruin; having been the prey of vandal hordes for five hundred years, the victim of great fires, and finally the target of the lightning bolt. The student reads in it the progress of the feudal ages, and in its ivy-hung remains contrasts the eternal rejuvenescence of nature and the instability of the proudest monuments erected by human hands to human glory. All the old influences seem to have died with the years. The embers now only smoulder amongst the ashes of forgotten learning and perished royalty.

Still the vicinity of Heidelberg is thronged by visitors in the season, but the busiest places are the well-ordered hotels. The sparkling waters and wooded heights and green forests are like so many fresh maidens, with all the exhilarating fascination of their pastoral home, still untarnished by the glare of metropolitan gaslight and the taint of social familiarity, proving the eternal youth of a recreative world.

Now Darmstadt has a population twice the number of Heidelberg, and as a natural sequence has quite a municipal attraction. In its handsome streets, fine squares, noble pleasure-grounds, valuable library, galleries of pictures, antiquities, and coins, a theatre, a palace, and the usual appurtenances of royal towns, it offers mostly the charm sought by tourists in greater cities. The whole neighborhood is crowded with the remains of the residences of nobility, reviving the harsh features of the olden time, when the masses were ruled by a few famous families, who enjoyed life without labor, and governed without brains. I think Germany was more subject to the feudal system than even France, at least there remain sterner evidences of the fact. Can we speak of liberty in a government where the land is owned and dominion vested in a few, while the people are ground to the earth by military exaction and taxation?

Modern Germany is a vast improvement on the past. Its literature is more powerful, its music more penetrating, its statesmanship more influential, its art more self-asserting, its manufactures more stupendous, than at any former period; and, though still a huge military nation, and a great barrack from Bohemia to the North Sea, still a mighty force for good, more useful to civilization than Austria, more progressive than Russia, and, of course, a resistless opposite to the fading and enervated country of the Turk. What struck me as I dwelt upon Darmstadt was that the people of Hesse should have been willing to fight for their old Grand Duke more than a hundred years ago, not for the wages paid to themselves, but to fasten English slavery upon the American colonies, and to let those wages go into the pockets of their local chiefs, who sold them for so much a head to the Hanoverian Georges. And yet from these very Hessians, and the redemptioners that came after them, our country received the founders of some of our most useful families. Pennsylvania was particularly reinforced by this element.

With such reflections I came into Frankfort, with its long and brilliant record as one of the free towns of the German confederation. It dates from the time of Charlemagne, and the atmosphere of wealth and dignity which pervades it is not only an indication of its commercial importance, but of its long continued financial ascendency and political independence. The influences that made Frankfort what it is, are patriotism, wealth, industry, energy, and commerce.

Frankfort is a royal garrison town set in a broad plain in the very heart of the Taunus range, that seems to close over it, and at the same time affords a multitude of leafy retreats where the rich Frankforters pass their summers. The city proper lies on the right bank of the Main; on the left is its suburb, that seems inhabited by quite another community. While the streets in the old portion of the town are crooked, narrow, dark, and dirty, those in the newer sections are broad, with an expression of perspective, flanked by handsome structures, florid with the art of the Renaissance, odorous and inviting by the many open squares planted with trees, where the winds from the bleak heights of the Taunus rustle among the full foliage and beautiful shadowed avenues, where the *belles petites* of the city saunter or linger under the great spreading branches, closely resembling in face and costume our better-class women at home. They are not walking advertisements like the fast Frenchwomen or the painted houris of London. Removed from the old cramped byways of the city, with their storied precincts, antique architecture, and commercial wharves, is the new Opera House, with its wealth of sculpture, columns and capitals, and its fine broad streets and extravagant houses, occupied by the uppertendom and foreign embassies. It is like a paradise, but it is very far away from all that tells us of Guttenburg, Faust, Goethe, or the Rothschilds.

Frankfort has many striking attractions, some of them worthy of a far more pretentious city. Next to the new Opera House, the Frankforter Hof, a hotel of fine proportions, is the boldest example. The old streets are alive with ancient story and renown. The house in which the original Rothschilds was born and lived, with its high steps and flat awkward façade, opposite an open platz, where the square-hipped women sold wilted vegetables in the twilight as I rode by, had a tongue for every stone, telling tales of the founder of the great Hebrew house of Mammon; the princes who deal with empires and kings as if they were so many figures on the great political chessboard. I was shown the house, 148 Judenstrasse, in which the progenitor of the gold-coining race lived, in the days when the Jews were closed within their own squalid purlieus every evening at eight o'clock, and throughout the entire Sabbath and holidays were not allowed to venture about the city under penalty of a heavy fine. This nefarious custom prevailed until the present century in the free city of Frankfort, and now the Rothschilds, who once were prisoners in their own city, not only wield sovereign power with their millions and billions, but occupy their place in parliaments, while their sons and daughters are gladly welcomed in marriage with the noblest families. Protestant sentiments hold dominion in Frankfort, but the great number of resident Hebrews is readily seen by a visit to any of the public resorts, where they compose the better part of the attendance. This proscribed race now rank amongst the best musicians, authors, painters, orators, statesmen, historians, scientists, and philosophers, not only in these Teutonic districts, but all over Europe.

In this same tumble-down, unswept, and ungarnished quarter are mementos of greater ones than the lordly money-changers. Opposite the northeast corner of the old cathedral stands an archaic slate-covered house, bearing a grotesque marble effigy and a Latin inscription upon its face. From a window in this antique structure the celebrated religious reformer addressed the multitudes on his way to Worms, and from the window still looks the face of Martin Luther in all its quaint and ludicrous stoniness. The house where the poet Goethe was born is more of an object of attraction than the superb colossal monument, with its allegorical reliefs and its chaste illustrations of his poems, to his glory, in the platz adjoining the Rossmarket, where is the massive cenotaph of Guttenberg, holding his types and surrounded by statues of other masters of the art preservative of all arts. Here then were the four monarchs of their day and time; Rothschilds, the father of the money kings; Luther, father of Protestant reform; Goethe, the father of poetic philosophy; and Guttenberg, the inventor of the art of printing.

These monuments and their pendent historical incidents suggested many pleasant reflections, but my visit to the Romerberg and its market-place in front, and its collection of wretched portraits in the *kaisersalle*, was a dismal disenchantment. I threaded my way through many dirty streets until I came to a great open, dusty, rusty, moth-eaten square and an equally decaying temple, which had lofty gables and broad doorways standing open. I entered the gaping vestibule or arcades,—all damp and dark and grimy. At first I thought it the rendezvous of rats, and imagined lizards and loathsome insects playing in and out the chinks of the pavement and walls after nightfall. I ascended a broad stair to my right and entered the *kaisersalle* or gallery of emperors, on the first floor. The portraits from the day of Charlemagne are without exception bad, yet precious to the mind, as every individual who entered that saloon was watched by two German women as if each was a famous professional thief. No one was allowed to make his exit until he had contributed something to the support of the sentinels of these travesties of the early German rulers. The strategy was only another version of the spider and the fly story. The Romerberg is the market place of every public rejoicing, and another of the former prescribed precincts of the Jews.

But there is one real work of art here, the inspiration of genius,—the group of "Ariadne on the Panther." This chaste and artistic fancy of Danneker is shown in an alcove of Mr. Bethman's museum. That gentleman purchased it for the sum of twenty thousand florins, and preserves it and several lesser casts and carvings in an addition to his own residence. The crimson drapery of the tabernacle was drawn aside by an old servant of the house, and the famous group appeared like a frozen poem in a sort of transcendent golden light, or *fata morgana*, that enveloped it and floated about it, yet every line and curve of the marble shone as distinctly as if it were cut in the strange amber glare. It had all the glow of life, and as the figure revolved upon the pivot of the pediment I imagined I could see the sinews of the limbs contract and relax, and the flesh quiver. The easy and mobile pose of the figure, the graceful lines, the almost sentient stone, the double poetry of life and beauty, the varied phases of expression, prove not alone the idealism of the artist, but the growing influence of his work. It has the great and enduring virtue that even the most celebrated conceptions of our modern artists lack,—it is not too large for a perfect type of womanhood. The limbs of the divinity are rather small and round, with that expression of luscious pliancy that we expect as the chief charm of the ideal woman. We never find the old marbles of the Greeks with rigidly curved limbs and a nether jaw that proclaims determination of purpose. Praxiteles and Phidias never made their Venuses and Junos after the pattern of an Amazon. The Goddess of Love, or the Angel Purity, the muses of Art and Music, were not created to fight wars and harrow up vast fields of agriculture. We must come to the later works to find conceptions of herculean strength and limbs that seem to have been developed in a calisthenic school.

LETTER LXXI.

The gambler with his dice has fled,
And pure and sweet now lies the land,
Where sweetest flowers their fragrance shed,
And grape vines wreathe in gold and purple band.
ANONYMOUS.

WEISBADEN, July, 1878.

HERE is another exquisite offspring of the gaming system. A fashionable German spa, a finished watering-place, a modern cluster of luxurious homes and lazy resorts, with none of the soft shadows of a pastoral retreat and with none of the gray tone that comes with age. A city that has sprung up since the era of electricity and steam; that looks as if it had been expressly constructed to please the tastes of the meretricious element that took possession of it before the fraternity of hazard was expelled from the kingdom, and as if its cost had been paid for out of their pockets. And though there is no bustle in the streets, everything looks new and garnished like a decoration for a holiday. Every one passes by with an invalid or indolent air, and many of the men on the streets have the easy, audacious, well-dressed, well-fed look of gamblers; such men as we have all seen at great stations and hotels; loungers, with an inert, supine expression; grand in flashing diamonds, glazed shirt-fronts, flashy neckerchiefs, hair oiled, and arranged after the latest tonsorial style, exquisitely trimmed finger-tips, and as they pass, the atmosphere is rife with the subtleties of frangipanni, ylang-ylang, or musk.

There are great hotels, parks where the ladies sun themselves after thermal baths, and sweet, secluded walks over an iron portico to the Trinkhalle, and Cursaal grounds glowing in flowering parterres, that are apt to chase away all morbid or immoral reflections; yet I cannot help the conviction that there is still a substratum of the old social composite underlying the present quiet affectation of convalescence.

Still there are many beautiful villas bordering the town, and excursions to the adjacent heights of Sonnenberg, Neroberg, and the Platte; or to the sanitary baths and waters of Schlangenbad and Schwalbach, both lying in green valleys noted for their medicinal and curative properties. The air at all of these health spas is clear and invigorating, though situated in dales richly wooded; and the bridle and carriage paths of the mountains afford rare views of the Rhine and Main, and the surrounding country, as we rise and fall with the undulations of the road; now in a narrow valley with comfort and plenty about us; and then on the hilltop, where the vines are trained to the summit, and the road cut through the fruitful vineyard, held at figures that would appear enough to purchase the rich acres themselves.

The ride from Frankfort to Wiesbaden is a short journey of an hour and a quarter, through a district literally bursting with the varied wealth of a bounteous and bountiful nature. The railway is one of the oldest in Germany, and its branches are numerous, reaching many historic towns and Roman settlements in the time of the Cæsars. A good story is afloat of General and Mrs. Grant while at Homberg, the most popular watering-place in the Rhineland. There are many remains of the Roman occupation before the Christian era; on a wooded height about one and three-fourths miles from the resort there is what once was an archaic cemetery. A number of tombs were excavated in the presence of the ex-President, and the urns containing the human ashes found in excellent preservation; the Roman coin placed on the lid of the burial vase according to Pagan custom, to pass the body of the deceased over the river Styx, still remained, and as the exhumer handed it to General Grant, he quietly remarked to his friend, General Badeau, "They are evidently not taking toll down there now."

Many amusing paragraphs are told of the soldier-President's visit to Europe. He has been highly and constantly honored. Kings, courts, parliaments, and great communities have been spontaneous in their tributes, yet through them all he has remained the same unaffected and unobtrusive republican. His reticence has been at times painful in the midst of noisy speeches, high-flown compliments, and the blazon of pageantry. It has even given offence to those who expected some demonstration in return for their loud welcome.

In passing from the red wines of Southern France and Italy to the white wines of the Rhine and Moselle, there is as great a difference in the growth and training of the vines as there is in the juice they yield. In the Hockheimer district, where the celebrated sparkling hock is manufactured, the vine is grown on tall arbors more closely resembling the American plant; and so valuable is this particular species that when the railroad was surveyed through the section, the contractors agreed to pay over two dollars and a quarter for each vine removed or destroyed during the necessary excavations. This was over forty years ago; to-day the wine ranks among the finest growths of the Rhine. So Wiesbaden is a prosperous, elegant town, and the centre of a region of surpassing fertility and loveliness. The climate is more perfect—that is, more healthful—than the southern countries, but it has nothing of the feverish, intoxicating influence of the regions bordering the Mediterranean and Ionian waters. Here we have an atmosphere that energizes and nerves the natives to labor; south, the world-famed salubrity enervates and renders slothful not only the sons of the soil but all who linger within its shadow.

Here orchards, vineyards, and mineral springs are the gifts of generous nature, while wide and sweeping roads, white and glittering palaces, and ranks of gigantic broadspread trees encircling green squares, radiant flowerpatches, and silvery fountains are the achievements of man.

Everywhere one may turn in Wiesbaden there is lavish proof of the gambler's liberality. Before the Emperor William closed them out they had already beautified the little German resort in many ways, and the monuments of their affluence are not only preserved, but supplemented by the city with new splendors.

In the grand hall of the Cursaal there are instrumental

concerts every Friday, and dancing every Saturday. But the park adjoining the long building is a much more popular rendezvous than the conversation hall. I walked among its gay parterres in the darkness of night, with nothing but the groups of lamps along the lake margin and the twinkling stars overhead to light up the glistening waters, where the white swans paddled and floated like animated snowdrifts, and the complete combinations of floriculture rose in mounds of bloom. The skill displayed in weaving the flowers by the scientific process of sowing the seed in particular devices has been reduced to the elegance of written characters; and as I passed away from the perfumed alleys the strains of the delicious music in the adjacent building came floating through the pines and dropped into the water like the melodious tinkle of liquid bells. I crossed the way, and under the shadow of the laurel and oleander, in large green tubs that stand close to the windows of the great hotels, I watched the pedestrians. Where were they all going? Very few females, but battalions of male stragglers fashioned after the model I have already presented.

Through a beautiful valley in the full flush of the summer afternoon I sought the Greek chapel. It is midway up the Neroberg, and we rode through vineyards, with here and there a little group of white cottages, like a flock of doves nestled in a dale between the hills, making a miniature world and community of its own. Then upon the summit of an elevation, over which the ripe fruit clambered in riotous confusion, stood a spacious stone mansion, the home of the princely owner of the rich lands it overlooked. It was very regal and exclusive in its majestic solitude, but it seemed cold and isolated at its height, while the cluster of humble homes below shone in the warmth of happy domesticity.

The chapel, erected by the Duke of Nassau in commemoration of his Muscovite wife, containing her mausoleum, stands alone upon a smoothly-shaven mound. In the form of a Greek cross, it is surmounted by five mosque domes or minaret towers, sparkling in golden contrast to the pallid façade. The interior is dazzling with decorations and the rich stuffs of White Russia. The floors, walls, and ceilings of pure white marble glow in stained glass and precious stones, enamelled screens from the native home of the duchess, and in a recess reclines the full-length monumental figure of the princess herself. Upon either side of the sarcophagus are statuettes of the twelve apostles, and at the corners sit the holy quartette, Faith, Hope, Charity, and Immortality; in the circle above soar angels, while between the arches stand the prophets and evangelists,— a costly, chaste, and highly suggestive combination of royal wealth and taste, and a fitting tribute to the pure daughter of the house of Romanoff. Yet the Duke married again and espoused the cause of Austria in 1866, and is now a fugitive in a foreign land, though still esteemed by the community to which he left a perennial source of profit in the souvenir to his dead spouse.

LETTER LXXII.

"I saw the blue Rhine sweep along—I heard, or seemed to hear,
The German songs we used to sing, in chorus sweet and clear,
And down the pleasant river, and up the slanting hill,
The echoing chorus sounded through the evening calm and still."
CAROLINE NORTON.

COLOGNE, August, 1878.

The sweetest memory I have of Wiesbaden is the odorous path over which we rode to Biebrich-on-the-Rhine. Although the first of August the air was as fresh and exhilarating as the last of September; for in these conservative countries we have all the glorious refocillating tone of autumn while our American friends are languishing in the lassitude of the so-called dog-days. With our baggage in a comfortable carriage we posted across a level highway, flanked by full-leaved chestnut trees, heavy with half-ripened fruit. The scene was not so picturesque and graceful as the French, nor so glowing and spirituelle as the Italian, nor so wild as the Swiss, but every rood was marked by the same German care and thrift. The ride was not long enough to prove tedious, and, when I reached the steamer station at Biebrich, I was eager to obtain my introduction to the much-sung stream of poets and troubadours. Mounting the upper deck of the "Merkins," that came puffing and propelling its huge and ungainly carcass through the dark waters, I was brought face to face with another magnificent estate of the Grand Duke of Nassau.

The deserted palace, and vast demesne stretching along the river shore, and extending far back into farm-lands and forests, is another proof that, until the consolidation of Germany, he was the good shepherd of all this district; he gave much and when expatriated he left much, as if to show that even in his banishment he desired to be remembered in his solitary gardens and vacant palaces. The terraces of the long barracks of buildings overlook the Rhine, while for a mile rearward a well-kept park grows into a mammoth picture, with its majestic timber and dense foliage lighted up by glowing flower-beds, where smooth walks and drives dissect well-shaven lawns, murmurous with the silver harmony of cascades and fountains, and sparkling with the glisten of marbles. And these, with the interior beauties of the mansion, are left alone to gladden the senses of strangers, in care of the servants and workmen retained by the luxurious exile.

The day, that had been cool and rayless as we rode through the sweet chestnut groves, had settled into a dull, disagreeable drizzle as we coursed up the Rhine. Perhaps the dismal atmosphere exercised a pronounced influence in disenchanting me with the historied water; or, perhaps, my expectations had swollen unreasonably with the ebullition of my fancy; but the afternoon was bad, the waters black, and the expected beauty vanished. I looked in vain for the sapphire blue in the stream over which I sailed; but, alas! I discovered no tone or shade that I might etherealize in even my wildest flights of imagination. The waters were not only dark with storm, but had a gray and grimy tone, as if full of alluvium, or a mountain deposit constantly drifting down from the Swiss Alps, borne in the torrents from St. Gothard's, or carried in the wake of the Rheinwald glaciers.

There is no beauty of flow nor majesty of volume to lend dignity to the stream. Strip it of its legends, its ruins standing on every side like grim skeletons of faded glory, its unequalled vines of Rheingau, its forests of Neiderwald, its castled crags of Drachenfels, and we would have nothing but a very contracted, sluggish current, crawling like a torpid serpent through a country really tropical in its profuse growth of the grape. The river seems as if it had drunk itself stupid with the juice of the seductive vine.

The course of the iron road follows the water's edge on either side; now and then we see the great mechanical fiery horse vanish into what I at first supposed to be the remains of some regal home of the centuries,—of which only a Gothic arch and a few towers remained,—and, being lost to us for a few seconds, emerge on the opposite side, and after passing a succession of these pretty cathedral domes and turrets, I discovered they were the entrances and exits to the tunnels through mountains jutting into the water. They are fresh and ornate with a vast deal of architecture, and seem a fitting place of worship for the limited population of the wine district. One little town after another studs the shore like white dots upon a green and golden surface; —hamlets of 600 to 1000 vine-growers and wine-makers. Yet the homes of the humble and the continuity of the small tracts in which the precious and costly Rhine wine is grown, seemed scarcely more frequent than the great estates of the German nobility,—alternately decaying and blossoming.

The boats are pleasant,—when I say pleasant, I do not mean that they approach the fresh-water steamers of America, but an improvement on the transport that brought me from Schaffhausen to Constance. The travellers of the best class Germans, largely interwoven with foreign tourists, were as well dressed, polite and deferential as the French, but the absence of the Gallic gabble and the all-pervading guttural Teuton spoken by cultivated women and men proclaims the perponderance of the classic German domination at Berlin, and the bold self-assertion of the German race.

The ride upon the Rhine was a revelation and a perennial fount of study, meditation, and speculation; from the chief lower embarkature at Mayence to Cologne it is crowded with incident and history and novelty to the stranger, and while my mind wandered and wondered over each consecutive event, the Germans between whom I was mortised were indifferent to their own traditions. Though I had read much of the mystic origin of the Rhine, and of its equally abstruse termination,—as no drop empties into the sea,—of its varied and rich products, and of its feudal castles and battlements, yet I had the craving curiosity for a more intimate knowledge of the historic *locale.*

The slopes of Johannisberger and Steinberger are small stretches, where the vines are grown upon terraced rocks and tended principally by monks; and the vineyards overlooked by the gray and rugged towers of the castles. Each small town has its special vine territory, but these two are the rival deities of the bacchanalian area. The old fort, "Cat," and the Mouse Tower, may be interesting objects to the average traveller, but this marvellous wine-yielding country can never lose point to the student.

The light white wines of the vicinage are the beverage, and while many have gained popularity from their intrinsic value, many owe much of their exalted reputation to their name. The Leibfraumilch, a Rhenish-Hessen wine, sells here for figures it no more commands by its superiority of quality alone than the Lachryma Christi of Italy. The Moselle wines,—and the sparkling ones are really fine,—are chiefly cultivated among the slate rocks. Champagne is a rare product of the Rhine, though there is a mammoth establishment in the environs of Wiesbaden. Sparkling wines are grown at Mayence, Hockheim, Rudesheim, Coblentz, and, indeed, in all the wine country, but the vintages are always small, and must of necessity be very far below the quantity that floods the different countries and is consumed under the original label sold here.

But this universal and plenary adaptation of the grape-juice has a beneficial effect upon the community. The light French, German, and Italian wines are procured for a trifle by the lower classes in their districts; they invigorate, but do not inebriate, and in these countries there is little or no intoxication. Brandy is rare wherever wine is the growth of the neighborhood, and even beer is rejected by the laboring classes. Those two busy Bs, that have wrought so much havoc and anguish in England and at home, are here unable to work their mischief side-by-side with the pure juice of the fruit, distilled from the fair fields of the Rhine, the Moselle, the Rhone, and the classic streams of Illyria. The climate is so conservative and healthful, the inhabitants so moderate, industrious, and frugal, that the wild emotions engendered by brandy, or the phlegmatic indolence born of beer, find no more constituency here than riotous saturnalias found among the Arcadians.

The Rhine abounds in pleasant retreats and villas of wealthy foreigners, old as the Mediterranean and the Alpine lakes. Dismantled castles and ruined fortresses are not alone the features of the celebrated stream; and had I never heard through poet or author or historian of the trascendent country, with its gentle vales lying between projecting rocks and fierce heights, the literature sold upon the boat and at the stations, as profuse as the tracts with which the passengers are bombarded *en route* to Monte Carlo, would have told me the most flattering tales of the enchanted region. Byron, Bulwer, and the Hon. Mrs. Norton are still conspicuous and popular. Here are the castles, and here the poets and poems glorifying the castles, each with its history, and each with its romance, each in the midst of a valuable region, each with its neighborhood nobility, and all photographed *ad nauseam*.

We came into Coblentz just as the Catholic church bells were chiming six, and in the sweet evening the melody fell over the water and rang through the hills as harmoniously as it had upon the holy lakes of Italy. At the confluence of the Rhine and Moselle, backed by hedging vineyards mountainward, the little Romish town lies in a triangular basin. Before me, on the opposite bank of the river, rose the massive and formidable fortress of Ehrenbreitstein. Rock upon rock was piled in the air, and fortification upon fortification reared their gray watches higher and higher, until mountain and stronghold seemed to have been created at one birth. I looked at the mighty bulwarks, and I looked at the guard, and I saw nothing else until the misty veil of twilight wrapped all nature in clouds.

Four miles from Coblentz, on a summit above the hamlet of Capellen, rise the spires and towers of Stolzenfels, palace of the Empress Augusta. On a beautiful Sabbath I rode over hill and dale; through vine arbors and golden wheat-fields; over broad table-lands, where not even carriage-wheels nor horses' hoofs had marked a path; over stretches of emerald herbage and by the rugged mountain-base, higher and further until the Rhine and Moselle lay sparkling beds of crystal below, while we were within the wall of the Fort Kaiser Alexander, where the guards were taking their humble meal of porridge, or washing their white jackets upon the rough stones. The village of Cappellen is a straight row of houses facing the railway. The ascent of Stolzenfels is made from here either on foot or "mit de donkeys," as the guard in charge informed us. The donkeys are miserable, browbeaten little creatures, decked as gayly as Alpine shepherdesses, and trot over the precipitous paths on their spindle-legs regardless of sharp corners, deep gorges, or perilous ledges. It does not require any particular equestrian talent to ride one of these tasselled and rosetted animals, as a neat little chair is fastened to his back for the tourist, and a peasant boy, to tickle the creature into wakefulness, acts as guide. The path was good, and as it was a gradual ascent of 310 feet above the Rhine I confidently depended upon Shank's mare. The pull was arduous, but I managed to keep pace with the visitors who preferred the mules. At last the plateau crowned by the machicolated battlements, and the hoary chapel steeples, was reached, and the doors opened unto us by the lady castellan; the baffled bullet of Nobling had prevented the royal family from occupying their summer home, so the brilliant chateau was left in the hands of the seneschals.

I entered a large vestibule, and in one corner saw twenty or more pairs of white felt moccasins, which each of the visitors was requested to don before entering the polished floors of parquetry in the several banquet and reception saloons. There are many historic suits of armor, the halberds and matchlocks of a hundred kings, and paintings by all the best Lowland artists. There are six memorial pictures relative to chivalry in the smaller salon, that could not but impress the stranger; they are of the Rhenish school, yet aglow with all the dazzling radiance of Rubens; Faith, illustrated by Godfrey de Bouillon at the Holy Sepulchre; Justice, typified by Rudolph of Hapsburg sitting in judgment on robber knights; Poetry, troubadours with Philip of Swabia and his queen on a pleasure excursion on the Rhine; Love, the Emperor Frederick welcoming his bride; Loyalty, Hermann von Siebeneichen sacrificing his life to save Frederick Barbarossa; Bravery, blind King John of Bohemia at the battle of Crecy; but, above all these, there is one, a fresco in the chapel, of Adam and Eve whose memory, like the wrinkles of care, will grow deeper with the years.

Stolzenfels overlooks the termination of the most romantic and contracted valley of the Rhine, and all the beauty of the section seems concentred at its feet and about its top. Churches stand at the marriage of the waters; pilgrim shrines upon rock-bound summits; quondam convents upon isolated islands; and back of all, beyond all, and above all, the impenetrable Ehrenbreitstein frowning; formidable in its proportions, sublime in its majesty.

The palace of the regal pair in the city is bowered in groves and gardens, and surrounded in the flowery walks thrown open to the people. Like most of the royal homes it is maintained in silent and vacant grandeur. Still though the monarchs cannot occupy their many castles, the many pleasant tales of the benevolence of the empress to her subjects somewhat temper the mad extravagance of this opulent and aristocratic system.

Upon the bridge of boats leading to the portals of Ehrenbreitstein I waited in the midday sun half an hour while a succession of craft drifted up and down the stream; the ascent is tedious, and though the grim fortress evokes a mingling of admiration and awe, it is sure to become tiresome to the American because of the omnipresence of military power. A fee for entrance goes to the treasury of the disabled veterans, and after passing an ostentatious succession of bars and barricades, and foolish fanfaronade, we made the ascent of the vantage-ground, where the young soldiers were drilling on the topmost parade, while others were beating their clothing clean on the crude stones near the pumps; Sunday seems to be wash-day in the garrisons. These poor fellows go through the dismal monotony of their slavery to the Emperor, and are remunerated with three or five cents a day for their services; while of such subjects as do not enter the army, the males are obliged to pay a tax of twelve dollars a year, and the females three. Well may we call our country free, and well may the poor of foreign nations hail it as a salvation where we have no great army to eat away the substance of the public weal, no tremendous forts guarded by gangs of martial serfs, and no tax upon the working classes, who cannot, either from their condition or their sex, become soldiers. View Ehrenbreitstein from the lower opposite only; from that point it inspires every lofty sentiment; we see only what is grand and fascinating because seemingly unattainable, and like one of the enchanted watch-towers of a fairy tale that might only be approached by supernatural aid; but having scaled its height and viewed its military discipline, there is a poison of imperative rule making the whole atmosphere a pestilence.

Waiting for the boat to go to Cologne, I studied a group of peasants on the quay. In all these countries the lower classes adhere to the dress of their station with apparent pride. Whether it be a white ribbon twisted in their hair, a blue blouse, a silver clasp in their plaits, or a blue kerchief about their necks, it is universally and happily adopted by the same damsel who would in America ape her mistress's train, and puffs, and bangles, and bang, three weeks after stepping from the emigrant ship.

From Coblentz to Cologne I found the country flatter and less interesting than the first part of my Rhine journey, and marked by a strange geological formation of pumice-stone. Many of the towns are attractive, but the nearer one draws to Cologne the more evident becomes the fact that you are passing from the land of the vine. Soon after leaving Coblentz, the seven mountains, Drachenfels, and other points made familiar by pen and pencil, showed themselves in undisputed position. Great crowds came on the steamer from their summer holiday, again presenting to view the better classes of Germany. Coming from their day's outing as they were, there was no sign of dissipation, nor the slightest degree of excess; many ladies bore the mark of high distinction, with all the grace of quiet dignity, which is ever more attractive than idle volubility.

As we approached Bonn, the university town, the trade of the country seemed to be rather in slate and a peculiar white stone, partaking of the volcanic character of the region, and used largely for building purposes. In the twilight this interesting city seemed much more populous than represented. Near all these German towns there are old palaces, monuments, extinct mines, and any number of ecclesiastical remains. Bonn was one of the first Roman fortresses, and is spoken of by Tacitus, and in its ancient minster several of its early German kings were crowned. In science, art, classical learning, and in general acquirement, this collegiate city maintains a high celebrity. It has recently become a favorite residence of the English, and now, lighted by a young moon, the steamer, after depositing most of her passengers, glided on to Cologne.

LETTER LXXIII.

"As I am rhymer,
And now, at least, a merry one,
Mr. Munis Rudisheimer
And the church of St. Geryon,
Are the two things alone,
That deserve to be known,
In the body- and soul-stinking town of Cologne."
COLERIDGE.

COLOGNE, August, 1878.

FAR off I saw the many lights of a great town, casting their yellow glare out upon the water, and defining clearly the contour of the semicircular city,—mirroring it against the fervent sky and dark-purple water as it never could have appeared to me had I not entered it by river and by night. From its shore it seemed a wild, rollicking place, and as I stepped upon its wharf—Sunday though it was—my conjectures were confirmed; the town was in general carnival. The riotous clatter of the streets seemed as if the entire population and its 14,000 troops in garrison were indulging in fierce saturnalia. Across the Rhine I heard the noisy brass band, and saw the moving figures in the jocund booths through the glittering lamps, while from the adjacent houses floated the hoarse voices of dissipated men and the shrill shrieks of excited women, making night hideous and our route a terror. In the military town the wildest license prevailed. The quarter about the wharves, through which we passed, was evidently infected by the most degenerate part of the community, judging by the *fracas*, and the soldiers that should have preserved order only added trumpet-tongued obscenity to the fray. It impressed one rather as a city just invaded by a conquering host, and in the hands of pillagers, than a quiet German town whose commerce had faded, where military rule reigns supreme. Nor was it any better when we at last reached the Hotel du Nord, a magnificent stone structure, with towering portals, stone corridors and stairways like a palace, and a busy court, with an odd boisterous medley of soldiers, servants, tourists going and coming, and the confusion of travel, like a world on wheels. Here I had gotten into another pandemonium of anarchy and tempest; a whirlpool, where symmetry and system were utterly ignored.

The Hotel du Nord is to Cologne what the Fifth Avenue is to New York, but the difference is as widespread as a cathedral to a madhouse. Porters in the act of precipitating huge burdens upon travellers, waiters rushing to and fro, and the manager screaming in a jargon of tongues, whilst in the midst of the imbroglio stands the startled guest tired and tossed and stunned. The architecture of the hotel is fresh and florid, seeming a work of the period when Cologne was in the flush of enthusiasm for Gothic art; while the upholstering decorations of the best chambers are as beautiful and expensive as palace adornments. But with all this prodigality and culture of art there was the plebeian tone that comes with indecorum, and the mercenary management of a proprietor who a few years ago was head-waiter, and who now "runs" it, not for the comfort of his guests but to fill his own coffers. The house crowds the profits of a year into three months, and hence the wild caravansera of Cologne. Its motto is: rapidity of action; the result: inattention, disorder, ill-manners, and interminable delay. The riotous scene at *table d'hôte* yesterday was a subject for Hogarth, and the ludicrous opposite to the graceful courtesy and refined plenty of the splendid establishment, the Cavour in Milan. There is a classic elegance pervading Northern Italy and the shores of Southern France met in no other Continental country. Be it only a flagon of Vesuvio or Capri for fifty centimes, a kilo of black bread, a blade of garlic, or a wafer of Bologna sausage, taken at the base of the volcano, or in the stableyard of a roadside inn of the Appian Way, there is an attic grace in the refined poverty, a mystic picturesqueness in the surroundings, which even the impurity and degeneracy of the lower classes of Italy cannot dispel. There is a certain luscious, luxurious ease and elegance never attained or approached by the same orders in Germany, where frolic is vulgar and poverty offensive.

I can look from my window at the interminable review of military in the great square of the Cathedral, and then watch the long line of plumed troops clatter over the iron bridge and dissolve amongst the forests and mountains across the Rhine. All day there are soldiers; and everywhere soldiers; now a great revolving train of artillery that shakes the earth like an earthquake, then a calvacade of horsemen, their iron hoofs clattering over the stones, then solid columns of infantry surging by; and all for what? Why this pestilential presence of war in a land of peace and plenty? And as I queried the kellner answered, "This martial monster is only to tax the poor, to feed royalty, to chill our hearts, to drive us from our Fatherland," and as he spoke his face glowed and his voice rang with hatred of the dark shadow of the omnipresent soldier. The gloomy raven saddens and maddens them and makes them an indifferent and dissatisfied people.

The Cathedral at Cologne is the offspring of Gothic art in the Middle Ages, which having passed through six centuries of gestation, is still incomplete. It is called the most magnificent edifice in the world; yet the architecture is not so complicated, nor has it the graceful airiness of the superb Dom at Milan, that seems a creation of the purest snow. It is the prime attraction, but its interior is most unclean. Having passed through many ages and survived revolutions it has grown old in its unfinished state. Of course, in all these years it has had a number of architects, but the schools and periods have not been mixed, although the rounded windows and doors, the groined and vaulted roofs, and the arch-connected pillars of the purely Romanesque, have been preserved. Its low naves lend a magnificent expression of distance, and its series of heights, and arches, and lofty domes a marvellous grace of altitude. This religious bauble, that has been supported by royalty, has been taken in hand by the government, and with private subscriptions and the proceeds of a lottery,—that is maintained specially to defray the pounds yet to be paid,—its completion, even to the topmost tower, is pledged within three years.

A walk through the new quarter of Cologne vividly recalls Paris; revealing a classic taste in domestic furniture, fashionable costumes, photographs, paintings, and engravings, fully equal to the local reputation for architecture and music. Long streets stretch away from the Cathedral that compare favorably, in point of shops, with Chestnut Street or Broadway, and the vast galleries making Maltese and Grecian crosses in the centre of the city, glowing in painted glass and florid capital, have cafés and bijouterie establishments that would put the gay metropolis to the blush. And in all these magazines tall bottles of the original Eau de Cologne of the old Farina firm stare one out of countenance. It is a pestilence—a sweet pestilence, nevertheless a pestilence—the way strangers are besieged by this historic manufacture from all quarters. It is the first thing thrust upon a new guest in the hotels; if he call for some personal necessity, from a pitcher of wash-water to a glass of beer, Seltzer, old rye, or Cognac, the Eau de Cologne is brought in by the answering *kellner*, and a sale is accomplished before the first desire is satisfied. Forever after he dreads the sight of the tall bottles that dress the shop-windows, or the little, wicker-covered flagons for sale. He has been deluded once, and avoids a second betrayal. There is much of the pure article to be obtained, but, like the superfluity of wines of the famous brand that float Germany, more than two-thirds of the deluge is spurious.

Cologne has, of late years, become the seat of scientific music, and it was a high plume in Gilmore's bonnet that he should have secured the applause of the citizen connoisseurs when he came over here several years ago. What of disappointment I experienced in the melody of Italy has been more than compensated by the divine harmonies of Germany. Not only is it a city of first-class musical societies and institutions, under the baton of such artists as Weber and Dr. Hiller, but the military airs, exquisitely rendered by the several bands of the German troops stationed here, are heard from *reveillé* to *tattoo;* so that with the incessant beat of the drum, toot of the fife, blare of the trumpet, and tramp of armed men, there is a surfeit of soldiers, and something too much of the whole fanfaronade. Nor do I wonder at the apparent indifference of the residents to the interminable pageant, when it is supported by the taxes and hard tasks of enforced servitude imposed upon a reluctant people.

LETTER LXXIV.

"A country that draws fifty feet of water,
In which men live as in the hold of nature;
A land that rides at anchor and is moored,
In which they do not live but go aboard."
BUTLER.

HOLLAND, August, 1878.

I FELT as I left Cologne for Amsterdam that I was descending to the seashore, and other characteristics could not have been more marked than the houses, language, dress, and currency of the Dutch. I fully realized for the first time the widespread difference between German and Dutch. The great hills and blue waters of the Rhine are lost in the low lands, the canals, the windmills, and the squatty red-roofed houses. The language is grotesque and painfully guttural, and a no nearer relation to the German than it is to the Danish or Swedish. It is not a patois or a hybrid of German as is popularly and erroneously supposed, but a cultivated dialect of purely Teutonic origin, with none of the ungrammatical features that constitute the body of a half-caste tongue. Canals and windmills are the objects of the low moorlands, and though there are many barges to enliven the waters, which are invariably covered by a green pestilential scum or stirred into muddy pools, the scene was not a pleasant one. It is all Dutch and heavy.

I was passing from the land of wine, but I was entering the heaven of painters. Yes! this very nondescript country almost gross and clownish, has an art all its own. With its other idiosyncrasies why should it not have an individual genius in its history? But the art is in pronounced contrast to the utter unsentimental face of nature in the Netherlands.

It seemed as if I had been transferred to another planet. It was all Holland, nothing of Germany was left; not even a memory, a tradition, or a custom. At the first station after crossing the Dutch frontier, the clerk in the railway office could not recognize a German gold piece; hesitated, and was obliged to call the entire official staff into council before he consented to change it into Holland coin. I had a similar adventure in a drug-shop at Amsterdam; my purchases made I offered the pharmaceutist a silver *mark* in payment, which he refused to accept for the reason that he did not know what it was! He turned it over as curiously in his palm as if I had brought it from Kamtschatka, and yet it was the currency circulating in the adjacent empire, not five hours' distant!

In every old country there are odd spectacles to the visitor; especially when the visitor is an American woman. The peculiarities unnoticed by the opposite sex quickly attract her attention. She sees and contrasts colors and shapes, furniture and decorations, change of food, dresses, and municipal mannerisms, that would pass utterly unrecorded by her brother, husband, or father.

Amsterdam, which originated in a few fishermen's huts on the Zuyder Zee, now the capital of Holland, is full of these contrasts. I have always heard it compared to Venice, but to liken Dutch Amsterdam to the glamour-veiled shores of Illyria is gross injustice. It has its labyrinthine canals, its multiplied islands, and its numerous bridges; but these are all stripped of the romance of their Italian protoplast by the Dutch architecture, Dutch women, and Dutch habits.

Still the pictures I took in by the wayside are the prettiest pieces of mosaic I have to store in my memory. Low fresh fields, with a pronounced inclination, sloped far away on every side, undivided by an elevation of earth and unmarred by a fence; the fair demesne of the prince is parted from the little paddock of the peasant by a narrow ditch of stagnant water that seems to breathe disease; on the broader channels boats and barges were plying their way and flying their gay colors, which aided the crimson roofs and long swaying arms of windmills to enliven the landscape; a multiplicity of cattle grazed in the soft summer afternoon, many roaming at will or wading in the morass, while hundreds were being milked by men or boys; yet, when I called for a glass of cream in the hotel they said they had none, from which I conceived what an article of commerce milk must be.

Amsterdam I loved to traverse; in the old and Jewish quarters there are establishments and sections resembling Chatham Street, New York; Seven Dials, London, and the Rue du Temple, Paris; then in the broader streets I studied the art and literature of the Lowlands. The houses are spacious, and closely resemble the homely brick structures of Philadelphia, polished and scrubbed with ultra care into painful cleanliness. The nurse and baby of an aristocratic family are not a more peculiar sight, and in more characteristic uniform, than the housemaid of the same domicile; while the abigail is decked in quillings and rosettes like a circus mare, the infantile appendage lies spread out dormant across her arms, the whole enveloped in an immense bridal veil; and the scrub girl or woman, or man, whichever I may term those who do the general labor of the household, for their dress ages them, and their constant and unnecessary work unsexes them to such an extent that I could make no estimate of age or gender,—this creature is invariably in a short black skirt, and a purple chintz sacque fastened about the waist by an apron, and white cap.

The quays are exquisitely paved and shaded by long columns of trees, while the boats and ships drift in the undredged canals; furnished with female cooks, washers, and laborers to push the floating tenements through the sluggish water; to manage the tiller or the helm; to load and unload, and in every case to mother the multitude of children sprawled over the decks.

This, with the other Holland towns, are depositories of Dutch art; and, while the Rijks Museum is considered the finest collection in the Netherlands, the array in the gallery at the Hague seemed to be more choice, though not so numerous. They are both truly national galleries, yet the Rijks contains many representations of events of national history. The two great pictures are the monographs, so to speak, of ancient political symposia. First, the "Banquet of the Arquebusiers" is more remarkable for the total effect produced by its vast size, and the aggregate of figures clustered with the many other details, than for beauty of outline. It celebrates the peace of Westphalia, and the twenty-five convivial diners are life portraits. On the opposite wall hangs Rembrandt's "Night-watch," a companion to the former. It is superb, as all things are that the pencil of that artist ever touched; a wonderful creation of grouped figures, diversified pigments, and mystic lights and shadows, which make it a whole gallery of art in itself. But the most curious and fantastic work of a very old Dutch master represents the Madonna in a black velvet dress, embroidered in seed pearls, and a blue velvet bodice, cut pompadour, while her wealth of shimmering crimped hair falls over her shoulders; the infant Christ lies upon her lap; he has a Chinese face; and two little boys, curled at her feet like star acrobats, have banged hair. To complete this ridiculous illustration one of the female members of the holy family sits near with an open Bible and a pair of eyeglasses! Now this was the first time I had ever seen a traditional fashion-plate of the Virgin's costumes, and thought the velvet and pearls rather inconsistent paraphernalia for an obscure carpenter's consort.

But the galleries of the Lowlands, like the dykes and sand-hills, that repel the threatened invasions of the sea, are numerous interesting old stories, and must be seen to be enjoyed. Like the crowding commerce, the trade and opulence, they are familiar pictures, never omitted by the painstaking statistician or the plodding compiler of the gazetteer.

I had been warned of the exorbitant prices of the Holland hotels, and soon realized the admonition. The water is execrable, indeed so offensive as to assert its potent odor when transformed into soup. The necessity of imported wines makes them equal the prices paid in America for the same article. Perhaps this is the chief reason for the marked sobriety of the Dutch as a race; while their excuse for using intoxicating beverages is sufficient, their safety may lie in the fact that they, like us, are obliged to pay for their wines in the shape of protective duties.

It was moonlight; my window overlooked a swamp, and the hordes of mosquitos came in and fed upon me like cormorants, so I determined to leave the pretty Dutch city as soon as I had visited the diamond polishing mills of Amsterdam. There are several of these establishments, but the one of which I speak is the most important in the densely settled Jewish quarter. A tall, vaporous, squalid structure loomed before us; passing through an equally impure courtyard filled by the mill employés,—male and female,—we ascended lofty flights of steps and passed through a succession of workrooms. The polishers impressed me more than the process, of which I only understood enough to render my visit interesting, not instructive. The machinery of the mills is driven by steam power, and the rough stone is polished by being pressed against a rapidly revolving iron disk dressed with a decoction of oil and diamond dust. When the stones are cut or sawn, the same mixture is used upon the hair wires, by which means they are split. The stone to be split is pressed into the top of a small stick covered with wax, and after a little nick is made by a fine file, the sharp edge of another diamond is pressed into the slight incision, until with wonderful accuracy and brilliancy the stone evenly bisects.

Of the four hundred employed in the establishment few had good faces. In consideration of the delicacy of their work, it was amazing and saddening to note the wild and depraved air of the girls, ranging from fourteen to twenty. They had a certain kind of Oriental, dark, unwashed beauty, where more of the brutal than the spiritual was developed. They evinced uncivilized pride in the tattooed decorations on their hands and arms; and where their brothers displayed one of these jewels; they, with a feminine love of extravagant embellishment, brocaded themselves with almost savage pride.

These mills are the estate of the Portuguese Jews of Antwerp and Amsterdam; they conduct the entire trade in the precious stones which are gathered at the Cape of Good Hope, and this must account for the eager avidity with which they seek and horde the gems. Amsterdam to the Hebrews is a second Jerusalem.

Rotterdam, the second commercial city of Holland, lies one and a half hour below Amsterdam, over the same even sandy country, presenting the same features of soil and production. With only one-third the population of the former city, it possesses treble its attractions in the life of its floating community. The houses are more antique, the architecture plainer, and the canals more populous. Most of the structures have a downward grade following the sinking earth to the sea, and on all the poorer avenues I find signs of hot coals and boiling water for sale; the lower classes purchase just enough of these requisites to make their tea and cook their potatoes for each repast. But there is something ineffably charming to sit in one of the crumbling brick bow-windows overhanging the canals and watch the aquatic life beneath.

What a medley and what a motley of curious custom and customers; yet this commonwealth is not of to-day nor yesterday; it is the growth of centuries. Families procreate through ages, and never have other homes than the cramped low-roofed cabins, nor other fields than brackish inlets, nor other woodlands than the forests of masts. Shortly after dawn this morning I rose to watch the progress of the day's domestic life. A family barge lay near; the mother first ducked her babies into the grimy, briny stream, that seemed to add only soilure to the bedaubed and beslobbered condition of the youthful progeny, then proceeded to perform her own ablutions by ducking her head over the side of the boat, until I feared in her perilous condition, not only for her life, but a sad *exposée*. The baker, the milkman, and the market boats came drifting in the tide, stopping at each of the floating homes at anchor, and the habitants of the river craft negotiated for their provisions from the cruising costermongers. One little transport has only a man and his canine companion for occupants; at evening he cooks his frugal meal with the canal water dipped in a tincup, and his little dog keeps him solitary company on deck while he smokes; in the morning the faithful animal is first on deck to watch for and apprise his master of the approach of the truck vendor. In the evening the families of the larger craft cluster on deck, and to the music of a well-played accordeon sing the religious refrains of the American Jubilee singers, who have been passing through these sluggish canals, gathering kreuzers for themselves and leaving their own quaint melodies among these Dutch sea-birds.

The perfect religious toleration of Holland is refreshing in contrast with the bigotry of the greater part of Europe; and while the artist may regret the fierce Puritan rage that swept many beautiful works from the churches of Amsterdam and the lesser towns of the Netherlands, there is ample compensation in the preservation of the forms and features of the victorious Dutch admirals, and the eminent champions of religious liberty portrayed by the immortal masters whose master-pieces have reflected so much honor on the Dutch Republic.

Here again I had a study in these exclusive people, with their guttural dialect, their apparent simplicity, and their real eccentricities, and a literature and art of their own.

The Dutch schools are of immortal renown, the German eminent, and the reflection surprising that this small kingdom, with an unimportant army, and comparatively small navy, controls its increasing commerce, and its vast distant possessions with all the quiet stolid determination of real Dutchmen.

Out beyond the treetops of the Boompjes the canal is thronged with vessels from every sea. Many moored to the wharf, and others moving in and out for or from foreign stations. Multitudes of the names flying on the pennons of these craft indicate their trading with the Dutch colonies of Samarang, Borneo, Sumatra, while their freight of sugar, coffee, spice, and rice strengthen the proclamation of the banners. The craft connected with the interior trade is largely manned, if I may be permitted the paradox, by women; all populous with vociferous babyhood.

I hadly feel that I may trust myself to speak of the Dutch seat of government, the Hague, in my present state of intense enthusiasm. Perhaps it was the recollection of the accounts of the melting heat at home in contrast with the delicious atmosphere in this beautiful political capital, and perhaps the vast difference between the former commercial towns, and this, the aristocratic rendezvous of refinement and culture. Not only the residence of the king, the legislative centre, the favorite home of the Dutch nobility, and the choice resort of those moneyed princes who have accumulated their fortunes by trading with the colonies in India, but the seat of art, and, by its nearness to the ocean, the spot most sought for by those who delight in the pleasures of the seaside; thus it has the double charm of metropolis and pastoral resort.

It is a city of broad streets, splendid residences, imposing squares, fine public buildings, and excessive and universal cleanliness. The canals are less numerous, and those that adorn the streets are so embellished by white stone quays and double colonnades of foliage as to render them a cheerful adornment. Home and foreign customs are charmingly interwoven, so I do not marvel that the rich come here to spend their money, the old prefer to close out their lives amid its enchanting surroundings and mystic memories, the scholar loves to linger in its libraries, galleries, and parks, and that the poor seem happier here in the air of gentle improvement. For centuries it has been the Court city, and though less absorbed in commerce, its great artists, the products of its mechanics, the dress of the better classes, and the evident superiority of the men, all point to its commanding influence at home and abroad.

The gods of Dutch idolatry in the realm of art are Rubens, Vandyke, Jordeans, Jan Steen, Rembrandt, Paul Potter, and while scarcely daring as a connoisseur to discuss their works, I was naturally anxious to see something of each in the region in which they lived, and labored, and died. Rembrandt's "School of Anatomy," painted two hundred and fifty years ago, and purchased by King William for the museum here, is a weird and wonderful work of fore-shortening. Paul Potter's famous "Bull" and Vandyke's "Magdalen," and Jan Steen's "Family Group," are the most impressive works in the gallery. There are many pictures with all the shaded and mellow gloom of the Dutch school, gems in themselves to be studied, but so startlingly beautiful and sad is the penitent Magdalen of the Flemish artist, in all the magnificence of melancholy loveliness, and with the dew of contrition lying like vaporous pearls upon her cheeks, that all others seemed dwarfed into insignificance by its omnipotence. Here begins a plentitude of Rubens, an introduction to the endless proofs of his genius. I mention these artists not to describe them or their works so much as to pay a tribute to the Flemish schools they represent with such exquisite finish and fidelity.

The good Queen Sophia, being dead, the royal family seems to be in bad odor with the people. The King is controlled by an elective Parliament, and his renegade son, Prince of Orange, riots his fortune away in the foreign capitals. The city is aglow with bridal arches and platforms and wreaths for the coming nuptial festivities of Prince Henry and his bride, who it is confidently hoped will succeed to the throne.

The late Queen's "home in the woods" is a healthy contrast to the sad state of royal morals. A mile and a half from the city, the Huis ten Bosch lies in a beautiful park completely isolated from other habitations, with the exception of a pretty villa on the same estate formerly occupied by our own John Lothrop Motley, the best historian of the Dutch republic. The royal residence was erected by the widow of the late Prince William Henry Frederick of Holland, in honor of his memory. The park is a labyrinth of shade, drive, wood, foliage, and waterfall; one of those mementos which revive the lavish opulence of the old Dutch princes and kings. As I came upon the palace

I saw only a square, awkward, brick dwelling with a great deal of white about it; I was very much impressed by the severe plainness, but surprise was changed to pleasure as I passed into and through the interior, where the diversity of apartments and decoration manifested a prodigality of taste and expenditure. In all the superb palaces there is a harmonious repetition of adornment. It is only the novelties that impress me. In the dining-room there were two mural oil paintings, executed in grisaille by De Witt, one hundred and fifty years ago; so in unison were the monotones of white and gray blent that they arrested and held my admiration with greater strength than the bright hues, dramatic attitudes, of more generally acceptable works. So entirely bizarre in tone, sentiment, and natural poise, though drawn and filled in upon canvas, they stood in relief, like statuary or stucco, but, unlike marble, seemed to breathe in the exquisite swell and motion of their proportions.

The *pièce de resistance* of the late Queen's castle is the orange salon; an octagonal hall, adorned on the eight sides and cupola with scenes from the life of Prince Henry, executed by artisans of the Rubens school. The effect is fine, but the figures are overcrowded, though boldly conceived and portrayed. The lofty sides of this salon evince the presence of careful preservation. But the potent attraction to an American is the faithful portrait of the New England scholar and historian of the Dutch republic, who endeared himself to the Queen and in the hearts of the people by his marvellous annals of their country. He with his family stood in such high favor with the Queen that the villa adjoining the royal residence was fixed for their home, parted only by a wicker bridge, which the American litterateur crossed every day to see his Queen; a most singular coincidence, in connection, is the fact that the amiable Queen and gentle historian, afterwards our Minister to Great Britain, died within three days of each other.

The Royal Bazaar at the Hague is a depository of bric-a-brac, and nowhere may a better insight be gained of the wealth of many of the ancestors of the richer Hollanders. Trading as they did and do with the Dutch colonies, and dealing with princes and potentates, vast sums were invested in fantastic art, and gold and silver ornaments, and various conceits in furniture. Many of the families still hoard the archaic treasures, while others have been forced to part with those collected into the four walls of the Bazaar. Such mammon princes as the Rothschilds come here and pay $10,000 for an ornament of silver, made seven hundred years ago, and belonging to the ancient nobility. An endless array of old Dutch pottery, and such relics as the prayer-books of Philippe le Bon, and Marie de Medici, and Catharine of Aragon; coins, medals, and cameos, old and priceless, extending far back into the Pagan eras. The relics and canonized trophies collected here prove the assiduity with which the vanished ages gathered and valued their souvenirs. Passing away from their original owners they are now for sale to the fashionable world, who adorn their mantels and proclaim their centuried lineage by these tangible but false tokens.

I passed a Sabbath day at Scheveningen, the fashionable seaside of Holland. It was a lovely cold day in August, and as I rode over the sand dykes to the North Sea the populace was flocking out to enjoy the sanitary breath of the ocean. A succession of dunes were passed resembling the bulwarks upheaved to thwart the invasion of a rebellious force. Chain after chain of these earthworks protect the cities of the Lowlands from the cruel sea. It is a town of great and numerous hotels, expensive shops, and fashionable cafés, especially in the region of the beach; but as I walked up in the precincts of the fishers' cottages I observed real frugal domesticity, and in the heart of the town great comfort and happiness.

The gray surf of the North Sea came heaving and boiling over the sands, which, as it receded, it left dry and sterile; a painful sight in remembrance of the verdure which keeps our beaches so fresh and bright. As I rode over the northern sands the icy breath of Lapland swept over the blue and scintillating waters of the far-out ocean. The bathers were in their hive-like straw basket or bathing boats and wagons, which were hauled into the surf on wheels. Those in the watch-boxes were protected from the counter-current of wind, that sweeps over the Netherlands like the mistral of Southern France, getting only the fragrance of the sea and sun. The absence of heat and non-existence of insects seemed to render unnecessary a salt-water baptism, and was a chilly spectacle. The great dunes impeded the mighty ocean from throwing its avalanche of water over the Netherlands.

As I rode through the shaded avenue to the capital the inhabitants of the antique village were out in Sunday regalia, picturesque to the last degree; the granddame was attired as the grandchild of six,—a full short black petticoat, white chemisette and sleeves, a small purple and white or blue and white plaid woollen kerchief folded over the bosom, and an apron, completed the costume. But the headgear is still more grotesque, and is called the "hochtdizer." A silver plate fits closely on the back of the head and just above the nape of the neck; it is fastened by two gilt horns or skewers on either side the face, and over all is a large white muslin cap.

In fact it was very much like a scene in a play. These happy, unpretentious people, in the strange old-time dresses, as they passed in and out the odorous alleys of the magnificent forest, seemed rather the actors in some prepared festival than the simple laboring people of the antique and unique fishing village. It seemed impossible that in the immediate vicinity of the brilliant and costly modern life of the capital the people should adhere so strictly to the customs of their ancestors.

LETTER LXXV.

> In Rubensland we find the dual fruit work,
> Of master artist, and pupil Vandyke;
> Both now lie shrouded in glory mute,
> And both in history are beloved alike.
>   ANONYMOUS.

ANTWERP, August, 1878.

THE way from the Hague to Antwerp is through a rich and fruitful country. Nothing in the topography differs from the great expanse of lowland in Holland, except the impenetrable forests of Belgium, with here and there little white hamlets squatted down upon their borders, and between their glades and in their shadows, like a warren of rabbits or flocks of quail; hamlets full of the romance of an invisible life; humble communes where the girls stitch their lives into fragile laces, to be dragged in the dust by the great lady who nothing knows or cares of the sorrow, and sadness, and heart-pangs, contained in every sprig and wreath of the woof she desecrates at night revels; villages where the youths tend the kine, while the old men are off

on the broad seas, and the old women hobble through life
in clattering sabots, counting their beads, and mumbling
Aves in their Flemish tongue, and ignorant, yet unsophisticated bigotry to the Holy Mother. They bow their knee
at the wayside shrine, invoke a pardon, lisp a hallelujah,
mutter a litany, and pass away as blindly confident in the
omnipotence of the Great Unknown as the Pagans were in
their Hermes. But these Brabant peasants often leave the
quiet shade of the gigantic forests, and through vale and
wood come, in their long-eared caps, silver ornaments, and
clicking, clashing, clapping, wooden shoes, beating a devil's
tattoo over the rough cobbles, to the great cities, to sell a
bunch of violets, or a shred of lace, at the doors of the majestic Cathedral or under the florid portals of the Hotel de
Ville. They come and sell their bouquets to a stranger, and
lose the flower of their chastity, and the fragrance of their
innocence in the whirlwind of the cruel, flattering metropolis; and then go back in discontent, or remain to sink
deeper and deeper into the mire, seeking gayer flowers, and
more ecstatic, wildering aroma among the poisonous airs
of a false society.

At the Belgian frontier the customs officers came to examine the baggage of passengers, and a solitary military
dignitary loomed dark upon the platform, while the yellow
and green and red lanterns of the brakemen gleamed along
the meadows, following the line of rail, like fire-flies in the
sombre gloom.

We rolled into the only seaport of the flourishing kingdom of Belgium on Sunday night, and at my first glimpse
I suspected it of the same indecorous revels that greeted
me at Cologne. At the station I inquired for my hotel;
the porter said it was about two squares above, and in his
care I concluded to trust my luggage, and foot the short
distance. I walked seven or eight long blocks, which
seemed to be alive with the people from beyond the bastions, eating and drinking in the cafés of this suburban
section, as I discovered it to be, as I continued inquiring
my way from pillar to post of the Flemish or Walloons
who understood little French. At last I got into a noble
street that looked as if there was a possibility of leading
me to my destination. Great structures of efflorescent
architecture lined the way, and on either side the foot
passages colossal lamps, in groups of three glaring pendants, lighted the avenue that seemed to stretch out in
interminable length. It was the Place de Meir, adorned by

the statues and homes of great artists and rulers; the Fifth Avenue of Antwerp. In an abrupt curve to my left I found my hotel in the midst of the trading quarter, and adjacent to the network of narrow, dirty, antique purlieus leading to the wharves of the Scheldt.

Antwerp is a port of vast commerce, much wealth, and some social prestige, and while the supremacy it enjoyed in the Middle Ages has faded with the years, its art remains to proclaim its mediæval ascendency, and establish its conceded influence. It is a fragment of a semicircle upon a stream which forms its chief advantage; it has few or no pavements, old market-places, trading shops of only ordinary status; a great middle class, and marine populace; a population that rests with closed offices and shops three hours in the middle of the day, and resumes business again in the afternoon. Yet it possesses its fine homes, its aristocracy, its zoological gardens, its parks, and above all its art schools, and the choice treasures of its national gods.

Overwhelmingly Catholic, it contains all the sacred gems of the Flemish painter Rubens, and his pupil Vandyke, whose flower of ripe genius endears it to the hearts of the Romish society of all countries. Master and protégé glorified the earlier part of the seventeenth century with their successive and successful labors. Both the favorites of princes, the elder pre-eminent for the excellence of his historical and sacred subjects, the younger for his royal portraits, scattered through the courts of the entire Continent. Rubens, though a Prussian by nativity, made Antwerp his residence and the theatre where he achieved his grandest glory. I fear many of the stupendous works bearing his signature, like the oceans of superior wines, are spurious. He may have conceived the models, and left them to receive flesh and clothing, and coloring and life, from his journeymen students, thus leaving a bad impression of some of the work said to be the great artist's. His inspirations are ever of the most sublime and broadest character, though there was often little delicacy or consonance of tone. Vivid coloring and brawny contortions—of the Michael Angelo school—seem to have been his peculiar talent, though his most celebrated disciple, Vandyke, acquired all the weird grace and mellow beauty his patron never possessed. In the works of the former there appears to be a stream of garish sunlight, that carnalizes the most pathetic theme; those of the latter have a soft twilight glamour that apotheosizes a profligate prince or sensuous duchess. Rubens's principal deficiency seemed to be his utter want of discrimination. Like all artists, whether painters, authors, or dramatists, he was wont to reward his favorites by placing them in the celestial spheres amongst the angels, and to punish his enemies by condemning them to the hottest flames of Gehenna. But, in that exquisite work,—his articulate monument to jealousy,—which he executed to perpetuate his own hatred and the faithlessness of his wife and scholar Vandyke, where he confines them in the liquid fire of the Stygian cave, he portrays the fallen angel with as much personal beauty as the deified Magdalen at the foot of the cross. Rubens's have all the bold flourishes and brilliant coloring of a liberal but crude mind; Vandyke shines brightest in his minutiæ and dignity of portraiture; a difference as widespread as the poles, yet they were preceptor and pupil.

In the Museum we see Rubens at home, as it were. Though the Cathedral claims his finest achievements, those of the Museum display greater accuracy of drawing. A vast wall of the building is occupied by the whole colony of Flemish artists, clustered in a group of fifty-two life-size portraits, executed by De Keyser, still alive, and though he steadily refused to insert his own figure upon earnest solicitation of the corporation, on the plea that the others were sanctified by death, when the composition was finished and his own was missing, but after loud importunity he consented to appear in the extreme background.

In an adjacent building was the exhibition of what seemed a more tangible proof of Belgian artistic enterprise and glory than the remarkable products of the ancient magicians. It was a specimen of the way in which the corporation of Antwerp encourages young students to emulate these immortal examples. In the school attached to the academy, and encouraged by the municipality, the poorest Brabant may, for a small sum, prepare himself to compete for the prize, which gives the winner the privilege of being sent to Rome, at the expense of the guild, to complete his education. The fruits of the labors of the six present rivals hung before a criticizing throng. The touching parable of the "Prodigal Son" was the subject under treatment, and each one had been left to work out his ideal alone, and when all were finished, a caucus of eminent artists convened and pronounced judgment; and now the victorious work hangs in the centre crowned with laurels.

There is scarcely a city or town of these old countries

that does not own such an institution, and yet with all our boasted liberal education in America we have yet to learn this great republican lesson.

Rubens's masterpieces in the Cathedral, the "Descent from the Cross," the "Elevation of the Cross," and the "Assumption" did not overcome nor impress me. There may have been something of disappointment in these works on account of my own inexperience, and something of too lofty expectations from the burden of adulation showered upon them; ort here may have been much in the counteracting radiance of the splendid decorations of the Cathedral itself, which had just been fully dressed for one of the numerous religious festivals, that led me to turn from the pictures to the body of the holy art-gallery.

Here, again, I noted the pageantry of the Catholic Church and the influence it wields. It rules the masses with the magic power of a caduceus, and whether the effect be upon the heart, the intellect, or the senses, if the result be beneficial, the cause is good. The majority of Papists go to church to enjoy the pictures, the exquisite stained glass windows, the bronzes, the banners, and the sweet music, but once having entered the sanctum they pray; no irrepressible longing to lay their hearts down before their Maker would have guided their steps into the Holy of Holies had it not been an art depository as well as the house of God.

The Cathedral is one of those Gothic fancies so prevalent in the church architecture of Catholic Europe. A wilderness of steeples and towers and flying buttresses. Inside, apart from the Rubens pictures and the painted windows, the amplitude of delicate and intricate wood carvings seem to be the loadstar. The elaborate tracery of the superb chapels, naves and chancels, is as marvellous and mystical a piece of art as the exterior of the Milan duomo. Religious ensigns in the pontifical colors floated from every pillar and post, and formed wreathed drapery from the dome; the clouds of incense symbolized a service which keeps itself forever before its worshippers.

The populace were out, like a great sea let loose, to welcome the Archbishop. It was a fine spree for them, but it was a decorous, sober, sincere frolic. No sloth, nor intoxication, nor profanity characterized the herd that swarmed through the lofty aisles of the Cathedral and filled the open squares of the city. Every age and station mingled in the jubilee, the poorest and the smallest seeming to sympathize with the event. The resplendent illumination in the evening in honor of the patron saint was the new ecstasy that supplemented the glory of the day.

What the Antwerpians call Mount Calvary deserves no better title than the Chamber of Horrors. In the court adjacent to St. Paul's a huge mound of rock and slag surmounted by a crucified Christ represents the sacred hill. Hideous prototypes of saints, angels, and patriarchs, stand at varied heights upon the projections, and surround the grotto intended to illustrate the sepulchre at Jerusalem, behind which a delineation of Purgatory gleamed, where the condemned stood neck-deep in flames behind iron bars. The entire conception was the fantasy of some ignorant bigot, and admirably disposed to make men turn back from the Catholic Church, who might have beeen converted by the other fascinations and displays. The statues without exception were repulsive, and the holy tomb, with all its wretched and tawdry painting of purgatory for a background, forms a chief object to inspire benighted adherents with awe, by a constant presentation of the terrors of eternal damnation. To intensify the ghastly and misshapen sight, several clothes-lines stretched from the tenement-houses adjoining, floated all the repulsive rags, just wrung from the washtubs, over the heads of the holy conclave.

LETTER LXXVI.

"And Ardennes waves above them her green leaves,
 Dewey with nature's tear-drops, as they pass,
Grieving, if aught inanimate e'er grieves,
 Over the unreturning brave."
                                CHILDE HAROLD.

BRUSSELS, August, 1878.

NOT an hour's ride on the rails from Antwerp to the little Paris, or hilly city of Brussels, as mountainous as a Swiss town hung upon the Alpine crags, and all the way is marked by the vagrant detachments of canals, the low white lands stretching away from the dunes of the Netherlands, and the tall poplars of France,

"Whose only boughs
Are gathered round their dusky brows."

There is little in the approach to these Lowland cities to stimulate the imagination, and it is only upon entering that I realized how it filled out the pictures of my fancy. The political capital of Belgium is indeed Paris, but Paris epitomized, Paris curtailed of its originality, and abridged of its fertile and varied proportions.

An exquisite city is Brussels, of art and architecture, of vast hotels, of marvellous manufactures, stations, cathedral, gallery, and palace. A mongrel city, so to speak; a half-cast, with French, Germans, and Dutch in its lineage; a court centre and an important commercial station; a city where the ducal pageants blend and harmonize with the traffic of the Zuyder Zee, the icy Baltic coast, and the far Indies; where the crimson and gold pennons, banners, and gonfalons floating from palace capitals and cathedral posts, seem a part of the national colors flying from the lofty masts, and the white sails swaying in the breeze of the canals and tributaries that flow away to the Scheldt; a city where the lowly peasant or burgher life drifting into the streets every morning from the forests of Ardennes or the woods of Soignies, or the plains of Waterloo, with its handful of violets and daisies, shred of lace, or milk-cart drawn by a big yellow dog, is far more interesting than the shrill-voiced bouffe singers at the Theatre de la Monnaie cutting their ambiguous antics, or the wealth in the Quartier Leopold, or the extravagant shops of the rues Royale, de la Regence, and de la Madelaine.

In the early morning the milk or bread wagons, drawn by dogs and driven by broad, square, brown Walloon women, clattering their sabôts and Flemish tongues in unison, fill the rugged hilly streets. Two canine brutes harnessed to the tongue and one under the miniature cart pull with all their might the burden up the hill, and when the mistress halts in the vicinity of her trade, each and every dog drops exhausted upon the white roads, but with the true instinct of that intellectual and faithful brute springs to his feet at the sound of his particular mistress's step. They serve their milk, flap the long tabs of their white caps and jingle the silver pendants in their ears, enter the shady, holy recesses of St. Gudule and pray to the Great Unknown, in the glow of the Belgian sun streaming through the golden and crimson glass of the marvellous windows, under the protection of the nimbussed cherubs, and in the seductive clouds of incense that reverently veil the angels of the dome, and return to their

Brabant groves and brakes to rehearse on the morrow the same programme that has been in course of action even from their infancy, and will be repeated until the sun of life is eclipsed behind the sorrowing shadow of death.

And these good Brabant people speak the Flemish or Walloon dialect, which is as incomprehensible to a Frenchman as it is to an Englishman, while the language of the upper classes, of government, the municipal laws and the literature, is French, and has been since the days Godfrey of Brabant armed himself with the holy cross and led the first crusade. There is some slight variation between the Walloon and Flemish tongues,—the former spoken by the northern Belgian, the latter by the peasants of the districts south of Liege and Brussels; but neither has a literature except in religious publications for the exclusive use of the under orders. The Walloons are an approach to the Irish, Scotch, or Swedes, while the Flemish are akin to the real Hollander, and the upper-tendom are French, or French mannered and French educated.

On an abrupt slope below the noble esplanade of the Rue Royale, where the military tramp and the royal carriages follow in close succession, with outriders and flying colors through the long sultry days, there rises a Gothic structure, with jutting angles and naves, ascended by vast flights of stone steps, and crowned by massive, square, unfinished towers, ornate with the florid intricate scrolls of the Corinthian chisel. The stained glass windows are the cynosure of the interior. They date from every era of time since the thirteenth century, and represent the successive rulers of Belgium in those days of cabal and discontent when the kingdom threw off yoke after yoke of foreign oppressors, and passed through a series of régimes, choosing its chiefs from among strangers. There are comparatively few sacred subjects portrayed upon these exquisite windows that arrest the attention of the world; yet this is the cathedral where the women sell figures of Christ within the vestibule, and the brown-eyed girl from Hougomont or Mont St. Jean barters away her soul on the steps without, under the eye of her Holy Mother and in the presence of her God.

One of the chief charms of Brussels is the monumental splendors of the streets. In this feature it seems almost an envious rival of the white capital of France. Perhaps it is because the little kingdom has so much of glory and strife and combat to relate in its history, and perhaps because the gallant citizens fancy this way of at once perpetuating the fame of their great ones and adorning their squares. Is not the equestrian statue of Godfrey de Bouillon, erected upon the spot where he exhorted the Belgians on to war for the Holy Sepulchre, a more fitting tribute to the centuried hero than some fantastic allegorical marble requiring inscribed explanation? The Place des Martyrs, back of the Rue Neuve, and approached through the Rue St. Michel, contains the cenotaph of the brave who fell in the autumn of '30. In a sunken gallery, or open tomb, are inclosed stone slabs recording the names of the martyrs. The figure of enfranchised Belgium surmounts a pediment guarded by angels of mercy and consolation and prayer, while Patria herself chronicles with her stylus the eventful days that unlocked her gyves, unbound her pinions, and gave her freedom; the base contains reliefs of a nation's oaths, its conflict, its gratitude, and its tombs. The Counts Egmont and Hoorne still stand before the Maison du Roi in all the stony calmness and majesty they displayed the day, three centuries ago, they met their treacherous fate, which really was the initial scene of the thirty years' tragedy that ended in bursting the Spanish halter. Opening from the Rue Royale, and on a vertical line with the celebrated mansion where sat "Brunswick's fated chieftain" on the calamitous night when a thousand "lamps shone o'er fair women and brave men," the Doric column of Congress loses its lofty head in the clouds. The fact which the heaven-kissing tower commemorates gave to Belgium its king, its liberty of press, freedom of education, immunity of associations, and latitude in public worship, and Belgium reciprocated by giving the cloud-capped memorial to the city.

But with all these unfading testimonials to the independence, valor, and genius of a country, the grotesque Fountain of the Mannikin is a greater municipal attraction. It is worshipped by the lower Flemish, and sought by strangers; it is pointed to by *valets de place*, and attired in fitting costume upon political or religious festivals. The Mannikin is a racy little diplomate, who changes his national sentiments with the springtide of public opinion, and therefore is ever a faithful subject of the enthroned régime, and dons a costume in consonance with his precepts. He has been a Frenchman, a Brabant, an Orangeman, a Revolutionist, and is now a loyal adherent of Leopold, of Saxe-Coburg. He always courts the ruling power and by his sycophant nature remains the favorite of the masses.

While Patria in her unloosed shackles, looking healthy and holy, may some day turn a green and sickly hue, or Egmont in his gold lace and feathers may be torn down from his pedestal and beaten into the defiling dust of the streets by the ungrateful and forgetting posterity of those for whom he suffered, and the Colonne du Congrés frown upon the threatening insurgents below, the Mannikin will reign in state, for he will be a constituent of the stronger faction.

The city is bathed in a sea of pomp and glee, for it is the festal season of the silver wedding of Leopold and his Queen Henrietta, and while the steeds from the royal stables, gay in gilt trapping and scarlet cloth, and the royal guard climb the steep streets, and the silver chimes of church towers make sweet melody, and the blare of trumpet and beat of drum reverberate through the crowded ways and galleries, and silks and laces and diamonds rival each other in shimmer and texture and radiance in the palace saloons, and orators endeavor to drown each other's voices and convictions in the public halls and parks, the peasants are trudging their leafy roads, where the shade of poplar and pine cast a holy mist around, to the great city to join in the pageant to their sovereign, a brilliant ovation where I catch glimpses of celebrated characters and meet frequent revelations of the manners and customs of the laboring multitude. I watched the parade of the Belgian free-schools and the Belgian Parliament, with their chiefs and leaders of the realm, as it wound about the broad boulevards that form the town into an ill-shaped triangle, like a brilliant-hued serpent, and passing before the royal family under the portico of the palace was lost in the roads leading away to the suburbs. Detachments from the far-away coal districts of Mons and Liege, the lace sections of Malines, the northern plains of Ghent and Bruges, and the southern sylvan shades of Ardennes came in fantastic dress to participate in the jubilee and offer precious gifts in homage to their monarch.

The communal pupils formed a vast army of childhood, and though the majority are Roman Catholic they are all instructed from a common fund, the training being thorough and practical, not religious. The girls flaunted their white dresses, long panties, and gay ribbons under the scrolled and gilded balconies of the metropolis, perhaps for the first and last time in life, and the boys marched like a miniature battalion of freedmen, in their gala suits and high hats, as proud of their introduction into their capital as an American girl of her presentation at Victoria's court. The future mothers and fathers of the kingdom chorussed their festive airs in exquisite harmony as they proceeded under the gold and crimson flags from their homes at Antwerp, Liege, Lille, Bruges, Ghent, Malines, Brabant, Luxembourg, Hainault, and Namur, cheered by the enthusiasm of the rapturous crowds and stimulated by the witchery of novelty; but as the Liberal deputies lately elected to the Belgian Parliament appeared they were greeted with a sterner and manlier ebullition of joy. And these men had vanquished the Ultramontanists at the late elections,—despite the overwhelming Catholicism of Belgium,—and instructed their King to organize a liberal or republican ministry!

All through the long days throngs of burghers pass to and fro in the halls of the Hotel de Ville, where the lace train and jewelled coronal to be presented to the Queen by her female subjects lay on exhibition, and all through the sunlight hours fine music bands march and countermarch in the glaring streets, white with the sand from the dunes of Holland,—military bands, showing a proficiency in the art such as I have heard in no other foreign capital, except at German Cologne. Yet, in the midst of this musical supremacy, it was not displeasing to hear that *our* Gilmore's orchestra fairly electrified the cultivated and censorious professors of music in the critical city of Brussels not long since, and while many unjust critics claim that the American leader's organization is composed of Germans, such has been the development of scientific music in the United States that some of the most valuable contributions to the operatic stage are native and to the manner born.

The revels and holidays of Catholic countries are unequalled for brilliancy, abandon, and universal participation. The inordinate love of dramatic effect, which has been fed by the garish show and scenic attributes of their church, creates a thirst for all attractions needing *figurantes* or *pulchinello*. The illumination in the evening was a grand sublimation or deification of the glories of the day. Great wreaths of mammoth flowers bridged the highways from pillar to post; arches of the national colors and various devices of many-colored lanterns filled the open places; bands and streamers of black and orange and crimson honeycombed the streets, floated from every window and rail of the habitations, and hung in festoons—looped and interwoven—over the façades of public structure and private home. The chalky pavements glare in a hoary resplendence, the atmosphere is a mystic splendor of prismatic hues, and the human herd dip and float in a foam of phosphorescence.

Among the honors extended to the Belgian King and Queen, upon the fête of their silver-wedding, the concert in the park of the Zoological Garden formed a conspicuous feature. A crush of people I met at the gates clamoring for entrance; there was a jostling and bustling of rude burghers and opulent citizens and under-officers of the peace. After some delay and a good deal of discomfort we accomplished our entrance within the pale, and, slowly taking our place in the ponderously-moving line, began the ascent of the path toward the radiant façade of the restaurant, under which the royal pair were to sit. It was a weird, nocturnal combination of illumination and serenade, with the lights shining in the grass like natural constellations, and the red-lighted shells looking down from between the tree-branches like great eyes, and yellow lamps shining in arches of glory. The decorations of colored fire were superb, but the pyrotechnical display did not surmount mediocrity, at least to me, for the memory of how I had feasted upon the supernal blaze of the Centennial Exhibition, and the meteoric effulgence of St. Peter's at Rome, was a bar to the enjoyment of lesser beacons.

The depots for the sale of India shawls and the brilliant depositories of laces have nothing at the exterior to indicate trade but a large brass-plate at one side of the entrance bearing the name of the firm, and at times the addition of the word *dentelles*. Both these productions deserve to be classed in the category of arts, as they take place with the higher sciences of oil-painting, engraving, sculpture, and *bric-à-brac*. The Netherlands have for centuries been in direct communication with India, and the wealthy firms own their manufactories of Cashmere shawls among the dusky nations of the East. A long apartment, like a lady's drawing-room, is used for the display, and the walls are decorated by prints and paintings of the inhabitants of the valleys of Northern Hindoostan, engaged in the various processes of the manufacture of the shawls; some at the looms, and some plying their wooden needles, and others steeped in rich, warm dye-stuff of the Orient. Do we marvel at the prices these goods demanded when we learn that

35*

it requires the fleece of ten goats and a year's work to produce a wrap of only ordinary quality and under size? Yet these goods may be purchased for a third less price here, from the Compagnie des Indes, than at our emporiums.

My first experience in the lace-shops left me disappointed and perplexed. They could not boast of the correspondingly and amazingly low figures of the shawls. If there is any one thing in which a woman may be said to possess instinctive knowledge it is in costume, detail and entire; therefore she is ever awake to the inconsistency of over-rates. The aristocratic lace and shawl manufactory of Brussels is never advertised; there is ever the all-pervading presence of quietude and concealment. I had made my purchase of Cashmeres and was consulting with a friend how I should carry them home without paying duty,—the adroit American female never pays impost. it is not in her code,—when the saleslady began to tell off the cost of her laces, like a Catholic counting her beads. What she threw before me were of the finest tissue, but all beyond my price. The attendant displayed a black thread mantle that had been ordered by one of the California money princesses, to cost $8000, and the duty at fifty per cent. would add $4000; but to escape this necessary imposition the garment remains at the depository until the lady millionaire calls for it and carries it home on her fair shoulders, and so cheats poor old Uncle Sam out of his rightful tariff. A flounce of point d'aiguille, costing two hundred and twenty-five dollars a meter, had each spray elevated from the foundation and the opening leaves of each rose consumed a day of the laceworker's time; labor which requires an artist for which she receives eighty cents per diem, while the workers of less subtile portions receive ten or fifteen cents of our money. What I saw was instructive but admonitory, and I hurried away from the airy fabrics with the weighty price. After many days' search I found the envied gossamer in the Rue des Paroissiens, where the finest textures may be procured at rates in moderate contrast to those of the Indian importers.

On a mound of earth adjoining the Zoological Garden I sought and found what looked to be an antique ruin. It was the home and studio of the erratic artist Wiertz while he lived, and is now the casket of his works and a national property. I had heard of the fantastic vagaries of this gifted man, and felt a natural hunger to feast upon the fruits of his weird genius *en masse*. The paintings that have won the fame of this strange being are the creations of a wild, imaginative brain, to which the owner seems generally to have allowed unlimited scope;—to use an Americanism, "let himself loose." He was an expert with intervals of insanity; often working with genuine inspiration, and oftener with a reckless dash and gross extravagance; yet from his portrait, painted at various ages, I saw a philosophical face, and far from any evidence of inebriety or insanity. The pictures in his gallery are all interesting and original emanations; most of the conceptions colossal and strongly indicative of developed personifications of the mania-à-potu. With the vivid coloring of Rubens, the distorted and brawny anatomy of Michel Angelo, the prodigious conceits of Carlyle, and the fanatic illusions of Poe, he was at once fascinating and spectral. It seemed very like a lunatic gifted with supreme but momentary power, throwing off his dark and brilliant vagaries upon canvas. Still there were some of his achievements that manifested a soft and touching sentiment, mystical and beautiful beyond expression. Many of his women seem to have been coined out of the melted love of his heart. The portrayed horrors of this man's frenzies are alone worthy a trip to Brussels.

It is strange that the thickly settled kingdom of Belgium, crowded with great events and numbers of distinguished artists, writers, and statesmen in its annals, would be obliged to take its kings from other countries. The father of the present King was Leopold of Saxe-Coburg, son-in-law of Louis Philippe, of France, and his wife was a princess of the house of Austria; so it may be said that neither are Belgians. Despite the disparity of not one Protestant to every five hundred Catholics, the Extremists were conquered by a large majority at the last election by the Liberals. The Queen is a Protestant, and her royal spouse is a moderate Catholic, quiet and domestic in his customs, while Henrietta is fond of the turf, horseflesh, sawdust, spangles, rush lights, and legs, which is equalized by her philanthropy, and though a grandmother, still drives four-in-hand and frequents the American circus.

* * * * * *

"The play is done, the curtain drops,
  Slow falling to the prompter's bell;
A moment yet the actor s'ops,
  And looks around to say—Farewell."

INDEX.

African slave trade, 15
Afterglow of Bernese Oberland, 332
Alcester, 62
Alhambra, 83
Allumination, May 1, 1878, 146
Altorf, 349
Amsterdam, 394
Antwerp, 402
Aquarium, London, 115
Arabs of London, 36
Arc de l'Etoile, 182
"Ariadne on the Panther," 376
Avenue de l'Opera, 139
Avignon, 218

Beau Séjour, Zurich, 356
Beecher, Henry Ward, 46
Beneficent organization, 35
Benevolence of a proprietress, 58
Bercy, 211
Berne, 325
Bernhardt, 191, 194
Bilton Hall, 21
Birmingham, 52, 56
Black Forest, 363
Boboli Gardens, 292
Bois du Boulogne, 183
Bond Street jewelry shops, 29
Bonivard, 324
Boompjes, 398
Borbonica, Museum, 290
Boulevards, 139
Brienz, 337
British Museum, 124
British patriotism, 84
British pauperism, 37
Brunig Pass, 344
Brussels, 407
Bull, John, taciturn, 20
Bull, Mrs. and her heifers, 27
Bullier, Jardin, 157
Burgundy vineyards, 211

Cabinet particulier, 198
Cadenabbia, Lake Como, 306
Café Royal, 23
Calais, 135
Campo Santo, 243, 245
Cannes, 229
Casino, 237
Catalans, 224
Catholicism in Switzerland, 349
Cave canem, 283
Chaillot Heights, 204
Champs Elysées, 181
Champs de Mars, 142, 200
Channel, crossing the, 134
Charlecote, 62
Chester, 52
"Chester Cup," 55
Chiffonnier, 147
"Christ leaving Prætorium," 33
Chr.stoforo Columbo, 241
Cimarosa, 81
"City of Richmond," 13
Claqueurs, 193
Coblentz, 385
Coiffure, English, past and present, 28
Cologne, the city, 388
Constance, Lake, 360
Coppet, 313
Corniche, 226
Costumes and Customs, English, 26
Côte d'or, 212
Covent Garden, London, 78
Coventry, 74
Crewe, 21
Criterion, bar, 24
Criterion Theatre, 89
Crystal Palace, 112
Cyprian goddesses, 284

Demon, *Rum*, the, 35

(417)

418 INDEX

Dijon, 213
Diomed Inn, 281
Docks at Liverpool, 17
Docks at Marseilles, 224
Doré Gallery, 33
Dream of Chillon, 316

Eaton Hall, 53
Ehrenbreitstein, 386
Émanuletta, 294
English churchmen, salaries of some, 46
English Literati, 105
English women, 27
Estates at Liverpool, 17
Ethelfleda, 70
Euston Square Station, 21
Euthanasia, 282
Evan's, 85
Exposition Universelle, a day at, 143, 205
Extract of Alderney, 63

Farrar, Canon, 46
Faubourg St. Antoine, 152
Ferney, 314
Figures of British pauperism, 37
Flaneurs, 139
Florence, 287
Fluelen, 350
Fog, London, 30
Forwood, reception of Mr. and Mrs., 16
Foundling Hospital, 46
Frankfort-on-Main, 374
French charities, 199
    caricatures, 151
    flats, 138
    labor, 148
    milliners, 150
    restaurants, 197
    shops, 198
Frogmore, 119

Geneva, 308
Genoa, 240
Giessbach, 340
Gluck, 81
Godiva, 75
Goethe, 375
Gold, power of, 91
Greek Chapel, 380
Grisette, 155
Grosvenor, Marquis of, 53

Guidecca, 297
Guttenberg, 375
Guy's Cliff, 71

Hague, 398
Handel, harpsichord of, 41
Hansom, 15
Hastings, 108
Hathaway, Anne, 62
Heidelberg, 373
Herald's College, London, 48
Holland, 392
Home of Frenchmen, 195
Hotel des Invalides, 167
Hotel, London and Northwestern at Liverpool, 15
House of Commons, 129
Huis ten Bosch, 399
Human intellect in Republican France 209
Hyde Park, 120
Hyères, 228

India House, 205
Interlaken, 333
Irving, Henry, 87

Jubilee Singers, 330
Judic, Madame, 193
Jungfrau, 337

Kaisersalle, 376
Kaltbad, 352
Kenilworth, 73
Kulm, 353

Lake dwellings, 358
La Scala, 304
"Last Supper," 305
Latin Quarter, 152
Lausanne, 326
Leamington, 73
Leicester Square, 82
Liberté, Egalité et Fraternité, 146
Lion of Luzerne, 348
Liverpool, 13
"Locked in and left," 20
London, 18
London, a walk through, 96
Lotteries of Marseilles, 221
Louvre, 173
Lully, 81
Lutetia, 152
Luther, 375

INDEX. 419

Luther, finger organ of Martin, 41
Luxembourg, 156, 176
Luzerne, 340
Lyceum Theatre, 87
Lyons, *croix-Rousse*, 210

Mabille, Jardin, 159
Madame Michel, 151
Mannikin, 410
Marché du Temple, 154
Marine Aquarium, 112
Marseilles, 217
Marshall and Snellgrove, 29
Mausolea of Titian and Canova, 301
Mendicants, scarred and scarified, 37
Mersey, 17
Milan, 302
Monaco, 231
Mont Cenis, 310
Mont-du-Piété, 154
Mont Pilat, 218
Monte Carlo, 231
Monte Pincio, 248
Motley, John Lothrop, 399
Mount Vesuvius, 278

Netherlands, religion of the, 397
New Place, 58
Nice, 227
Notre Dame Cathedral, 156
Notre Dame de la Garde, 222
Notre Dame de Lorette, 140
Nouvel Opera, 189

Oak Lodge, 89
Opera, London, 79
Oxford Music Hall, 86

Paesiello, 81
Palace of the Doges, 299
Palais Royale, 141
Palestrina, 81
Paris, 132
Parliament Palaces, 128
Pauperism, English, 37
Pere la Chaise, 169
Peter Robinson, 29
Petrarch and Laura, 218
Phillips, J. O. Halliwell, 60
Piccini, 81
Pigeons of St. Mark, 300
Pitti Palace, 289
Pompeii, 279

Pont de Jena, 203
Ponte Vecchio, 291
Prince of Wales, pavilion, 202

Quai d'Orsay, 203

Rajah Holapore, 292
Regent's Park, 121
Rest Roubion, 226
Restaurants, London, 91
Rhine Falls, 359
Rhine, from Biebrich to Cologne, 381
Rialto, 297
Rienzi, 219
Rigi, 350
Rome, 246
Rothschilds, home of, 375
Rotterdam, 396
Roulette, 238
Rue de la Roquette, 169
Rugby, 21

Salve, 283
Santa Croce, 289
Schaffhausen, 360
Scheveningen, 401
Seagulls, 13
Sefton Park, 17
Servant-girlism, 186
Shakespeare House, 57
Shakespeare's birthplace, 60
Shottery, 62
Silk factories of Lyons, 215
Slave trade, 16
Soap factories, 17
South Kensington Museum, 38
Staffel, 352
Stanley, Dean, 43
Station bars and booking offices, 18, 19
Stoke Poges, 119
Stolzenfels, 385
Stratford-on-Avon, 57
Strasburg, 339
St. George's Hall, 14
St. James Park, 121
St. James's Hall, 86
St. Leonards-on-Sea, 110
St. Lorenzo, 289
St. Marco, piazza and cathedral, 298, 299
St. Peter's Cathedral, 252
Sydenham Hill, 112

Tapestry of Bayeux, 110
Tell's Chapel, 349
Thames, its course through Richmond, Kew, Hampton Court, etc, 100
Theatres, London 90
Theatres, Paris, 189
Thun, 334
Toulon, 228
Tower Hill, 96
Travelling carriages. English, 19
Trinity Chapel, Stratford-on-Avon, 59
Trocadéro, 200
Turin, 309
Tussaud, Madame, gallery and career, 31

Underground railway, 30

Valley of Marne, 212
Venice, 293
Versailles, 178

Vesuvian Bay, 277
Vevay, 320
Villa Borghese, 249
Virtue and Vice, in London, 34
Vitznau, 350

Wales, poor of, 37
Walloons, 403
Warwick, 61, 64, 65
Wealth and poverty of London, 34
Weisbaden, 377
Westminster Abbey, 24, 25
Westminster Hall, 131
Westminster, Marquis of, 53
Westminster Palace Hotel, 22
Wiertz Gallery, 414
Windsor,—town and castle, 116, 117, 118, 119, 120
Wood sculptures, 339

Zug, Lake, 353
Zurich, 354

www.ingramcontent.com/pod-product-compliance
Lightning Source LLC
Chambersburg PA
CBHW022111290426
44112CB00008B/629